Property Tax Relief

Property Tax Relief

Steven David Gold

Drake University

LexingtonBooks
D.C. Heath and Company
Lexington, Massachusetts
Toronto

Library of Congress Cataloging in Publication Data

Gold, Steven David.
  Property tax relief.

  Includes index.
  1. Property tax credit—United States—States.
I. Title.
HJ4120.G64   336.2'2'0973   79-1723
ISBN 0-669-02917-3

Published simultaneously in Canada.
Printed in the United States of America.
International Standard Book Number: 0-669-02917-3
Library of Congress Catalog Card Number: 79-1723

To my parents

Contents

List of Tables

Preface

This book arose from my involvement in a fierce property tax controversy in Iowa several years ago. In 1976 the state found itself with about $50 million which had to be used for property tax relief. Nearly every type of relief measure imaginable was considered, and the wrangling dragged on for two years. As a member of the faculty at a university located near the Capitol, I was deeply involved in suggesting alternatives, issuing studies of proposals by others, and writing expository articles for the major state newspaper.

I found that the available public finance literature was of limited utility. One problem was a paucity of timely material describing in useful detail the programs employed in other states. Another shortcoming was huge gaps concerning analysis of specific relief alternatives, such as homestead exemptions and limitations on local spending. A third drawback was that many writers were politically naive, advocating programs such as deferral with little political appeal. Most damaging, programs were often analyzed in isolation: no relatively comprehensive framework was available for comparing alternatives.

My intention was to write a book which will be useful to a wide audience. Hopefully it will be of interest to economists and political scientists concerned about state and local public finance (and their students), to legislators and other government officials, to interest groups involved with these issues, and to members of the general public who desire an understanding of current local tax issues. Because of this diverse audience, some compromises have been necessary in terms of content and style. Technical terminology has been kept to a minimum but not completely avoided. Hopefully that which remains will not put off the nontechnical reader. My general plan has been to avoid technical material when it was not clearly policy-relevant but to include it when it was practically important.

Because political considerations usually make it necessary to adopt something less than ideal policies, no attempt is made to lay out a blueprint of ideal property tax relief. Nevertheless, an effort is made to distinguish among policies which are more or less desirable.

In describing the property tax relief programs in various states, I have started with existing surveys by groups such as the Advisory Commission on Intergovernmental Relations (ACIR), Abt Associates, the Department of Agriculture, the International Association of Assessing Officers (IAAO), and the Census Bureau. I supplemented this information with three separate mail surveys of each state: on participation and costs of circuit breakers, on participation in farm tax relief and changes in the composition of assessed valuation, and on effective tax rates and an overview of all relief programs. The results of these surveys are reported in chapters 3, 5, and 15. Additional data were obtained in follow-up telephone communications and were incorporated in these and other chapters.

I am indebted to many people for help in this project. Special mention should go to Gerald Auten, Diane Fuchs, and Russ Murray, who commented on most of the chapters and offered many useful suggestions. Roy Saper also went far beyond the call of duty in providing information about the property tax situation in Michigan.

I am also grateful to many people for providing information and/or commenting on one or more chapters, in particular John Behrens, Michael Bell, Bob Ebel, Tom Hady, Nan Humphrey, Herman Ingram, Sandra Kanter, Sharon Levin, Russ Lidman, Art Lyons, Will Myers, Tom Muller, Bill Neenan, Lowell Norland, George Reigeluth, Ray Reinhard, John Shannon, Ross Stephens, Frank Tippett, Dean Tipps, Joan Towles, Roger Vaughan, Ronald Welch, Ray Whitman, and Hazel Young.

I also appreciate very much the typing and moral support of Linda Haugh, Sharon Jilany, and Susanne White as well as the just plain moral support of Tuwana Brown. The book could not have been written without the encouragement and patience of my wife, JoAnn.

Much of the work on this book was done while I was at The Urban Institute in 1978 and 1979 on a sabbatical leave. I am grateful to George Peterson for making its facilities available. Part of my financial support during this period was from a National Science Foundation Science Faculty Professional Fellowship. Earlier support was provided by a grant from the Drake University Research Council.

The views expressed here are my own and do not necessarily reflect those of any other person or organization.

1 Introduction

Even before Proposition 13 raised interest in property tax relief to new heights, most states had made significant changes in their property tax systems in the 1970s. With homes and farms rising in value at rates not experienced for decades, the property tax was put under unprecedented strain. Legislators and governors responded by enacting a myriad of reforms. Circuit breakers were initiated and expanded, homestead exemptions were raised, preferential assessment of farmland became widespread, new schemes for classification of property types were contemplated, new types of limits were placed on local budgets and tax revenues, local nonproperty taxes increased in use, and states increased financial aid to local governments, especially school districts.

As the preceding list suggests, the fifty states employ a vast array of methods of providing relief from property taxes. Although many of these methods individually have been the subject of valuable studies, there has been a dearth of analysis which compares the alternative forms of property tax relief in a general framework. That is the purpose of this book.

This book has three objectives: to describe the various types of relief policies which are in use, highlighting key design issues; to summarize the major existing analytical literature on these policies; and to draw conclusions about the strengths and weaknesses of the alternative policies, placing them in a general framework.

Property tax relief represents a change in the tax system. It is any action which reduces net property tax paid by individuals or businesses below what it would have been if no action had been taken to change the system. Thus, relief may be granted even though property taxes rise—as long as the rise is less than that which would have occurred without the relief.

Relief must be distinguished from reform. *Reform*—defined as any action which improves the property tax system—is in the eye of the beholder. What is reform to one person may be a worsening of the property tax to another.

Relief and reform do not necessarily go hand in hand. There may be relief without reform or reform without relief. An example of relief without reform would be an across-the-board cut in tax rates. On the other hand, an improvement of assessment accuracy would bring reform without relief, raising taxes for some and reducing them for others.

This book is concerned with the major types of relief, whether or not they represent reform in the author's opinion. Before we analyze the specific forms of relief, several preliminary topics must be discussed. First, there is an explanation

1

of how the property tax system operates. This is followed by an overview of relief methods used. The third and fourth sections present an overview of both the criteria by which the relief measures will be evaluated and key assumptions which govern how relief is viewed. Chapter 2 discusses geographic patterns of property tax use and changes in those patterns in recent years.

How the Property Tax System Works

> In the United States, "the" property tax is comprised of fifty-one separate state-local property tax systems, each subject to numerous legal and extra-legal variations and each changing in some fashion over time—through constitutional revision, enactment of statutes and ordinances, changes in administrative procedures, court decisions, and changes in the capabilities of tax administrators.... It is humanly impossible to comprehend all the variations in law, economic impact, and assessment practices that do exist, much less keep up with the changes.[1]

This quote from Richard Almy, director of research for the International Association of Assessing Officers (IAAO), suggests the magnitude of the problem of attempting to describe the contemporary property tax. Each state has different property tax laws, which are complex and changing. To make matters worse, actual practice often differs greatly from what the law dictates and varies widely within each state; and on many important questions, the information on practice is woefully incomplete. So this section simply provides a global overview of law, practice, and results. To reduce verbiage, the words *usually* and *in most cases* are used only occasionally, although they could be inserted in every sentence except those which are tautological.

Property Tax Mechanics

There are several terms to define: taxable property, assessed value, assessment ratio, exemptions, credits, and nominal and effective tax rates.

Taxable property is, naturally enough, that property which is subject to property taxation. It consists primarily of land and buildings, which is called real property. Over the years there has been a trend toward increasing exemption of nonreal, or personal property, so that now eight states exempt it entirely and most of the others exempt it partially.[2] Real property owned by religious, charitable, government, and educational organizations is also exempt in many cases. Property exemptions are discussed in chapter 12.

Assessed value is a property's value for tax purposes, as determined by a tax assessor. Most states legally assess property on a fractional basis, specifying that the assessed value should be a certain percentage of a property's actual value.

Assessors can use three approaches to determining value, referring to (1) sales of comparable property, (2) the cost of reproducing the property, or (3) the income derived from the property. Since there are many more sales of homes than of other types of property, usually residential assessments are related to sales, while assessments of business property are related to costs or income. Agricultural property is usually given preferential treatment, its assessment being based on the value of land in agricultural use rather than its market value, which is usually higher.

When assessed value is divided by a property's market value, the result is called the *assessment ratio*. Usually property is supposed to be treated uniformly, but a number of states set unequal standards for particular types of property, favoring residential and agricultural properties, a system referred to as classification. In practice, assessment ratios generally are far below what the law says they should be. They are also not consistent, with great variation from one piece of property to another, even when one is comparing similar properties. This disparity gives rise to widespread dissatisfaction with the quality of assessment administration. When the IAAO surveyed its membership (most of whom are assessors) in 1973, 68 percent characterized the overall quality of assessment administration as either "relatively poor" or "very poor."[3]

Poor administration implies that property burdens are not distributed equitably. Property owners living in the same government jurisdiction and owning property with the same market value should pay the same tax, but they will not if their assessment ratios differ, as they usually do.

The quality of assessment administration varies greatly across the country. In some states, it is relatively accurate; in others, not. In some states, assessments are regularly raised to keep up with rising property values; in others, a boom in the price of homes may have no effect on assessments because they are so seldom changed. Ironically, areas where assessors do a good job are apt to have more political problems with property taxation than places where assessors rarely update assessments.[4]

From 1971 to 1976 the assessed value of locally assessed real property rose more than 80 percent in eighteen states and 30 percent or less in thirteen states. While some of this difference can be accounted for by varying economic conditions, most of it is due to nonuniform assessment practices.[5]

Calculation of Tax Liability: A
Micro Perspective

States frequently grant *partial exemptions* to certain properties, depending on the nature of the property and the characteristics of the owner. Such exemptions are subtracted from the assessed valuation before the tax to be paid is calculated.

After exemptions are subtracted, the remaining assessed valuation is multiplied by the *nominal tax rate.* This tax rate is the sum of the property tax rates levied by all local governments (and, rarely, the state government) which rely on property taxes. It is often called a millage rate and is expressed as a certain tax per $1,000 of assessed valuation. For example, a millage rate of 150 means that there is a 15 percent nominal tax rate on what remains of assessed valuation after subtracting exemptions ($150/$1,000 = 15 percent). Multiplying this nominal tax rate by net assessed value yields the gross property tax.

One more step is sometimes necessary to determine how much property tax is to be paid—subtraction of *tax credits.* These credits can be deducted either before the property tax is paid or at a later time when a special form (which may be the income tax return) is filed. When the value of a credit depends in part on the income of the taxpayer, it is called a *circuit breaker.* The amount which is left after subtraction of credits is the net property tax.

The difference between exemptions and credits should be emphasized. *Exemptions* are subtracted from assessed value before the gross tax is calculated; *credits* are subtracted from the gross tax.

The final basic concept is the *effective tax rate,* the net tax divided by the market value of the property. In comparing tax burdens, the effective tax rate, rather than the nominal tax rate, is important, since the effective rate reflects exemptions, credits, and differences in assessment ratios, none of which are shown by the nominal rate.

Consider the example presented in table 1-1: Place A has a nominal tax rate of $200 per $1,000 of assessed valuation, an assessment ratio for homes of 20 percent, and a credit for homeowners of $500. Place B has a nominal tax rate of $30 per $1,000 of assessed valuation, a 10 percent assessment ratio, and no exemptions or credits. Place C has a nominal tax rate of $100 per $1,000 of assessed valuation, an assessment ratio of 50 percent, and an exemption for homeowners of $10,000. Suppose that the average home in each place is worth $50,000. Despite the great differences in nominal tax rates and other tax provisions, the tax on such a home is the same in all three places, as is the effective tax rate.[6]

*Calculation of Tax Liability: A
Macro Perspective*

The analysis up to this point has concentrated on the tax from the perspective of individual taxpayers. Additional insight can be obtained from taking the view of the tax users—governments. Property taxes are usually paid to a number of different jurisdictions, the most important being a city, county, and school district. Property taxes may also be paid to states and to special districts with functions such as recreation, higher education, assessment of property, and so

Table 1-1
Illustrative Tax Computation for a $50,000 House

Place	Nominal Tax Rate	Assessment Ratio (Percent)	Exemption	Credit
A	$200 per $1,000	20	0	$500
B	30 per $1,000	100	0	0
C	100 per $1,000	50	$10,000	0

Place	A	B	C
Market value	$50,000	$50,000	$50,000
X Assessment ratio / 100	0.2	1.0	0.5
= Assessed valuation	$10,000	$50,000	$25,000
− Exemption	0	0	$10,000
= Value subject to tax	$10,000	$50,000	$15,000
X Nominal tax rate / $1,000	0.2	0.03	0.1
= Gross tax	$ 2,000	$ 1,500	$ 1,500
− Credit	$ 500	0	0
= Net tax	$ 1,500	$ 1,500	$ 1,500
÷ Market value	$50,000	$50,000	$50,000
= Effective tax rate	3%	3%	3%

forth. Since the boundaries of these jurisdictions are often different, people who live in the same city may be subject to different property tax rates since their school district or special districts are not the same. At any rate, the nominal tax rate to which each property owner is subject is found by adding the separate tax rates of several layers of governments.

In order to see how these tax rates are determined, consider a single government. Its tax rate is found by dividing the property tax revenue which it needs by the assessed value of all the property contained within it (minus exemptions, if any). The property tax revenue to be raised is found by subtracting its nonproperty tax revenue (state and federal aid, revenue from charges and license fees, and nonproperty taxes) from its planned expenditures.

Table 1-2 provides an illustration. The local government's total expenditures are $12 million, and it has $4.5 million of nonproperty tax revenue available, leaving $7.5 million to be raised from the property tax. Since its taxable assessed valuation is $250 million, the nominal tax rate is 3 percent.[7]

Table 1-3 shows how the tax to be paid by each class of property is set. In this example, the total tax base of $250 million consists of $125 million residential property, $75 million business property, and $50 million farm property. Since homes are half of the tax base, they pay half of the tax; business owns 30 percent of the taxable property and pays 30 percent; farms represent

Table 1-2
Illustrative Determination of Local Government Tax Rate

Expenditures	$12,000,000	
Nonproperty Tax Revenue	−$ 4,500,000	
State aid		$2,000,000
Federal aid		250,000
Charges		1,500,000
Local sales tax		750,000
Revenue to be raised by property tax	7,500,000	

$$\frac{\text{Revenue to be raised from property tax}}{\text{Taxable assessed valuation}} = \text{Nominal tax rate}$$

$$\frac{\$\ \ 7,500,000}{\$250,000,000} = 0.03$$

The tax rate is 3 percent, or $30 per $1,000 of assessed value.

20 percent of the total and pay a similar percentage. Within each taxing jurisdiction, taxes are distributed in proportion to assessed values.

One possible source of confusion should be mentioned. The composition of the tax base in each taxing jurisdiction determines tax burdens, not the composition of the total tax base of the state. Thus, farm property usually pays a smaller percentage of property taxes statewide than its proportion of the tax base because most property taxes are levied by local units of government and tax rates in rural areas, where most farms are located, tend to be lower than in urban areas.

This brief sketch of how the property tax system operates suggests three ways in which across-the-board tax relief can be given:

Table 1-3
Example of Distribution of Taxes among Classes of Property

	Assessed Value	Percentage of Total
Residential	$125,000,000	50
Business	75,000,000	30
Farms	50,000,000	20
Total	$250,000,000	100

	Tax at 3 Percent Rate	Percentage of Total
Residential	$3,750,000	50
Business	2,250,000	30
Farms	1,500,000	20
Total	$7,500,000	100

1. Reduce local government expenditures (by state-imposed controls, state or federal assumption of certain local functions, or independent local action).
2. Increase state or federal aid to local governments.
3. Increase charges or nonproperty taxes of local governments.

In addition, relief can be given to particular types of property in these three ways:

1. Increase exemptions for certain kinds of property.
2. Increase credits for certain kinds of property.
3. Set a lower assessment ratio for certain types of property than for other types.

Note that simply reducing assessment ratios across the board does not provide any relief. Nominal tax rates can be raised to offset such a decrease. Likewise, limiting nominal tax rates does not provide any relief if assessment ratios are allowed to increase as an offset. If the nominal tax rate or the assessment ratio is lowered *while the other is held constant,* property tax revenue will be restricted. This is a seventh method of providing relief.

All these means of relieving property taxes imply costs, in terms of reduced local government expenditures (which means lower services, unless efficiency can be increased in proportion to reduced spending), higher nonproperty taxes or charges at some level of government, or increased property taxes for the nonfavored classes of property. Table 1-4 provides examples of the third possibility—that property tax relief for one class of property results in higher taxes for other classes. It shows that if there is a homestead exemption or if agricultural property has a lower assessment ratio than other types of property, property taxes will rise for the nonfavored types of property because the tax rate will be raised to make up for the lost revenue.

In the original situation, farm property is 20 percent of the tax base and homes and business are 40 percent each. With total assessed value of $100 million and $3 million to be raised from property taxes, the tax rate is 3 percent; farms pay $600,000, and the other two classes pay $1.2 million each.

When the homestead exemption lowers residential taxable assessed values from $40 million to $30 million homes are just one-third of the tax base, with farms two-ninths and business four-ninths. Since the taxable assessed valuation is now only $90 million, a tax rate of 3 1/3 percent is needed to raise $3 million. Home taxes fall, but those on business and farms rise.

A similar result occurs if farms are assessed preferentially. If agricultural assessed value drops to $15 million while other properties are assessed as in the original situation, the tax rate will rise to 3.16 percent, resulting in lower farm taxes and higher taxes for home and business.

Whether the shifting of tax burdens is sizable depends on the composition

Table 1-4
Examples of Tax Breaks for Particular Types of Properties

	Farms	*Homes*	*Business*	*Total*
Original Situation				
Assessed value	$20,000,000	$40,000,000	$40,000,000	$100,000,000
Tax Rate $\dfrac{\$3,000,000}{\$100,000,000}$ = 3 percent				
Tax	$ 600,000	$ 1,200,000	$ 1,200,000	$ 3,000,000
Homestead Exemption				
Assessed value	$20,000,000	$30,000,000	$40,000,000	$ 90,000,000
Tax Rate $\dfrac{\$3,000,000}{\$90,000,000}$ = 3 1/3 percent				
Tax	$ 666,667	$ 1,000,000	$ 1,333,333	$ 3,000,000
Preferential Assessment of Farmland				
Assessed value	$15,000,000	$40,000,000	$40,000,000	$ 95,000,000
Tax Rate $\dfrac{\$3,000,000}{\$95,000,000}$ = 3.16 percent				
Tax	$ 473,684	$ 1,263,158	$ 1,263,158	$ 3,000,000

of the tax base, as explained in subsequent chapters. The major point here is that the cost of property tax relief is always borne by someone. It does not fall like manna from heaven.

State Aid to School Districts: The
Property Tax Connection

No analysis of how the contemporary property tax system operates can ignore the role of school aid. The crucial role of state aid to school districts does not stem from the fact that it represents the largest single category of state expenditure. The reason that school aid is so important is that in the great majority of states school aid is at least partially a function of local assessed valuation. School districts with lower assessed valuation per pupil receive greater state aid, in order to move the distribution of resources in the direction of greater equality.

According to a tabulation by the Education Commission of the States, in 1979 forty-six out of fifty states used school aid formulas which incorporated the local property tax base as one determinant of school aid. Twenty of these states had foundation plans, twelve had guaranteed tax base programs, and the others had some sort of hybrid plan. The four states which did not consider assessed valuation were Alabama, Mississippi, Hawaii, and North Carolina.[8]

Since foundation plans are the most common ones, they are used as an example of how assessed value affects school aid. In a foundation plan every school district is guaranteed a certain level of revenue per pupil (the foundation level) provided that it levies a property tax at a specified rate. State aid is equal to the difference between the foundation level of spending and the revenue generated by the required tax levy. For example, suppose the guarantee is $1,000 of revenue per pupil and that the required tax rate is 0.5 percent. A school district with $100,000 of property per pupil would receive $500 aid per pupil, a school district with $150,000 of property per pupil would receive $250, and a district with $200,000 of property per pupil would receive no aid.

Effect of Inflation on Tax Shares of Different Classes of Property

Some of the major strains affecting the property tax in the 1970s can be traced directly to inflation. Had there been no inflation, the property tax would look much different today.

If inflation affected all types of property equally and if school aid were not a function of property values, inflation would not pose a problem for the property tax. Effective tax rates and the shares of the property tax bill paid by different classes of property would not be affected.

But not all types of property have been equally affected by inflation in the 1970s. Home values have risen faster than those of business property, and farm values have jumped faster than those of homes. Unless the ground rules of the property tax system are changed, these differing rates of inflation imply that farm taxes will rise faster than average and business taxes slower than average, with taxes of homeowners somewhere in between.[9] In other words, the shares of the total tax bill borne by each class of property will shift.

The potential tax shifts are very large when property values change rapidly, as they have in the 1970s. The average value of farmland more than doubled from 1970 to 1976, and in some states it more than tripled. Home values have been rising more than 10 percent per year.[10] The actual tax shifts which occur depend on the composition of the tax base in each local jurisdiction. In an urban area with hardly any farmland, the major tax shift is away from business and to homes; in an area with agricultural and residential property but little business, the shift is away from homes and to farms. If virtually all the property in an area is farmland, no significant shift of taxes to farms from other classes of property can occur.

Appendix 1B summarizes evidence that the composition of the property tax base in many states did change during the 1970s, with single-family homes becoming a larger proportion of the total.

The property tax element in school aid complicates the situation further. When assessed values rise, there is a substitution of local property tax for state school aid.[11] Thus, even in a rural area with nothing but farm property, rising farm values lead to higher property taxes. In an urban area with a balance between homes and business property, the higher residential taxes resulting from the tax shift away from business are exacerbated by the school aid loss.

All these developments can be averted by the timely application of property tax relief. That was the course in states such as Iowa. But in California and other places, timely legislative action was not forthcoming. Tax revolt was the result.

This discussion suggests an eighth method of providing property tax relief—limit the assessment changes which are allowed to occur.

Overview of Relief Measures Used

The eight alternative methods of relieving property taxes can be categorized in several ways. One basic distinction is between measures which are targeted at particular classes of property and those which are not. Credits, exemptions, and differential assessment ratios (including limits on the growth of assessments) can be used to target relief. Aid from higher levels of government, local nonproperty taxes, and limits on spending and taxing (including limits on their increases) lower the amount of revenue to be raised by property taxation and reduce property taxes for all classes of property without distinction.

A second distinction can be made between measures which require an appropriation of state funds and those which do not. State aid to local governments and assumption of local functions are the only two measures which must be state-financed, but credits usually are as well. Exemptions, preferential assessment of farmland or other property, and limits on assessment increases may also involve indirect costs to the state by increasing school aid costs (since they reduce or hold down assessed valuation). Other measures, like local nonproperty taxes and controls on local spending or taxing, do not entail state expenditures.

A third method of distinguishing among relief alternatives is to consider how their effects vary. Measures differ, for example, in the extent to which they interfere with local autonomy, affect fiscal disparities among jurisdictions, or increase or reduce the progressivity of the tax system.

Table 1-5 summarizes the use of the major forms of property tax relief in each state. From left to right, the relief mechanisms are as follows. Homestead exemptions and credits, shown in the first two columns, are exemptions or credits for homeowners. Ten states also provide credits for renters. Circuit breakers, shown in the third column, are credits whose value depends on household income and property taxes paid. Usually renters are eligible as well as homeowners. Classification, in the fourth column, is a system in which certain types of real property are taxed at lower rates than other types. Local sales and incomes taxes, in the fifth and sixth columns, enable local governments to diversify their revenue sources and thus tend to reduce property tax levies.

State-imposed limits, in the next four columns, take numerous forms. The oldest and most widespread limit applies to local government tax rates, but it is not shown in the table. Limits which are included relate to property tax levies (or revenue), local government spending, and assessment increases. Full disclosure procedures, which do not absolutely limit taxes but do require special publicity and hearings before they can be raised, are also shown.

State aid and assumption of local functions provides considerable relief by substituting state funds for local property taxes. This type of relief is closely related to the proportion of state-local taxes which is collected by the state government. The rank of each state on this measure is shown in the final column.

Many types of relief are not included in table 1-5 because of space limitations but are covered in later chapters. Examples are exemptions for business, charitable, personal, and rehabilitated residential property, user charges, deferral, and income tax deductions for property taxes paid. Tax relief for agricultural property is omitted because it is nearly universal.

Framework for Evaluating Relief Measures

A number of questions can be asked about each form of relief:

1. Eligibility—does it benefit all property taxpayers or just a limited group? If benefits are limited, what is the distinguishing characteristic for identifying recipients: type of property owned (residential, agricultural, and so on), income, or other (age, disability, veteran status, and so forth)?
2. Given the eligibility, what determines the magnitude of benefits received? If benefits are not equally distributed, they may be a function of the amount of property owned, the gross property tax payment (which depends on the local tax rate and the amount of property owned), or the gross property tax payment and income.
3. Neutrality—does the aid have any significant effects on the actions of individuals as producers, consumers, voters, and so on?
4. Is the program difficult or expensive for the government to administer or for individuals to comply with?
5. Is the cost of the relief obvious or obscure (that is, easy or difficult to calculate)? Is it fixed or may it vary considerably from year to year? Is the program itself readily comprehensible?
6. Does the relief have important objectives other than property tax relief, such as equalization of government fiscal capacities or service levels, preservation of land in certain uses, encouragement of homeownership, or preventing the elderly from having to move because of property taxes?

Table 1-5
Property Tax Relief Mechanisms Employed by States, 1979

| State | Homestead Exemption or Credit | | Circuit Breaker[a] | Local Taxes | | | State-Imposed Limits[e] | | | | Percentage of State-Local Taxes Collected by State (Rank)[f] |
	All Ages	Seniors Only		Classification	Sales	Income	Levy	Spending	Assessment	Full Disclosure	
New England											
Connecticut	X		S	X[b]							11
Maine[d]	X	X	S								32
Massachusetts		X		X			CMS	CMS			6
New Hampshire		X									1
Rhode Island	X	X	S								21
Vermont			A								20
Midwest											
Delaware		X				X[b]	C				49
District of Columbia					—	—				X	—
Maryland	X		A	X		X[b]			X	X	16
New Jersey[d]	X	X	A			X[b]		CMS			2
New York		X	A		X	X[b]					4
Pennsylvania		X	S			X					26
Great Lakes											
Illinois	X	X	S	X[b]	X						13
Indiana[c, d]	X	X	S			X	CMS				29
Michigan			A			X	CMS				24
Ohio[c]			S		X	X	CMS				9
Wisconsin[c, d]	X		A				CMS	S			35
Plains											
Iowa	X		S	X		X[b]		S			23
Kansas			A		X		CMS	S	X		15
Minnesota[d]	X		A	X	X[b]		CM	S			38

	1	2	3	4	5	6	7	8	9	10	
Missouri	X				X						14
Nebraska	X	X	S		X	x^b	CM	S			7
North Dakota			S		X			S			33
South Dakota			S					S			3
Southeast											
Alabama	X		S	X	X	x	C				41
Arkansas	X	X			X					X	44
Florida	X	X			X						27
Georgia					X	x					28
Kentucky					X	x	CMS				42
Louisiana				X	X		CMS	S			37
Mississippi	X	X			X						45
North Carolina					X						40
South Carolina				X	X		CMS				43
Tennessee				X X	X						30
Virginia				X							22
West Virginia			S							X	46
Southwest											
Arizona[d]	X		S	X	X		CMS	CMS			25
New Mexico			S/Ag		X		CMS	CMS			48
Oklahoma	X		S		X						36
Texas	X				X					X	17
Rocky Mountain											
Colorado	X		S		X		CMS	S	X		5
Idaho			S						X		34
Montana	X	X		X				S			13
Utah[d]	X	X			X		CMS	S		X	31
Wyoming	X				X						18
Far West											
Alaska	X				X						50
California[d]	X	X	S		X	x^b	M	S	X		10
Hawaii[d]	X			X						X	47

Table 1-5 continued

State	Homestead Exemption or Credit		Circuit Breaker[a]	Classification	Local Taxes		State-Imposed Limits[e]				Percentage of State-Local Taxes Collected by State (Rank)[f]
	All Ages	Seniors Only			Sales	Income	Levy	Spending	Assessments	Full Disclosure	
Nevada	X		S		X						19
Oregon[d]			A	X		X[b]	CMS		X		8
Washington		X			X		CMS				39

Sources:

Columns 1 to 3: Advisory Commission on Intergovernmental Relations, *Significant Features of Fiscal Federalism*, 1976-77 ed., vol. 2, table 73; and Abt Associates, *Property tax Relief Programs for the Elderly: A Compendium Report* (Washington, D.C.: 1975), pp. 112-37.

Column 4: International Association of Assessing Officers, "Classified Property Tax System in the U.S."

Columns 5 and 6: Advisory Commission on Intergovernmental Relations, *Significant Features of Fiscal Federalism*.

Columns 7 to 10: International Association of Assessing Officers, "Property Tax Limits"; Advisory Commission on Intergovernmental Relations, *State Limitations on Local Taxes and Expenditures*; Education Commission of the States, *School District Expenditure and Tax Controls*.

Column 11: Advisory Commission on Intergovernmental Relations, *Significant Features of Fiscal Federalism*, 1978-79 ed.

All columns: survey by author during May-June 1979.

Certain types of relief are not shown, such as relief for farm property, deferral of homeowner taxes, tax rate limits, and relief for business property.

aS = only senior citizens eligible; A = all ages are eligible.

bUse of this form of relief is restricted to a small number of localities.

cThe state provides a credit which pays a certain percentage of all property taxes; in Wisconsin, only taxes due to above-average rates receive the credit.

dThe state provides a credit for renters.

eState-imposed limits: S = schools, M = municipalities, C = counties.

fPercentage of state-local taxes collected by the state is a measure of the degree to which the state government has relieved local governments of the burden of financing services, which usually leads to lower property taxes. States ranked with high numbers indicate a large state role and low numbers a modest state role. This measure is for 1977, and all other data are for 1979.

gIn addition to a property tax circuit breaker for senior citizens, New Mexico has another circuit breaker which is based on all state-local taxes paid.

Criteria

After each question has been answered for each type of relief, it can be evaluated in terms of the following criteria:

1. Horizontal equity. There should be equal treatment of equals.
2. Vertical equity. There should be appropriate treatment of households at different levels of economic well-being.
3. Efficiency. Any changes in the economic behavior of recipients are in a socially desirable direction.
4. Administrative and compliance cost. The cost to the government of dispensing relief and to recipients of applying for it should be low.
5. Visibility and understandability. The relief should be easy to trace; it should not be so complex that its provisions are difficult to comprehend without exceptional effort.
6. Appropriateness. The goals of the program should be proper ones for the government to seek with its limited resources.
7. Cost-effectiveness. The benefits of the program relative to the costs compare well with alternative means of achieving the goals of the program.
8. Political marketability. The program should be feasible both to enact and to administer politically.

Few, if any, programs are likely to receive top marks on all these criteria. After the relief alternatives are weighed according to these criteria in succeeding chapters, the conflicts among them are discussed in chapter 16.

The relative importance of these criteria is a matter of value judgment, but it is widely agreed that two of the most important are horizontal and vertical equity. Much more attention is devoted to discussing the distributional effects of relief measures than to other criteria. The differences among policies in terms of efficiency, administrative cost, and compliance cost appear to be relatively minor.[12] Each criterion is important for some relief alternatives and is brought into the analysis whenever relevant.

In terms of vertical equity, economists differentiate among progressive, proportional, and regressive taxes, according to whether the ratio of tax paid to income rises, remains constant, or falls as household income rises. Likewise, tax relief is progressive if it represents a higher proportion of income for poor than for rich families.

Tax relief alternatives fall into several categories. Most progressive are those which provide all their benefits to households with relatively low incomes. Next come those for which the average benefit falls as income rises. Programs which provide equal absolute benefits to all are also relatively progressive, because the relief is a higher proportion of income for those with low incomes. Even relief measures which provide higher benefits to the rich than to the poor are progressive if the ratio of relief to income is higher for people with low income. Regressive relief measures represent a higher proportion of income for the rich than for the poor.

The progressivity of property tax relief depends not only on which type of relief measure is being considered but also on how progressive or regressive the property tax is itself, which is a somewhat controversial subject. Appendix 1A outlines the issues involved in this controversy. Because its heavy burden on households with below-average income is considered one of the most serious defects of the property tax by the author, programs which favor households with relatively low income are viewed favorably in this book.

Fundamental Questions

Attitudes toward particular relief measures or relief in general depend on a number of assumptions. Fundamental disagreement exists about the answers to some questions, so there can never be unanimity about these policies.

Is the Property Tax Inherently Defective or Basically Sound?

Until the late 1960s, the attitude toward this tax among both economists and the general public was generally hostile. Surveys indicate that the general public has not changed its mind,[13] but within the economics profession there has been a considerable shift of opinion. The major reason for the more favorable attitude is that the view of the tax's incidence has changed. Formerly, the property tax was viewed as being rather regressive. Now many economists consider it to be progressive. Even those who still accept the idea of regressivity believe that widely used estimates in the 1960s exaggerated the degree to which landlords and businesses passed taxes on to tenants and customers, one of the important sources of regressivity.[14]

A related source of controversy stems from the ability-to-pay principle of taxation. Critics of the property tax claim that the relationship between ability to pay and property ownership is very weak for many reasons: Income is the best measure of ability to pay because all taxes must be paid from income; it is not fair to tax unrealized capital gains; an unfair burden is placed on the elderly, whose property wealth is often not matched by commensurate high income; much property ownership is offset by heavy indebtedness, but it is gross property ownership which is taxed; and so many kinds of property are exempt that the tax is unfair to the property which remains subject to tax.

Defenders of the property tax argue that it does measure a dimension of ability to pay. They maintain that the property tax rightfully imposes burdens on many of the wealthy who take advantage of income tax loopholes to avoid much of their tax liability; that persons with high wealth and low current income can borrow to meet their property tax liability; and that property ownership is strongly correlated with a family's normal income, which is a better measure of economic well-being than income in a single year.

Adherents of taxation according to benefits received also can be found on both sides of the property tax argument. Critics claim that only a small share of public service benefits are property-related rather than individual-related. Defenders deny this argument and claim that the tax provides a mechanism for society to capture a portion of the windfall gains created by various public investments.

The last major criticism of the property tax is that it is an antihousing levy: housing is a necessity of life, and yet it is subject to heavier taxation than anything else a consumer can buy. This point loses much of its force when it is recognized the federal income tax is strongly biased in favor of housing consumption. Besides, it appears as if in many places improvements to property do not result in higher assessments, thus avoiding an important disincentive effect which is frequently mentioned.[15]

Most defenders of the property tax concede that, as it exists, it is a defective fiscal instrument, but that it should be repaired rather than phased out. Almost everyone favors more accurate assessments to improve the tax's equity, and many favor circuit breakers or deferral to help those with high ratios of property to income. Critics liken this to prescribing band-aids for cancer.

*To What Extent Should Redistribution of Income
Take Place at the Subnational Level?*

There is a fairly strong consensus among economists that redistribution of income can best be accomplished at the national level, where one does not have to be concerned about the migration of high-income people out and low-income people in.[16] This consideration places a constraint on how redistributive state and local tax policies can be. However, there is a mitigating factor—the deductibility of state and local taxes in determining federal tax liability. Because of this deduction for income, sales, and property taxes, the incentive of a high-income person to escape high state-local taxes is significantly reduced. For example, suppose that state-local taxes are $1,000 higher in one state than in a neighboring one. For a family whose marginal tax rate is 40 percent, these extra taxes lower the federal tax bill by $400, leaving a net cost of $600.

In considering how redistributive to make its taxes, a state which is not satisfied with the degree of income redistribution accomplished by the federal government must be concerned about how its tax system compares to those in neighboring states. Studies indicate that most state-local tax systems are regressive but in varying degrees.[17] There is little evidence that existing differentials in tax rates lead many people to move from one place to another.[18]

How Much Control Should Be Centralized at the State Level?

On the premise that the government closest to the people best knows their desires, local autonomy is a value which has long been cherished. However, autonomy may conflict with other goals. An increasing number of states have imposed controls on the taxing or spending decisions of local governments. These controls imply that democratically elected officials cannot be trusted to follow the desires of their constituents.

Autonomy can also be impaired in other ways, such as when a state tax substitutes for a local one or when the state assumes responsibility for a function which was previously handled locally.

How Much Relief Is Desirable if It Results in Reduced Services or Increases in Other Taxes?

It was pointed out earlier that property tax relief is rarely a "free lunch." As one writer has put it, "property tax relief is sales tax aggravation, or income tax or payroll tax aggravation."[19] He might have added "or service reduction" or "property tax aggravation for someone else." Unless the relief is matched by an increase in governmental efficiency, someone suffers as a result.

Should Shifts of Property Tax Shares or One-Year Jumps in Tax Bills Be Moderated?

It was explained earlier how inflation can redistribute property tax burdens, raising them for some persons and lowering them for others. A policy goal in numerous states has been to avoid such sharp increases and decreases. This policy extends the adage "an old tax is a good tax" to "an old tax burden is a valid tax burden, and it should not change too much too fast." This position is inconsistent with the view that fairness requires uniformity of treatment of all types of property and that those whose property appreciates in value are better off and should pay more tax than those who have not been so lucky.

Conclusions

The answers to the five questions are controversial. The author will not expose his own opinions to the reader on four of them. However, on the first question the author feels compelled to say that he agrees with those who want to reform the property tax rather than replace it. While those states with extremely high tax rates can use some across-the-board relief, elsewhere the prescription is different. In many states the property tax needs fine-tuning, not a complete overhaul. It needs a scalpel, not a sledge hammer.

One ought to compare alternative property tax relief methods with other politically feasible policies. All policies (including the status quo) have defects, so they should not be criticized in isolation. Discussing property tax relief is usually an exploration in the realm of the second-best, if not the third-best, or the lesser of two evils. It is important to keep one's eye on a theoretical ideal policy, but it is naive and futile to stop there.

This book proceeds from the assumption that property tax relief will be granted. Going beyond the question of whether to give relief, it concentrates on the questions how and for whom.

One basic justification for this approach is political. In many states, the pressure for property tax relief is so great that something must be done. The more positive attitude toward the property tax of many economists has made very little impression on the public consciousness. Until it does, property tax relief may be a political imperative.

Aside from political considerations, there are strong grounds for believing that there should be property tax relief. One set of reasons relies on the traditional criticisms of the property tax in economic literature. First, the property tax is regressive with respect to current income, at least up to an income level which covers a majority of families and individuals. Second, in many old, declining central cities the property tax base has been relatively stagnant even in the inflationary 1970s. Income and sales are more satisfactory bases for revenue because their growth rate is higher. Third, except for the portion falling on land, the property tax distorts the allocation of resources by discouraging capital investment. The empirical importance of the third argument is uncertain.

Another approach to justify property tax relief is based on how the local government finance system is affected by inflation. While the term *taxflation* is usually used with reference to the income tax, in some states it is equally applicable to the property tax. In this context *taxflation* may be defined as a situation in which inflation causes residential property taxes to rise faster than the local government spending required to maintain a constant level of services. It has two sources. Inflation drives up the assessments of homes much more than the assessments of businesses because they are assessed in different ways. Thus, the tax burden shifts from business property to homes. In addition, the school aid system may also contribute to property taxes' rising faster than school spending because as assessed values rise, the state's aid to school districts usually declines.

This concept of taxflation both resembles and differs from taxflation of the income tax. The latter kind of taxflation occurs when income tax liabilities rise faster than income because of the interaction between inflation and a progressive tax rate structure. Even though a person's income adjusted for inflation has not risen, the tax liability may. Property tax taxflation can, but does not necessarily, involve residential property taxes becoming a larger fraction of income. The property tax tends to rise faster than local government spending for the two reasons noted; but if local spending is increasing slowly, the property tax might not become a larger fraction of personal income. The tendency for property tax taxflation to occur will also be counteracted if nonproperty tax revenue, such as federal or state aid or local nonproperty taxes, is increasing at a high rate.

Much of the property tax relief which has been provided during the 1970s does nothing more than cancel the effects of taxflation. It offsets a shift of the tax burden adverse to homeowners and a shift in the tax mix toward greater reliance on property taxes relative to state revenue. In a sense, this property tax relief is as much "fiscal sleight of hand" as the income tax cuts which Congress regularly enacts to offset taxflation of the income tax—the tendency of the average tax rate to increase because of inflationary increases in nominal income. This property tax relief, like the income tax relief, merely tends to offset "excessive" increases in taxes and may leave the taxpayer no better off than before the bout of taxflation.

Not all property tax relief is of this sort. Many states have gone far beyond measures which merely offset taxflation. Our intention is simply to point out that counteracting taxflation is the purpose of a considerable amount of relief.

Notes

1. Richard R. Almy, "Rationalizing the Assessment Process," in *Property Tax Reform* ed. George E. Peterson (Washington, D.C.: The Urban Institute, 1973), p. 175.

2. The treatment of personal property depends on its type. In 1976 commercial-industrial personal property was at least partially taxed in forty-seven states, agricultural in forty-two states, and residential in twenty-six states, according to the Census Bureau. A 1978 survey found that more personal property is exempt. See chapter 12.

3. Almy, "Rationalizing," p. 175.

4. For indicators of the quality of assessment performance, see Advisory Commission on Intergovernmental Relations, *Significant Features of Fiscal Federalism,* 1978-79 ed., table 37 (Washington, D.C., 1979).

5. States in which assessments rose more than 80 percent include Alaska, Arizona, Colorado, Delaware, District of Columbia, Florida, Georgia, Hawaii, Iowa, Maine, New Jersey, North Carolina, South Carolina, Texas, Utah, Virginia, Washington, and Wisconsin. States in which the increase was due to a change in legal assessment ratios are omitted. States in which assessments rose 30 percent or less are Alabama, Illinois, Indiana, Kansas, Louisiana, Missouri, Montana,

Nebraska, North Dakota, Oklahoma, Pennsylvania, Tennessee, and West Virginia. See John O. Behrens, "Again Some Facts for a Tax under Attacks" (Paper delivered at conference of National Association of Tax Administrators, Madison, Wisconsin, June 12, 1979).

6. A home which is not worth $50,000 would not pay the same tax in each place. For example, a $40,000 home would pay the following amounts of tax: $1,100 in place A, $1,200 in place B, and $1,000 in place C. The example in the text was not intended to suggest that different combinations of assessment ratios, tax rates, exemptions, and credits necessarily produce the same result, but that they may do so.

7. The illustration in table 1-2 assumes that cash reserves remain unchanged from year to year and that there is no borrowing. For a limited period expenditures could exceed new revenues received by reducing cash reserves, but that is not possible indefinitely.

8. Kent McGuire et al., "School Finance at a Fourth Glance" (Denver: Education Commission of the States, 1979).

9. This section assumes that farms are assessed according to their market value rather than use value.

10. Data on farm values are from U.S. Department of Agriculture, "Farm Real Estate Market Developments," Washington, D.C., January 1978, and on home values from National Association of Realtors, *Existing Home Sales: 1978* (Washington, D.C.: 1979), p. 3. The median sales price of existing single-family homes rose 69 percent between 1973 and 1978. The average price of an acre of farmland rose from $204 to $474 in the continental United States from March 1971 to November 1977; during the same period it rose from $392 to $1,250 in Iowa.

11. In some states this does not occur because the state appropriation for school aid is a fixed amount. Rising assessed valuation leads to a redistribution of aid but not a reduction of the total amount. Examples are Missouri and Vermont.

12. If there are significant differences, they have generally not been documented. The limited extent to which property tax relief affects residential, business, and farm actions is discussed in chapters 3 to 6. More generally, the welfare loss due to nonneutral taxation has been shown to be relatively small in the literature following Arnold C. Harberger, "The Measurement of Waste, " *American Economic Review, Papers and Proceedings,* vol. 54, pp. 58-76. As for administrative and compliance costs, they occasionally may be significant (as in the administrative cost of certain types of personal property taxation), but usually they are relatively small in relation to the amount of relief provided.

13. Advisory Commission on Intergovernmental Relations, "Changing Public Attitudes on Governments and Taxes: 1978," (Washington, D.C.: 1978) shows that people in the United States generally rate the property tax as "the worst tax—that is, the most unfair." In May 1978, 32 percent of persons polled

selected the property tax for this honor, followed by: 30 percent, federal income tax; 18 percent, state sales tax; 11 percent, state income tax; and 10 percent, do not know. The property tax was also least popular in 1973, 1975, and 1977.

14. See appendixes 1A and 1B for a discussion of these issues.

15. George Peterson et al., *Property Taxes, Housing and the Cities* (Lexington, Mass.: Lexington Books, D.C. Heath, 1973). This book concluded that the property tax does exacerbate slum conditions by reducing maintenance expenditures financed out of cash flow. In addition, many owners believe that improvements lead to increased assessments even though they seldom do.

16. See, for example, Wallace E. Oates, *Fiscal Federalism* (New York: Harcourt, Brace, Jovanovich, 1972).

17. Stephen E. Lile, "Family Tax Burdens Compared among States and among Cities Located within Kentucky and Neighboring States" (Bowling Green: Western Kentucky University, 1975), crudely estimates the incidence of each state's tax structure. For a more refined overall estimates, see Joseph A. Pechman and Benjamin A. Okner, *Who Bears the Tax Burden?* (Washington, D.C., The Brookings Institution, 1974).

18. A number of studies have found that migration is affected by differences in tax burdens, but most of the studies have serious methodological shortcomings, such as using per capita burdens as a measure of the level of taxation. See R.J. Cebula, "The Migration Impact of State and Local Government Policies: A Survey of the Literature in the United States," *Urban Studies,* forthcoming.

19. Mason Gaffney, "An Agenda for Strengthening the Property Tax," in *Property Tax Reform,* ed. G.E. Peterson, p. 65.

Appendix 1A:
Property Tax Incidence

The recent literature on the incidence of the property tax is voluminous. This appendix reviews the major issues for the nonspecialist in public finance.[1]

In the 1960s the conventional view was that the portion of the property tax on buildings and other improvements is mostly passed on to consumers and the portion of the tax on land is borne by its owner. The resulting distribution is regressive over the income levels which cover most taxpayers because consumption expenditures (both housing and nonhousing) tend to increase more slowly than income as income rises. The reason that consumers bear most of the tax on improvements has to do with the mobility of capital. If a tax in one jurisdiction lowers the rate of return on investment below its normal level, capital will flee. Investment which remains will earn higher pretax returns than previously, and prices paid by consumers will be higher and payments to land and immobile workers and other suppliers will be lower.

In contrast with this "old" partial view of the economy, the "new view" recognizes that the property tax is used throughout the economy. Since the supply of capital nationally is relatively fixed, to the extent that the property tax is a uniform national tax it is borne by the owners of capital. The portion of the tax which is levied at a rate above the national average rate produces "excise"-type effects similar to those under the old view (such as higher prices and lower wages), while any tax which is at a rate below the national average tends to result in the opposite types of effects.[2] As a rough approximation, the tax is borne in proportion to ownership of capital.

It is tempting to leap to the conclusion that a tax whose burden is proportional to property ownership must be progressive, since most property is owned by the rich. However, data for 1972 show that such a tax is regressive up to the $10,000-$15,000 income level and progressive above that level.[3] Since most families had an income below $15,000 in that year, the tax was regressive for the majority of people in the United States. No recent estimates are available, but the income level at which the tax changes from regressive to progressive probably occurs at a considerably higher level because of inflation.

After an initial period of confusion, it is now generally believed that both the new and old views are correct in certain situations. If one is contemplating a national change in property tax use, the general equilibrium view is appropriate, so the tax is borne by owners of capital. However, if a single state or local government raises or lowers the level of its property tax, this change is best viewed from the perspective of the old view.

A second major challenge to the idea that the property tax is regressive is based on the permanent-income concept, which relates taxes to a household's normal income rather than its actual income in a particular year. Because people tend to maintain their spending habits when their income temporarily rises or falls, consumption-related taxes appear more regressive when related to actual current income than when compared to normal income. For example, a well-to-do family which happens to have low income one year is unlikely to move to a different house, so their property tax appears high relative to their current income even though the family is not in real economic distress. On the other hand, while the permanent-income viewpoint has some appeal, several economists have argued (and their sentiments are undoubtedly shared by many noneconomists) that taxes have to be paid out of current income, so that past or future income is irrelevant. Even a family whose income is only temporarily depressed may be in sufficient difficulty to justify some temporary relief. Moreover, many of the households with relatively low incomes are permanently at that level.[4]

Many other considerations can be introduced. One economist has argued that the property tax has led many communities to restrict the supply of low-income housing for fiscal reasons, which has raised housing costs for families with below-average income, and that this considerably increases the regressivity of the tax.[5] Another points out that the ratio of rent to market value tends to be lower for housing rented by the affluent, reducing the regressivity of the tax.[6] Others argue that if the imputed rent of homeowners is included in the calculation of their income, the regressivity of the tax is reduced.[7]

In summary, it appears that with respect to current income the property tax is generally regressive for the majority of taxpayers, whether one refers to the new view or the old view. However, the incidence pattern varies from place to place depending on such factors as the degree to which assessments are biased against low-value property, the level of the tax rate relative to the national average, the composition of the tax base, and the mobility of local factors of production.

A final issue relates to capitalization, the process by which property values are determined on the basis of the discounted benefits and costs which accrue to property owners. If property taxes are fully capitalized, the benefits of property tax relief will be reflected in higher property values. Thus, persons who acquire the property once the relief is already in effect do not benefit from it because their initial purchase price has been raised.

At first glance capitalization seems to confound the common objective of property tax relief of aiding particular groups of taxpayers. It is not certain, however, that full capitalization occurs. Moreover, since the decision must be made each year to continue providing particular types of property tax relief, their benefits may be viewed as being annually renewed, even if they were initially capitalized.

Notes

1. The most accessible discussion of these issues are in Henry Aaron, *Who Pays the Property Tax?* (Washington, D.C.: The Brookings Institution, 1975); Dick Netzer, "The Incidence of the Property Tax Revisited," *National Tax Journal* 23 (December 1973):515-535; and Charles E. McLure, "The 'New View' of the Property Tax: A Caveat," *National Tax Journal* 30 (March 1977):169-75.

2. Thus, it is important whether tax rates are above or below average in places with high income. Using county data, Aaron found that in half of sixteen states which he studied there was a significant correlation between average income and property tax rate. In all these cases, tax rates increased less than in proportion to income. Such calculations yield biased estimates of the relationship between tax rate and income because within counties there is often a negative correlation, as Aaron showed in a number of New Jersey counties. A common situation is for central cities to have higher incomes and tax rates than rural areas but lower incomes and higher tax rates than most suburbs. What is needed is data on household income, home value, and tax rate. Unfortunately, surveys of income and home value generally do not obtain direct information on tax rates. See Aaron, *Who Pays the Property Tax?* p. 46; Abt Associates, *Property Tax Relief Programs for the Elderly: An Evaluation* (Washington, 1975) p. 65.

3. Charles Schultze et al, *Setting National Priorities: The 1973 Budget* (Washington, D.C.: The Brookings Institution, 1972), p. 445. Allan Odden and Phillip E. Vincent reached a similar conclusion in case studies of several states. See their *The Regressivity of the Property Tax* (Denver: Education Commission of the States, 1976).

4. Aaron, *Who Pays the Property Tax?* pp. 34-38. Netzer, "Incidence Revisited," pp. 528-30.

5. Bruce K. Hamilton, "Capitalization and the Regressivity of the Property Tax: Empirical Evidence" (Unpublished paper, October 1978).

6. George E. Peterson, "The Regressivity of the Residential Property Tax" (Working Paper 1207-10, October 1972).

7. James N. Morgan et al., *Income and Welfare in the United States* (New York: McGraw Hill, 1962).

Appendix 1B:
The Changing
Composition of the
Property Tax Base

A survey was conducted in which state tax officials were asked to provide information on changes in the composition of assessed valuation during the 1970s. Many states either did not have such information or failed to provide it, but usable responses were received from thirteen states. In ten of those thirteen states, single-family homes became a larger proportion of the total property tax base. Results are summarized here.

California: Homes rose from 31.6 to 41 percent of net assessed value between 1973-1974 and 1977-1978, taking into account credits for homesteads and inventories.

Colorado: Homes rose from 41.2 percent of assessed valuations in 1970 to 45.3 percent in 978.

District of Columbia: Between 1976 and 1978 single-family residences rose from 40.5 percent of all taxable realty to 49.3 percent.

Idaho: Homes increased as a proportion of the property tax base from 24.8 percent in 1970 to 26.3 percent in 1976 to 31 percent in 1978.

Iowa: Taking into account credits, the proportion of property taxes impacting on homes rose from 30 to 33.4 percent between 1970 and 1976-1977.

Kentucky: Between 1973 and 1976, the proportion of assessed valuation consisting of homes rose from 28.7 to 31.1 percent.

Michigan: Homes rose from 48.2 percent in 1970 to 54.4 percent of assessed valuations in 1978, primarily because of new exemptions for personal property.

Nebraska: Homes rose from 31.2 percent of assessed valuations in 1970 to 34 percent in 1978.

Rhode Island: Between 1969 and 1976 the proportion of assessed valuation accounted for by homes rose from 40.9 to 43.4 percent.

Wisconsin: Homes rose from 43.2 percent of assessed valuation in 1970 to 48.9 percent in 1977.

The three states in which the proportion of single-family homes in the total property tax base did not change were Minnesota, Pennsylvania, and New Jersey.

The figures reported in a number of states may not reflect changes in the proportion of taxes paid because neither exemptions and credits nor tax rates are taken into account. However, in Iowa both credits and tax rates are considered, and in California credits are taken into account.

Another shortcoming of the statistics is that they do not differentiate between changes in assessed valuations due to net new construction and changes due to price increases or decreases.

2 Variations of Property Tax Use over Time and among States

Sensational reports of property tax increases and seemingly oppressive burdens grab headlines, but they often give a misleading impression of typical property tax levels and trends. They can also steer policy in the wrong direction. This chapter examines recent data on property tax revenue to set the stage for the analysis of relief programs. It is divided into four sections: the role of the property tax in state-local fiscal systems, aggregate national trends in property taxes, measures of state property tax burdens in 1977, and changes in these state measures in recent years.

Relation of Property Tax to Other State-Local Revenue

The property tax should be viewed as one element of the entire state-local revenue system. The first part of this section describes the extent to which the property tax is used by each level of government and how it relates to other revenue sources. Second, there is a description of the major sources of local government revenue in each state. Third, the relationship between the level of property taxes and the level of other state-local revenue sources is analyzed. The first two subjects deal with the composition of revenue, while the third compares state-local revenue to personal income in each state.

School districts are the heaviest users of property taxes, accounting for more than two out of every five dollars levied. Municipalities and counties are the next most important users of the tax, claiming one-fourth and one-fifth of property tax revenue, respectively. Townships, special districts, and states combined receive only one-eighth of all property tax dollars. As table 2-1 shows, these proportions did not change much during the 1970s, although over the longer run the city share has fallen and the school share risen.

Table 2-1 also shows that all three major types of local governments receive less than half of their general revenue from the property tax. Once again, schools are most dependent on the property tax, with 42 percent of their revenue coming from it. The property tax accounts for only one-third of county general revenue and one-fourth of city funds. All these proportions have declined steadily, both in the 1970s and over a longer period.

Table 2-2 reports the sources of revenue for all local governments in 1976-1977, 1970-1971, and 1957. States are excluded because of their low

Table 2-1
The Role of the Property Tax in Financing Various Levels of Government,
Selected Years
(percent)

	Distribution of Property Tax Revenue by Level of Government			Proportion of General Revenue from Property Tax		
	1977	*1971*	*1957*	*1977*	*1971*	*1957*
All state and local governments	100.0	100.0	100.0	21.9	26.1	33.7
Counties	20.6	20.1	20.3	31.1	37.4	46.5
Municipalities	25.0	26.5	33.4	25.7	32.8	46.3
School districts	42.5	42.6	34.6	42.0	45.7	50.1
Townships	6.0	5.5	5.8	56.8	62.8	63.6
Special districts	2.3	2.3	2.2	13.1	19.7	29.1
States	3.6	3.0	3.7	1.3	1.3	2.4

Source: U.S. Census Bureau, *City Government Finances in 1976-77, 1970-71* (Washington, D.C., 1978, 1972); U.S. Census Bureau, *1972 Census of Governments*, vol. 6, no. 4: *Historical Statistics on Government Finances and Employment* (Washington, D.C., 1974).

reliance on property taxation. As noted, the relative importance of the property tax has waned during this period. It accounted for nearly half of general revenue in 1957 but only slightly more than one-third in 1977. No other major source of general revenue increased at such a slow rate.[1] Federal aid increased much faster than any other revenue source, with local income and sales taxes also well above average.

Table 2-3 reveals the great diversity in the means by which local governments are financed. States in which local governments rely heavily on state aid, nonproperty taxes, and user charges tend to have relatively low property taxes. There are clear regional patterns. In the South there is heavy reliance on state aid and local user charges; in the Middle Atlantic states, on local income taxes; and in the West, on local sales taxes. But in New England no revenue source other than the property tax is used much.

The revenue raised by state and local governments can be divided into two categories—the property tax and all the rest, including both taxes and user charges but excluding federal aid. In this analysis both are expressed as a percentage of income in order to hold fiscal capacity constant. Two questions will be considered:

1. Do states with low (high) property taxes compensate by having high (low) tax burdens in other respects, or are the nonproperty tax burdens similar to those for property taxes?
2. How do rankings in terms of property tax burdens compare to overall tax burden rankings?

Table 2-2
Sources of Local Revenue, 1976-1977, 1970-1971, and 1957
(billions of dollars)

Type of Revenue	1976-1977	1970-1971	1957
General Revenue	$178.979	$91.964	$25.531
Federal and state aid	76.948	34.472	7.664
Federal aid	16.637	3.391	0.343
State aid	60.311	31.081	7.321
Revenue from Own Sources	$102.031	$57.491	$17.886
Taxes	74.794	43.434	14.286
Property	60.275	36.726	12.385
Income	3.752	1.747	0.191
General Sales	5.417	2.339	1.031
Selective sales	2.815	1.323	0.679
Other	2.534	1.298	
Current charges	18.977	9,819	3.580
Miscellaneous revenue	8.259	4.239	
Utility and Liquor Store Revenues	$ 15.559	$ 7.545	$ 3.062

Source: U.S. Census Bureau, *City Government Finances in 1976-77, 1970-71* (Washington, D.C., 1978, 1972); U.S. Census Bureau, *1972 Census of Governments* (Washington, D.C., 1974), vol. 6, no. 4: *Historical Statistics on Government Finances and Employment.*

Table 2-4 shows the ten highest and ten lowest states in terms of property tax per $1,000 of personal income. Four of the ten states with the lowest property taxes (Louisiana, Delaware, New Mexico, and Hawaii) have very high burdens in terms of other taxes; only one of the ten lowest-property-tax states (Arkansas) is below average for other taxes. Thus, a state cannot be very low on both scales.

But the opposite is not true. Three of the ten highest-property-tax states are also in the top ten in terms of other taxes. In two cases (Wyoming and Alaska) heavy taxation of minerals accounts for the high property tax revenue. New York stands alone as a state which ranks very high in both property and nonproperty tax burdens. Overall, only five of the ten states with the highest property tax burdens are below average in reliance on other revenue sources. New Hampshire, New Jersey, and Massachusetts do have low nonproperty tax burdens, but one cannot generalize from them.

Nonproperty tax revenue is much more important in accounting for each state's overall ranking than is the property tax. Among the ten states with the lowest overall burdens, Arkansas is the only one with especially low property taxes. The lowest overall state, Missouri, ranked seventeenth from the bottom in property taxes and sixth from the bottom in other revenue. Although it ranked third highest in terms of property tax, New Hampshire was the lowest in other revenue sources, and overall its burden was the second lowest.

At the high end of the overall rankings, five states (Alaska, New York,

Table 2-3
Variations in Sources of General Revenue for Local Governments, 1977

State	Proportion of General Revenue from		Proportion of Own-Source General Revenue from						
	Federal Aid	State Aid	Total	Property	Taxes		Other	Charges and Miscellaneous
					Sales	Income		
New England								
Connecticut	8.2	19.4	87.2	86.5	0.0	0.0	0.8	12.8
Maine	19.8	33.6	83.5	82.8	0.0	0.0	0.6	16.5
Massachusetts	11.4	22.8	86.7	86.1	0.0	0.0	0.5	13.3
New Hampshire	8.6	15.1	84.1	82.5	0.0	0.0	1.6	15.9
Rhode Island	15.4	25.2	91.5	90.7	0.0	0.0	0.8	8.5
Vermont	8.1	22.2	87.8	86.6	0.0	0.0	1.1	12.3
Mideast								
Delaware	16.7	42.6	59.3	50.4	0.0	6.2	2.7	40.7
District of Columbia	58.0	0.0	86.9	19.5	16.7	30.2	20.5	13.1
Maryland	11.0	35.6	75.6	49.6	0.0	18.3	7.7	24.4
New Jersey	8.0	25.7	85.5	76.9	0.0	0.0	8.6	14.5
New York	6.2	39.8	79.7	54.6	11.6	9.1	4.5	20.3
Pennsylvania	11.4	31.1	76.5	50.6	0.0	16.6	9.2	23.5
Great Lakes								
Illinois	8.4	29.3	79.0	64.8	7.2	0.0	7.0	21.0
Indiana	7.1	38.4	70.9	68.5	0.0	1.9	0.5	29.1
Michigan	9.9	33.4	69.3	63.6	0.0	4.1	1.6	30.7
Ohio	7.7	33.1	70.4	54.8	1.5	11.9	2.2	29.6
Wisconsin	5.6	48.5	69.3	68.3	0.0	0.0	0.9	30.7
Plains								
Iowa	6.9	37.3	67.2	65.2	0.0	0.0	2.0	32.8
Kansas	7.6	25.8	68.2	64.2	1.2	0.0	2.8	31.8
Minnesota	8.6	43.6	62.0	59.7	0.2	0.0	2.2	38.0
Missouri	12.8	24.1	71.1	49.5	7.1	4.6	9.9	28.9
Nebraska	7.2	20.7	68.4	63.7	2.6	0.0	2.1	31.5
North Dakota	6.2	35.8	63.9	61.6	0.0	0.0	2.3	36.1
South Dakota	8.4	16.8	78.0	70.6	3.5	0.0	3.9	22.0

Southeast							
Alabama	11.3	36.7	49.0	19.5	14.5	2.1	12.8	51.0
Arkansas	11.9	40.0	52.7	47.9	0.1	0.0	4.6	47.3
Florida	10.2	33.8	56.7	47.8	0.0	0.0	8.9	43.3
Georgia	12.0	26.5	58.1	47.1	4.3	0.0	6.7	41.9
Kentucky	13.0	35.9	64.1	42.7	0.0	16.2	5.1	35.9
Louisiana	10.3	38.3	60.4	30.2	25.5	0.0	4.6	39.6
Mississippi	9.3	44.7	48.1	45.3	0.0	0.0	2.8	51.9
North Carolina	10.6	48.2	66.7	54.9	10.4	0.0	1.4	33.3
South Carolina	10.5	39.0	58.5	54.5	0.0	0.0	4.0	41.5
Tennessee	11.8	29.5	63.8	43.3	13.9	0.0	6.6	36.2
Virginia	11.6	31.9	78.5	54.2	8.1	0.0	16.3	21.5
West Virginia	8.7	47.5	64.9	53.2	0.0	0.0	11.8	35.1
Southwest							
Arizona	8.6	37.2	73.1	59.3	10.2	0.0	3.6	26.9
New Mexico	13.3	53.1	57.1	46.6	3.8	0.0	6.7	42.9
Oklahoma	13.5	34.8	64.8	45.3	16.3	0.0	3.3	35.2
Texas	8.5	27.7	69.4	59.6	6.1	0.0	3.7	30.6
Rocky Mountain							
Colorado	7.0	29.3	73.2	55.6	13.9	0.0	3.8	26.8
Idaho	8.8	38.1	64.6	62.9	0.0	0.0	1.8	35.4
Montana	7.7	29.0	73.7	70.8	0.0	0.0	2.9	26.3
Utah	9.2	38.3	72.6	59.3	9.8	0.0	3.5	27.4
Wyoming	4.1	29.1	66.4	61.0	4.0	0.0	1.4	33.6
Far West							
Alaska	7.6	40.3	61.9	48.7	12.1	0.0	1.2	38.2
California	6.6	35.2	77.3	65.9	6.4	0.0	5.1	22.7
Hawaii	29.6	8.7	78.7	63.0	0.0	0.0	15.7	21.3
Nevada	5.5	28.0	60.0	40.4	4.8	0.0	14.8	40.0
Oregon	13.4	25.3	72.4	66.7	0.0	0.0	5.8	27.6
Washington	12.4	34.4	56.2	39.2	7.0	0.0	10.0	43.8

Source: U.S. Census Bureau, *Governmental Finances in 1976-77* (Washington, D.C., 1978).

Table 2-4

The Relationship between Property Tax Revenue and Other State-Local General Revenue Excluding Federal Aid, 1976-1977

State	Revenue per $1,000 of Personal Income (Rank)		
	Property Tax	Other Revenue	Total Revenue
Lowest Property Tax			
Alabama	$ 11.76 (1)	$132.78 (40)	$144.54 (14)
Louisiana	18.73 (2)	150.82 (46)	169.55 (33)
Delaware	19.06 (3)	141.02 (43)	160.08 (27)
West Virginia	20.98 (4)	123.77 (31)	144.75 (15)
Kentucky	21.11 (5)	124.60 (33)	145.71 (16)
New Mexico	21.71 (6)	160.50 (50)	182.21 (45)
Arkansas	22.56 (7)	113.49 (20)	136.05 (4)
Oklahoma	23.99 (8)	124.28 (32)	148.27 (18)
Hawaii	24.07 (9)	155.74 (49)	179.81 (41)
South Carolina	25.17 (10)	122.85 (17)	148.02 (17)
Highest Property Tax			
Alaska	134.81 (51)	168.34 (51)	303.51 (51)
Massachusetts	74.24 (50)	102.79 (9)	177.03 (38)
New Hampshire	65.70 (49)	65.67 (1)	131.37 (2)
California	65.14 (48)	122.64 (28)	187.78 (46)
Montana	64.30 (47)	114.51 (22)	178.81 (40)
New Jersey	63.36 (46)	88.43 (3)	151.79 (21)
New York	63.30 (45)	154.19 (48)	217.49 (50)
Wyoming	52.98 (44)	151.50 (47)	214.48 (49)
Vermont	61.97 (43)	126.75 (35)	188.72 (47)
South Dakota	60.19 (42)	111.09 (16)	171.28 (35)
Lowest Overall Revenue			
Missouri	32.54 (17)	97.44 (6)	129.98 (1)
New Hampshire	65.70 (49)	65.67 (1)	131.37 (2)
Ohio	38.34 (23)	93.39 (4)	131.73 (3)
Arkansas	22.56 (7)	113.49 (20)	136.05 (4)
Indiana	39.21 (27)	97.85 (7)	137.06 (5)
Virginia	31.26 (16)	107.04 (12)	138.30 (6)
North Carolina	25.88 (11)	112.63 (19)	138.51 (7)
Illinois	45.09 (31)	94.84 (5)	139.93 (8)
Texas	38.55 (25)	102.79 (10)	141.34 (9)
Tennessee	26.89 (13)	114.53 (23)	141.42 (10)
Highest Overall Revenue			
Alaska	134.81 (51)	168.34 (51)	303.15 (51)
New York	63.30 (45)	154.19 (48)	217.49 (50)
Wyoming	62.98 (44)	151.50 (47)	214.48 (49)
Minnesota	43.94 (29)	148.40 (45)	192.34 (48)
Vermont	61.97 (43)	126.75 (35)	188.72 (47)
California	65.14 (48)	122.64 (28)	187.78 (46)
New Mexico	21.71 (6)	160.50 (50)	182.21 (45)
North Dakota	38.82 (26)	143.19 (44)	182.01 (44)
Arizona	55.29 (38)	124.94 (34)	180.23 (43)
Wisconsin	49.29 (35)	130.82 (39)	180.11 (42)

Source: U.S. Census Bureau, *Governmental Finances in 1976-77* (Washington, D.C., 1978).

Wyoming, Vermont, and California) were also among the top ten in terms of property tax burdens. New Mexico is the only state which has very low property taxes and yet has a high overall burden.

It is not surprising that other taxes and user charges are more important than the property tax in the overall rankings, since property tax revenue accounts for only 28 percent of general revenue other than federal aid.

Indicators of Property Taxation

Since no single measure can adequately describe property tax use, five measures have been employed in the remainder of this chapter:

P_1 Property tax revenue as a proportion of state-local revenue

P_2 Property tax revenue per capita

P_3 Property tax revenue per $1,000 of personal income

P_4 Property tax as a percentage of the market value of homes (the effective tax rate on homes)

P_5 Property tax as a percentage of the market value of farm real estate (the effective tax rate on farms)

Interpretation of the first three measures is complicated because of differences among states in the composition of their taxable property tax bases. For example, in the average state 59.2 percent of taxable property was residential in 1976, but that proportion varied from 30.2 percent in North Dakota to 72.3 percent in Maryland. Acreage (which is mostly farmland) accounted for only 1.3 percent of taxable property in Rhode Island but 55.8 percent in North Dakota, averaging 11.9 percent. Commercial and industrial property also varied widely, representing 38.9 percent of taxable property in New York and only 10.8 percent in South Dakota. In the average state it was 24.2 percent of the tax base.[2] Although some taxes levied on business property are shifted to residents, a sizable proportion may be exported to nonresidents.

Another difficulty in comparing tax burdens is that data on the composition of the assessed valuation of property do not necessarily indicate how the tax burden is distributed. For example, farm property is generally located in rural areas where tax rates are usually below average. Tax credits and partial exemptions must also be taken into account.

Another problem is that the statistics used in this chapter reflect property taxes collected and do not take into account rebates or deductions which taxpayers may receive after paying their taxes. Since only a few states provide for circuit breakers to be subtracted directly from property tax bills,[3] they are generally not reflected here. Likewise, the tax savings realized by homeowners who itemize deductions on their income tax returns are also not considered. The omission of deductibility is much more serious than not considering circuit breakers, since the benefits in 1977 were, respectively, $4.8 billion and $950 million. Since most other exemptions and credits are reflected directly in property tax payments, they are taken into account in these figures.

Other problems with the data on property tax use are discussed in appendix 2A.

Aggregate National Trends

There has been a long-term movement away from reliance on the property tax, and that trend accelerated in the 1970s. In fact, the 1950s and 1960s can be considered an aberration in that property tax revenue grew faster than personal income and the market values of homes and farms. The trends are encapsulated in table 2-5.

The proportion of state-local revenue which is derived from property taxation has declined steadily, from more than 50 percent prior to 1940 to 37.8 percent in 1962, 31.7 percent in 1972, and 28 percent in 1977. In order to isolate the effects of decisions by state and local governments, these figures exclude federal aid. If it were included, the decline would be even more dramatic, since federal aid has increased rapidly.

The first column of table 2-5 shows that property tax revenue has risen substantially, but the third column reveals that most of the recent increase was due to inflation and population increases. From 1972 to 1977, per capita revenue did not increase at all in inflation-adjusted dollars.

Per capita property tax collections increased 5.5 percent per year from 1942 to 1957, 5.7 percent per year from 1957 to 1967, and 9.3 percent per year from 1967 to 1972. In each of these periods the growth was considerably greater than the rate of inflation. But from 1972 to 1977 per capita property tax revenue rose at only a 7 percent annual rate, approximately equal to the inflation rate.[4]

The early 1970s were pivotal years.[5] From 1957 to 1972 the effective tax rate on homes climbed from 1.34 to 2.12 percent. Farm taxes had been fairly steady at about 1 percent of market value from 1950 to 1965 before edging up to 1.10 percent in 1972. Thereafter, both fell. The tax rate on homes dropped from 2.12 to 1.67 percent in 1977, and the tax rate on farms fell from 1.10 to 0.74 percent. Thus, the farm tax rate fell considerably faster than the home tax rate, 32 versus 21 percent. In 1978 the rate on homes dropped further, to 1.51 percent.

The ratio of property tax revenue to personal income peaked in 1972 and also declined. Two measures relating tax revenue to income follow somewhat different courses. In the median, state revenue per $1,000 of personal income fell from $45.06 in 1972 to $38.93 in 1977. The decline in the aggregate average

Table 2-5
Historical Statistics on Property Tax Use

Year[a]	Property Tax Revenue				Property Tax per $100 of Market Value	
	Total (Billions)	As a Proportion of State-Local General Revenue (Excluding Federal Aid) (Percent)	Per Capita (1967 Dollars)	Per $1,000 of Personal Income	Homes[b]	Farm Real Estate[c]
1977	62.535	28.0	158.91	42.85	1.67	0.74
1976	57.001	28.4	155.39	43.24	1.84	0.78
1975	51.491	28.4	149.57	42.76	1.89	0.82
1974	47.705	28.8	152.42	43.22	1.90	0.96
1973	45.283	30.0	161.69	45.40	2.07	1.05
1972	42.133	31.2	161.01	46.77	2.12	1.10
1971	37.852	31.9	150.07	45.59	1.98	1.08
1970	34.054	31.3	142.92	44.02	1.93	1.05
1969	30.673	32.2	137.83	42.87	1.85	1.01
1968	27.747	33.0	132.67	42.30	1.87	0.98
1967	26.047	34.4	131.08	42.99	1.80	0.98
1962	19.054	37.8	112.74	44.53	1.51	1.00
1957	12.864	37.5	88.73	37.82	1.32	0.95
1948	6.126	39.8	57.95	30.76	1.14	0.87
1936	4.093	55.0	76.94	63.46	NA	1.11
1927	4.730	66.1	76.42	59.46	NA	1.16
1902	0.706	72.1	34.30	34.95	NA	NA

Source: U.S. Census Bureau, *Governmental Finances*, various years, and U.S. Census Bureau, *1972 Census of Governments* (Washington, D.C., 1974), vol. 6, no. 4: *Historical Statistics on Governmental Finances and Employment*, columns 1-4; Department of Housing and Urban Development, *Series Data Handbook Covering Section 203b Home Mortgage Characteristics* (Washington, D.C., 1978), column 5; Department of Agriculture, *Farm Real Estate Taxes*, various years, and Jerome M. Stam and Ann G. Sibold, *Agriculture and the Property Tax* (Washington: Department of Agriculture, 1977), p. 51, column 6; income and price data from U.S. Census Bureau, *Historical Statistics of the United States: Colonial Times to 1970* (Washington, D.C., 1975) and *Statistical Abstract of the United States* (Washington, D.C., 1978).

aFiscal year, for columns 1 to 4; calendar year, for columns 5 and 6.

bFor existing homes with newly issued FHA-insured mortgages under the Section 203 program.

cFor year in which tax is collected.

has been considerably slower, from $46.77 to $42.85. The explanation is that large states such as New York and Massachusetts ran counter to the national trend and pulled up the aggregate average but had little effect on the median.

Many factors account for these trends. The high rate at which local government spending increased tended to push tax burdens up. The halt to this spending spree following the 1973-1975 recession tended to lower tax burdens in 1977.[6] The major factor working to reduce reliance on the property tax was the increase in state and federal aid to local governments. Even though property tax relief was often not one of the stated goals of increasing this aid, it was one of the results. Local nonproperty taxes also relieved pressure on the property tax. Finally, the rapid increase in the market values of homes and farms during the 1970s contributed strongly to reductions in effective tax rates.

Property tax relief measures other than increased state and federal aid and nonproperty taxes influenced the aggregate property tax picture to only a limited extent up to 1977. Although tax and spending limitations had important effects in a number of states, prior to Proposition 13 their impact on nationwide totals was relatively small. Circuit breakers had only a small impact. Use value assessment of farmland had an important effect on farm property taxes but not on the overall totals. The other types of relief generally had only minor effects because their spread came at the very end of the period under study. The major exception is another type of relief not reflected in the table—the deductibility of property taxes in figuring federal and state income taxes.

Variations among States in 1977 and 1978

Table 2-6 presents statistics on how each state and the District of Columbia ranks on each of the five indicators of property tax use. Tables 2-7 and 2-8 list the states which have extremely high or extremely low rankings on at least two of these measures. All data are for 1977 except for the effective tax rate on homes, which are for 1978.

Tables 2-7 and 2-8 show the states which have either extremely high or extremely low rankings on at least two of these measures. Several significant points are suggested by these tables:

1. Certain states have consistently high or low rankings. The ones with high rankings may be considered the top candidates for property tax relief.

2. The high tax states are sprinkled across three areas—the Northeast, Midwest, and Far West—with the strongest regional representation from New England, where only Maine is not a high tax state.[7]

3. California stands out as one of the four states—New Hampshire, New Jersey, and Massachusetts are the others—which prior to Proposition 13 had a consistently high ranking. This may indicate that the tinder for a Proposition 13 type of conflagration is not present in many other states.

4. The eleven states with the lowest property taxes are all located south of the Mason-Dixon line. This includes not only five states in the Deep South but also border states Delaware, West Virginia, and Kentucky and Western states Oklahoma, New Mexico, and Hawaii.

Several factors account for the variations in overall property tax use. As table 2-3 demonstrates, states vary in the diversity of their revenue sources. States where localities receive substantial state aid or make heavy use of local nonproperty taxes tend to have lower property taxes. A second factor is the level of government spending. In 1977 per capita local spending ranged from $1,339 to $434 per person, and places with higher spending tend to have higher taxes.[8] The magnitude of the property tax base is a third influence. Places with a large per capita tax base can obtain revenue with lower effective tax rates than places with small tax bases, but being property-rich, they tend to have higher property tax burdens in relation to income and population. Finally, state-imposed limitations on local spending or taxing can also influence the overall use of the property tax.[9]

There are three reasons why certain states are extremely high or low on some indicators and not so extreme on others. First, differences in the composition of the property tax base may favor or hurt agricultural and residential property. States like Alaska and Montana are very high on P_1, P_2, and P_3 but not P_4 or P_5 because of the substantial revenue received from business property. (In Alaska, the oil boom more than quadrupled property tax revenue in 1976.) A second factor is the availability of nonproperty tax revenue. New York is the best example of a state where high property taxes are accompanied by heavy use of other taxes as well. Thus the proportion of its revenue derived from property taxes is not particularly high, while other indicators are among the highest in the nation. Finally, states may affect relative farm and home tax rates by the exemptions, credits, and assessment practices which they employ.[10]

Recent Changes in State Use

Although property tax revenue has been increasing annually in most states during the 1970s, its rise has generally been slower than that of other state and local revenue, income, and the values of homes and farms. Thus, in most states most of the measures of property tax burdens discussed in the previous sections have been declining. But the rate of decline has varied considerably from state to state. Some states have experienced rising burdens according to certain measures.

Two of the most extreme states are Minnesota and New York. In Minnesota the property tax's proportion of state-local revenue fell from 39.0 percent in 1962 to 27.3 percent in 1971 and 18.1 percent in 1977. During the 1971-1977 period, per capita property taxes adjusted for inflation fell 14 percent and the proportion of personal income claimed by the property tax fell 22 percent. The effective tax rate on farms fell 45 percent and on homes 32 percent, from 2.05

Table 2-6
Five Measures of Property Tax Burdens or Usage, 1977 and 1978[a]
(Rank in parentheses, with 1 being lowest.)

State	Property Tax Revenue (51 ranked)			Property Tax per $100 of Market Value	
	As a Proportion of Total State-Local Revenue (Percent)	Per Capita	Per $1,000 of Personal Income	Homes (only 50 Ranked)	Farm Real Estate (only 50 Ranked)
New England					
Connecticut	32.2 (47)	$ 412.52 (46)	$ 55.92 (39)	1.84 (40)	0.91 (36, tie)
Maine	20.2 (27)	237.79 (23)	44.94 (30)	1.53 (31)	1.13 (42)
Massachusetts	32.8 (48)	491.44 (50)	72.24 (50)	3.57 (50)	1.70 (50)
New Hampshire	36.8 (51)	382.45 (44)	65.70 (49)	2.34 (45)[e]	1.14 (43)
Rhode Island	24.2 (39)	326.63 (37)	52.06 (37)	NA[c]	1.31 (45)
Vermont[b]	23.2 (33)	330.64 (38)	61.97 (43)	1.93 (41)[e]	1.22 (44)
Mideast					
Delaware	9.1 (5)	134.02 (9)	19.06 (3)	0.88 (7)	0.16 (2)
District of Columbia	8.2 (2)	240.28 (24)	29.28 (14)	1.26 (20)[e]	NA
Maryland	18.4 (23)	265.47 (28)	38.54 (24)	1.72 (38)	0.50 (17)
New Jersey	33.7 (49)	468.11 (49)	63.36 (46)	3.15 (49)	0.96 (40)
New York	23.5 (36)	448.21 (47)	63.30 (45)	2.89 (48)	1.62 (49)
Pennsylvania	17.0 (17)	201.13 (18)	21.03 (15)	1.84 (39)	0.83 (33, tie)
Great Lakes					
Illinois	24.9 (40)	330.80 (39)	45.09 (31)	1.70 (36)	0.95 (39)
Indiana	23.4 (34)	242.07 (25)	39.21 (27)	1.43 (24)	0.59 (20, tie)
Michigan[b]	23.0 (32)	331.89 (40)	49.28 (34)	2.63 (47)	1.61 (48)
Ohio	23.6 (37)	249.38 (26)	38.34 (23)	1.17 (13)	0.75 (29, tie)
Wisconsin	22.0 (30)	298.75 (32)	49.29 (35)	1.96 (42)	1.56 (46, tie)

Plains									
Iowa	23.5	(35)	290.80	(31)	46.71	(33)	1.52	(30)	0.83	(33, tie)
Kansas	25.1	(41)	299.23	(33)	46.57	(32)	1.19	(15)	0.75	(29, tie)
Minnesota[b]	18.1	(22)	271.01	(29)	43.94	(29)	1.52	(29)[e]	0.82	(32)
Missouri	19.0	(24)	193.11	(16)	32.54	(17)	1.38	(22)	0.57	(20, tie)
Nebraska	28.2	(46)	356.82	(42)	58.94	(41)	2.40	(46)	0.91	(36, tie)
North Dakota	15.8	(15)	223.58	(21)	38.82	(26)	1.13	(11)	0.66	(25)
South Dakota	25.8	(44)	306.82	(34)	60.19	(42)	1.65	(35)	0.94	(38)
Southeast									
Alabama	5.8	(1)	59.65	(1)	11.76	(1)	0.73	(5)	0.14	(1)
Arkansas	11.8	(10)	109.25	(3)	22.65	(7)	1.51	(28)[f]	0.37	(9)
Florida	19.7	(26)	211.02	(20)	35.19	(19)	1.16	(12)	0.67	(26)
Georgia	17.2	(18)	189.54	(14)	34.70	(18)	1.25	(17)	0.54	(19)
Kentucky	10.6	(8)	112.58	(5)	21.11	(5)	1.26	(18)	0.39	(11)
Louisiana	8.2	(3)	99.16	(2)	18.73	(2)	0.51	(2)	0.24	(4)
Mississippi	11.2	(9)	116.20	(7)	26.03	(12)	1.08	(10)	0.32	(6)
North Carolina	13.6	(12)	139.71	(11)	25.88	(11)	1.26	(19)	0.41	(12)
South Carolina	14.1	(13)	128.34	(8)	25.17	(10)	0.83	(6)	0.35	(8)
Tennessee	14.2	(14)	141.38	(12)	26.89	(13)	1.28	(21)	0.46	(16)
Virginia	17.5	(20)	194.26	(17)	31.26	(16)	1.22	(16)	0.45	(15)
West Virginia	10.3	(7)	112.21	(4)	20.98	(4)	0.55	(3)	0.18	(3)
Southwest									
Arizona	25.1	(42)	317.03	(36)	55.29	(38)	1.62	(33)	0.81	(31)
New Mexico	8.7	(4)	113.45	(6)	21.71	(6)	1.39	(23)	0.25	(5)
Oklahoma	12.0	(11)	134.76	(10)	23.99	(8)	0.96	(8)	0.38	(10)
Texas	21.8	(29)	232.65	(22)	38.55	(25)	1.63	(34)[f]	0.44	(14)
Rocky Mountain									
Colorado	22.7	(31)	314.17	(35)	49.47	(36)	1.62	(32)	0.52	(18)
Idaho	17.9	(21)	204.67	(19)	37.44	(21)	1.50	(26)	0.62	(24)
Montana	25.6	(43)	361.89	(43)	64.30	(47)	1.19	(14)	0.61	(22, tie)
Utah	16.0	(16)	190.61	(15)	36.79	(20)	0.98	(9)	0.61	(22, tie)
Wyoming	21.7	(28)	402.22	(45)	62.98	(44)	0.67	(4)	0.43	(13)

Table 2-6 continued

	Property Tax Revenue (51 ranked)			Property Tax per $100 of Market Value	
State	As a Proportion of Total State-Local Revenue (Percent)	Per Capita	Per $1,000 of Personal Income	Homes (only 50 Ranked)	Farm Real Estate (Only 50 Ranked)
Far West					
Alaska	35.3 (50)	1,317.94 (51)	134.81 (51)	1.45 (25)	0.87 (35)
California	27.6 (45)	457.85 (48)	65.14 (48)	1.98 (43)d	1.56 (46, tie)
Hawaii	9.5 (6)	166.70 (13)	24.07 (9)	0.50 (1)	0.33 (7)
Nevada	19.1 (25)	285.62 (30)	41.39 (28)	1.71 (37)f	0.72 (28)
Oregon b	24.0 (38)	353.03 (41)	57.53 (40)	2.15 (44)	1.03 (41)
Washington	17.4 (19)	255.47 (27)	38.04 (22)	1.50 (27)c	0.71 (27)

Source: Columns 1 to 3: U.S. Census Bureau, *Governmental Finances in 1976-77.* (Washington, D.C., 1978). Column 4: Estimated from Federal Housing Administration reports on existing homes with new FHA mortgages. Column 5: U.S. Department of Agriculture, *Farm Real Estate Taxes: 1976* (Washington, D.C., 1978). This report covers taxes levied in 1976 and collected in 1977.

aData for 1977, except for home tax rates, which is for 1978.

bThese states have relatively large circuit breakers which lower property tax burdens for many citizens. Other circuit breakers have considerably narrower coverage.

cThe last year for which data are available for Rhode Island is 1974, when the tax rate was 2.27 percent (rank: 44).

dAverage for entire year; only 1.15 in fourth quarter, reflecting Proposition 13.

eFigure obtained directly from state officials, not FHA.

fAccuracy of this tax rate is questionable, as explained in appendix 2A.

Table 2-7
States with Highest Property Taxes
(Numbers indicate rank, with low numbers indicating highest taxes.)

State	P_1	P_2	P_3	P_4	P_5
New Hampshire	1	8	3	6	8
Vermont[a]	19	14	9	10	7
Massachusetts	4	2	2	1	1
Rhode Island	13	15	15	8	6
Connecticut	5	6	13	11	14 tie
New York	16	5	7	3	2
New Jersey	2	2	6	2	11
Michigan[a]	20	12	18	4	3
Wisconsin[a]	22	20	17	9	5 tie
Nebraska	6	10	11	5	14 tie
Montana	9	9	5	37	28 tie
Oregon[a]	14	11	12	7	10
California	7	4	4	8	4 tie
Alaska	2	1	1	26	17
South Dakota	8	18	10	16	13
Wyoming	24	7	8	47	38

Source: P_1, P_2, P_3: U.S. Census Bureau, *Governmental Finances in 1976-77* (Washington, D.C., 1978). P_4: Unpublished data on mortgages on existing single-family homes insured by FHA under Section 203b. P_5: U.S. Department of Agriculture, *Farm Real Estate Taxes: 1976* (Washington, D.C., 1978).

Note:

P_1:   Property tax revenue as a proportion of state-local revenue, fiscal year 1977

P_2:   Property tax revenue per capita, fiscal year 1977

P_3:   Property tax revenue per $1,000 of personal income, fiscal year 1977

P_4:   Property tax as a percentage of market value for homes, calendar year 1978, except for Rhode Island, for which rank is for 1974 (in 1978, only fifty states are included in rankings)

P_5:   Property tax as a percentage of market value for farm real estate, calendar year 1977

[a]   A circuit breaker lowers tax burdens for many households but is not reflected in this table.

to 1.39 percent. Near the other end of the spectrum is New York. From 1971 to 1977 real per capita property taxes and the proportion of income taken by the property tax each rose 16 percent. While the effective tax rate on farms dropped 15 percent, it rose 6 percent for homes.

As already noted, the early 1970s marked a major turning point. The number of states with an effective tax rate on homes over 2 percent rose from four in 1958 to fifteen in 1966 to twenty-three in 1971. Then it receded to sixteen in 1975 and six in 1978. Between 1966 and 1971 the effective tax rate on homes rose in every state except four, but by 1978 only 20 states still had higher rates than in 1966. Three of them were in the Northeast (Massachusetts,

Table 2-8
States with Lowest Property Taxes
(Numbers indicate rank among states, with low numbers indicating lowest taxes.)

State	P_1	P_2	P_3	P_4	P_5
Delaware	5	9	3	7	2
West Virginia	7	4	4	3	3
Kentucky	8	5	5	18	11
South Carolina	13	8	10	6	8
Alabama	1	1	1	5	1
Mississippi	9	7	12	10	6
Louisiana	3	2	2	2	4
Arkansas	10	3	7	28	9
Oklahoma	11	10	8	8	10
New Mexico	4	6	6	23	5
Hawaii	6	13	9	1	7

Note:
P_1:   Property tax revenue as a proportion of state-local revenue, fiscal year 1977
P_2:   Property tax revenue per capita, fiscal year 1977
P_3:   Property tax revenue per $1,000 of personal income, fiscal year 1977
P_4:   Property tax as a percentage of market value for homes, calendar year 1978, except for Rhode Island, for which rank is for 1974 (in 1978, only fifty states are included in rankings)
P_5:   Property tax as a percentage of market value for farm real estate, calendar year 1977
a   A circuit breaker lowers tax burdens for many households but is not reflected in this table.

Source: P_1, P_2, P_3: U.S. Census Bureau, *Governmental Finances in 1976-77* (Washington, D.C., 1978). P_4: Unpublished data on existing single-family homes insured by FHA under Section 203b. P_5: U.S. Department of Agriculture, *Farm Real Estate Taxes: 1976.*

New Jersey, New York), eight in the South (Alabama, Arkansas, Florida, Kentucky, Louisiana, Mississippi, South Carolina, and Virginia), and nine in the rest of the country (Alaska, District of Columbia, Idaho, Michigan, Nevada, New Mexico, Oregon, Texas, Washington).

Another way to demonstrate how pervasive has been the trend toward lower property tax use is to note the small number of cases in which measures increased after 1971. Between that year and 1977 the property tax became a higher proportion of state-local revenue in only three states and of personal income in only twelve states. The effective tax rate increased in just eight states for homes and in not a single state for farms.[11]

There are some clear regional patterns, as indicated in table 2-9. The two regions which formerly had the highest property tax levels followed distinctly different paths during the 1970s. The seven Plains states made the greatest strides in the direction of reducing property taxes, but New England had the largest increase in property taxes, both in per capita terms and as a percentage of income. In fact, New England was the only region in which the property tax became a larger proportion of personal income between 1971 and 1977. The

Table 2-9
Changes of Property Tax Measures over Time by Region
(median percentage changes)

Region	P_1 1971-1977	P_2 1971-1977	P_3 1971-1977	P_4 1971-1978	P_5 1971-1977
New England	−12	72	8	−23[a]	−38
Mideast	−18	56	−5	−11	−32
Great Lakes	−23	45	−11	−21	−17
Plains	−27	29	−21	−39	−40
Southeast	−11	63	−7	−13	−26
Southwest	−13	54	−12	−16	−27
Rocky Mountain	−12	54	−9	−34	−41
Far West	−14	53	−3	−9	−26

For states composing each region see table 2-6. For definitions of P_1 through P_5 see table 2-7.

[a]Only three states included.

twelve states of the Southeast, which traditionally have had the lowest property taxes, moved somewhat closer to the national averages, since their deemphasis of property taxation was relatively slight.

Conclusions

The patterns described here can be used in three ways. They identify which states are the top candidates for relief. New York, New Jersey, and Massachusetts—with high and rising property tax burdens—seem to be the ripest for relief, but other problem states can also be identified. In addition, the findings of this section point out the states which have already achieved substantial relief; in subsequent chapters we discuss in detail the mechanisms adopted to achieve these results. Finally, the patterns observed provide valuable perspective by enabling readers to see where their own state stands in comparison to national norms.

One of the major generalizations which can be made based on the material in this chapter is that the property tax situation in various states differs greatly. There are great differences in terms of the amount and type of property and the degree to which it is taxed. Consequently a property tax relief program which is appropriate in one state may be totally out of place in another.

Notes

1. For the entire 1957 to 1976-1977 period, one relatively unimportant revenue source did grow more slowly than property taxes—local taxes which

were not on property, income, or sales. But in the 1970s, even this group of taxes rose faster than the property tax.

2. U.S. Census Bureau, *1977 Census of Governments,* vol. 2; *Taxable Property Values and Assessment/Sales Price Ratios* (Washington, D.C.: 1978) pp. 51-52.

3. Connecticut, Idaho, Maryland, Ohio, and North Dakota were the only states using this procedure in 1977. Iowa has since adopted it.

4. Advisory Commission on Intergovernmental Relations, *Significant Features of Fiscal Federalism, 1978-1979 Ed.* (Washington, D.C.: 1979) table 42.

5. Netzer dates the more rapid rate of decline for the property tax from the "middle and late 1960s" based on an analysis of the extent to which it was used as a means of financing expenditures in which it ordinarily played a role. See Dick Netzer, "The Property Tax in a New Environment" (Delivered at Conference on Municipal Fiscal Stress, March 8-9, 1979).

6. Local government spending increased from 6.2 to 9.1 percent of gross national product between 1959 and 1976. But in fiscal 1977, local spending rose only 6.1 percent, a sharp drop from the average increase of 10 percent in the previous five years. U.S. Department of Commerce, "Survey of Current Business," May 1979, p. 17; U.S. Census Bureau, *Governmental Finances,* selected years; U.S. Council of Economic Advisors, *Economic Report of the President: 1978* (Washington, D.C.: 1979).

7. In his analysis of this subject as of 1962, Netzer mentioned two reasons why variations in property tax use tend to follow regional lines: neighboring states tend to have similar economies, values, and histories; and states are more likely to emulate nearby states than distant ones in developing tax policies. See Dick Netzer, *Economics of the Property Tax* (Washington: The Brookings Institution, 1966), p. 89.

8. The highest state was New York, and the lowest was Arkansas. U.S. Census Bureau, *Governmental Finances in 1976-77,* (Washington, D.C.: 1978) tables 13 and 17.

9. Appendix 2B reports on a statistical analysis of factors influencing property tax levels across the nation. A more detailed regression analysis of variations in property tax levels among counties in one state found that rates depended on the per capita market value of property, median family income, the proportion of the population of school age, urbanization, and population change. Both increases and decreases in population, if they were large, exerted upward pressure on property taxes. The market value of property per capita was positively related to property tax revenue as a fraction of income and to per capita property tax revenue, but negatively related to the effective tax rate. See Steven D. Gold, "Geographic Variation of Property Tax Burdens: The Case of Iowa," *Nebraska Journal of Economics and Business* 16 (Spring 1977):55-72.

10. See chapters 3 to 7.

11. Vermont, Arizona, and Alaska are the states in which the proportion of

general revenue from the property tax increased. The states in which property taxes became a larger fraction of personal income are New Hampshire, Vermont, Massachusetts, Rhode Island, New York, New Jersey, Virginia, South Carolina, Georgia, Oregon, Arizona, and Alaska. Oregon drops off the list when its circuit breaker is considered.

Appendix 2A:
Comments on Data

All the data used in this chapter are approximations. Measures P_1, P_2, and P_3 are estimated on a sample basis by the Census Bureau; P_4 is based on existing homes with new mortgages insured by the Federal Housing Administration (with five exceptions); and P_5 is estimated by a survey of local officials.[1] Despite their imperfect accuracy, they are the best indicators of property tax burdens available.

Except in five states, all the figures are for gross property taxes before subtraction of circuit breakers. When these relief measures are considered, the decline in property taxation is even greater than indicated here, since circuit breakers are a recent development. In the few states where circuit breakers are significant, these data significantly exaggerate tax burdens. In 1977 circuit breakers covered 12.5 percent of property tax liability in Minnesota, 8.8 percent in Oregon, 9.1 percent in Michigan, 4.8 percent in Vermont, 7.2 percent in Wisconsin, and much lower percentages in other states. The proportion of residential property taxes covered was, of course, higher. In Michigan, one of the most generous states, the circuit breaker paid approximately 29.5 percent of the property tax for households which received it, but only about 41 percent of all households were covered. Minnesota and Oregon are the only two states in which more than half of all households received a benefit from the circuit breaker, as shown in the next chapter.

As statewide averages, the measures of property taxation do not reflect wide variations which may exist for individual taxpayers within a state. One source of such variation is differences in tax rates; it is common for some jurisdictions to have tax rates two or three times as high as other jurisdictions in the same state. Even within a single jurisdiction, tax rates vary because of nonuniform assessment practices and exemptions and credits. While it is obvious that circuit breakers cause the tax rate to vary for different households, the same is true of many other tax relief measures. Exemptions and most non-circuit-breaker credits produce greater percentage tax reductions for owners of homes with relatively low values. For example, suppose that there are two homes worth $40,000 and $80,000, respectively, and that each is subject to a 2 percent tax. If assessments are equal to market values, their taxes would be $800 and $1,600, respectively. If there were a state-financed homestead exemption which covered the tax on $10,000 of assessed valuation, their taxes would be reduced to $600 and $1,400, respectively. Now their effective tax rates would no longer be equal, with one home being taxed at 1.5 percent of its value and the other at 1.75 percent.

Another potential problem concerns the effective tax rates for homes. Homes with FHA mortgages, on which the measures are based, tend to have somewhat lower prices than the average home which is sold, primarily because there is an upper limit on FHA mortgages (raised from $45,000 to $60,000 in late 1977). Since low-priced homes tend to be assessed at a higher percentage of their market value than high-priced homes, homes with FHA mortgages might tend to have higher effective tax rates than the true average. Offsetting this tendency are tax credits and exemptions, which tend to lower tax rates most for lower-value homes.

The data used in the book are for the largest FHA program, known as Section 203b. These data do not include FHA activities which are particularly aimed at low-income households or require especially low downpayments.

As a check on their accuracy, the effective tax rates on homes estimated from FHA data were compared with similar tax rates estimated by the Census Bureau in 1976. The correlation between the FHA rate and the Census Bureau rate for the largest city in each state is high ($r = .79$). Both sources indicate that West Virginia, Louisiana, Alabama, and Hawaii have the lowest home tax rates, and that Massachusetts and New Jersey have the highest rates. However, in fourteen states and the District of Columbia there is a large discrepancy.

In five states the difference between the tax rate in the largest city according to the Census Bureau and the statewide average according to FHA data can be attributed to the fact that the largest city's tax rate differs considerably from the statewide average. In Colorado and New York, Census Bureau data show that most cities have a much higher property tax rate on homes than the largest city, while in Kansas, Ohio, and Indiana the reverse is true.

In two other states, Washington and Minnesota, there is also an indication that the tax rate in the largest city is much different from the state average, but not enough other cities are covered by the Census Bureau data to be confident that this accounts for the large discrepancy between it and FHA. According to the Census Bureau, the tax rate in Washington is lower and in Minnesota higher than according to FHA data.

In six states and the District of Columbia there is a large discrepancy between the tax rates indicated by the two sources, but the Census Bureau does not report on enough cities other than the largest one to account for the disparity. According to the Census Bureau, tax rates may be much lower in Arkansas, Texas, the District of Columbia, and Nevada and much higher in North Dakota, Delaware, and Maine than FHA figures indicate.

In Iowa there is also a large discrepancy, with the Census Bureau indicating a considerably higher tax rate than FHA data. This case illustrates another reason why the two indicators could differ. The effective tax rate on homes fell particularly sharply in Iowa between 1975 and 1978 because of an increase in the homestead credit and other programs. Since the Census Bureau tax rate is for a period two years earlier than the FHA rate, part of the difference is due to timing.

Officials in all states were requested to comment on the effective tax rates on homes which were calculated from FHA data. In Minnesota, Washington, and the District of Columbia, officials indicated that the FHA figures differed considerably from those based on their own studies. In these three cases tax rates shown in table 1-6 are those provided by state officials. In addition, officials in New Hampshire and Vermont reported tax rates although FHA data for those states were not adequate for estimating any tax rates. Thus, in those five cases, FHA rates are not reported in table 2-6.

The table also notes three states (Arkansas, Texas, and Nevada) in which there is strong reason to suspect that the FHA tax rate is misleading although no better alternative is available. In these three states the FHA rate is considerably different from the Census Bureau tax rate in the largest city of the state, and the ranking of the Census Bureau rate is closer to state's ranking on the other four property tax indicators in table 2-6.

In the great majority of the other states either Census Bureau and FHA tax rates are similar or state officials confirmed the accuracy of the FHA tax rate.

A serious omission from the measures of property tax use is an indicator dealing with taxation of business property. Unfortunately, no reliable, up-to-date figures are available showing business tax rates.[2]

Notes

1. Farm data are reported according to the year from which they are levied, which is usually the year prior to that in which they are collected, so that the years referred to in this book are lagged one year from those reported in *Farm Real Estate Taxes.* This procedure is adopted from Jerome M. Stam and Ann G. Sibold, *Agriculture and the Property Tax* (Washington, D.C.: Department of Agriculture, 1977), Agricultural Economic Report no. 392, p. 9.

2. One recent study which purports to measure each state's tax effort in taxing commercial-industrial property actually does not do so. Its measures for commercial-industrial property are extremely similar to those for residential property. See D. Kent Halstead, *Tax Wealth in Fifty States* (Washington, D.C.: National Institute of Education, 1978), p. 29. See chapter 6 this book for evidence that the relative treatment of commercial-industrial property varies greatly from state to state.

Appendix 2B:
Regression Analysis of
Property Tax Use

Table 2B-1 shows that much of the variation among states in property tax use can be explained by three variables—the level of local government spending, the diversification of revenue sources, and the size of the property tax base. Property tax measures are higher, the greater the level of local spending and the smaller the proportion of general revenue derived from nonproperty tax sources such as federal aid, income taxes, sales taxes, and user charges. Per capita spending and the proportion of personal income devoted to property taxation are also directly related to the market value of property per capita, indicating that states with large amounts of property tend to have more property tax revenue and the proportion of personal income devoted to property taxation related to the size of the tax base.

Diversification of revenue sources explains much more of the variation in each measure than either of the other two variables.

Table 2B-1
Regression Analysis of Property Tax Use

Dependent Variable	Number of States	Constant	Per Capita Spending	Reliance	Property Base	R^2
Property tax revenue per capita	51	116.9	0.0211* (3.21)	−1.46* (6.02)	0.00119** (1.80)	63
Property tax revenue as proportion of personal income	51	179.3	0.0167* (2.95)	−2.00* (9.64)	0.00112* (1.96)	.77
Effective property tax rate for homes	48	6.77	0.00078* (3.00)	−0.062* (5.98)	−0.00007* (2.33)	.52

Sources of data: Per capita spending and reliance: U.S. Census Bureau, *Governmental Finances in 1976-77.* (Washington, D.C., 1978). Property base: U.S. Census Bureau, *1977 Census of Governments*, vol. 2: *Taxable Property Values and Assessment/Sales Price Ratios* (Washington, D.C., 1978), table 9. Dependent variables: Described in text.

t statistics in parentheses. * = Significant at .05 level ** = Significant at .10 level.

Independent variables:

Per capita spending: Per capita direct general expenditure other than for capital outlay

Reliance: Proportion of state-local general revenue from sources other than property taxation

Property base: Per capita market value of all assessed ordinary real estate

3 The Residential Circuit Breaker

A circuit breaker is a form of property tax relief in which benefits depend on both income and property tax payments. Its advocates compare it to its electrical namesake—when there is an overload relative to income, the circuit breaker shuts off the property tax system. It is potentially the most progressive form of property tax relief, offering the possibility of eliminating the tax's regressivity (or, as some would have it, increasing its progressivity). Although the circuit breaker has spread rapidly in the past fifteen years, it is not without its critics.

Description

A circuit breaker usually takes one of two forms—the threshold or the sliding scale. The ACIR, a leading proponent of circuit breakers, defines them as follows:

> Under the *threshold approach*, an "acceptable" tax burden is defined as some fixed percentage of household income (different percentages may be set for different income levels), and any tax above this portion of income is "excessive" and qualifies for relief. Under the *sliding-scale approach*, no threshold is defined. Rather a fixed percentage of property tax... is rebated for each eligible taxpayer within a given income class; the rebate percentage declines as income rises.[1]

Consider an example of each type. The Vermont threshold formula provides relief as follows, subject to a maximum benefit of $500 per household:

Income	*Relief*
Under $4,000	Property tax in excess of 4 percent of income
$4,000 - 7,999	Property tax in excess of 4 1/2 percent of income
$8,000 - 11,999	Property tax in excess of 5 percent of income
$12,000 - 15,999	Property tax in excess of 5 1/2 percent of income
$16,000 - and over	Property tax in excess of 6 percent of income

The Iowa sliding-scale circuit breaker for elderly households operated this way in 1979:[2]

Income	*Relief*
Under $2,000	100 percent of property tax
$2,000-2,999	95 percent of property tax
$3,000-3,999	85 percent of property tax
$4,000-4,999	70 percent of property tax
$5,000-5,999	55 percent of property tax
$6,000-6,999	40 percent of property tax
$7,000-7,999	30 percent of property tax
$8,000-8,999	25 percent of property tax
$9,000-9,999	20 percent of property tax

Thus, a family with income of $2,500 and a property bill of $400 would receive relief of $300 in Vermont ($400 minus 4 percent of $2,500) and $380 in Iowa. A tax bill of $600 and income of $8,500 would produce relief of $175 in Vermont ($600 minus 5 percent of $8,500) and $150 in Iowa. There would be no relief in either state for a household whose income was $20,000 and property tax $1,000.

Some circuit breakers use formulas other than the sliding-scale or threshold approaches. The essential features for a program to be classified as a circuit breaker are that (1) benefits are related to income and property tax payments and (2) the program is financed by nonproperty tax revenue.[3]

The circuit breaker's benefits are usually paid through a refund check after a household has filed an application, but in a few states the relief is subtracted directly from the property taxbill.

History, Current Extent of Use, and Costs

Twenty-eight states and the District of Columbia provide a circuit breaker in some form.[4] This is an impressive tally considering that in 1970 there were just five circuit breakers and that the first one was adopted in 1964.[5]

Circuit breakers are common throughout the country except in the South. Eleven of the twenty-two states without circuit breakers are in the South, four in the Northeast, six in the West, and only one in the Midwest. Most of the non-circuit-breaker states have relatively low property taxes on homes. The four major exceptions are Massachusetts, New Jersey, Nebraska, and New Hampshire. Only four other non-circuit-breaker states have above-average tax rates.

Programs differ considerably in their coverage, as indicated in table 3-1, which summarizes the major features of existing circuit breakers. Most of them are only for elderly households, although nine have no age limit. Twenty-three states extend eligibility to both homeowners and renters; five are only for homeowners. (States which include renters make the assumption that some

Table 3-1
Circuit Breaker Programs in 1977 and 1979

State	Income Ceiling	Average Benefit	Per Capita Cost	Percentage of Households Receiving Benefits[a]
All ages, homeowners and renters				
District of Columbia[b]	$20,000[c]	$220	$ 5.85	7
Kansas[d]	13,000	NA	NA	NA
Michigan	none	223	30.24	41
Minnesota	none	156	33.94	66
New York	12,000	NA	NA	NA
Oregon	17,500[e]	148	31.20	60
Vermont	none	210	16.08	23
Wisconsin	14,000[f]	206	10.31	15
All ages, homeowners and elderly renters				
Maryland[g]	none	248	5.03	6
				Percentage of Elderly Households Receiving Benefits[a]
Elderly, homeowners and renters				
California	12,000[h]	216	4.25	26
Colorado[k]	8,300[i]	187	4.20	44
Connecticut[j]	6,000	244	7.96	50
Illinois[k]	10,000	250	8.85	55
Indiana[k]	5,000	29	0.16	8
Iowa[k]	10,000[l]	115	3.34	35
Maine	6,000[m]	209	4.06	22
Missouri	7,500	125	1.46	14
Nevada	11,000	128	2.20	27
New Mexico	16,000	91	0.93	19
North Dakota[k]	8,000	119	2.01	21
Pennsylvania[k]	7,500	142	4.99	46
Rhode Island	8,000[n]	52	NA	NA
Utah	7,000	95	0.75	16
West Virginia	5,000	14	0.01	1
				Percentage of Elderly Households Receiving Benefits[a]
Elderly, homeowners only				
Arkansas	8,000	76	0.36	5
Idaho[k]	7,500	231	4.67	33
Ohio[k]	10,000	135	4.26	47
Oklahoma[k]	6,000	86	0.13	2
South Dakota[k]	7,375[o]	99	2.17	27

Source: Advisory Commission on Intergovernmental Relations, *Significant Features of Fiscal Federalism*, 1978-79 ed. (Washington, D.C., 1979). Additional data obtained from survey of states by author. Number of households is from U.S. Census Bureau, *Current Population Reports, Demographic, Social and Economic Profile of States: Spring 1976* Series p. 20, no. 334 (January 1979), p. 25. (*Table notes continued on next page.*)

Table 3-1 continued

Notes: Classification of program and income ceiling are for 1979, but other data are for 1977, except in the District of Columbia.

aThese percentages are approximations based on the number of households in the spring of 1976 and program statistics for fiscal year 1977. Estimates for elderly programs do not consider that some programs include participation by nonelderly persons such as the blind or disabled.

bFinancial data for the District of Columbia are for 1978.

cAlthough this ceiling applied to all households in 1979, in 1978 the maximum income for nonelderly households was $7,000.

dNonelderly households are eligible only if they include at least one child under the age of 18.

eIn 1978 income ceiling was $16,000.

fIn 1978 income ceiling was $9,300.

gPrior to 1979, only homeowners were eligible.

hNet income ceiling is $12,000 for homeowners and $5,000 for renters.

iFor married persons; ceiling for single persons is $7,300.

jParticipation data include households in elderly freeze program.

kHouseholds in which the head is disabled are also eligible.

lIn 1978 ceiling was $9,000.

mFor married persons; ceiling for single persons is $5,000.

nIn 1978 ceiling was $7,000.

oFor married persons; ceiling for single persons is $4,625.

portion of rent represents property tax passed on to the tenant by the landlord.) The seven places with the broadest eligibility, covering homeowners and renters with no age limit, are the District of Columbia, Michigan, Minnesota, New York, Oregon, Vermont, and Wisconsin.

There is a tendency for circuit breakers to expand after they are introduced, particularly by increasing the ceiling on relief payments, raising percentages in sliding-scale programs, or boosting the maximum income for participation. In several states, coverage expanded by including renters (where originally only homeowners were eligible) or the nonelderly (where at first only the aged were covered).

Benefits range from moderate to meager. The highest average benefits are for elderly households in the District of Columbia ($285 in 1977). The benefits in the median state are $135 per recipient, and they fall as low as $14 in one state. Although circuit breakers are sometimes viewed as an income transfer program, they are rather small compared to such programs as social security, public assistance, and unemployment compensation.

There is a regional element in the setting of benefit levels. The eight states with the lowest average benefits are all adjacent to states which do not have any circuit breaker program at all.[6]

The highest per capita costs in 1977 were in Minnesota ($33.94) and Michigan ($30.24). In most states, the costs are relatively low; the only other states in which cost per capita exceeds $10 are Oregon, Vermont, and Wisconsin.

The last column of table 3-1, which shows the percentage of households receiving circuit breaker benefits, reflects both the structure of programs and the response to them. Many households do not benefit because either their income is too high or their property tax payment is too low. Others do not participate even though they are eligible because they are unaware of the program or for other reasons.

Nationally, the total cost of circuit breaker programs more than doubled between 1974 and 1977 to $950 million, and the number of claimants increased 69 percent to 5,113,000. By contrast, property tax revenue rose only 31 percent, which was about the same rate at which income rose. The growth in circuit breaker costs occurred because more states had programs, many states liberalized benefit schedules, and participation rates rose as knowledge spread that the programs were available.

The aggregate impact of circuit breakers is not large. They covered less than 2 percent of total property taxes paid and less than 5 percent of residential property taxes in 1977.

Little information is available on the cost of administering circuit breakers. A 1974 survey estimated that administration costs were 2 percent or less of benefits paid in most of the twelve states surveyed.[7]

Design Issues

The circuit breaker is one of the most complicated types of property tax relief, requiring decisions about a large number of issues. This complexity arises in part from the flexibility of the circuit breaker, since it affords a wide range of choice with regard to who receives benefits and how much they receive.

The circuit breaker can be designed to make the property tax proportional, progressive, or regressive; it may limit benefits to the very poor or to those of average means, or it may allow households with high income to participate; its benefits may be high or low; it can be limited to the aged or extended to all families, restricted to homeowners or extended to renters as well. All depends on the objectives of the designers and the available resources.

We discuss first eligibility, second the level and distribution of benefits, and finally technical issues such as the treatment of the family and the definition of income.

Eligibility

The issue of eligibility raises four major questions and several minor ones.

Income Ceiling. Most states place an upper bound on the income of households which may participate in the circuit breaker, ranging from $5,000 to $20,000.

The rationale for having an upper limit is to target relief to those believed to be in greatest need. Even states with no limit (Maryland, Michigan, Minnesota, and Vermont) provide relatively little assistance to high-income households because of the way in which the circuit breaker is designed and the tendency for residential property taxes to fall as a fraction of income as income rises. The issue boils down to a political judgment as to whether it is desirable to provide any assistance to households at high income levels with unusually large property tax bills; as demonstrated later in this chapter, the cost of providing relief to such persons frequently is not very large.

Some persons consider it very important to limit circuit breaker benefits to the poor,[8] but most states place the income maximum above the federal poverty line. This practice is very reasonable in view of the niggardliness of the federal definition of poverty, the fact that regressivity extends above the poverty line, and the vague distinction between the poor and the near-poor.

Table 3-2 shows the distribution of income limits as of 1974 and April 1978. During that period the median income limit rose from $6,900 to $8,200. In 1978 only seven states had an income limit of $6,000 or less, a reduction from twelve in 1974.

Age As noted earlier, most circuit breakers are limited to the elderly, with eligibility usually beginning at age 65 but sometimes at 60 or 62, and for widows and widowers even earlier. This practice is consistent with the deeply ingrained notion that persons experiencing income distress are more deserving of government assistance if they are old than if they are not.[9]

Even if the circuit breaker is not limited to the elderly, older households receive a disproportionate share of benefits because the property tax claims a larger share of their income than it does for younger households, as table 3-3 shows.

Table 3-2
Maximum Income for Households Eligible for Circuit Breaker

	Number of States	
Income Limit	1974	1978
$6,000 or less	12	6
$6,001-8,000	5	7
$8,001-10,000	3	6
$10,001-15,000	1	3
$15,001-20,000	1	3
None	3	4

Source: 1974: Advisory Commission on Intergovernmental Relations, *Circuitbreakers.* 1978:*Significant Features of Fiscal Federalism*, 1978-79 ed. (Washington, D.C., 1979).
In cases where there was a split income limit for single and married persons, the limit for married persons was used.

Aside from political considerations, the grounds for favoring the elderly are weak. It is true that elderly households have lower average incomes than the nonelderly; on the other hand, elderly households tend to be smaller, have relatively high net worth, and are likely to have paid off their home mortgage. Elderly homeowners, on the average, spend about the same proportion of their income on housing as younger households.[10] To some extent, by providing relief to the elderly, states may actually be providing benefits to their children by reducing the support their parents needs. Nor is it true that most low-income elderly people live totally on fixed incomes. Social security and SSI, two of their major sources of income, are indexed so that they rise in proportion to the increase of consumer prices.

In rebuttal, it can be pointed out that much of the net worth of the elderly is in the form of their home and is thus not available for taxpaying purposes. This suggests the need for deferral, not forgiveness, of taxes, but the elderly have shown that they do not like the idea of placing a lien on their home and are very reticent about participating in deferral programs.

One common argument for favoring the elderly is to ensure that they will not be forced to give up their home because of taxes. Some writers have questioned this goal on the grounds that younger families could make more

Table 3-3
Real Estate Taxes as a Percentage of Family Income for Elderly and Nonelderly Single-Family Homeowners, by Income Class: 1970

Family Income[a]	Real Estate Tax as a Percentage of Family Income		Exhibit: Number of Homeowners (Percentage of Total)	
	Elderly (Age 65 and over)	Nonelderly (Under 65)	Elderly	Nonelderly
Less than $2,000	15.8	18.9	74.5	25.5
$2,000-2,999	9.5	10.1	70.3	29.7
3,000-3,999	8.0	7.2	59.1	40.9
4,000-4,999	7.3	5.5	48.6	51.4
5,000-5,999	6.2	5.1	32.0	68.0
6,000-6,999	5.8	4.3	25.4	74.6
7,000-9,999	4.8	4.1	13.3	86.7
10,000-14,999	3.9	3.7	6.4	93.6
15,000-24,999	3.3	3.3	5.4	94.6
25,000 or more	2.7	2.9	9.8	90.2
All incomes	8.1[b]	4.1[b]	20.2	79.8

Source: U.S. Bureau of the Census, *Residential Finance Survey, 1970* (conducted in 1971), special tabulations prepared for the Advisory Commission on Intergovernmental Relations. Real estate tax data were compiled for properties acquired prior to 1970 and represent taxes paid during 1970.
[a]Census definition of income (income from all sources). Income reported received in 1970.
[b]Arithmetic mean.

efficient use of the housing. It is doubtful whether there is a real problem here. The record indicates that the elderly move much less frequently than younger households, and taxes are seldom the reason when they do move.[11]

The question is not whether many elderly households need assistance. They do. The issues are whether elderly families and individuals need help more than younger people with similar income, and whether assistance for the elderly should be tied to housing rather than provided in a form enabling them to decide for themselves where their greatest needs lie.

Occupancy. The great majority of circuit breakers (twenty-four of twenty-nine) extend benefits to renters as well as homeowners. This practice is certainly appropriate, but the best means of doing so is in dispute. The method used in most states is to treat a fixed proportion of rent as if it represented property tax. The most common percentage employed is 20 percent, but it varies from 30 percent in Illinois to 6 percent in New Mexico. This procedure is very crude, since it does not reflect variations in local tax rates and the ratio of property value to rental payments, which affect the proportion of rent for which the property tax is responsible. While improvements in this procedure are feasible, an arbitrary assumption about the extent to which the property tax is shifted to tenants would still be necessary.[12]

The treatment of rent has also been criticized because it usually provides renters with smaller benefits than homeowners. According to one estimate, in Wisconsin it would be necessary to treat 32.6 percent of rent as property tax to provide equal benefits for homeowners and renters. This criticism views the circuit breaker as an income supplement rather than a tax relief measure.[13]

The occupancy and age eligibility issues are interrelated in that a high percentage of low-income homeowners are elderly. Inclusion of renters has a much greater impact on total program cost if the nonelderly are eligible.

Definition of Household Unit. Most states define the recipient household as a one- or two-person family.[14] Conflicting criteria come into play here. For the sake of evenhandedness, it is desirable to include income from all persons living together except renters in determining benefits. But such a policy is difficult to police. Moreover, sometimes not all persons in a common living unit pool their incomes. It seems desirable to at least include all income of dependents. This issue is of much greater importance for general circuit breakers not restricted by age, since elderly households are less likely to have more than two members than are younger households.[15]

Other Eligibility Issues. Lots of additional conditions on eligibility may be imposed. Some states with elderly circuit breakers extend them to the disabled or blind. On the other hand, students and public assistance recipients are sometimes expressly excluded. Maryland rules out anyone with more than $200,000 worth of assets. Many states have a residency requirement.[16]

The Level and Distribution of Benefits

The general form of a circuit breaker involves a rebate R of a percentage r of tax paid T in excess of a proportion p of income Y, where both r and p may vary with income. Thus,

$$R = r(T - pY)$$

The elements which may be manipulated are: p, the threshold percentage; r, the proportion of "excess taxes" rebated; the maximum amount of taxes T to be considered; the maximum rebate R which may be received; and the maximum income Y eligible to participate.[17] The last variable has already been discussed.

The choices of p and r determine the progressivity or regressivity of net tax burdens. For example, if both are constant and r is less than 100 percent, the resulting incidence will be regressive (assuming that the initial incidence is regressive). If it is desired to make net burdens proportional or progressive, either p must increase as income rises or r must fall. The specific values which p and r must assume in order to achieve a given degree of progressivity or regressivity depend on the income elasticity of property tax payments.[18]

Sliding Scale versus Threshold Formula. The only differences between a sliding scale and threshold circuit breaker[19] are that in the sliding scale p is zero and r must decline as income rises. Table 3-4 shows how the structure of benefits differs under sliding-scale and threshold formulas, using the Iowa and Vermont circuit breakers as examples. The sliding scale gives relatively more relief to households at each income level with lower property taxes; the threshold gives relatively more relief to households at each income level with higher property taxes. In order to determine which pattern is preferable, it is necessary to consider the main reasons why a household might have relatively high property taxes:

1. It devotes a large quantity of resources to housing because it needs space for a large number of children.
2. It devotes a large quantity of resources to housing because it is wealthy.
3. It devotes a large quantity of resources to housing because it places a high value on housing as compared to other things which it could buy.
4. Its community has a small property tax base per capita, requiring higher property tax rates than in property-rich areas.
5. Its community chooses to provide a high level of services, requiring higher tax rates than if services were just average.

Some of these reasons favor the threshold, while others favor the sliding scale. Reasons 2 and 5 weigh against giving more aid to families with the highest property taxes, since the high property taxes reflect relatively great benefits

Table 3-4
Illustration of Benefits under Sliding-Scale and Threshold Formulas

Income	Gross Property Tax	Net Property Tax[a]		Benefit[a]	
		Sliding Scale[b]	Threshold	Sliding Scale	Threshold
1,500	$ 200	$ 10	$ 60	$190	$140
	600	30	60[d]	570	540[d]
	1,000	50	60[d]	950	940[d]
5,500	200	90	200	110	0
	600	270	247.50	330	352.50
	1,000	450	247.50[d]	550	742.50[d]
9,500	200	160	200	40	0
	600	480	475	120	125
	1,000	800	475[d]	200	575[d]
13,500	200	200	200	0	0
	600	600	600	0	0
	1,000	1,000	742.50	0	257.50

[a]Benefit =gross property tax − net property tax.

[b]The sliding-scale formula is that for the 1979 Iowa elderly circuit breaker.

[c]The threshold formula is that for the Vermont circuit breaker. The provision which limits the maximum benefit to $500 is ignored in this illustration.

[d]In the actual Vermont circuit breaker, benefit would be lower and net property tax higher because of the $500 maximum benefit per household.

received or high ability to pay; they favor the sliding scale. Reason 4 weighs in favor of helping those with high property taxes and thus favors the threshold.[20] However, aid to governments is a more appropriate tool than circuit breakers for dealing with the problems of intercommunity fiscal disparities.[21] To the extent that public service benefits are directly related to home values, reason 3 weighs in favor of the sliding scale; to the extent that such benefits are unrelated to home values, reason 3 weighs in favor of the threshold. As for reason 1, the best way to deal with it is by providing personal credits on the income tax and by making circuit breaker benefits a function of family size.

This discussion leads to an inconclusive result because the relative importance of reasons 1 through 5 is uncertain. Additional points may be made on behalf of either formula. A defect of the sliding-scale approach is that it may leave some low-income families with high property tax burdens relative to their income while extending relief to other, higher-income families whose taxes are not excessive relative to their incomes. On the other hand, the sliding scale guarantees that no one at a higher income level will receive benefits when someone at a lower level does not, thus providing greater vertical equity. In addition, while households at each income level with greater wealth receive greater benefits, this pattern is less pronounced for the sliding-scale than for the threshold approach.[22]

An important practical consideration is the amount of revenue available to pay for the circuit breaker. Particularly if the program is not confined to low-income groups, the sliding-scale approach tends to be more costly because it gives relief from the first dollar of property tax paid while the threshold provides relief only on that portion of the property tax which is treated as being "excessive."

Maximum Benefits. Every state uses some mechanism to limit the benefits which a household may receive. The simplest method is also the most commonly used—placing a ceiling on benefits directly. The next most common device is to limit the amount of property taxes eligible for reimbursement. The latter method tends to restrict benefits for higher-income families more than a direct limit on benefits would.[23] However, the distinction is blurred because many states which limit benefits also lower the limit as income increases.

Under most circuit breaker formulas only a small number of recipients are affected by the maximum benefit level. But a maximum is important to prevent large payments in unusual cases.[24]

Coinsurance. One effect of a circuit breaker is to relieve local citizens of a portion of the cost of services financed by property taxation. Such an effect is not unique to the circuit breaker, since deductibility of property taxes in determining income tax liability has the same impact. However, the circuit breaker can potentially be much more powerful than deductibility.[25] If r, the proportion of excess taxes which is rebated, is 100 percent, qualified citizens will not bear locally any of the cost of increased property taxes. This opens up the possibility that one negative side effect of a circuit breaker is that local spending might expand more than it otherwise would, interfering with neutrality.

Most states, if they permit rebates of 100 percent of taxes at all, limit this rate to the elderly and very low-income households. Setting rebates below 100 percent is sometimes referred to as coinsurance. Another factor tending to limit the circuit breaker's effect on voting behavior is the low limit on maximum benefits in most states.

There is some evidence that the behavior of some voters is affected by a circuit breaker. The identical bond issue was first defeated and then passed in Troy, Michigan, with the initiation of that state's circuit breaker occurring during the interim of one month between the votes.[26] A survey of Michigan school administrators found that most of them mentioned the circuit breaker in their campaigns in support of tax measures.[27]

Other Design Issues. One other design issue is relatively uncontroversial. In nearly all states the circuit breaker is financed at the state rather than the local level. This is appropriate for a device which redistributes tax burdens among individuals. However, this is not a particular advantage of the circuit breaker, since it is also true of many other forms of relief.

Three additional specific design issues are important: the definition of income, the treatment of net worth, and the treatment of family size. All involve serious tradeoffs among evaluative criteria—horizontal and vertical equity often conflict with administrative and compliance cost. Unfortunately, efforts to fine-tune the circuit breaker tend to increase its complexity. The simple is often the enemy of the fair.

From the point of view of horizontal equity, it is desirable to define income broadly, and most states do so. Many of the major types of income excluded from the income tax usually must be included in income for circuit breaker purposes—examples include income from social security, public assistance, and interest on municipal bonds.[28]

A related issue is whether net worth should be taken into account as a measure of needs. A major criticism of circuit breakers, as discussed in the next section, is that wealthy people with low current income may be eligible. As Aaron has stated,

> Because property tax payments are related positively to ownership of real property, a major part of net worth for most households, circuitbreaker relief is related negatively to household income and positively to net worth. . . . Gaffney has put the point acidly: "Those that become welfare cases should be treated by the welfare system on an impartial basis, without special favor to property owners. To use property tax relief as a substitute for welfare is to distribute welfare in proportion to net worth, surely an odd notion."[29]

While most writers agree that some recognition of net worth is desirable, it faces two practical difficulties: measures of wealth are difficult to verify, and the increased complexity of the application process may discourage households which do have real need. Defenders of omitting net worth also argue that even people with substantial net worth may have cash-flow difficulties, and that most wealth is in the hands of households whose incomes would disqualify them from circuit breaker benefits.[30]

In practice, most states ignore assets. A 1975 survey found only eight states out of twenty-four which considered net worth in designing their programs. The authors praised Iowa's approach, in which 10 percent of net worth in excess of $35,000 was added to income for determining benefits.[31] Shortly thereafter, Iowa repealed this provision.

The final design issue is how family size should be treated. Although it would be desirable in the interest of fairness, most circuit breakers do not differentiate between large and small households. A simple procedure would be to allow personal exemptions of $750 per person, as on the federal income tax. A more elaborate approach would establish different benefit schedules for varying family sizes.[32]

Analysis of Circuit Breaker Benefits

Because there is a theoretical tradeoff between the number of persons covered and average benefit levels, one might expect that states having more restrictive eligibility standards would have higher average benefits. But this is not true. States which are more liberal in coverage also are more generous in setting benefit levels. As table 3-5 indicates, states which impose no age limits tend to provide higher average benefits than states which limit eligibility to the elderly. In addition, states with programs for elderly homeowners have lower average benefits than states where circuit breakers cover both elderly renters and homeowners.

Despite the popularity of circuit breakers in the 1970s, little information has previously been collected on how the benefits of these programs are actually distributed. In order to fill this gap, a survey was conducted of the twenty-nine jurisdictions with circuit breakers.

A major goal was to determine how average benefits differ by income level. There is little question that circuit breakers are progressive in the sense that their benefits are a greater percentage of income for low-income households than for those with higher incomes.[33] However, it is not necessarily true that circuit breakers are more progressive than alternative tax relief mechanisms such as homestead credits. Depending on how they are designed and other factors, average circuit breaker benefits may increase as income rises. In fact, estimates of proposed national circuit breakers by Henry Aaron and Abt Associates predicted that benefits would be above average at high levels of income.[34] A homestead credit, on the other hand, could be equal at all income levels, as Iowa's was until 1976.

There are four factors which influence whether average circuit breaker

Table 3-5
Circuit Breaker Coverage and Benefit Levels, 1977

Average Benefits	All Ages		Elderly Only	
	Homeowners Only	Homeowners and Renters	Homeowners Only	Homeowners and Renters
Under $100	0	0	3	5
$100-$149	0	1	1	6
$150-$199	0	1	0	1
$200 or more	1	4	1	4
Median	$248	$208	$98	$127

Source: Advisory Commission on Intergovernmental Relations, *Significant Features of Fiscal Federalism*, 1978-79 ed. (Washington, D.C., 1979).

Note: In several cases, benefits are for years other than 1977. New York is omitted because of lack of data.

benefits increase or decrease as income rises. The first consideration is the design of the circuit breaker. If it rebates a constant percentage of property tax payments in excess of a uniform threshold level of income, benefits may rise as income increases even though the property tax is regressive. For example, suppose that a circuit breaker covers all property tax in excess of 3 percent of income and that the relationship of income to property tax is as follows:

Income	Property Tax
$ 5,000	$ 400
10,000	600
20,000	1,100

Although the property tax is regressive, circuit breaker benefits are $250, $300, and $500 at income levels $5,000, $10,000, and $20,000. Benefits decline as a percentage of income as income rises, but they increase in absolute terms. This result can be avoided by designing the circuit breaker so that the threshold rises or the proportion of tax rebated falls as income rises.

A second factor which might cause average benefits to be higher for high-income households is the treatment of renters. Families and individuals who rent usually receive considerably lower benefits at each income level than do homeowners.[35] Since renters are concentrated at the low end of the income scale, there is a tendency for average benefit to increase with income.

Besides these two aspects of how the circuit breaker is structured, the distribution of benefits also depends on the relationships among household income, the value of homes, and tax rates. One factor which sometimes tends to increase benefits for the affluent is that property tax rates may be higher in the cities or towns where they live. The ratio of home value to income also must be considered. Home values are close to proportional to normal income, but they are usually a higher proportion of current income for households with below-average incomes than for richer households.[36] The available data on actual circuit breakers deal with current income only.

The results of the survey allay fears that a large proportion of circuit breaker benefits goes to the rich. While average benefits to recipients do increase as income rises in several states, there are many programs with the opposite pattern. In cases where the average benefits of recipients at high income levels are above those at lower income levels, the proportion of high-income households which receive any benefits is low. Besides, twenty of the twenty-nine states limit the maximum income for participation to $11,000 or less.

Results of the survey are summarized in greater detail in appendix 3A. It clearly demonstrates that the benefits of all existing circuit breakers go mostly to households with below-average income. There is not a single state where more than half of the payments in 1977 went to households with incomes over $10,000.

One reason why the existing circuit breakers concentrate their benefits on those with below-average income more than estimates by Aaron and Abt Associates predicted is that most programs have an income ceiling, a rising threshold, or a falling proportion of excess taxes rebated as income rises.[37] In addition, Southern states tend to have low property tax burdens and low average incomes, so that a national circuit breaker would provide relatively small benefits to them in view of their income alone. Within a single state, benefits are likely to be more progressive than nationally.

Although this survey found that existing circuit breakers have benefits which are skewed heavily in favor of low-income households, not all circuit breakers necessarily have such a distributional pattern. For example, a circuit breaker proposal which was narrowly defeated in California in 1977 provided approximately 75 percent of its benefits to households with incomes over $10,000. The program's benefits were still progressive, since these households paid 87 percent of the homeowner property taxes, but it was designed to provide the lion's share of relief to the middle class.

As table 3-6 shows, it concentrated benefits in the $10,000-$30,000 income range, providing little relief to homeowners with income in excess of $30,000.[38]

Evaluation

In the annals of circuit breaker literature, most of the comment is friendly. The outstanding critic of the circuit breaker approach to tax relief is Henry Aaron.

One of the Aaron's major attacks is related to a point mentioned above, that at a given income level the circuit breaker provides greater relief as net worth increases. This is undoubtedly true and is a defect of the circuit breaker.

In a similar vein, Aaron states that "many of the neediest households will not receive aid, while some households with substantial wealth will qualify for relief."[39] Here Aaron is on very weak ground. The first part of the statement

Table 3-6
Distributional Impact of a Circuit Breaker Narrowly Defeated in California in 1977

Income Class	Percentage of Homeowners	Percentage of Homeowner Property Taxes	Percentage of Benefits from Circuit Breaker
Under $10,000	17.7	12.7	24.6
$10,000-$30,000	64.8	63.3	70.0
$30,000-$40,000	10.1	11.7	5.4
$40,000 and above	7.5	12.2	—
Total	100.0	100.0	100.0

Source: California Tax Research Project, *The Circuit Breaker: A California Tax Research Project Analysis* (Sacramento, 1978).

may be true for a national circuit breaker limited to the elderly which does not extend relief to renters, but it is not true for a state circuit breaker which covers all age groups and includes renters. In a sliding-scale circuit breaker, all low-income households receive benefits if they apply for relief; a threshold circuit breaker might miss some low-income households, but only if the threshold level is high, property tax rates are low, and the family does not spend much on housing. Many needy households in some states apparently do not receive aid, but this is because of poor publicity for programs, not the inherent nature of the circuit breaker.

The second part of Aaron's statement points out that some wealthy households qualify for relief. The same can be said of every other type of property tax relief in use. The difference between the circuit breaker and other programs is that it is much less true for the circuit breaker. The other chapters of this book show how most types of property tax relief provide disproportionate benefits to the rich. The material in appendix 3A documents that existing circuit breakers provide most of their benefits to households with below-average income.

A related issue concerns the incidence of the property tax. According to Aaron, "The intellectual rationale for circuit breakers rests on the alleged regressivity of the property tax." He describes the incidence theory currently influencing public officials as "an atavistic attachment to naive and obsolete theory in defiance of published theoretical advances that demolish the previous orthodoxy."[40] The two major advances to which he refers are the general equilibrium analysis of the property tax and the permanent-income hypothesis.

Those who continue to regard the property tax as regressive are not necessarily "slaves of some defunct economist" whose legacy is "indefensible analysis."[41] Aaron's analysis was initially developed for a national circuit breaker; from that point of view, it is appropriate to use a general equilibrium model, which under certain assumptions leads to the conclusion that the property tax is borne by the owners of capital and is progressive. However, from a single state's position, a partial equilibrium analysis is more appropriate, and the excise tax effects which it incorporates may yield the conclusion that the property tax is regressive.

The other major theoretical development referred to by Aaron is to view the incidence of the property tax in relation to permanent income rather than current annual income. Such a change definitely reduces the regressivity of the residential property tax and may make it proportional or progressive. However, it can be argued that current income is at least as relevant to tax policy as permanent income.[42]

More than one writer has denied Aaron's assertion that the case for the circuit breaker rests on the regressivity of the property tax. According to the Advisory Commission on Intergovernmental Relations,

. . .there would be a need for property tax relief even if the tax were proportional—or even progressive—if the absolute level of the tax worked a hardship on some persons. A reasonable analogy is the need for exemptions to shield subsistence-level income under an income tax that features sharply progressive rates.[43]

All the discussion thus far concerns the allegation that the circuit breaker aids the wrong households. A second major criticism is that the circuit breaker provides disproportionate assistance in areas where local governments rely heavily on property taxation rather than other revenue sources.[44] Once again, this charge has more validity against a national relief program than one administered at the state level. There is much less variation in taxes used within states than among states.

A third criticism of circuit breakers by Aaron is that they reduce the incentive for low-income persons to raise their incomes: as income goes up, relief goes down. However, it can be shown that generally the marginal tax rates are low, so that this is not a serious problem.[45]

Another problem, already alluded to in the section on design issues, is that a circuit breaker may affect voting behavior, increasing the willingness to vote in favor of spending increases. This problem is most severe if there is a threshold formula with no limit on benefits and no coinsurance provision, but it can be greatly reduced by careful design of the circuit breaker. There is little evidence that this is a serious problem in actual practice.

Two other criticisms are easily dismissed. One study criticizes circuit breakers because they provide no incentive to reform the administration of the property tax.[46] The same is true of almost every other form of relief. Another argument is that the circuit breaker encourages expansion of the property tax[47] and tends to retard the shift to sales and income taxes. First, this argument may be wrong, since sales or income taxes are the most likely source of revenue to pay for circuit breaker relief.[48] Second, it may be desirable to revive the property tax; many students of government finance regard this tax as vital to maintenance of local government autonomy.[49]

One major problem has not received sufficient public scrutiny. As it is actually administered, the horizontal equity of the circuit breaker is far from what it should be, because many eligible households apparently fail to participate. Data on this problem are sketchy but suggestive. A 1974 ACIR survey estimated that the percentage of eligible households which were in the program averaged 69 percent in states with elderly circuit breakers and 82 percent in states with no age limit.[50] However, some of these rates are probably overestimates.[51] Abt Associates, which has conducted the largest survey of circuit breaker activity, found the data inadequate for estimation of participation rates but stressed the need for a well-organized outreach program to stimulate participation. Fortunately, the participation rate does tend to rise as familiarity with the program increases, and outreach programs can be effective. But as long as many eligible households are not in the program, its reality falls significantly short of its potential.[52]

In the overall evaluation of the circuit breaker, perhaps the two most important factors are the urgency which is felt with regard to relieving taxes for households with relatively high property taxes in relation to their income and one's sense of political realities. The circuit breaker is potentially the most progressive form of property tax relief. The ability of the circuit breaker to target relief is a great virtue in the eyes of many,[53] but it is a wasted virtue to those who want across-the-board relief.

Political acceptability is a crucial consideration. Aaron admits that it tempts him, but instead he advocates deferral, a housing allowance, and comprehensive income maintenance,[54] none of which have the apparent political momentum or appeal of the circuit breaker. Some circuit breaker advocates concede that it is not the ideal solution but that it is much preferable to the practical alternatives.[55] In fact, the circuit breaker's tendency to target relief on behalf of those with low and moderate income is a political liability in legislatures where the interests of the upper middle class and the wealthy are on the minds of many lawmakers. In Michigan, this problem was overcome by making the circuit breaker part of a package that included business tax breaks and an increase of income tax exemptions, which favored higher-income groups.[56] As already mentioned, a circuit breaker considered by the 1977 California Legislature was modified in order to confer greater benefits on middle-class suburbanites.

In a general analysis, the circuit breaker must be viewed as one form of relief for homeowners and renters in competition with the other types of relief discussed in subsequent chapters. Two questions have to be confronted: How much relief should go to homeowners and renters as opposed to other property taxpayers? Is the circuit breaker the most appropriate device for aiding homeowners and renters? The second question is discussed in the next chapter following the analysis of other types of residential property tax relief. The first question is considered in the final chapter.

The circuit breaker provides a means of integrating the property tax with income. It is a means of overcoming the often-heard complaint that the property tax is not based on ability to pay. It automatically cushions the impact of taxes when property values rise. It has much to recommend it.

Notes

1. Advisory Commission on Intergovernmental Relations, *Property Tax Circuitbreakers: Current Status and Policy Issues* (Washington, D.C., 1975), pp. 3-4.

2. This discussion ignores the fact that in Iowa the benefit of the

homestead credit is subtracted from the circuit breaker, so that the circuit breaker provides less benefit than it would in isolation.

3. Thus, locally financed homestead exemptions are excluded even if their benefits depend on income.

4. Unless otherwise noted, the descriptive statements in this chapter are based on Advisory Commission on Intergovernmental Relations, *Significant Features of Fiscal Federalism* 1978-79 ed., Washington, D.C.: 1979, tables 43 and 44. Its tally of circuit breaker states is thirty plus the District of Columbia. However, it includes Hawaii and Arizona, which are not counted here. Hawaii's program is a renter credit, and Arizona's credit for low-income elderly households is no longer related to property taxation in any respect, although it formerly was.

5. Wisconsin was the first state to adopt a circuit breaker. Credit for originating the idea is attributed to Harold Groves by Kenneth E. Quindry and Billy D. Cook, "Humanization of the Property Tax for Low-Income Households," *National Tax Journal* 22 (September 1969):359. Dates of adoption of circuit breakers are as follows: 1964, one; 1967, two; 1969, one; 1970, one; 1971, five; 1972, two; 1973, eight; 1974, three; 1975, one; 1976, one; 1977, three; 1978, one.

6. Arkansas, West Virginia, Indiana, New Mexico, and Oklahoma all border on the large block of Southern states with no program; Utah is adjacent to Wyoming, Rhode Island to Massachusetts, and South Dakota to three non-circuit-breaker states.

7. Abt Associates, *Property Tax Relief Programs for the Elderly: A Compendium Report* (Washington, D.C.: Department of Housing and Urban Development, 1975), pp. 86-91.

8. Marc Bendick, "Designing Circuit Breaker Property Tax Relief," *National Tax Journal* 27 (March 1974):26-27.

9. See Thomas R. Ireland and William E. Mitchell, "A Public Choice Analysis of the Demand for Property Tax Circuit-breaker Legislation," *Public Finance Quarterly,* (October 1976), pp. 379-94, for a discussion of reasons for favoring senior citizens. For a negative view of preferential treatment of the aged, see Mason Gaffney, "An Agenda for Strengthening the Property Tax," in *Property Tax Reform*, ed. George E. Peterson (Washington, D.C.: The Urban Institute, 1973), pp. 68-69.

10. Renters are much worse off than homeowners. While the median elderly renter in metropolitan areas spends over 30 percent of income on housing, the median elderly homeowner spends only 17 percent of income on housing costs. Michael Gutowski and Tracey Feild, *The Graying of Suburbia* (Washington, D.C.: The Urban Institute, 1979), p. 32. See also Raymond J. Struyk, *The Housing Situation of Elderly Americans* (Washington, D.C.: The Urban Institute, 1976); Abt Associates, *Property Tax Relief Programs for the Elderly: An Evaluation* (Washington, D.C., Department of Housing and Urban

Development, 1975), pp. 16-41; and Gaffney, "An Agenda for Strengthening the Property Tax," pp. 68-69.

11. Gutowski and Feild, *The Graying of Suburbia* p. 53.

12. W. Norton Grubb and E. Gaerth Hoachlander, "Circuit-breaker Schedules and Their Application in California," *Policy Analysis,* Summer 1978, pp. 328-33.

13. Billy D. Cook, "The Circuit-Breaker Approach for Granting Property Tax Relief with Special Emphasis on Wisconsin and Minnesota," in Advisory Commission on Intergovernmental Relations, *Financing Schools and Property Tax Relief* (Washington, D.C., 1973), p. 181.

14. Abt Associates, *Property Tax Relief Programs for the Elderly: Final Report,* (Washington, D.C.: Department of Housing and Urban Development, 1976), p. 97.

15. Bendick, "Designing Relief," pp. 24-25. Abt Associates, *Final Report,* pp. 97-102.

16. Abt Associates, *A Compendium Report,* is the broadest survey of circuit breaker provisions; its information was gathered in 1974 and early 1975. It is the basis for statements in this section.

17. Grubb and Hoachlander, "Circuit-breaker Schedules," p. 325.

18. Ibid., p. 327.

19. This section closely follows Steven D. Gold, "A Note on the Design of Property Tax Circuitbreakers," *National Tax Journal* 29 (December 1976):477-81.

20. Bowman believes that in view of large variations in within-state tax bases, this reason often "swamps" other factors; therefore, he favors the threshold approach. See John H. Bowman, "Property Tax Circuit-Breakers: Continuing Issues Surrounding a Popular Program," *Journal of Economics and Sociology,* forthcoming.

21. This point is demonstrated in Dick Netzer, "State Education Aid and School Tax Efforts in Large Cities," in *Selected Papers in School Finance: 1974* (Washington, D.C.: Department of Health, Education, and Welfare, 1974), pp. 135-232.

22. Bowman claims that another disadvantage of the sliding-scale approach is that it involves notch effects because a $1 change in income will result in a much larger change in tax relief in certain cases. However, Grubb and Hoachlander point out that the threshold may involve a substantial notch if it incorporates an income ceiling. See Bowman, "A Popular Program," and Grubb and Hoachlander, "Circuit-Breaker Schedules," p. 336.

23. There are two reasons. First, the parameter r may decrease as income rises. Second, high-income households tend to have high property taxes, which would increase their circuit breaker benefits it there were no maximum.

24. See, for example, Larry D. Schroeder and David L. Sjoquist, "Alterna-

tive Circuit-Breaker Programs: An Analysis of the Size and Distribution of Benefits," *Public Finance Quarterly* 6 (October 1978):409.

25. The net cost of deductible property taxes is found by multiplying the property tax by one minus the marginal income tax rate. For example, the net cost of $100 property tax for someone in the 36 percent marginal tax bracket is $64.

26. Abt Associates, *Final Report,* p. 52.

27. Robert Kleine, personal correspondence.

28. However, gifts, life insurance benefits, and relief in kind are usually excluded from the income measure. For details, see Abt Associates, *A Compendium Report,* p. 40. See also Bendick, "Designing Relief," p. 25.

29. Henry J. Aaron, *Who Pays the Property Tax?* (Washington, D.C.: The Brookings Institution, 1975), p. 76.

30. See Bowman, "A Popular Program"; Advisory Commission on Intergovernmental Relations, *Property Tax Circuitbreakers,* p. 16; Abt Associates, *A Compendium Report,* pp. 47-51; and Bendick, "Designing Relief," p. 27.

31. Abt Associates, *A Compendium Report,* p. 48.

32. Bendick, "Designing Relief," pp. 25-26.

33. If the property tax is regressive, a credit which rebates some proportion of property tax payments in excess of a specified percentage of income is a greater percentage of income for low-income households than for high-income households. Given the regressivity of the property tax, the only ways in which circuit breaker benefits could be an increasing function of income would be for the proportion of excess taxes rebated (r) to rise or for the threshold ratio of tax to income (p) to fall as income rises, which is contrary to all existing programs.

34. Henry J. Aaron, "What Do Circuit-Breaker Laws Accomplish?" in, *Property Tax Reform* ed. G.E. Peterson, p. 56, and Abt Associates, *An Evaluation,* p. 75.

35. See, for example, Abt Associates, *A Compendium Report,* p. 25. This relationship was also found in the survey reported on in this chapter.

36. Evidence on these points is discussed in appendix 1A.

37. The Abt estimates also were marred by lack of data on the actual tax rate on each home in the sample, so that countywide averages were used. See Abt Associates, *An Evaluation,* p. 65.

38. The statistics cited refer only to the portion of the circuit breaker for homeowners.

39. Aaron, "Circuit-Breaker Laws," p. 64.

40. Ibid., pp. 58-60.

41. Ibid., p. 53.

42. See appendix 1A for a discussion of the incidence of the property tax.

43. Advisory Commission on Intergovernmental Relations, *Property Tax Circuitbreakers,* p. 16.

44. Aaron, "Circuit-Breaker Laws," p. 64.

45. Ibid., p. 65; Grubb and Hoachlander, "Circuit-breaker Schedules," pp. 334-35.

46. Larry D. Schroeder and David L. Sjoquist, "Property Tax Relief through Circuitbreakers," *International Assessor* 43 (May 1977):6.

47. Ibid., p. 6; Aaron, "Circuit-Breaker Laws," p. 64.

48. In fact, all the states with general circuit breakers derive an above-average percentage of their general revenue from income taxation. Advisory Commission on Intergovernmental Relations, *Significant Features,* table 46.

49. James A. Maxwell and J. Richard Aronson, *Financing State and Local Governments,* 3d ed. (Washington, D.C.: The Brookings Institution, 1977), pp. 134-38; Bowman, "A Popular Program."

50. Advisory Commission on Intergovernmental Relations, *Property Tax Circuitbreakers,* p. 5.

51. See the appendix of this chapter.

52. Abt Associates, *A Compendium Report,* pp. 60-67. The Oregon circuit breaker, which was accompanied by a major publicity campaign, has a particularly high participation rate. But participation in Maryland initially was only 25 percent of that expected, and in the District of Columbia it was even lower. Wisconsin also had much lower participation than originally expected.

53. Bendick, for example, is particularly forceful on this point, in "Designing Relief," pp. 26-28.

54. Aaron, *Who Pays?* pp. 78-79; Aaron, "Circuit-breaker Laws," p. 64.

55. Bowman, "A Popular Program"; Gold, "A Note," p. 481; Bendick, "Designing Relief," p. 24.

56. See the discussion of this point in chapter 14.

Appendix 3A:
Survey of Distribution
of Benefits

In October and November 1978, a mail survey was conducted of all states with circuit breakers in order to obtain information on the distribution of benefits from existing programs and participation rates. Responses were received from every state except one, which was contacted by telephone.

Numerous states either had no distribution information at all or else reported only the distribution of participants among counties.

The most important result of the survey was to document that most circuit breaker benefits go to households with relatively low incomes. Before the survey was conducted, it was already known that most circuit breakers have relatively low income ceilings (that is, maximum income for eligibility). But in the states which have either a relatively high ceiling or none at all, it is possible that households with relatively high income will receive a disproportionate share of benefits. In fact, some hypothetical estimates of national circuit breakers suggest that benefit per recipient would increase as income goes up.

Two factors account for the distribution of circuit breaker benefits among income levels—benefits per participant and the proportion of households at each income level which are participants in the program. In most states, as table 3A-1 shows, benefit per participant tends to fall as income rises. In addition, the proportion of households at each income level who receive benefits tends to decrease as income goes up. As a result of these two patterns, a high proportion of benefits go to households with relatively low incomes.

Table 3A-2 reports more detailed information on the seven programs which had ceilings of $12,000 or higher. Clearly there are great differences among them. Maryland, Michigan, and Minnesota distribute benefits more widely among income groups than the other states. But in all cases a majority of benefits go to households with incomes under $10,000. Moreover, in all cases, more than 70 percent of the benefits go to households with incomes under $15,000 which was close to the national median income in 1977.

Now we briefly discuss each of the six major programs.

District of Columbia. Average benefits in the $15,000-$20,000 income group were higher than at any other level, but only 9.4 percent of the beneficiaries were in this income range.

No data are reported separating benefits to renters and homeowners, and the relatively low benefits for renters may be an important element in explaining the average benefit pattern. (Only 15 percent of rent is counted as a property tax equivalent, one of the lowest percentages used in any circuit breaker.)

Table 3A-1

Relation of Circuit Breaker Benefit per Recipient to Household Income

Arkansas	No data on average benefit or participation by income level
California	Average benefit falls as income rises
Connecticut	No data on average benefit or participation by income level
District of Columbia	Average benefit trendless to $15,000, then rises
Idaho	No data on average benefit by income level
Illinois	No data on average benefit by income level
Indiana	U-shaped pattern, but average tends to fall as income rises
Iowa	Average benefit falls as income rises
Kansas	No data on average benefit or participation by income level
Maine	Average benefit increases from lowest income level to $2,000-$4,000 level, then is relatively constant to $6,000
Maryland	Average benefit falls as income rises
Michigan	Average benefit tends to increase as income rises, for both elderly and general programs
Minnesota	Average benefit falls as income rises except at very highest income levels
Missouri	No data on average benefit by income level
Nevada	Average benefit falls as income rises
New Mexico	U-shaped pattern, but excluding lowest income level (under $1,000), average benefit rises to $10,000 income and then is roughly constant
North Dakota	Average benefit falls as income rises
Ohio	Average benefit increases slightly from lowest income level to $3,000-$5,000 and then tends to fall
Oklahoma	No data on average benefit or participation by income level
Oregon	Average benefit falls as income rises
Pennsylvania	Average benefit falls as income rises
Rhode Island	Average benefits are roughly constant
South Dakota	No data on average benefit or participation by income level
Utah	No data on average benefit or participation by income level
Vermont	U-shaped pattern
Wisconsin	Average benefit tends to fall as income rises

Source: Survey of states conducted in October-November 1978.

Note: The average benefit equals the circuit breaker benefit per person in the program. Persons who are ineligible or who are eligible but do not participate are not considered.

Maryland. Average benefit falls as income rises in this circuit breaker, the only large one which did not cover renters during the period studied. The city of Baltimore and two counties in suburban Washington accounted for 68.4 percent of benefits and 61.4 percent of participants in 1978, even though they had only 50.3 percent of the population of the state.

Michigan. As income increases, average benefits tend to rise but the proportion of households receiving benefits tends to fall. These patterns exist in both the

Table 3A-2
Distribution of Circuit Breaker Benefits in States which Extend Eligibility above $12,000 Income, 1977 and 1978

Place (Year Filed)	Income Ceiling (dollars)	Percentage of Payments to Households with Income under		Percentage of Households Receiving Benefits with Income under	
		$10,000	$15,000	$10,000	$15,000
District of Columbia[a] (1978)	20,000	63.2	88.3	64.2	90.6
Maryland[b] (1978)	None	56.3	88.5	46.3	82.9
Michigan[c] (1977)	None	55.8	72.3	51.0	68.5
Minnesota (1977)	None[d]	52.0	72.9	46.8	66.4
New Mexico[e] (1977)	16,000	82.3	98.9	86.5	99.1
Oregon (1977)	15,000[f]	82.3	100.0	68.8	100.0
Vermont (1977)	None	84.4[g]	97.7[h]	84.1[g]	97.8[h]

Source: Survey of states.

[a]Data are only for elderly; younger households eligible only to $7,000 income in 1978.

[b]Program only for homeowners in 1978.

[c]Omits small programs for disabled and others.

[d]Implicit ceiling of $36,000 for nonelderly households.

[e]Program is only for elderly households.

[f]Ceiling raised to $17,500 in 1979.

[g]Estimate based on average for percentage under $8,000 income and under $12,000 income; understates true percentage which is above midpoint.

[h]For $16,000 income, because $15,000 was unavailable.

senior citizen and the general circuit breakers. Besides the factors mentioned in the chapter, part of the explanation is that farmers may count all their property tax payments toward the circuit breaker, and that distorts the relationship of income to benefits for homeowners and renters. See chapter 14 for more details.

Minnesota. Average benefits tend to decrease as income rises up to $35,000. But for the very small number of recipients above that income level, average benefits are much higher than for other income groups.

The distribution of benefits is strongly influenced by a credit for 45 percent of gross residential property tax payments up to a maximum of $325 (since raised to a higher level) which is subtracted from taxes before circuit breaker calculations are made. Since this credit tends to increase with income, it reduces circuit breaker benefits most for high-income households. Nonsenior citizens with income over $36,000 would not be eligible for the circuit breaker unless they neglected to apply for their homestead credit.

Oregon. Average benefits decrease as income rises. This clear result is related to the unusually simple design of the Oregon circuit breaker. The state refunds all property taxes up to various maximums which decrease as income rises.

Vermont. There is a U-shaped benefit distribution, but the number of beneficiaries at high income levels is small. Among renters benefits decline steadily as income increases, but the U-shaped pattern exists among homeowners and for the total program.

Another subject covered in the survey was the proportion of eligible households which participated in the program. The results of the survey confirm previous indications from an ACIR study that many eligible households do not participate, either because of a lack of information or for some other reason, and they raise questions of the reliability of the ACIR estimates. In the present survey most state officials (who were selected because they had previously provided information on circuit breakers to the ACIR) declined to make any estimate. Those who did often emphasized that they were only rough approximations or "guesstimates." Rates were reported as follows:

	Percent
Idaho	95
Illinois	70
Indiana	27
Iowa	80
Maine	64
Michigan	90
New Mexico	50
Ohio	85
North Dakota	71 (only among homeowners)
Oregon	"substantially all"

To sum, in most states with a high income ceiling the benefits do tend to increase at some high income level for the small number of households which receive benefits. Nevertheless, circuit breakers generally do succeed in targeting relief to households with relatively low incomes.

4

Residential Property Tax Relief by Means Other than Circuit Breakers

This chapter covers a wide variety of programs which may be considered alternatives to the circuit breaker, to other relief measures, and to one another. Their purposes vary from alleviating taxes for certain meritorious groups to encouraging particular types of behavior. Judgments on them rest on two issues—whether their goals are appropriate and how each instrument compares to the other means available for achieving those goals.

Description

The most widespread form of relief for homeowners is the *homestead exemption*, which provides for exemption of a specified amount of a home's assessed value from the tax base. For example, if a home's assessed value is $30,000 and the homestead exemption is $3,000, its owner will pay taxes on just $27,000. Homestead exemptions may be made available to all homeowners or limited to the elderly, veterans, or some other group.

A closely related device is the *homestead credit*. It differs from the exemption in that it is subtracted from the gross property tax rather than from assessed value. It is usually state-financed, in contrast to the exemption, which is generally state-mandated but locally financed.

There are two principal types of homestead credits. The most common is similar to an exemption in that it covers the taxes on a certain number of dollars of assessed valuation. Several states have recently adopted a credit which covers a certain percentage of each homeowner's tax bill, subject to a maximum in some cases.[1]

Property tax *deferral programs,* used in a few states, allow certain homeowners to postpone paying all or part of their property taxes. However, a lien is placed on the property, and deferred taxes must be repaid when the property is sold, given away, or transferred at the time of death.

A little used method of relief is the *tax freeze*. It provides that residential property taxes shall not increase after a homeowner reaches the age of 65.

Several states extend relief not only to homeowners but also to renters by means of a *renter credit* against the state income tax. The credit is usually either a flat amount or a percentage of rent, subject to a maximum payment.

Finally, many states provide for *exemption* from assessment of the increase in value because of the *rehabilitation* activity on homes or rental property.

History, Current Extent of
Use, and Costs

Homestead Exemptions and Credits

Homestead exemptions or credits exist in thirty-seven states and the District of Columbia. Every state which does not have a circuit breaker does have either an exemption or credit for homeowners. Fifteen states and the District of Columbia have both a circuit breaker and an exemption or credit.[2]

According to table 4-1, most states favor elderly households. Fourteen states limit homestead relief to them, and fifteen others provide a more liberal exemption or credit for them. Only eight states and the District of Columbia make no distinction.

Most of the early homestead programs were adopted as property tax relief measures during the Depression and covered all homeowners. New Jersey in 1957 was the first state to provide an exemption solely for the elderly. By 1965, twelve states had exemptions or credits with no age limit, and six others had programs solely for the elderly.[3] Since that time the number of states with homestead programs more than doubled. At first, most of these new programs were limited to the elderly. At the same time, eight states with programs which formerly disregarded age added new provisions favoring older households. However, in the late 1970s the trend was away from programs limited to senior citizens, as the District of Columbia, New Jersey, Utah, Oregon, Illinois, Massachusetts, Wisconsin, Indiana, Montana, Maine, and Wyoming added programs without age restrictions (often retaining older programs exclusively for the elderly).

Another new development in the 1970s is a credit which pays a certain percentage of property taxes for homeowners. Minnesota was the first state with such a program. Its credit paid 45 percent of the tax bill up to $325 until it was raised in 1979. Similar programs were enacted in 1979 in Utah, Oregon, Wisconsin, and Indiana. The Utah credit has a minimum of $100 and a maximum of $400.

Table 4-2 summarizes the state circuit breaker and exemption/credit programs. As expected, there is a tradeoff. States which have no exemption or credit are certain to have a circuit breaker; if there is a circuit breaker, the state is less likely to provide an exemption or credit. There is also a relationship between the existence of a circuit breaker and the homestead program's age limit. States with no circuit breaker are more likely to have homestead programs favoring the elderly than circuit breaker states. This reflects the strong tendency to do something special for the elderly; if the circuit breaker already favors them (as most do), the homestead exemption can be more even-handed.

Financing arrangements for homestead programs vary from state to state. Fifteen states have locally financed programs, fifteen are state-financed, and in eight states financing is part state and part local. Five of the local programs

Table 4-1
Homestead Exemption and Credit Programs, 1979

State	Income Limit	Financing
No Age Restrictions		
Arizona	No	State
District of Columbia	No	State
California	No	State
Iowa	No	State
Maine	No	State
Minnesota	No	State
Oklahoma	No[a]	Both
Oregon	No	State
Wisconsin	No	State
Senior Citizens Receive a Larger Exemption or Credit than Others		
Alabama	Partial[b]	Both
Florida	No	Both
Georgia	Partial[b]	Local
Hawaii	No	Local
Illinois	No	Local
Indiana	No	Both
Louisiana	No	State
Massachusetts	Partial[b]	Local
Mississippi	No	State
Montana	Partial[b]	Both
Nebraska	Partial[b]	State
New Jersey	Partial[b]	Both
Texas	No	Both
Utah	Partial[b]	Both
Wyoming	Partial[b]	State
Only for Senior Citizens		
Alaska	No	State
Delaware	Yes	Local
Kentucky	No	Local
New Hampshire	Yes	Local
New York	Yes	Local
North Carolina	Yes	Local
North Dakota	Yes	Local
Rhode Island	Yes	Local
South Carolina	No	State
South Dakota	Yes	Local
Tennessee	Yes	State
Virginia	Yes	Local
Washington	Yes	Local
West Virginia	No	Local

Source: Advisory Commission on Intergovernmental Relations, *Significant Features of Fiscal Federalism,* 1976-77 ed. (Washington, D.C., 1977); Abt Associates, *Property Tax Relief for the Elderly* (Washington, D.C., Department of Housing and Urban Development, 1975); reports from individual states.

[a]There is no income limit for the basic exemption, but there is for an extra exemption.

[b]There is no income limit for the program without age restrictions, but there is an income limit for at least part of the program for senior citizens. Eligible persons may participate in both programs.

Table 4-2

Relation to Homestead Programs to Circuit Breakers, 1979

Homestead Program's Treatment of Age Groups	States with Circuit Breakers	States without Circuit Breakers
All ages equal	California, Iowa, Maine, Minnesota, Oklahoma, Oregon, Wisconsin, D.C.	Arizona
Elderly receive preferential treatment but nonelderly receive some benefits	Illinois, Indiana, Utah	Alabama, Florida, Georgia, Hawaii, Louisiana, Massachusetts, Mississippi, Montana, Nebraska, New Jersey, Texas, Wyoming
Only elderly receive benefits	New York, North Dakota, Rhode Island, South Dakota, West Virginia	Alaska, Delaware, Kentucky, New Hampshire, North Carolina, South Carolina, Tennessee, Virginia, Washington
No program	Arkansas, Colorado, Connecticut Idaho, Kansas, Maryland, Michigan, Missouri, Nevada, New Mexico, Ohio, Pennsylvania Vermont	None

Source: Advisory Commission on Intergovernmental Relations, *Significant Features of Fiscal Federalism*, 1976-77 ed. (Washington, D.C., 1977); Abt Associates, *Property Tax Relief for the Elderly* (Washington, D.C., Department of Housing and Urban Development, 1975); reports from individual states.

Note: All property owners in Indiana, Ohio, and Wisconsin receive a credit, but these credits are not included in this table because they are not limited to residential property.

(including one state where financing is shared) are optional; the rest are state-mandated. Generally programs for the elderly are locally financed, while those for all homeowners are financed by state governments.

A 1977 survey reported that states distributed $880 million to reimburse localities for homestead programs.[4] This sum is within 10 percent of total state expenditures for circuit breakers in that year.

There is no sense in comparing the amounts of assessed value which are exempted, because assessment practices vary widely. For example, Louisiana's $5,000 exemption excluded close to $50,000 of a home's value from taxation in Baton Rouge in 1976, since the assessment ratio was about 10 percent, but Florida's $5,000 exemption excluded approximately $6,250 from taxation in Orlando, where the assessment ratio was close to 80 percent.[5]

Two recent surveys could not obtain estimates of average benefits or costs in many states, but those data which were collected indicate that the benefits are often rather meager. Benefit per recipient exceeded $200 in only three of thirteen states surveyed, reaching a peak of $466 in Massachusetts (which has the highest property tax rates in the country). Program cost per capita was highest in Massachusetts and South Dakota ($5.18 and $5.15, respectively), but it was less than $2 in fourteen of the twenty states surveyed.[6]

Several states which expanded their homestead programs in the late 1970s have more expensive programs. Iowa's homestead credit, which was approximately doubled in 1976, has a per capita cost of over $26 and an average benefit of $125. For Minnesota comparable figures are $40 and $271, respectively. The Oregon and Utah credits are also relatively large.

Veteran's Exemptions or Credits

Thirty-one states provided veteran's exemptions or credits in 1973. The number of such programs grew steadily from the period directly after World War II, when they first became popular, to 1964. From that year to 1973, the date of the most recent survey, there was no further increase.

Provisions vary considerably. In about half of the states, the exemption applies only to veterans who are partly or completely disabled. Several states also limit eligibility to those with low income and/or low property value. Usually eligibility is limited to those who served in the armed forces during wars or other specified periods of national emergency.[7]

Deferral Programs

Eight states and the District of Columbia have deferral programs. By far the largest is in California, where $12.7 million in taxes was deferred in 1977-1978, the program's first year in operation. However, the number of participants and the value of taxes deferred dropped after Proposition 13 took effect. This experience shows conclusively that participation is sensitive to how onerous taxes are. As of 1973, the largest of the five programs in operation was Oregon's, with only 283 participants.

Other places with deferral programs are Florida, Colorado, District of Columbia, Massachusetts, Oregon, Texas, Virginia, and Utah. In most cases the program is locally financed, with California and Oregon being among the exceptions in which the state bears the cost. In Virginia and Utah the program is available only in localities which choose to offer it; in other states deferral is mandated by the state government.

All the programs are limited to elderly homeowners.[8]

Tax Freezes

Connecticut has a tax freeze for the elderly, but households must choose whether they want to participate in it or the circuit breaker. Once they choose the circuit breaker, they may not reenter the tax freeze. Total benefits paid under the tax freeze are considerably higher than those under the homeowner component of the circuit breaker.

Minnesota provided a tax freeze for senior citizens for several years, but it was eliminated in 1977 when benefits under the circuit breaker were increased. Some localities in Rhode Island and Virginia also have local tax freezes.[9] Arkansas enacted one in 1979.

Renter Credit

Ten states provide income tax credits for renters—Arizona, California, Maine, Minnesota, Indiana, Hawaii, New Jersey, Oregon, Wisconsin, and Utah. The programs are of recent vintage. Minnesota's $120 credit (or 10 percent of rent if lower), was the most generous as of 1975. Unlike deferral and tax freeze programs, renter's credits are available to all age groups. However, in cases when renters do not pay income tax, they usually do not benefit from the credit. In New Jersey it is estimated that 500,000 renters per year do not receive the credit for that reason.

The Oregon, Wisconsin, Maine, and Utah credits were passed in 1979 as companions to new homestead credits. Just as the credits for homeowners pay a fixed percentage of the property tax, the renter credits pay a fixed percentage of rent. In Utah the credit may vary from $100 to $400.[10]

Exemptions for Rehabilitation

Twenty-five states have enacted legislation which enables cities to exempt from reassessment for defined periods the increase in a residence's value resulting from rehabilitation. Participation is restricted in various ways, including the nature of rehabilitation work, the type of structure, the geographic area, and the characteristics of the residents. Most of these programs were initiated in the 1970s.[11]

Design Issues

Three major design issues are related to all types of relief oriented to residential property:

1. Should relief be financed from local property tax revenue or from some other source?
2. What formula should be used to determine how much relief is provided?
3. Should eligibility be restricted in some fashion?

These issues are discussed first in the context of homestead exemptions and credits. Additional issues concerning other types of residential relief are discussed in the following section.

Source of Finance

The two most common types of relief are exemptions financed locally from property tax revenue and credits financed from other taxes. The difference between an exemption and a credit is that the first is subtracted from assessed value and the second is subtracted from the gross property tax payment.

A locally financed exemption involves two kinds of costs:

A local tax shift: It changes the proportionate composition of the property tax base and therefore shifts property taxes to nonresidential property.

A school aid impact: It reduces assessed value per pupil and therefore increases state aid to the school district.

The local shift imposes a cost on nonresidential property; the school aid impact entails a cost to the state.

The magnitude of the local tax shift caused by a homestead exemption depends on the amount of nonresidential property in a jurisdiction and the amount of property tax revenue to be raised. The effect of the exemption is to reduce the total property tax base and therefore to require a higher nominal tax rate in order to raise the same amount of revenue as if there were no exemption. (See table 1-4 for an example of how an exemption increases taxes for nonresidential property.) If there is not much nonresidential property to which the tax burden can be shifted or if the total property tax load is light, the exemption is of less value than if there is considerable nonresidential property and property tax revenue is high.

It is important to recognize that in this context nonresidential property includes rental housing. Thus, a locally financed homestead exemption shifts a portion of the tax burden from homeowners to renters, who on the average have lower income.[1][2]

If a millage limit exists, an indirect effect of an exemption is to reduce local government revenue potential. If the exemption is high relative to home values and if there is little nonresidential property, this limitation can be very significant, forcing a large reduction in government spending.

On the other hand, a credit which is financed by nonproperty tax revenue does not affect the property tax rate. It does not increase taxes on nonexempt property or affect local government revenue from the property tax.

If an exemption is fully financed by the state, it is equivalent to a credit financed by the state. For example, if a state-financed exemption of $5,000 is provided, the state pays directly to the locality the taxes due on the first $5,000 of each home's value. There is no local tax shift and no effect on revenue raising potential.[13] Therefore, in the following discussion, *exemption* refers only to locally financed exemptions and *credit* includes state-financed exemptions.

As noted in chapter 3, it seems appropriate that state-mandated relief should be financed by the state. One reason is that redistribution activity should be financed at the highest feasible level of government. Another is that the cost and benefit of the relief are obvious and easily calculable rather than implicit and difficult to measure.

Credits are nearly always financed by the state government, but they need not be. A local government could finance a homestead credit with revenue from a sales or income tax, and its effects would be similar to those of a state-financed credit. New Jersey is apparently the only state with a homestead credit financed out of property tax revenue itself. All homeowners who are senior citizens may subtract $100 from their property tax payment.

Relief Formula

The credit offers more variations than the exemption. The most common system is for the credit to be equal to the tax on a specified amount of assessed valuation. However, it may also be a flat amount for all eligible households or a certain percentage of the gross property tax bill. Unless it is a flat amount, the credit provides more relief where tax rates are higher. If central cities have the highest tax rates, followed in order by suburbs and rural areas, benefits vary accordingly.

The chief formula issue in designing an exemption is whether it should apply to all taxes or to just those levied by certain types of governments. Except where exemptions are on a local-option basis, there seems to be little reason for differentiating in this manner.

Restricted Eligibility

A common method of limiting eligibility is to require that participating homes be occupied by their owners. The District of Columbia reduced the number of eligible properties by over 35 percent in 1979 by adding this restriction to its homestead exemption program. The proportion of absentee homeowners is likely to be considerably lower in most places, but this example illustrates how seemingly minor details may be very significant.

Numerous states restrict eligibility to households with relatively low incomes, home values, or net worth, which is appropriate if the aim is to reduce or eliminate the regressivity of the property tax at the low end of the income scale. However, such provisions cause undesirable "notch" effects, with sudden cutoffs of eligibility when the income limit is reached.[14]

The most common restriction is to limit eligibility to senior citizens. Income and age restrictions are interrelated. None of the twenty-two programs which do not contain an age limit place a limit on the income of participants. But nearly two-thirds of the twenty-nine programs which are limited to senior citizens also limit the income of participants, and the limits are low—none exceeding $7,500.

Other Programs

Each of the nonhomestead programs involves some distinct design issues in addition to the ones already discussed.

Some veteran's exemptions or credits apply only to disabled veterans, while others do not contain such a restriction. These programs also differ with regard to the dates of service which qualify a veteran for the benefits.[15]

A key issue in deferral programs is the interest rate charged on deferred taxes. Some state programs provide for no interest, but Massachusetts charges 8 percent interest. Massachusetts also limits the deferral to 50 percent of the claimant's equity in the property.[16]

The existing renter's credits are either a flat amount or a percentage of rent subject to a maximum, but other formulas are possible. For example, a credit proposed in Iowa related the renter's credit to the value of the homestead credit. In that way benefits depend on the local tax rate but not on how much rent is paid.

Exemptions of housing rehabilitation from reassessment confront a host of design issues. Aside from restrictions on participation, designers must decide how much value can be exempted and how long the exemption is to last.

Evaluation

Appendix 4A provides a highly simplified numerical illustration of how some aspects of the distribution of benefits differ for a homestead exemption, two kinds of homestead credits, a circuit breaker, and two other types of property tax relief. The reader may refer to the appendix for clarification of some of the major points in the following discussion.

Homestead Exemption or Credit

It has already been argued that a state-funded exemption is equivalent to a credit and that credits are superior to locally financed exemptions because their distributional effects are clearer and it is preferable to finance relief at higher levels of government. Therefore, this section concentrates on the contrast between the homestead credit and its next closest alternative, the circuit breaker.[17]

Circuit Breaker or Homestead Credit

Vertical and Horizontal Equity. Homestead credits vary greatly in terms of how their benefits are distributed. The most common type of credit, one which pays the tax on a certain amount of assessed valuation, provides an equal benefit to all homeowners within each taxing jurisdiction. However, since the benefit depends on the tax rate, homeowners in some places receive greater benefits than those in others. For example, in 1977 the California homestead credit was worth $170 in rural Imperial County (where the tax rate was low) and $223 in San Francisco.[18]

Such credits tend to reduce the regressivity of the property tax among homeowners (or to increase its progressivity) because they constitute a larger proportion of income for low- than high-income households. This is true by definition *within* each jurisdiction (where the tax rate is constant) and is also true *among* jurisdictions unless the tax rate rises more than in proportion as community income rises, which is not usually the case.[19] Although these credits reduce regressivity, they may be greater in absolute terms in high-income areas if tax rates are higher in them.

A credit which pays a certain percentage of taxes for all homeowners is much less progressive than a credit which pays the taxes on a certain amount of assessed value. Affluent households will have large benefits because their homes tend to be more valuable and therefore subject to more tax. But as a percentage of income, the benefits from such a credit will be greater for low-income households if the residential property tax is regressive.

The fairness of a property tax relief program which incorporates a homestead credit depends heavily on whether there is a companion credit for renters. If renters are not included in the program, its progressivity and horizontal equity are both undermined. Since circuit breakers usually do cover renters as well as homeowners, the following discussion assumes that a homestead credit is accompanied by a renter credit. Otherwise, the case for the circuit breaker is much stronger.

It is impossible to generalize about how much difference there is between the distribution of benefits at various income levels of "the" homestead credit and "the" circuit breaker because each has many variations. The comparison also depends on the relationships among income, home value, and tax rates, which vary from state to state. Nevertheless, homestead credits are generally not as progressive as circuit breakers of the type currently provided.

It is easier to compare the horizontal equity of the homestead credit and the circuit breaker. There is much less variation in benefits for households at each income level when a homestead credit of the usual type is provided. Holding income constant, usually circuit breaker benefits depend on both the tax rate and the value of each home, while homestead credits depend only on the tax rate.

While this generalization is valid for nearly every circuit breaker and for the great majority of homestead credits, there are exceptions. Oregon's circuit breaker refunds all property taxes up to various maximums which decrease as household income rises. The maximums are sufficiently low that most home-owners at each income level receive the same benefits. As for homestead credits, the benefits of those which pay a certain percentage of tax liability depend both on a home's value and on the tax rate. But if a fairly low maximum homestead credit is set, home value will not affect benefits for most households.

The differences between these two relief mechanisms are relatively slight compared to how much they each differ from other types of property tax relief such as aid to local governments or classification. In fact, there is no need to make an either/or decision. Many states have circuit breakers alongside their homestead programs, thus enabling them to provide some benefits to everyone while giving extra relief to certain targeted groups of taxpayers. The interaction between the exemption and circuit breaker often reduces significantly the net cost of the circuit breaker.

Other Considerations. A homestead credit has two other advantages: It is easier for the public to understand and comply with, so that low participation is not a problem; and it is administratively simpler, since income does not have to be verified. On the other hand, the circuit breaker is attractive in that it automatically cushions tax burdens when inflation forces them up faster than income. With a threshold circuit breaker, net taxes rise more slowly than gross taxes; with a homestead program, net taxes rise faster than gross taxes in percentage terms. If a homestead credit is to offset a tendency for residential property to bear a greater proportion of the tax burden,[20] it must be raised periodically by legislation.[21] A circuit breaker automatically deals with this problem.

Another advantage of circuit breakers is that they depend on tax payments rather than assessed valuations. In states where assessment standards are not uniform, homestead exemptions are undesirable because their value will be higher in places where assessments are a low proportion of market values. A $5,000 exemption covers $10,000 of a home's value if homes are assessed at half of their market value but $15,000 if the assessment ratio is one-third. This problem also plagues credits which are based on assessed valuation but not credits such as those which depend on tax payments.

The answer to the question of which relief mechanism—the circuit breaker or homestead exemption—is preferable and how it should be designed depends on priorities about who should get relief. In most cases the circuit breaker is more progressive and bestows greater benefits on those with more valuable homes at each income level. Which of these characteristics is more important and whether they count as advantages or disadvantages are matters of taste. Some persons think that those with the highest taxes should receive greater relief, while others want to target relief to those who pay the greatest proportion of their income in property tax, and yet others prefer a relatively even distribution of benefits.

Deferral and Tax Freeze

Each of these programs has appeal under certain conditions. In an ideal system of taxation and government spending, deferral may make more sense than outright forgiveness of taxes. But advocacy of deferral unaccompanied by other policies may imply acceptance of an unwarranted shift in the distribution of the tax burden away from businesses and toward homeowners. Total reliance on deferral may also mean forgoing an opportunity to make the state-local tax system somewhat less regressive. Deferral has two other strikes against it in its relative administrative complexity and the unwillingness of most senior citizens to use it when it is available. However, deferral is an attractive policy in its own right, though not necessarily as a substitute for other tax relief policies. Particularly if they are unwilling to provide adequate relief for low-income homeowners in other ways, states should consider deferral programs. They should not be restricted to senior citizens.[22]

A tax freeze is a very crude device for aiding the elderly. On one hand, it may leave many households with very high tax burdens in relation to their income. On the other hand, unless it is strictly limited to households with low incomes, it may afford relief to families or individuals who do not need it. However, a freeze has the virtue of simplicity and can be a useful supplement to other relief for the low-income elderly in states where other relief programs are meager.

Veteran's Exemption of Credit

Property tax relief is an extremely poor method of providing assistance to veterans for many reasons. Only veterans who are property owners benefit; the poorest veterans get nothing. The amount of relief received depends on how high the local tax rate is. Even veterans who had safe wartime jobs far from the areas of battle often receive aid, although veterans who had similar jobs during peacetime receive none. Finally, compensation for veterans should be taken care of by the federal government, which has responsibility for the armed forces, not by states and localities.[23]

Some of these criticisms can be vitiated to some extent if eligibility is limited to disabled veterans and if relief is conditioned on income and is equal across the state. Even with such provisions, there are much better ways of showing our appreciation for veterans than by granting them property tax exemptions or credits.

Renter's Credit

A high priority in the area of tax reform is to redress the discrimination against the renter under both income and property taxes. As long as homeowners retain their tax breaks, the renter's credit should be widely used to offset the favoritism which now exists.

The major arguments for not aiding renters are that homeownership should be encouraged because of the social benefits which it allegedly produces and that landlords do not shift property taxes to tenants. The first argument is dubious because the social benefits of homeownership are unproved and factors other than property tax relief are the key considerations in deciding whether to buy a home. The second argument is not supported even by the "new view" of property tax incidence in cases where the local tax burden is higher than the national average.[24]

Exemptions for Rehabilitation

Many of these programs are predicated on the assumption that the fear of reassessment is an important deterrent to rehabilitation of property. There is little foundation for such a belief in most places, since assessors rarely reassess property when improvements are made. Even if property is reassessed, the additional tax avoided by a temporary exemption is relatively slight at tax rates which prevail in most places. Although these exemptions are often described as "urban revitalization" measures, whether much rehabilitation activity takes place is not likely to be much affected by them. It is not surprising that the participation rate among eligible properties is less than 1 percent in most cities with these programs.[25]

Conclusions

The tax instruments discussed in this chapter have several different objectives: to fine-tune the incidence of the property tax, to reduce (or to avoid an increase in) the proportion of the property tax borne by homeowners, and to change behavior. The last objective can be dismissed—there is little evidence that these measures, in the magnitude with which they are currently used, have much effect on how people act. The other two objectives are legitimate. With regard to the first, a strong case can be made for reducing the heavy burden of the property tax on low- and moderate-income families and individuals. Finally, it is justifiable to be concerned about the proportion of the tax load borne by various classes of property. Where the existing property tax system is operating in a manner to increase the share of taxes paid by homeowners, it may be appropriate to change the way in which the system operates to offset some of or all such tax shifts.

Notes

1. A third type of credit which is occasionally provided is a uniform amount for all homeowners. Montana and Maine provided such credits in 1979 for all homeowners, and New Jersey has offered that kind of credit for veterans for many years.

2. This section relies heavily on the description of programs in Abt Associates, *Property Tax Relief Programs for the Elderly: A Compendium Report* (Washington, D.C.: Department of Housing and Urban Development, 1975), pp. 112-137, and Advisory Commission on Intergovernmental Relations, *Significant Features of Fiscal Federalism,* 1976-77 ed., vol. 2, pp. 109-116. More current data are used for the District of Columbia, Iowa, New Jersey, Utah, Oregon, Illinois, Arizona, Massachusetts, Wyoming, Indiana, Wisconsin, Maine, and Montana.

3. As of 1965, Sliger identified twelve states with general homestead programs and Chen listed six with exemptions or credits strictly for the elderly. See Bernard F. Sliger, "Exemption of Veterans' Homesteads," and Yung-Ping Chen, "Property Tax Concessions to the Aged," both in *Property Taxation— USA,* ed. Richard W. Lindholm (Madison: University of Wisconsin Press, 1969), pp. 213-223 and 225-235, respectively.

4. U.S. Census Bureau, *1977 Census of Governments,* vol. 6, no. 2: *State Aid to Local Governments,* (Washington, D.C., 1979) table 5.

5. U.S. Census Bureau, *1977 Census of Governments,* vol. 2: *Taxable Property Values and Assessment/Sales Price Ratios,* (Washington, D.C., 1978) table 19.

6. Advisory Commission on Intergovernmental Relations, *Significant Features,* 1976-77; Abt Associates, *A Compendium Report.*

7. "The Erosion of the Ad Valorem Real Estate Tax Base," *Tax Policy* 11 (1973):19-21; and Sliger, "Veterans' Homesteads."

8. Abt Associates, *A Compendium Report,* pp. 97-102; information provided by California Department of Finance. Proposition 13 obviously reduced the volume of deferrals.

9. Abt Associates, *A Compendium Report,* pp. 102-105. Telephone calls with Lance Staricha in Minnesota and Philomena Chiodo in Connecticut.

10. Abt Associates, *A Compendium Report,* pp. 107-109; Advisory Commission on Intergovernmental Relations, *Significant Features,* 1976-77, pp. 109-16; information from William Asplund in Utah and Richard Yates in Oregon. New Jersey Commission on Government Costs and Tax Policy, *Summary Recommendations and Subcommittee Reports,* December 1977, p. viii.

11. George A. Reigeluth et al., "Comparison and Summary of Property Tax Relief Programs for Housing Rehabilitation" (Urban Institute Working Paper 1130-03, September 29, 1978), pp. 1-24; and International Association of

Assessing Officers, "Urban Property Tax Incentives: State Laws" (Research and Information Series, August 1978).

12. Larry D. Schroeder and David L. Sjoquist, "Property Tax Exporting and the Differential Incidence of the Homestead Exemption," in *Metropolitan Financing and Growth Management Policies,* ed. George F. Break (Madison: University of Wisconsin Press, 1978). This paper, the most sophisticated analysis of the incidence of homestead exemptions in the literature, uses a general equilibrium theoretical framework to demonstrate that such exemptions lead to exporting of a significant amount of the property tax's burden to nonresidents.

13. Thus, it is very misleading for the Census Bureau to refer to exemptions as "removing" property from the tax base, as it does in U.S. Census Bureau, *Taxable Property Values,* 1977, p. 29. This error is frequently committed.

14. Nineteen of the thirty-eight states with programs (including the District of Columbia) impose an income ceiling on at least a portion of their homestead program. Thus, the circuit breaker is not the only device which targets relief to the needy.

15. As of 1965, in about half of the states with veterans' homestead programs eligibility was limited to veterans who were partially or totally disabled. Sliger, "Exemptions of Veterans' Homesteads," p. 214.

16. Abt Associates, *Property Tax Relief Programs for the Elderly: Final Report* (Washington, D.C., Department of Housing and Urban Development, 1976), pp. 61-65; Abt Associates, *A Compendium Report,* pp. 97-102.

17. Many of the statements about credits also apply to exemptions, though sometimes to a different degree. For example, both a credit and an exemption for $X of assessed valuation are progressive among homeowners, but the exemption produces smaller tax savings because it is usually accompanied by an increase in the tax rate. Likewise, if a homestead exemption or credit is not accompanied by a renter credit, there is a serious horizontal inequity.

18. Dean Tipps, "The Circuit Breaker: A California Tax Research Project Analysis" (Sacramento: California Tax Reform Association, 1978).

19. For evidence on this point, see appendix 1A.

20. The conditions under which the tax burden shifts to residential property are discussed in the analysis of taxflation in chapter 1.

21. Kentucky's homestead exemption is indexed to the consumer price index, which partly overcomes the problem discussed. Between 1974 and 1979, it rose from $6,500 to $10,200. Kentucky Department of Revenue, *Annual Report: 1976-1977.*

22. A strong advocate of deferral is Henry J. Aaron, *Who Pays the Property Tax?* (Washington, D.C.: The Brookings Institution, 1975), p. 77. More critical views are expressed in Advisory Commission on Intergovernmental Relations, *Property Tax Circuitbreakers* (Washington, D.C.: 1975), p. 17. See also Abt Associates, *A Compendium Report*, pp. 97-102.

23. Sliger, "Exemptions of Veterans' Homesteads," and James R. Prescott and Gene Gruver, "Veteran's Property Tax Exemption: Incidence and Policy Alternatives," *Land Economics* 47 (November 1971):410-413.

24. See appendix 1A.

25. Reigeluth et al., "Comparison and Summary.[11]

Appendix 4A:
Simplified Illustration
of Differences among
Certain Programs

Many statements about the differing effects of various types of relief mechanisms can be illustrated by numerical examples. Although they are highly simplified, such examples can be useful to enhance understanding.

Suppose that the town of Alpha consists of only four homes, whose property taxes provide all government revenue. The residents are U.R. Rich, whose income is $60,000 and whose home is worth $80,000; M.C. Bighouse, whose income is $20,000 and whose home is valued at $48,000; M.C. Smallhouse, whose income is also $20,000 but whose home is worth only $42,000; and I.M. Poor, with an income of $10,000 and a home valued at $30,000.

The town of Beta consists of four residents with exactly the same incomes, home values, and names as Alpha. The only difference between the towns is that the property tax rate in Alpha is 1 percent, while in Beta it is 1½ percent. Thus, property taxes are as follows: Alpha's U.R. Rich, $800; Beta's U.R. Rich, $1,200; Alpha's M.C. Bighouse, $480; Beta's M.C. Bighouse, $720; Alpha's M.C. Smallhouse, $420; Beta's M.C. Smallhouse, $630; Alpha's I.M. Poor, $300; and Beta's I.M. Poor, $450. The property tax is regressive because it is a higher proportion of income for the rich than for the poor.

The state has $1,000 which it wants to use for property tax relief. It has three prime options: (1) a homestead credit which covers $10,000 of assessed valuation on each home; (2) a homestead credit which pays 20 percent of everyone's tax bill; and (3) a circuit breaker which pays all property taxes which exceed 2 percent of income. There is also a possibility that the state might simply (4) mandate that all homes should receive a $10,000 homestead exemption with no state financing.

For comparative purposes, the effects of (5) increasing state aid to local governments and (6) limiting local property tax rates can also be considered.

Homestead Credit for $10,000
Assessed Valuation

Benefits would be $100 for each resident of Alpha and $150 for each resident of Beta. This benefit is calculated simply by multiplying the tax rate by the value of the exemption. Since the Alpha tax rate is lower, benefits there are lower, but all homeowners in each town benefit equally with their fellow citizens.

Homestead Credit for 20 Percent of Tax Bill

Benefits would be as follows:

	Alpha	Beta
U.R. Rich	$160	$240
M.C. Bighouse	96	144
M.C. Smallhouse	84	126
I.M. Poor	60	90

Notice that within each jurisdiction the benefits now increase directly as home value and income rise. This alternative is much less progressive than the first one. However, because the property tax is regressive, the benefits are a higher proportion of income for lower-income households. As in the first case, benefits are 50 percent greater in Beta than in Alpha because the property tax rate is 50 percent higher.

**Circuit Breaker which Pays Taxes in Excess
of 2 Percent of Income**

In this case, benefits would be as follows:

	Alpha	Beta
U.R. Rich	$ 0	$ 0
M.C. Bighouse	80	320
M.C. Smallhouse	20	230
I.M. Poor	100	250

In absolute terms, benefits vary inconsistently across income levels. No particular importance should be attached to the fact that in Alpha average benefits fall as income rises, while in Beta they rise in going from $10,000 income to $20,000 income and then fall in going to higher incomes. If U.R. Rich had an income of $40,000 rather than $60,000, his benefit in Beta would be higher than for anyone in either town. In absolute terms, the pattern of benefits across income levels is also sensitive to how the circuit breaker is designed. However, as a percentage of income, circuit breaker benefits will normally be higher for low-income households than for others. (See the discussion of this point in chapter 3.)

If benefits are compared at each income level rather than for different income levels, one sees that the circuit breaker results in greater benefit inequalities than the homestead credit, both within and across jurisdictions. The circuit breaker is particularly generous to households with high property taxes as opposed to low property taxes.

Homestead Exemption for $10,000
of Assessed Valuation

To some extent, the effects of an exemption depend on how much non-residential property is located in the jurisdiction. Suppose, to take the most extreme case, that there is none. Now each town will lose one-fifth of its tax base. To maintain its revenue, Alpha must raise its tax rate to 1 1/4 percent, while Beta's tax rate must rise to 1 7/8 percent. Only the effects in Alpha will be shown; the results in Beta are similar.

Now, U.R. Rich's $80,000 home is taxed on only $70,000 of value, but because of the higher tax rate his taxes are now $875, which is $75 higher than they were initially. His three fellow citizens fare better, realizing gains of $5, $20, and $50, respectively. Thus, all that the exemption did was to redistribute the local tax burden, making it more progressive. However, no one got nearly as much benefit as from a $10,000 homestead credit.

Now suppose that half of the property tax base is nonresidential property. In this case, the tax rate will have to be raised only to 1 1/8 percent in order to avoid a decline in revenue. Because business property taxes rise, the benefits to the homeowners in Alpha are, respectively, $23, $56, $64, and $78. Once again, benefits are greatest on the property with the lowest value, but they are still much lower than for a credit.

This example is simplified by assuming that assessed valuation does not affect state aid to school districts and that there is no state-imposed limitation on tax rates.

Increased State Aid to Governments

The effect of state aid is to lower the local property tax rate. Assuming that Alpha and Beta receive equal amounts of aid, that each town's tax base is divided evenly between residential and nonresidential property, and that all the aid is used for tax relief, tax rates can be lowered 1/8 percent in Alpha and 1/12 percent in Beta. In each town U.R. Rich will receive $100 of tax savings, M.C. Bighouse will save $60, M.C. Smallhouse will save $52.50, and I.M. Poor will save $37.50. The total savings to homeowners is only $500, with an equal amount of relief going to nonresidential property. If some of the aid is used to increase local government expenditures, tax relief will be even less.

Within each town the distribution of benefits is proportional to the amount of property tax paid, just as in the case of the homestead credit which paid 20 percent of each household's property tax. However, Alpha fares relatively better in this case than Beta. Now each town benefits equally, whereas with the homestead credits and circuit breaker the town with the higher tax rate received greater benefits.

Tax Rate Limit

This is another form of relief which does not necessarily place a burden on the state budget. If the state limited tax rates to 1 percent, this would have no effect in Alpha but would sharply reduce Beta's taxes. Benefits would be in proportion to taxes paid, with U.R. Rich saving $400 and the others saving smaller amounts. With such a sharp decline in Beta's revenue, the state would probably replace some of the lost funds with its own money. Thus, there would be a substitution of state for local revenue. This is similar to what occurred in California when Proposition 13 passed.

5 Property Tax Relief for Agriculture

Many people are concerned that urban expansion is causing a large amount of farmland to be converted to other uses. Property taxes represent a high proportion of income for many farmers. For these and other reasons nearly all states give some sort of tax break to agricultural property, usually by prescribing that its assessment should be based on use value rather than market value. These laws have proliferated rapidly since the first one was passed by Maryland in 1956. Although research on the effects of differential assessment is hampered by the inadequate recordkeeping in most states, numerous studies have cast doubt on its efficacy as a device for preserving farmland. The laws are considered more effective in achieving their other purpose—to increase the income of owners of farmland.

Many states aid not only land used for farming but also forests and other types of open-space land such as marshes and recreational land. While the issues raised by these programs in many respects are similar to those for farms, they are not discussed here.[1]

A few states use mechanisms other than differential assessment to aid farmland, and those alternatives are described and analyzed in this chapter.

Description

Differential assessment laws are usually divided into three types: A *pure preferential assessment law* provides simply that land is valued according to its current use. No penalty is exacted if it is later converted to another use. A *deferred tax law* differs from pure preferential assessment in that when land use changes, a penalty tax is levied against the land or its owner. This penalty is sometimes referred to as a rollback tax or a recapture provision. In a *restrictive agreement*, the landowner and the local government agree to restrict use of the land in return for a low assessment.

Table 5-1 illustrates the mathematics of pure preferential assessment and deferred tax laws. It is assumed that in 1970 a farm was worth $1 million, that it increased in value 10 percent per year, that it was subject to a 1 percent nominal tax rate, and that it was converted to a nonagricultural use in 1979. Its assessed value was set at $500,000 in 1970 on the basis of its estimated use value at that time. It was reassessed annually thereafter, and each time its assessment was raised 5 percent because use value had risen that amount.

Table 5-1

Example of How a Differential Assessment Program May Affect Taxes on a Farm

Year	Market Value	Assessed Value	Tax Savings
1970	$1,000,000	$500,000	$ 5,000
1971	1,100,000	525,000	5,750
1972	1,210,000	551,000	6,590
1973	1,331,000	579,000	7,520
1974	1,464,000	608,000	8,560
1975	1,611,000	638,000	9,730
1976	1,772,000	670,000	11,020
1977	1,949,000	704,000	12,450
1978	2,144,000	739,000	14,050
1979	2,358,000	776,000	15,820
Total			$96,490

Note: *Assumptions*

Market value grows 10 percent per year.

Assessed value grows 5 percent per year.

Nominal tax rate is 1 percent.

Tax savings are the difference between tax at 1 percent rate on market value and assessed value.

Columns 1 and 2 of the table show the assessed value and market value of the land each year. Column 3 shows the annual tax savings, which is the difference between a tax of 1 percent on the market value and a similar tax on assessed value. This estimate is based on the assumption that in the absence of differential assessment the assessed value would equal the market value.

Over the ten-year period, the market value of the farm rises from $1,000,000 to $2,358,000 and the assessed value increases from $500,000 to $776,000. The total tax paid is $62,900. However, this tax is $96,490 less than that which would have been paid if there had been no preferential assessment. Using a 10 percent discount rate, the present value of the tax saving is $59,084, which may be compared to the present value of the tax actually paid, $40,924.

If the differential assessment program provides for the payment of deferred taxes when the use of the property changes, the subsidy for 1979 and a number of previous years must be repaid. For example, if the recapture provision covers three previous years, $53,340 would have to be repaid. If interest is charged on past subsidies at a 5 percent rate, the total penalty would rise to $57,056. Thus, even with the recapture provision in effect, the landowner has benefited from the differential assessment program, because the recapture applies only to a limited number of years and the interest rate charged is below the market rate.[2]

Another method of aiding owners of farmland is by means of a tax credit. Since credits are usually state-financed, in effect the state government is paying a portion of the property tax for the owners of farmland. In some cases credits vary according to the owner's income, so that they are a form of circuit breaker.

As explained in chapter 7, some states classify real property so that certain classes are taxed at lower rates than others. All these states include farmland in one of the most favored categories, thus providing relief for farms along with other types of property such as homes. However, classification differs fundamentally from differential assessment in that assessments of classified property should rise in proportion to market value, whereas assessments based on use value may rise faster or slower than market value.[3]

Finally, relief may be given to owners of farms by exempting personal property from taxation.

History, Current Extent of Use, and Costs

History

The oldest aid to farmland other than classification is Iowa's agricultural land tax credit. It was started in the 1940s when many school districts were consolidating. When farm areas merged with towns, the result usually was higher farm property taxes because agricultural areas, having greater property valuation per pupil, originally had lower tax rates. The credit was designed to partially offset these higher farm taxes.

The first state to adopt use-value legislation was Maryland in 1956, followed by Florida in 1959; Connecticut, Hawaii, and Indiana in 1963; and New Jersey in 1965. The number of states with such laws swelled from six in 1965 to twenty-four in 1970, thirty eight in 1975, and forty-four in 1978.[4] The only six states without differential assessment laws are Michigan, Georgia, Alabama, Wisconsin, Mississippi, and West Virginia. Michigan and Wisconsin have circuit breaker programs specifically for farmland, and the four Southern states all have extremely low tax rates on farms even without any preferential law. See table 5-2.

The increase in tax relief programs for agricultural property can be attributed to four factors. First, many persons are concerned about the loss of farmland due to urban expansion and other factors. Second, for a long period farm property taxes took an ever-increasing share of farm income, which was considered unfair in many quarters. Third, farm property values shot up extremely fast in the 1970s. Finally, the widespread de facto policy of assessing farms far below their market value was challenged by the movement toward reform of assessment practices which brought assessments into closer conformity with the law; in this context, differential assessment laws were needed just to maintain the status quo.

Evidence that use-value laws initially changed assessments relatively little can be obtained by comparing states which had such laws in 1971 with those

Table 5-2
Provisions for Assessment of Property for Agricultural, Open-Space, and Associated Explicit Uses, by State: 1976 and Subsequent Periods

State	Provisions Affecting Assessed Value Applicable to Explicitly Specified Uses	State	Provisions Affecting Assessed Value Applicable to Explicitly Specified Uses
Alaska	Deferred taxation	Montana	Deferred taxation
Arkansas	Use-value assessment only	Nebraska	Deferred taxation
California	Use-value assessment only	Nevada	Deferred taxation
	Contracts and agreements	New Hampshire	Deferred taxation
Colorado	Use-value assessment only		Contracts and agreements
Connecticut	Use-value assessment only (sometime classified as deferred taxation, because of conveyance tax)	New Jersey	Deferred taxation
		New Mexico	Use-value assessment only
		New York	Deferred taxation
Delaware	Use-value assessment only		Contracts and agreements
Florida	Use-value assessment only	North Carolina	Deferred taxation
	Contracts and agreements	North Dakota	Use-value assessment only
Hawaii	Deferred taxation	Ohio	Deferred taxation
	Contracts and agreements	Oklahoma	Use-value assessment only
Illinois	Deferred taxation	Oregon	Use-value assessment only
Indiana	Use-value assessment only		Deferred taxation
Iowa	Deferred taxation	Pennsylvania	Contracts and agreements
Kansas	Deferred taxation	Rhode Island	Deferred taxation
Kentucky	Deferred taxation	South Carolina	Deferred taxation
Louisiana	Use-value assessment only	South Dakota	Use-value assessment only
	Contracts and agreements	Tennessee	Deferred taxation
Maine	Deferred taxation	Texas	Deferred taxation
Maryland	Deferred taxation	Utah	Deferred taxation
	Contracts and agreements	Vermont	Deferred taxation

Massachusetts	Deferred taxation
Minnesota	Deferred taxation
Missouri	Use-value assessment only
Virginia	Contracts and agreements
Washington	Deferred taxation
	Deferred taxation
	Contracts and agreements
Wyoming	Use-value assessment only

Source: U.S. Census Bureau, *1977 Census of Governments*, vol. 2: *Taxable Property Values and Assessment/Sales Price Ratios* (Washington, D.C., 1978), pp. 286-287.

Terms (based on review of applicable legal provisions):

Deferred taxation—Change from benefited (explicitly specified) use activates tax on value differences, for specified periods, plus any interest specified.

Contracts and agreements—Agreements providing for limitations on use over specified periods, as part of explicitly specified use-value assessment determination.

which did not. Farm real estate in the twenty-six states which did not have such laws at that time was generally underassessed more in relation to other real estate than in the twenty-four states with use-value legislation. While the assessment ratio for farm property averaged 70 percent of the assessment ratio for all property in non-use-value states, it averaged 76 percent in states with use-value legislation.[5] In addition, the assessment ratio of farmland increased proportionately more in states with use-value legislation during the 1961-1971 period than it did in states without such legislation.[6]

Current Extent of Use

It is difficult to count the programs of each type because some states offer alternative programs, and penalty provisions apply in some situations but not in others. Pure preferential assessment is in effect by itself in twelve states, and deferred taxation is in effect by itself in twenty-one states. One state has a contractual program which stands alone. Three states combine use-value assessments with contracts, while six states combine deferral with contracts, and one has both a pure preferential assessment program and a deferral program. Table 5-2 shows how the Census Bureau describes the programs; its classification has been followed here with a few exceptions.[7]

Altogether, thirty-one states provide that a landowner who received use-value assessments and changes the use of his land is liable for tax penalties.[8]

Four states use credits to provide farm tax relief. Michigan's farm circuit breaker (begun in 1974) rebates property tax in excess of 7 percent of household income, but it is open only to persons who enter into a ten-year contract to maintain the land for farm purposes. Benefits from Wisconsin's farm circuit breaker (begun in 1978) depend on whether a county has zoning and land-use plans. Participating farmers must sign a contract, and there is a provision for collection of deferred taxes if land use changes.[9] Finally, Iowa and Minnesota provide a credit for all owners of farmland regardless of income.

In addition to the twelve states which classify property overall, some states have special provisions for some farmland which are so minor that they usually are not characterized as classification. For example, Iowa law specifies that farmland located within cities is subject to a low maximum tax rate.

Costs

Differential assessment laws involve several different kinds of costs. In most cases there is no explicit cost to state government associated with the program, but that is misleading in several respects.

One cost of differential assessment arises from redistribution of local property burdens away from agriculture and to other classes of property. This local tax shift occurs in the sense that taxation is a "zero-sum game": If one group pays lower taxes because its assessed valuation is reduced, another group must pay higher taxes because its share of total assessed valuation is increased. Primarily the owners of property in the towns near farm areas bear this cost.

Ironically, this local tax shift cannot occur if an area is completely agricultural; in that case, the only results of differential assessment of farmland are (1) to shift the tax burden to owners whose investment is heavily in farm buildings and taxable personal property and away from farmers whose investment is land-intensive, and (2) to shift the tax burden away from owners of land whose value is most inflated by nonagricultural influences and to persons whose land's market value is close to its use value.[10] In other words, lower assessed values lead to higher nominal tax rates, and taxes are unchanged.

Whether the local tax shift is considered to be large also depends on the perspective taken. For example, if there is only a small amount of farm property in a jurisdiction, it may experience a large reduction in taxes while other property has only a relatively small increase, since the savings for owners of farmland are spread over a large amount of nonfarm property.[11]

Case studies which have measured increases in tax rates and local tax shifts resulting from differential assessment indicate that their magnitude varies considerably within a state. One study in Florida estimated that in thirteen counties the increase in the tax rate was less than 2 percent, in seventeen counties it was between 2 and 6 percent, in six counties it varied from 6 to 10 percent, and in only three counties was it higher (exceeding 25 percent in only one county). Research in 151 New Jersey municipalities showed that tax rates increased much more there. In about one-third of the cities, the tax rate increased less than 10 percent, in 43 percent of the cities it rose 10 to 30 percent, and in one-fourth of the cities it increased more than 30 percent.[12]

In general, the size of the tax shift depends on the proportion of the tax base which is nonfarm property and on the magnitude of the gap between assessed value with and without the differential assessment program.

A second cost of differential assessment occurs if the state reimburses localities for revenue lost because of lower agricultural valuations. California, New York, and Alaska provide for such payments, although appropriations often fall short of payments implied by enabling legislation. In New York no payments have been made, and in California they have replaced considerably less than the 50 percent of lost revenue which was originally envisioned.

Third, by reducing assessed valuations below what they would be if property were valued according to its market value, usually the cost of state aid to school districts is increased. As explained in chapter 1, state school aid generally varies inversely with per pupil property valuation.[13] While the magnitude of this cost will vary from state to state depending on both the difference between market value and use value and the structure of the school aid program, it is quite substantial in many states.[14] While this cost is directly attributable to differential assessment of farmland, the benefit of the higher school aid goes to all property owners in school districts which contain farm property, since the aid permits a lowering of the overall tax rate.

A fourth type of cost may result from changes in land-use patterns. To the extent that land near urban areas remains in farm use because of these laws when its highest and best use is to be developed, differential assessment interferes with the pattern of urban development. For example, housing developments might be forced to "leapfrog" around farmland, resulting in a checkboard pattern of development. As explained later in this chapter, in practice this cost is relatively unimportant because differential assessment laws apparently do not have a great impact on land use.

All these types of costs depend on how much farmland participates in the program. In ten states virtually all farmland is automatically assessed at use value (Arizona, Colorado, Idaho, Indiana, Iowa, Maryland, North Dakota, Oklahoma, South Dakota, and Wyoming),[15] but in others applications must be submitted, so that not all land participates. Owners may not sign up their land for the program for one of three reasons: They cannot meet the program's requirements, they choose not to commit themselves to the conditions attached to the program, or the program offers little or no benefit to them.

In many states, participation is far from complete. However, reports from states such as California and Michigan indicate that after a slow start participation tends to increase significantly as familiarity with the program increases. In New York and North Carolina, participation increased sharply to counties where property was revalued, but statewide not much land has participated because ordinary farm assessments are so low.[16]

Two important qualifications should be stated about estimates of how much differential assessment costs. First, it is often not clear what the assessment on farm property would have been in the absence of use-value legislation. As noted, farms have generally been granted an extralegal form of differential assessment, with assessed value considerably below market value. In many cases use-value legislation has simply tidied up the tax system by legalizing the de facto situation. Second, the cost of differential assessment is not constant but will tend to grow over time as long as the difference between market value and use value expands. Of course, the costs of relief must be weighed against its benefits, which are discussed in a later section.

Personal Property Taxation

Another source of tax relief has been a trend toward exempting much of farm personal property. As of 1978, all but eighteen states either had already exempted or were in the process of exempting livestock; only twenty-two states fully taxed farm implements; and nineteen fully taxed inventories of seed, feed, and fertilizer. Many of these exemptions had been granted in the preceding decade. Between 1968 and 1978, sixteen states exempted livestock, eleven exempted equipment, and ten exempted seed, feed, and fertilizer.

Farm personal property taxes have been declining as a proportion of total farm property taxes since 1952, when they were 22 percent of the total. By 1975 personal property taxes had declined to 14.4 percent of farm property taxes.[17]

The Role of Farm Taxes in the Total Property Tax Picture

Farm taxes play a small role in the property tax systems of most states. In 1977 farm real estate taxes accounted for less than 5 percent of property tax collections in twenty-four states and for 5 to 10 percent in fifteen states. Farm real estate paid 10 to 20 percent of property taxes in seven states, and more than 20 percent in only four states (Iowa, North Dakota, South Dakota, and Nebraska).[18] Their significance is much greater within local areas than state-wide.

Design Issues

Who, and What Is Eligible?

Gloudemans has summarized the definition of farmland as follows:

Permitted farm uses typically include the growing of crops, vegetables, fruit trees, flowers, and ornamentals; the raising of livestock, poultry, fur-bearing animals; the production of forage, grain, and apiary products; and the keeping of bees. Contiguous woodlands and wastelands which contribute to the viability of the total commercial unit are also included.[19]

Most states limit eligibility in one way or another. Requirements usually take one of five forms: previous agricultural use, minimum number of acres, minimum gross income, minimum net income as a percentage of total income, and zones and preserves. The objective of these provisions is to target aid to genuine farmers or to places which merit special assistance. Here is a quick rundown of these provisions, as described by Gloudemans.[20]

Previous Agricultural Use. Approximately half of the states with use-value assessment programs require that to be eligible, land previously must have been used for agriculture. Requirements vary from two to eight years.

Minimum Number of Acres. Seventeen states set a minimum number of acres for inclusion in the program, with the figure varying from 5 to 25 acres.

Minimum gross income. At least seventeen states require eligible land to produce a minimum gross income. Although the highest requirement is $10,000, the usual minimum ranges from $1,000 to $2,500. This minimum is easier to achieve for large holdings than small parcels, so some states make the income requirement vary according to the number of acres in the farm. It is seldom difficult for any landowner to satisfy these provisions, whether he is a bonafide farmer or a land speculator.

Minimum Proportion of Income from Farming. One approach to limiting participation to bonafide farmers is to require that some proportion of the landowner's income be derived from farming. Texas has had the most stringent requirement, 50 percent, but that provision is expected to be liberalized or dropped completely following the passage of a constitutional amendment in 1978. Alaska retains a limit of 10 percent of income, which is a reduction from the original level of 25 percent. Several other states consider this factor under certain circumstances in conjunction with other restrictions. The main problem with these limits is that so many farmers derive substantial income from nonfarm sources that a fairly low percentage must be set if many bonafide farmers are not to be excluded. In fact, farm operators derive more income from nonfarm sources than from farming itself. This provision is one reason why participation in Texas's program was very low before its recent revision. (Another reason may be that land was already assessed preferentially so that there was little advantage in entering the program.)[21]

Zones and Preserves. A number of states require that eligible land be located within specific zones or preserves. These districts are usually defined on the basis of their value as agriculture, not because of any threat to them by expanding urban areas. In California and New York these areas are designated by local officials. In Hawaii and Oregon land must be zoned for farm purposes. Wisconsin's circuit breaker provides more liberal benefits if the county of the participating farmer has adopted a land-use plan and zoning. Several states deny use-value assessment to lands which have been subdivided or zoned for nonagricultural purposes or for which applications to carry out such changes are pending.

Minnesota is exceptional in the stringency of its eligibility criteria. Its preferential assessment program generally requires that a minimum percentage of income be derived from farming, although exceptions are made for "family farm corporations" and for close relatives and persons who recently retired from farming. Its farm tax credit limits eligibility to 320 acres and provides considerably larger benefits to owner occupiers than to absentee landlords.

In general, it can be stated that in a substantial majority of states eligibility standards are not very stringent. The exceptions are states like California and New York, with districting, and Texas and Alaska, with their percentage of income limits.

Credits versus Differential Assessment

Although credits are outnumbered by differential assessment programs by a ratio of more than 10 to 1, they have a number of advantages. First, a distinction must be made between the circuit breaker and other credits. According to its advocates, the advantage of a circuit breaker is that it targets relief to low-income farmers who are most burdened by the regressive property tax.[22] However, the argument for circuit breaker relief of farmers is considerably weaker than for homeowners and renters. The main reason is that farmers can manipulate how much income is reported from year to year because they may use cash accounting. (Farmers also share with other self-employed persons the opportunity to obtain income tax advantages by mingling their personal and business expenses and by underreporting income.) By timing their sales of output and purchase of inputs, farmers can bunch their income in a particular year in order to qualify for circuit breaker benefits. Even without such techniques, farm income fluctuates considerably from year to year, and thus any particular year's income is less reliable as an indicator of a taxpayer's economic well-being than it is for nonfarmers. These fluctuations also make the cost of a farm circuit breaker particularly unstable from year to year.[23]

Iowa and Minnesota are the only states which provide a non-circuit-breaker tax credit for owners of farmland. Such a credit provides the advantages of credits discussed below without the shortcomings of a circuit breaker. A credit can easily be designed to target relief, for example by making it higher in places with relatively high tax rates or by setting a ceiling on the maximum relief which a single person may receive.[24]

An important advantage of a credit as opposed to differential assessment is that its cost is explicit and easy to calculate, in contrast to the difficult-to-measure, indirect subsidy provided by differential assessment. Tax credits appear annually in the state budget, whereas the implicit cost of differential assessment is hidden. It is best to have tax expenditures out in the open.[25]

Credits are usually state-financed, whereas differential assessment is almost always financed locally. This is an advantage because relief which is state-mandated should normally be state-financed as well.

Credits are administratively much less cumbersome than use-value assessment, since they do not require estimates of a hypothetical value, what land is worth solely for its agricultural value.[25] They also facilitate the recapture of benefits if land use changes.

The credit approach also makes it administratively easier to place a limit on the value of the farm tax break if that is desired. For example, credits can easily be limited to a certain number of acres or to a certain dollar value, thus avoiding open-ended benefits to wealthy landowners.

Thus credits have numerous advantages over differential assessment. Credits which are not in the form of circuit breakers are preferable to farm circuit breakers. The main virtue of differential assessment is the intellectual aura which surrounds it: it seems more justiable to provide an assessment which eliminates nonfarm influences than to provide an ad hoc credit. But when the results of the alternative policy tools are contrasted, it seems that the credit can accomplish the same things as differential assessment and do it better.

How Use Value Is Measured

Conceptually there are two approaches to determining farm use value. One which is seldom used bases the assessment on sales of comparable property where nonfarm influences are absent. One problem with this approach is that there may not be many such sales. In addition, according to some authors, there are many motives for buying farmland other than the desire to derive current income from it (for example, it serves as a hedge against inflation and as an income tax shelter), and it is impossible for an assessor to determine the true reason for which it is bought.[27] A third reason why this method is unpopular is that it might not produce an assessed value which is below market value, which would defeat the purpose of use-value legislation according to some of its proponents.

Therefore, the method usually used to determine use value is to capitalize the net income derived from the land, according to this formula:

$$V = \frac{I}{r}$$

where V is the use value of property, I is average income derived from the land, and r is a capitalization rate.

Income should be averaged over a period of years because of its volatility from one year to the next. Income can be based on the cash rent or share rent for land or owner operator's net income. Most states direct assessors to use soil productivity ratings in determining use value. Whatever approach is taken, the calculation of income confronts many knotty problems and complicates the assessment process considerably. Arbitrary decisions are inevitable, as in Maryland where the assessment depends on the soil's productivity for growing corn, even though that crop is not typically raised in certain regions of the state.[28]

The capitalization rate used has a great impact on the amount of subsidy which is provided by use-value assessment. Although no survey is available summarizing state practice, capitalization rates vary at least from 5 percent in one state to 11 1/2 percent in another.[29]

A recent theoretical analysis of the capitalization rate issue by Kent concluded that the most appropriate approach is the "band of investment" method. This method takes a weighted average of the prevailing interest rates on farm mortgages and the return which could be obtained on a nonfarm investment, with the weights reflecting the respective proportion of total farm value covered by borrowed money and the farmer's own equity investment. The effective property tax rate must be added to this average to obtain the capitalization rate.[30]

Kent rejects the most widely used approach to determining the capitalization rate, the "built-up rate" method, which consists of adding several different rates reflecting the return on a safe investment, a risk premium, and so forth. He agrees with several other authorities that components such as the risk premium are too speculative to use.[31]

However, Kent's analysis as well as typical state practice is undermined because of his reason for rejecting the third approach to setting the capitalization rate, which is to base it on the market. Since the rate of return on farm investments for farm use is considerably lower than the rate on other investments in the economy, basing the capitalization rate on it would give relatively little subsidy compared to the higher rates obtained by using other approaches. Kent quotes approvingly an Oregon report which states that ". . . utilizing the average rate of return for comparable properties. . .would leave the farmer right where he started."[32] This statement is an exaggeration: it is not true where urban influences have driven up the price of farmland, and it may not even be true where speculation has raised farm values; in those cases the value for farm use will be lower than the market value. But the statement is correct that relying on the actual rate of return in agriculture produces a relatively high use-value figure because the capitalization rate is so low. Kent and most states regard it as self evident that this fact disqualifies this approach, but that is true only if one has a preconceived notion that use value must be considerably less than market value.

Penalties

There are two reasons for applying penalties when land use changes: to provide an extra incentive not to make such conversions and to make the program fairer to nonparticipants.

Thirty-one of the forty-four use-value states provide for penalties if a landowner who has received use-value assessment changes the use of his land, as do the two circuit breaker states. In twenty-eight states the penalty takes the form of a repayment of tax savings during a number of preceding years.[33] No state assesses a penalty when property ownership changes without a change of use.

At the beginning of this chapter an example was presented showing how a typical deferral penalty operates. In that example, the penalty recaptured considerably less than the total benefit which had been granted by the differential assessment program for two reasons: the deferral covered only a limited number of years, and the interest rate charged was below the market rate. Both conditions are characteristic of actual deferral programs.

All states with rollback taxes require that benefits be repaid for the current year and a certain number of previous years. The rollback penalties are as follows:

Required in

Two years	four states
Three years	six states
Four years	four states
Five years	six states
Seven years	four states
Ten years	two states

In addition to being one of the two states with the ten-year rollback (Maine is the other), Hawaii also provides for a twenty-year rollback in certain cases.[34]

Four states penalize changes in land use in other ways than by a rollback tax, and three states with rollback provisions provide other penalties in certain cases. For example, if a landowner in California cancels an agreement to preserve land free from development before his ten-year contract expires, he must pay a penalty of 12 1/2 percent of current market value. Gloudemans argues convincingly that it is preferable for penalties to take this form rather than repayment of back taxes, because with this approach it suffices to determine market value in only one year instead of for a period of years.[35] He suggests that even if a rollback penalty is used, assessors should not be required to make annual estimates of market value for all participating property because "the added time and effort is not justified." Penalties for previous years could be calculated when property changes use on the basis of sales of comparable nearby property.[36]

Eleven of the rollback states impose interest penalties, varying from 5 percent in Alaska to 10 percent in Hawaii and Washington.

There is widespread agreement that rollback tax penalties do not provide a significant deterrent in most cases to changing land use. "Since the size of the penalty depends on the divergence of market value from use value, the larger the potential rollback tax penalty, the larger the potential capital gain association with a change in land use."[37] This is particularly true because most rollback penalties are rather small in comparison to the benefits of use-value assessment.

Nevertheless, rollback taxes are appropriate. As a report prepared for the Council on Environmental Quality concluded,

> Without a rollback provision preferential assessment laws provide a free ride for the speculator, at the cost of others whose taxes are increased to make up for the loss in revenue. It is only fair that this lost revenue be made up to the public when conversion occurs. In the interest of fairness, interest should be charged and at a rate equal to the rate which other taxpayers would have had to pay in order to provide the lost revenues. . . . The rollback period should be at least 10 years, and, preferably, the entire period during which tax savings were enjoyed.[38]

Although this report did not say so, its logic implies that penalties should be applied when property changes owners as well as when it changes use. When property is sold, an owner of farmland realizes a capital gain on his investment, and he should be treated like any other investor, regardless of how his land is to be used subsequently. Therefore, it seems reasonable that he should have to pay back past subsidies which he has enjoyed. However, no states do apply rollback penalties when land changes ownership without changing use.[39]

Contracts or Restrictive Agreements

If the purpose of the differential assessment program is to preserve land in agricultural use, a restrictive agreement is a useful feature because it commits land to farm use for a period in the future. California and Hawaii have the strongest contract provisions among the differential assessment states, and Michigan has a similar requirement for participation in its circuit breaker. All three require a commitment of at least ten years. In California and Hawaii approval of a local government is needed to enter the program or to leave it (except with a ten-year wait), and land may participate only if it is in designated districts. Hawaii has a program for which urban land is eligible that requires a twenty-year commitment and makes the assessment one-half of use value. In Michigan, approval of state and local governments is needed.[40]

Besides the states mentioned thus far, nine others provide for contracts.[41] In those states landowners are legally entitled to use-value assessment as long as they meet the applicable requirements.

Evaluation

The two major motives for giving property tax relief to owners of farmland are to preserve farmland and to enhance the income of farmers. However, most of these programs do little to accomplish the first and are clumsy methods of achieving the second.

Preserving Farmland

There is no doubt that a considerable amount of farmland is annually converted to other uses. The Department of Agriculture estimates that 2.5 million acres of cropland is converted each year to nonfarm uses. However, this loss is partially offset by the conversion to farm use of about 1.5 million acres per year of formerly nonproductive farmland.[42]

The problem is worst in the Northeast and Southeast. From 1950 to 1972, nine states (Maine, New Hampshire, Massachusetts, Rhode Island, Connecticut, New Jersey, West Virginia, South Carolina, Georgia) had a net decrease of more than 30 percent of their acreage of taxable farmland, nine states (Vermont, New York, Pennsylvania, Maryland, Virginia, North Carolina, Tennessee, Alabama, Michigan) lost 20 to 29 percent, six (Wisconsin, Ohio, Kentucky, Delaware, Mississippi, Arkansas) lost 10 to 19 percent, and six other states (Florida, Louisiana, Indiana, Illinois, Minnesota, and Missouri) lost more than 1 percent.[43]

Nationally, the net decrease in taxable acreage was 8 percent. The loss would have been much greater were it not for the substantial amount of land which was converted to productive farm use. Peterson and Yampolsky point out that the new farmland which has been created in the past thirty years has come at the cost of substantial public investment in irrigation and reclamation projects. It is not known how those costs compare to the cost of preserving farmland at the urban fringe.[44]

Given the increases in farm productivity which have occurred and which may be expected to continue, the conversion of farmland nationally is no threat to the national food supply in the foreseeable future.[45] So why is there a need for a policy of farmland preservation? The most common answer has to do with the loss of farmland at the urban fringe. But this raises other questions, as Thomas Hady has pointed out:

> If the purpose is to preserve farmland, what kinds of farmland and in what locations? For example, are we principally worried about land for growing certain specialty crops? Or is all land adaptable to agriculture—even if it takes 640 acres to support one cow—to be included? Do we include all farmland of a given type, including that which may be, for example, immediately adjacent to the freeway and 5 miles from downtown Washington? In preserving open space, what is our purpose? Are we looking for recreational property? Trying to protect scenic views? Trying to protect coastal wetlands? Or merely trying to channel urban development into a particular pattern? . . . It is important to ask

not only whether these laws preserve farmland or open space but also whether they preserve the right farmland and open space.[46]

One implication of these comments is that preferential assessment should be given only to property in specific districts as part of a broad policy to preserve them. Few state laws are framed and implemented in this way. California's law does limit eligibility to property in specified agricultural districts, but most of those districts are in rural areas where they face little threat from growing cities.[47]

Another reason which is sometimes suggested for states to preserve farmland is the alleged danger of loss of self-sufficiency in food production. Food is supposedly better and cheaper if it does not have to be transported a great distance, as it would have to be if local food production were diminished. This argument applies most strongly in the Northeast, where the decrease of farmland has been greatest. However, after surveying the evidence, Peterson and Yampolosky conclude as follows:

> In most cases it would seem that production can be transferred from one geographic region to another without undue burdens being placed on the consumer, either in terms of product quality or prices—although more than a few gourmets aver that Long Island potato fields, like French vineyards, are irreplaceable. A number of farm products—including milk, egs, fruits, and vegetables—are best marketed on a local or regional level. Local supplies of these products may be threatened by continued farmland conversion.[48]

Other reasons for preserving farmland include protection of traditional rural values and an aesthetic preference for farmland over suburban subdivisions.[49]

Regardless of the reason for desiring to preserve farmland, it appears that differential assessment is not by itself a very effective means of preserving it. The main reason is that the financial benefit which it provides is relatively small compared to the capital gain that can be realized by selling to a developer. At the urban fringe, the land's value for nonfarm use tends to be substantially higher than in agriculture. Gloudemans shows that use value assessment can delay the date of conversion for land whose market value exceeds its use value but for which the highest and best use is agricultural; but eventually even such land will tend to be converted despite its differential assessment.[50]

Stocker explains the lack of impact on land-use decisions in a different way. He argues that differential assessment does not affect land use because its benefits are capitalized into land value. Thus, while differential assessment lowers out-of-pocket costs in the form of property tax, it increases the implicit opportunity cost of holding land. It leads to an increase in wealth for the landowner but does not affect the calculus of whether to sell or hold land.[51]

Another reason why differential assessment has little effect on land use is that it often simply ratifies the previously existing situation of de facto preferential assessment for farms, as explained earlier.

Increasing the Income of Farmers

Property tax paid represents a considerably higher fraction of income for farmers than for nonfarmers. In 1976 farm real estate taxes represented 6.3 percent of the total personal income of the farm population versus 4.6 percent for the entire country. This understates relative farm property taxes because personal property tax levies are not included for farmers although they are counted in the national total.

There is a widespread impression that farm property taxes have been increasing as a percentage of farm income. This was true from 1945 to 1971 when they rose from 2.5 to 6.9 percent of farm income, but since then taxes have risen slower than income, averaging 5.4 percent of income from 1972 to 1976.[52]

These figures understate the magnitude of the problem for some farmers and overstate it for others. Owners of farmland at the urban fringe tend to pay much higher property taxes than others. In the late 1960s, taxes per acre levied on farms inside metropolitan areas averaged more than three times those in counties adjacent to metropolitan areas and more than seven times those in other counties.[53]

An example demonstrates the tax squeeze felt by some farmers if assessments are based on market values. Farmers A and B each own farms worth $200,000 in their agricultural use and can derive a net income before paying property tax of $20,000. Farmer A is not located near any large cities. Since the effective property tax rate on his farm is 0.5 percent, his property tax is $1,000 and net income after property tax is $19,000. Farmer B's farm is near a metropolitan area, so its market value is much higher, $1 million. Since the effective tax rate is 1.5 percent on his farm, his property tax is $15,000, leaving him a net income of only $5,000. These calculations are shown:

	Farmer A	*Farmer B*
Farm value of real estate	$200,000	$ 200,000
Market value of real estate	200,000	1,000,000
Effective property tax rate	0.005	0.015
Property tax bill	$ 1,000	$ 15,000
Net income	20,000	20,000
Less property taxes	1,000	15,000
Net after property taxes	19,000	5,000
Property taxes as a percentage of net income	0.05	0.75

While the property tax takes 5 percent of farmer A's income, it amounts to 75 percent of farmer B's. While farming may be a viable proposition for farmer A, it does not pay for farmer B.[54]

Data on the ratio of property tax levied on farms to farm personal income ignore three important considerations—capitalization, variations in economic status within the farm sector, and absentee ownership of farm property.

It is generally believed that property taxes on land are capitalized, which is to say that they are reflected in lower land values.[55] Thus, someone who recently purchased a farm would have paid a lower price because of the property tax burden which could be expected. However, farms sell relatively infrequently, and most farmland has not been purchased recently.

It is often asserted (although not documented) that owners of farms may have a cash flow problem because it is difficult to borrow against equity to pay taxes. Differential assessment programs which incorporate a deferral provision are meant to deal with this situation.

A second important consideration is the diversity in wealth and income within the farm sector. The 162,000 largest farms, which represent only 6 percent of all farms, account for more than half of total farm sales. Since larger units tend to be more productive, assessed value is probably not as concentrated as production, but there is a wide gulf between affluent farmers and others.[56]

Finally, a large amount of farmland is not operated by its owner. In 1969 about 37.5 percent of all farmland was rented, with higher percentages in states with the most valuable land.[57] Some of the non-owner-operated land is owned by other farmers, so that the tax on it can still be related to farm income, but about 33.5 percent is owned by nonfarmers. It is misleading to relate taxes on farmland owned by such persons (or businesses) to farm income because their incidence is not on farmers since the tax cannot be shifted. Likewise, in evaluating programs for property tax relief for farms, one must distinguish between the interests of farmers and those of owners of farmland (the two groups overlap but are not identical).

If the objective is to boost the income of struggling farmers, existing differential assessment laws are very inefficient mechanisms in several respects.[58] First, they generally provide benefits to all owners of farmland, whether they are farmers or not. Minnesota, Texas, and Alaska have been exceptions in that they required certain percentages of the taxpayer's income to be derived from farming, but Texas has dropped that provision. Until recently Texas also excluded corporations from eligibility; that is a crude device for restricting benefits, since many bonafide farmers are incorporated and many nonfarmers are not incorporated.

Second, laws generally do not concentrate their benefits on farmers for whom property taxes are a particularly heavy burden because of unusually high tax rates or because the taxes take a high percentage of income.

A third flaw is that no limit is placed on benefits. Within a taxing jurisdiction, benefits almost always increase as the value of property owned goes up. If the objective were to assist struggling farmers, a maximum could be placed either on the number of acres or value of property which could receive differential assessment or credits or on the subsidy itself.

The easiest quantity to limit is acreage, but it is also the least appropriate, since it fails to distinguish between good and poor land. The value of eligible property could be limited without too much difficulty, but the limit would have to be periodically adjusted to account for inflation. The subsidy itself would be easy to limit if credits were used, but it would be much more cumbersome to restrict the subsidy from differential assessment because calculations would be much more complex.

If there is a desire to target benefits to certain owners of farmland rather than provide them to all, some difficult design issues must be confronted. Many farmers supplement their income with substantial earnings from nonagricultural jobs, so that if a minimum percentage of income to be derived from farming is set, it cannot be too high. Much land is owned by farmers and rented out or is owned by retired farmers or their children, and there is a reluctance to treat them like other absentee landlords. If a ceiling is placed on benefits in some fashion, there would be a tendency to divide farms into smaller units to maximize subsidies received.[59] The opportunity for such behavior could be limited by applying the ceiling to households rather than to individuals.

These problems are not insurmountable. The law could state that only owners of farmland who actually farm their own property are eligible, that there is a maximum subsidy which can be received and only one person per household is eligible. While it is impossible to devise a law in which benefits go to all the right people and to them only, it is certainly possible to target benefits with greater precision than present laws do.

Conclusions

Although there are several excellent studies of differential farmland assessment, most are somewhat out of touch with the reality of farm property tax relief programs in that they tend to overemphasize the goal of preserving farmland relative to the goal of enhancing the income of farmers. They also tend to overemphasize the situation facing the farmer at the urban fringe relative to that which confronts the rural farmer. The impact of many state laws is not felt on land near cities but on land far from cities.

One might suppose that for farms in rural areas use value would be approximately equal to market value. That is not how it works out in many states, for two reasons: The procedures adopted for measuring use value make it artificially low, and a major force driving up farm property values has been not pressure from expanding cities but rather speculation.

The value of farmland has soared in the 1970s. Between 1971 and 1977 the average value per acre of farm real estate rose 132 percent.[60] This inflation was sparked by the sensational increase in farm income in 1973, when it more than doubled. But since that year farm income has not continued to rise. In fact, it has fallen sharply. Nevertheless, farm property values have continued to rise, perhaps on the speculative assumption that farm income in the future will fare much better than it has in the past.

Use-value assessment has shielded owners of farmland from the higher property taxes which would have been levied on them if assessments had kept up with farm market values. Farm real property tax rose 43 percent from 1971 to 1977 while the total market value of farm real property increased 122 percent.[61] Although nonfarm property value went up less, its property tax rose 67 percent in the same period. Thus, while owners or farmland enjoyed an increase in their share of total property wealth, they were also able to enjoy a decrease in their share of property taxes. It is not an exaggeration to say that they could have their cake and eat it too.

While it has been very effective in enhancing the income of owners of farmland, differential assessment has had relatively little impact on land use in the urban fringe. The three investigators who have made the most extensive studies of this subject are unanimous. One describes its effectiveness in this regard as "at best, unproved."[62] Another says that it has "only a very limited effect."[63] A third concludes that "with respect to the goal of retarding the conversion of farm and other open land, differential assessment is marginally effective and its cost in terms of tax expenditures is . . . so high as to render it an undesirable tool for achieving this goal."[64]

What policies should be implemented? Non-circuit-breaker credits are preferable to differential assessment because they are easier to administer and their effects are clearer. Relief should go only to land which produces sufficient income to show that it really is used for farming.

If it is desired to preserve farmland at the urban fringe, differential assessment should be supplemented by other measures, such as zoning or a system of transferable development rights.[65] Relief should not be available statewide, but should be restricted to particular districts threatened by urbanization. Contracts committing owners to continued farm activity should be required.

If it is desired to aid struggling farmers, relief should be limited to those who derive a significant proportion of their income from farming. A maximum should be placed on the amount of relief which any household can receive. When property is sold or changes use, a penalty should be assessed which approximates the benefits previously received, including interest charged at the market rate.[66]

The policies suggested here are contrary to the interests of persons and businesses which own large amounts of valuable farmland. Perhaps that is why actual policies diverge so greatly from the ones outlined. But another factor is that gullible urban residents have voted for such policies in the belief that these would preserve farmland without understanding what their true effects would be—little effect on land use but a large effect on the wealth of owners of farmland.[67]

Notes

1. E.C. Pasour, Jr., and D.L. Holley, "An Economic Analysis of the Case against Ad Valorem Property Taxation in Forestry," *National Tax Journal* 29 (June 1976):55-64.

2. This example is oversimplified in several respects. For example, the tax rate would be the same with and without differential assessment only if farmland represents a very small proportion of the total tax base. If farmland is a significant share of the tax base, the tax rate would have to be higher if differential assessment were in effect in order to maintain government revenue. It is also unrealistic to assume that in the absence of differential assessment the property's assessment would equal its market value; in fact, it would normally be lower. However, the assumptions of a decreasing effective tax rate over time and faster growth of market value than use value are consistent with recent experience.

3. Although Iowa's limits on assessment increases are categorized in chapter 7 as a form of classification, the statement in the text is not true in Iowa, since farm assessments do not rise in proportion to market value.

4. Robert J. Gloudemans, "Evaluating Alternative Use Value Farmland Assessment Laws" (Paper presented at a seminar at Topeka, Kansas, February 24, 1977), p. 1; U.S. Census Bureau, *1977 Census of Governments,* vol. 2: *Taxable Property Values and Assessment/Sales Price Ratios,* (Washington, D.C., 1978), pp. 286-287.

5. Robert J. Gloudemans, *Use-Value Farmland Assessments: Theory, Practice and Impact* (Chicago: International Association of Assessing Officers, 1974), pp. 29-30.

6. Thomas F. Hady, "Differential Assessment and the Preservation of Farmland, Open Space, and Historic Sites," in International Association of Assessing Officers, *Use-Value Assessment and the Preservation of Farmland, Open Space, and Historic Sites* 1975, p. 5.

7. The tabulation follows the Census Bureau with these changes: Idaho and Arizona (not included by the census) are counted as having pure preferential assessment, and Michigan and Wisconsin are not included because their circuit breaker programs do not affect assessments; also, Connecticut is classified as having a deferral program. Sources used in addition to the census are Coughlin et al., "Differential Assessment of Real Property as an Incentive to Open Space Preservation and Farmland Retention," *National Tax Journal* 31 (June

1978):166-167; and U.S. Department of Agriculture, *Farm Real Estate Taxes: 1976* (Washington, D.C., 1978), p. 23.

8. Gloudemans, "Evaluating," p. 10; Iowa added deferral to its law in 1977. Gloudemans counts Connecticut, which has a conveyance tax, among the states with penalties, and it is included in the tabulation of states with deferral in the previous paragraph.

9. Details on Michigan's circuit breaker are from Advisory Commission on Intergovernmental Relations, *Property Tax Relief for Farmers: New Use for Circuit Breakers,* August 1974, and material provided by the Michigan Department of Natural Resources. Description of the Wisconsin program is based on information provided by James Plourde.

10. See Coughlin et al., "Differential Assessment," pp. 170-72, and John C. Keene et al., *Untaxing Open Space* (Washington, D.C., Council on Environmental Quality, 1976), chapter 5.

11. Gloudemans and Keene had a semantic disagreement about whether shifts were "large." See John C. Keene, "The Impact of Differential Assessment Programs on a Tax Base," pp. 40-61, and Robert J. Gloudemans, "Discussion," pp. 64-68, in International Association of Assessing Officers, *Use-Value Assessment and the Preservation of Farmland* (Chicago, 1977).

12. Keene, *Untaxing Open Space,* pp. 91-93; see also Hoy F. Carman and Jim G. Polson, "Tax Shifts Occurring as a Result of Differential Assessment of Farmland: California, 1968-69," *National Tax Journal* 24 (December 1971):449-457.

13. This point is not mentioned in the major studies of differential assessment by Hady, Gloudemans, or Keene et al. John N. Kolesar and Jaye Scholl, *Saving Farmland* (Princeton, N.J.: Center for the Analysis of Public Issues, 1975), does mention it but considers it a minor point (p. 10). Its importance depends on whether farm property is a large proportion of the total property tax base, on how rapidly it is increasing, and on the formula by which school aid depends on assessed valuation.

14. For example, a change in the method of valuing farmland in Iowa resulted in extra school aid costs to the state of $50 million or more in the first year it was in effect, 1979-1980. In 1978 Minnesota (whose ordinary preferential assessment program has a low participation rate) passed a law requiring use-value assessment for purposes of distributing state school aid. However, the level of assessments does not affect school aid in rural areas which in some states receive no aid because their tax rate is low, a minimum level set by the state.

15. Gloudemans, "Evaluating," p. 8; Arizona has been added to the list cited in this source.

16. A survey of all states was conducted by the author to obtain data on the extent to which landowners participate in use-value assessment programs. Most states did not have such data available, nor could they estimate the reduction in farm assessments due to use-value assessment. See Carman and

Polson, "Tax Shifts," p. 450; D.F. Neuman and E.C. Pasour, *Agricultural Use-Value Taxation in North Carolina* (Raleigh: North Carolina State University, 1978); information was also obtained in letters from Roy C. Saper, economic analyst, Michigan Department of Management and Budget, and Hollis A. Swett, director, Office for Local Government Liaison, State of New York.

17. Steven J. Zellmer and Calvin A. Kent, "Trends in the Taxation of Personal Property," *State Government,* Winter 1979, pp. 13-15; Ann G. Sibold, *Taxes Levied on Farm Personal Property, 1960-72* (Washington, D.C.: Economic Research Service, U.S. Department of Agriculture, Agricultural Economic Report no. 321, January 1976); Jerome M. Stam and Ann G. Sibold, *Agriculture and the Property Tax* (Washington, D.C.: Department of Agriculture, Economic Research Service, Agricultural Economic Report no. 392, November 1977), pp. 18-19.

18. The proportions were calculated by dividing the taxes levied on farm real estate (as reported in Department of Agriculture, *Farm Real Estate Taxes: 1976,* pp. 10-11), by the total property tax collections (as reported in U.S. Census Bureau, *Governmental Finances in 1976-77).* As explained by Stam and Sibold, *Agriculture and the Property Tax,* p. 9, data in *Farm Real Estate Taxes: 1976* refer to the year taxes are levied, which is usually one year before they are collected.

19. Gloudemans, "Evaluating," p. 5.

20. Ibid., pp. 5-8. These descriptions apply only to the forty-one states with programs identified by Gloudemans.

21. Telephone conversation with Dan Brody, staff member of Texas General Assembly, December 11, 1978, provided details on Texas programs. Statistics on income from nonfarm sources are from Lee Bawden et al., "Income and Wealth Data as Indicators of Well-being for People Engaged in Farming," *Agricultural and Rural Data* (Economic Statistics Committee, Agricultural Economics Association, May 1977), p. 94.

22. Allyn O. Lockner and Han J. Kim, "Circuitbreakers on Farm Property Tax Overload: A Case Study," *National Tax Journal* 26 (June 1973):233-240; Fred C. White et al., "Comparison of Property Tax Circuit Breakers Applied to Farmers and Homeowners," *Land Economics* 52 (August 1976):355-362.

23. See James W. Haughey et al., "The Michigan Property Tax Circuit-breaker: Design and Cyclical Sensitivity" (unpublished mimeographed article) for comments on cyclical variations of circuit breaker costs; also, Douglas O. Stewart, "Comparison of Property Tax Circuit-Breakers Applied to Farmers and Homeowners: Comment," *Land Economics* 54 (August 1978):390-396, for additional criticisms of farm circuit breakers.

24. For example, the Iowa credit varies according to the amount by which the school property tax rate exceeds a prescribed level, thus providing greater assistance in property-poor areas.

25. For a discussion of the concept of tax expenditures, see Stanley Surrey, *Pathways to Tax Reform* (Cambridge, Mass.: Harvard University Press, 1971).

26. Advisory Commission on Intergovernmental Relations, "Property Tax Relief for Farmers: New Use for Circuit Breakers," August 1974.

27. Calvin A. Kent, "Determination of Capitalization Rates for Mass Appraisal of Farmland under the Use-Value Approach," *Assessor's Journal* 11 (June 1976):92-93.

28. Gloudemans, *Use Value,* pp. 15-16.

29. Kent, "Capitalization Rates," p. 92.

30. Ibid., pp. 91-100.

31. Kent cites the International Association of Assessing Officers and the American Institute of Real Estate Appraisers on this point. Ibid., p. 94.

32. Ibid.

33. Gloudemans ("Evaluating," p. 10) counts twenty-five states but does not include Iowa, which added a deferral feature to its differential assessment program in 1978.

34. Gloudemans, "Evaluating," p. 12-13; Coughlin et al., "Differential Assessment," p. 168, is another source on this and related program characteristics.

35. Ibid., p. 16.

36. Ibid., pp. 14-15.

37. Ibid., p. 23; see also Keene et al., *Untaxing Open Space.*

38. Keene et al., *Untaxing Open Space,* pp. 76, 121.

39. The argument for applying rollback taxes when there is a change of ownership but not of use would be weaker if farm tax relief actually had a significant effect on land-use decisions. Since such effects are apparently small, equity considerations are dominant, and they favor rollback when ownership changes.

40. Gloudemans, "Evaluating," pp. 9, 14.

41. Ibid., pp. 9-10.

42. George E. Peterson and Harvey Yampolsky, *Urban Development and the Protection of Metropolitan Farmland* (Washington, D.C.: The Urban Institute, 1975), p. 6.

43. Gloudemans, *Use Value,* p. 11.

44. Peterson and Yampolsky, *Urban Development,* p. 9.

45. In view of the high rate of increase of farm productivity and the low-income elasticity of demand for farm products, the decrease in farm acreage is not surprising.

46. Hady, "Differential Assessment," p. 5. Reprinted with permission.

47. Carman and Polson, "Tax Shifts"; Roy Saper (letter cited in note 16) reports that land in Michigan's circuit breaker program averaged 22.7 miles from an urban center of 25,000 or more population; studies cited in Keene et al., *Untaxing Open Space,* chapter 4.

48. Peterson and Yampolsky, *Urban Development,* p. 9.

49. Ibid., p. 11.

50. Gloudemans, *Use Value,* pp. 39-41.

51. Frederick D. Stocker, "The Impact of Ad Valorem Assessment on the Preservation of Open Space and the Pattern of Urban Growth," in International Association of Assessing Officers, *Use-Value Assessment and the Preservation of Farmland*, p. 29.

52. Department of Agriculture, *Farm Real Estate Taxes: 1976,* p. 22, and Stam and Sibold, *Agriculture and the Property Tax.* The latter report points out that although they represent a larger percentage of income for farmers than for others, property taxes are a smaller percentage of wealth. The effective property tax rate on farm property, 0.6 percent, is less than half of that on nonagricultural property, 1.4 percent.

53. Gloudemans, *Use Value,* p. 10; the study cited covered 1964 to 1968, but no more recent figures are available. Another indication of how variable is the impact of property taxes on farmers is that in 1976 real estate taxes exceeded 15 percent of net farm income in eighteen states and were less than 5 percent in seven states. Department of Agriculture, *Farm Real Estate Taxes: 1976,* pp. 20-21.

54. This example is modified from one developed by Gloudemans, *Use Value,* pp. 10-11. The numbers have been changed to make them somewhat more realistic. The effective tax rate is higher for farmer B because his community's tax base is smaller and a higher level of services is provided in it.

55. See, for example, E.C. Pasour, "The Capitalization of Real Estate Taxes Levied on Farm Real Estate," *American Journal of Agricultural Economics* 57 (November 1973):539-548.

56. U.S. Congressional Budget Office, *Public Policy and the Changing Structure of American Agriculture* (Washington, D.C., 1978), p. 10.

57. U.S. Department of Agriculture, *Farmland Tenure Patterns in the United States* (Agricultural Economic Report no. 249), pp. 2-3.

58. Similar conclusions are implied by Gloudemans, "Evaluating," p. 27, and Hady, "Differential Assessment," p. 6.

59. Such an effect was predicted when Congress placed a limit on certain federal crop subsidies in the early 1970s.

60. Department of Agriculture, *Farm Real Estate Market Developments,* July 1978, p. 18.

61. Ibid., p. 22. Department of Agriculture, *Farm Real Estate Taxes: 1976,* p. 9.

62. Hady, "Differential Assessment," p. 5. See also Thomas F. Hady and Ann Sibold, *State Programs for the Differential Assessment of Farm and Open Space Land* (Department of Agriculture, Agricultural Economic Report no. 256, 1974).

63. Gloudemans, "Evaluating," p. 28.

64. Keene et al., *Untaxing Open Space,* p. 115.

65. Transferable development rights are advocated, for example, by Kolesar and Scholl, *Saving Farmland,* pp. 38-43, 50.

66. Spokespeople for farm interests argue that it is inconsistent to require owners of farmland to repay benefits when owners of homes and other property are not subject to deferral. This point has some validity as long as the magnitude of the benefits received is comparable. However, when owners of farmland receive much larger benefits, the case for deferral in farm relief programs is stronger.

67. See Kolesar and Scholl, *Saving Farmland,* for an example of how saving farmland was used as the theme to gain support for the enabling constitutional amendment in New Jersey, although that has not been the differential assessment law's major effect.

6 Property Tax Relief for Business

Property tax relief for business differs from most of the other subjects discussed in this book in several respects. For one thing, much of it is offered at the local rather than at the state level, with little monitoring by state government. Frequently relief results from informal agreements between businesses and local officials which grant preferential treatment to certain parcels of business property but not to others in order to attract new industry to the community. Consequently, it is more difficult to describe and measure than most other forms of relief. In addition, business property frequently feels the brunt of the costs of relief which is provided to homes and farms. In such cases, it receives "negative relief." Finally, property taxes paid by businesses are often shifted to consumers or others and thus constitute "hidden taxes." In contrast, taxes on homes and farms are generally believed to be borne by their owners.

The Role of Business Property Taxes in Relation to Other State and Local Taxes[1]

The treatment of business is very important because businesses own a large proportion of taxable property. In 1977 an estimated 34 percent of property taxes had an initial impact on business. This ratio has been falling, since it was 39.5 percent in 1967 and 45.1 percent in 1957.

Property taxes have also been shrinking relative to other state and local taxes paid by business. Their share was 48.1 percent in 1957, 45.1 percent in 1967, and 34.4 percent in 1977.[2] At the same time, taxes impacting on business have been declining in relation to taxes paid by individuals. Business taxes dropped from 40 percent of total state-local taxes in 1957 to 33.6 percent in 1977. (The same thing was happening at the federal level as social security payroll taxes rose rapidly and corporation income taxes rose slowly.)

Thus, business property taxes have been a declining proportion of a relatively slow-growing revenue source (the property tax) and a declining proportion of business taxes, which themselves are becoming less important in relative terms. Business property taxes accounted for only 11.5 percent of state-local tax collections in 1977 compared to 19.3 percent in 1957.

Several factors are responsible for the decreasing role of business property taxes. The assessed valuation of commercial and industrial property has increased more slowly than values of other property.[3] In part, this is because inflation has driven up home values and assessments much more rapidly than business assessed values. Another contributing factor is formal and informal "tax breaks" granted to attract new industry. Business also benefited from the trend toward exemption of personal property. Unfortunately, there are no reliable statistics quantifying how important tax concessions have been in relation to factors such as uneven rates of new construction of various types of property, changes in assessment practices affecting businesses and homes, and other developments. As explained in a later section, it is not even clear whether on the average business is over- or under-assessed relative to other types of property. The situation varies from state to state, within sections of individual states, and even for various properties in the same city or county.

Description

Formal exemptions for new or expanding businesses take several forms.[4] They may cover all property or only certain types, such as buildings or equipment (sometimes of particular kinds, such as for pollution control). They may also be limited to particular industries. They may be for the entire value of the property or for only a limited portion of it. They may last for only a short period or continue for as long as fifteen years. Their availability may be limited to specific geographic areas, such as the blighted sections of cities, and may be at the discretion of local governments. Usually they are provided only to new investments or expansions of existing businesses or to new companies moving into existing facilities. Sometimes the revenue which is lost is replaced by the state government.

In addition to or instead of an exemption, business may be attracted by a guarantee that taxes will not be raised for a specified number of years.

Permanent relief also is provided by exemption from personal property taxes. (Personal property is property other than real estate. Business personal property usually consists mainly of inventories, office equipment, and certain machinery.) In some states all personal property is exempt, but more often only particular kinds, such as inventories or machinery, are not taxed. Many states have partial exemptions, and a number are gradually phasing out the personal property tax over a period of years.

Besides these formal relief programs, businesses sometimes receive informal tax breaks through negotiation with assessors or other local or state officials.

History, Current Extent of Use, and Costs

Exemptions for New Investment

Exemptions have a long history. The first exemption of property for commercial reasons dates from Connecticut in 1649. In Colonial and pre-Civil War days, property tax exemptions were more common in the North than in the South, where direct payments to industry were the preferred instrument of subsidy.[5]

Information available on business exemptions is far from complete. According to one recent survey, twenty-six states attempt to attract new industry by offering exemptions on land and buildings and twenty-seven states offer exemptions on equipment, as shown in table 6-1. In several cases use of exemptions is limited to specific geographic areas. In New York and Michigan, for example, the exemptions are for companies locating in low-income urban areas. In other states, exemptions are offered to particular industries, as, for example, in Alabama where poultry and animal feed industries are eligible for special exemptions beyond those available to most other companies.[6]

Of the exemptions for land and buildings, ten are available for all investments and sixteen are limited to certain industries, locations, or types of buildings. Nearly all the states with exemption programs are either in the South or in the northern tier of states stretching from New York to Washington and Oregon.

Most of the same states also offer exemptions for equipment and machinery. However, they are joined by three New England states and three scattered elsewhere. Only four states provide exemptions for land and buildings but not for machinery and equipment.

Few, if any, states collect information on the cost of exemptions granted. Since the state government rarely reimburses localities for revenue lost because of exemptions, localities attempt to recoup the revenue by raising the property tax rate, thus passing the cost of the exemptions to taxpayers whose property is not exempt. If tax rate limitations prevent such a rise, local governments may have to reduce their spending, so that the cost of an exemption program is likely to be reduced services.[7]

Exemption of Personal Property

As described in chapter 12, the personal property tax has been undergoing substantial erosion for many decades. Because intangibles and nonbusiness tangible personal property are a relatively small proportion of the remaining

Table 6-1
States Offering Tax Exemptions for Business Real and Personal Property, 1979

State	Land and Capital Improvements	Equipment and Machinery
Alabama	Full	Full
Connecticut		Partial
Delaware		Full
Georgia	Partial	
Illinois	Partial	
Indiana		Full
Kansas	Partial	Partial
Kentucky	Partial	Partial
Louisiana	Partial	Full
Maryland	Partial	Full
Massachusetts		Full
Michigan	Partial	Full
Minnesota	Partial	Full
Mississippi	Full	Full
Montana	Full	Full
New Hampshire		Full
New Jersey	Full	Partial
New York	Partial	Partial
North Dakota	Partial	Partial
Ohio	Full	Full
Oklahoma	Partial	Full
Oregon	Partial	
Pennsylvania	Full	Partial
Rhode Island	Full	Full
South Carolina	Full	Full
South Dakota	Full	
Tennessee	Partial	Partial
Texas	Partial	Partial
Virginia	Partial	Partial
Washington		Full
Wisconsin		Full

Source: Conway Publications, Inc., *Industrial Development* 14, no. 1 (January-February 1979): 5, 7, with permission.
Note: In 1979 Iowa enacted a partial exemption for land and capital improvements.

personal property tax base, a further phase-out of personal property taxation in most states largely impacts on the business sector.[8]

Many states have taken steps in recent years to exempt much of the inventories, machinery, and equipment of commercial and industrial enterprises. Seventeen states enacted exemptions for at least certain types of business personal property between 1968 and 1978. There were only fifteen states with no business exemptions at all in 1978, and only twenty states taxed inventories without exemptions.[9]

When states exempt personal property, they often replace a portion of the revenue which localities lose as a result of their smaller tax base.[10] To the extent this is done, the cost of phase-out comes from the state general fund rather than from other property taxpayers. Consequently, the burden of paying for the exemption is distributed much differently from the situation in which there is no state financing.

Design Issues

As the following section explains, there is very little evidence that property tax exemptions have much influence on business location decisions, so that there is little point in a detailed discussion of design issues.

One consideration which does deserve mention is that exemptions are likely to be more effective in influencing business investment decisions, the less widespread they are. If exemptions are available in only a limited area, they are more likely to attract business investment. Even when geographically restricted, they are often ineffective in influencing business location decisions.

Other factors which should be considered are the horizontal equity, neutrality, and administrative cost of business taxes. Personal property taxes in particular have been criticized on all these counts. They strike some industries very hard and others lightly. In order to avoid them, businesses may engage in inefficient activities, such as drawing down inventories in advance of the date when taxes are assessed. They are expensive to administer. Thus, the personal property tax is far from ideal as a method of taxing the business sector.

Evaluation

Several questions must be addressed in weighing tax exemptions for business:

1. What are the reasons for taxing business and how much tax should it pay?
2. How is business property treated relative to other property?
3. Should incentives be used to attract and retain business? If so, are property tax incentives the appropriate tools to use for this purpose?

Reasons

Brazer has identified four reasons for taxing businesses that do not violate the economic criterion of neutrality, which proscribes measures interfering with efficiency in the allocation of resources.[11] First, taxes are a means of paying for services provided by the government to business. Since it is generally desirable for prices to reflect the full cost of production of goods and services, taxes can be viewed as user charges. Second, taxes may capture location rents which arise when a location is so advantageous that it yields a return in excess of that which could be realized elsewhere. Taxes on such rents will not cause any shifts in economic activity because the rents are, by definition, surpluses. Third, taxes may cover external diseconomies of production caused by the firm, for example air and water pollution. While these three reasons would exhaust the grounds for taxing business if they were observed by all governments, a fourth reason exists in practice when other jurisdictions tax business at a higher rate than can be justified on the above grounds. Allocational efficiency may be improved in such a situation if the locality taxes business at a level similar to that which prevails elsewhere. Otherwise, more resources may be employed in the low-tax jurisdiction than would be dictated by nontax considerations.

In fact, taxes paid by business seem to be considerably in excess of those which can be justified by the first three reasons. That this is so is indicated by the many studies which show the fiscal advantage realized by communities when they attract certain types of industries.[12] However, some persons argue that business benefits from access to an educated pool of labor, and since education accounts for approximately half of local spending, inclusion of such benefits has a great effect on the tax-benefit ratio of business.

Additional considerations are often of practical importance in explaining the popularity of business taxation. First, it provides a means of exporting much of the local tax burden. Taxes on business are borne by its owners, its suppliers (including its workers), or its customers. For firms which produce products that are not locally consumed, a high proportion of the tax is likely to be borne by nonresidents. For example, in one of the most widely cited studies of tax exporting, McLure estimated that 20 to 25 percent of property taxes are not paid by state residents in the short run and 10 to 20 percent are exported in the long run.[13]

The other factor behind the popularity of business taxation is the ambiguity surrounding its incidence—who really pays it. According to Netzer, one of the implicit objectives of policymakers seems to be to "disguise the tax burden borne locally, by collecting a high fraction of property taxes from business property, with the tax shifted to consumers, employees, and owners in ways that are close to invisible."[14] A related factor, which is inconsistent with the invisibility viewpoint, is the naive belief that businesses have "ability to pay" of their own or, alternatively, that business taxes are paid by their owners, who are mostly wealthy. Thus, raising business taxes makes the tax system more progressive.[15] Depending on market conditions, this perception may be correct to some extent,[16] but using business as a conduit to tax the rich is very inefficient. The portion of the tax which is shifted forward to consumers (which is often sizable)[17] constitutes a tax which is not only regressive but also capricious in the horizontal distribution of its burdens.

Thus, there is a potpourri of reasons for taxing business, some theoretical and others pragmatic. Many of these reasons do not necessarily favor the property tax as the ideal instrument for taxing business. In fact, the value-added tax is preferable in at least two important respects. It is likely to be more neutral, since it favors neither capital- nor labor-intensive firms, and it is thought to be more closely related to the value of services received by firms than the property tax. However, whatever the abstract merits of value-added versus property taxation, there is unlikely to be a major shift from one to the other because of the changes in tax burdens which would ensue and the large institutional changes which would be involved.[18]

Treatment of Business Property
Vis-à-Vis Other Types

It is difficult to generalize about the property tax treatment of business as opposed to other property. Perhaps the best recent data are the Census Bureau sample of properties sold during a six-month period in 1976. The average assessment ratio nationally was 31 percent for all property and 35.7 percent for business property.[19] In thirty-five out of forty-two states for which results were reported, the ratio of assessed value to market value was higher for commercial-industrial property than for all types of property. In seventeen states the average assessment ratio for commercial-industrial property was more than 20 percent higher than for all property. Since only five of these states had a legal system of classification which called for business property to be assessed higher than most other property in 1976, there may have been illegal discrimination against business property.[20,21] (See table 6-2)

However, the validity of the Census Bureau data as an indication of the general level at which business property is assessed is open to serious question. Large parcels of business property are sold much less frequently than other property, necessitating a different approach to valuation of such properties than is used for valuing homes. While assessments on residential property are frequently determined by referring to sales prices, assessments for commercial and industrial property are usually based on the cost of reproducing the property or the capitalized value of income derived from it. Even when business property is sold, the true price is often difficult to determine because of the complicated terms relating to the method and timing of payments and other considerations which may be involved. A final problem with the Census Bureau data is that it excludes all transactions involving prices of more than $750,000. While its original sample did not include many such transactions, property with a value in the $750,000-plus range accounts for a large amount of the total value of business property.[22]

Careful case studies provide the greatest insight into how business is treated under the property tax. One study in Boston found a sharp distinction between old and new business property. The effective property tax rate on new commercial property, most of which had received explicit tax concessions when

Table 6-2
Inequalities in Average Assessment Ratios for Various Classes of Real Property with Value under $750,000

	Assessment Ratios (Percent)		
State	Commercial-Industrial	Single-Family Residential	All Types
Large Bias against Commercial-Industrial Property[a]			
Alabama (C)[b]	16.7	10.6	10.8
Indiana	18.5	16.1	14.8
Louisiana (C)	19.8	9.0	9.6
Massachusetts[c]	59.8	42.3	42.3
Minnesota (C)	27.8	22.3	21.5
Mississippi	13.9	10.5	9.6
Missouri	20.8	17.2	15.7
Nebraska	25.5	18.2	18.6
New York	35.2	23.7	27.2
North Dakota	8.5	6.5	6.5
Pennsylvania	27.8	16.8	17.9
Rhode Island	58.5	41.1	43.7
South Carolina (C)	4.8	3.2	3.3
Tennessee (C)	27.6	15.0	16.2
West Virginia	39.3	24.9	25.4
Wisconsin	64.1	49.5	49.3
Wyoming	13.3	10.1	10.1
Small Bias against Commercial-Industrial Property[a]			
Arkansas	9.4	10.1	8.6
Colorado	19.3	18.1	16.8
Georgia	32.3	31.4	30.8
Illinois[d]	29.6	26.3	26.0
Iowa	82.4	71.8	70.2
Kansas	13.3	12.7	12.3
Kentucky	72.1	74.0	72.0
Maine	64.3	55.5	53.5
Michigan	41.5	40.5	40.6
New Jersey	73.0	67.3	67.6
New Mexico	18.2	17.9	17.1
North Carolina	66.4	61.2	63.6
Ohio	31.1	28.0	27.3
Oregon	82.6	74.8	71.5
South Dakota	29.8	28.0	25.6
Texas	17.1	14.2	13.8
Virginia	33.1	32.9	32.8
Washington	77.5	64.0	64.2
Bias in Favor of Commercial-Industrial Property			
California	17.1	17.7	17.2
Connecticut	40.1	42.2	42.1
Florida	57.9	60.0	59.4
Idaho	8.9	9.4	9.1
New Hampshire	58.2	61.1	58.9
Oklahoma	8.7	12.4	9.9
Vermont	31.3	32.2	31.8

Source: U.S. Census Bureau, *1977 Census of Governments*, vol. 2: *Taxable Property Values and Assessment/Sales Price Ratios* (Washington, D.C., 1978), table 9.

Table 6-2 continued

Note: No data on the commercial-industrial assessment ratio were available for Alaska, Arizona (C), Delaware, District of Columbia, Hawaii (C), Maryland, Montana (C), Nevada, or Utah. See text for discussion of interpretation of this table. Assessment ratios are size-weighted.

aA large bias is one in which the commercial-industrial assessment ratio is more than 20 percent higher than the assessment ratio for all types of property.

b(C) indicates that this state had a system of classification in effect when the data were collected in 1976.

cMassachusetts voters approved a constitutional amendment which permits classification in 1978.

dOnly one county in Illinois—Cook County—classified property.

it was built, was 3.7 percent, while the rate on old commercial property was 10.6 percent. Overall, the tax rate on commercial property averaged 8.2 percent compared to an average rate of 5.5 percent for residential property.[23] In some other places, however, new business property is treated similarly to other new property, which is to say it is overtaxed relative to older property, the assessment of which was in some cases set decades earlier.[24]

A case study in suburban Washington, D.C., found that apartments were actually underassessed when their assessments were compared to sales prices, although a state report had indicated the opposite situation. The discrepancy occurred because the state report had given equal weight to small structures with only a few units and large buildings with hundreds of units.[25] This case demonstrates the need for caution in drawing conclusions about the manner in which business property is treated in comparison with other kinds of property.

There are undoubtedly cases in which business property on the average is overassessed, but how common this situation is and the magnitude of the typical overassessment are unclear from data which are presently available. Because of the different approaches that are often used for residential and business property because of the infrequency of sales of nonresidential property, answers to these questions are likely to remain controversial.

In addition to the extralegal discrimination against business which may exist, commercial and industrial property is adversely affected in two other ways. As explained in chapter 4, more than half of the states provide property tax exemptions for homeowners. To the extent that these exemptions are locally financed, their cost is shifted to other types of property, most of which is business property. In addition, more than a dozen states classify their property tax system. Most classification systems were enacted to preserve an extralegal pattern of assessments which was threatened by a legal mandate to conform to the law. The frequency with which states have turned to classification is evidence that such extralegal discrimination often has existed. Classification is discussed in chapter 7.

Incentives to Attract Business

Three questions are involved here: Is it desirable to attract business to a particular area? Are any incentives which government can provide effective in reaching their objective? How do property tax incentives compare to other methods of attracting business?

Most analyses begin with the assumption of the desirability of attracting business. In fact, if business makes investments in an area, it will benefit some segments of the population, harm others, and leave others no better or worse than before. Property owners may realize capital gains as a result of prosperity, unemployed workers may get jobs, and other workers and consumers may benefit from upgrading of work and shopping opportunities. But persons on fixed incomes and workers whose skills are not particularly in demand may be disadvantaged by higher rents and price markups, and everyone may be harmed by increased pollution and congestion. Moreover, many of the new jobs may go to nonresidents. When the goal is to avoid economic decline rather than to stimulate dynamic growth, there is less doubt that attracting investment is desirable, but the distribution of gains and losses still tends to be very uneven.[26]

Even if the desirability of attracting business is granted, there is no point in offering incentives if they are ineffective in attracting business. A great many studies have examined this question, using various techniques, samples of states and localities, and time periods. The consensus of these studies is that incentives to attract industry have very little effect. In the words of one recent article, "Taken as a whole, these incentives probably represent a serious misallocation of resources. In the main, government is subsidizing firms for performing activities they would have undertaken in any case."[27]

There are several reasons why tax incentives are generally ineffective. Most importantly, taxes are not usually a major consideration in deciding on plant locations. The cost and quality of the labor supply, access to transportation, and proximity to markets or raw materials rank as the most important considerations in location decisions for most firms. Factors such as the price and availability of capital and energy, the regulatory environment, government services, disamenities such as crime and pollution, and cultural opportunities also play a role in location decisions along with taxes.

State and local taxes usually represent only a small percentage of total costs. It is true that they represent a much larger percentage of profits, but their deductibility for federal corporation income tax purposes means that nearly half of the tax savings from a tax subsidy are eaten up by higher federal taxes. Moreover, only the differentials in rates are relevant to location decisions. These differentials tend to be much smaller within regions than among regions.[28]

There are two other major reasons why differentials in state and local taxes are not more important. First, they are sometimes related to variations in services, so that companies may find that their savings due to a low tax rate are offset by extra costs resulting from the poor quality of services such as fire and police protection, roads, and sewage treatment. In addition, to the extent that property tax differentials (including tax incentives) are capitalized, land values will tend to be higher in places with low business taxes, offsetting the tax advantages.

Despite the generally negative conclusions summarized here, two important caveats are needed. First, some studies which downplay the significance of taxes indicate that "business climate" does have a major impact on location decisions. This somewhat elusive concept certainly refers to the perception as to whether city officials tend to impede or facilitate business operations, but it may reflect even more. Due and Schmenner, authors of two of the most often cited studies of taxes and location decisions, both say that businessmen apparently look at a city's tax structure as an indicator of the overall business climate.[29]

When businessmen in ten large cities were surveyed recently about factors which encouraged or discouraged them to stay or expand in their present location, the factors considered most important were the city government's attitude toward business, the crime level, the adequacy of public facilities and services, the market demand for their product, and the quality of the city's schools. All of these factors except for one are related to nontax aspects of city government activities.[30]

A second qualification is that, according to some studies, taxes do frequently play a major role in deciding where to locate within a region or metropolitan area. In this view, taxes or other incentives are unimportant in selecting the region of the country of the location of a plant; but once this decision has been made, taxes may become a significant factor, because factors such as the quality and cost of labor and access to markets and transportation are relatively uniform within a small region. However, some studies do not find that taxes are important even at this local level.[31]

The preceding discussion has reflected the available literature, most of which has been concerned with tax incentives. States and localities also attempt to attract business in other ways, such as with industrial development bonds or special business-oriented services.

Industrial development bonds are advantageous for business because state and local governments can borrow at a lower rate of interest than a private company because the interest is exempt from federal income tax. One recent study found that, although tax incentives were ineffective, certain bond programs did seem to have a significant effect in attracting industry.[32]

Services provided for business can also have a significant cost impact, but because of the diversity of services which may be provided and their ad hoc character, it is difficult to measure their effect on location decisions. Examples include extending sewer and water facilities to a new industrial location, constructing railroads and highways, and providing free or subsidized technical training for prospective employees.[33] Some cities also lease property to companies on favorable terms.

Thus, taxes are only one of several tools which have been used in a attempt to attract business.[34] Likewise, property taxes are only one of a number of taxes employed to provide incentives. It is understandable for property tax incentives to be prominent because, as explained earlier, the property tax is usually the largest tax paid by business. However, tax incentives can also be provided through the sales tax (exempting new equipment and/or raw materials), and the personal income tax has been viewed as a factor in business location decisions as well.[35] Studies have generally not differentiated among these various taxes in indicting tax incentives as ineffective.

Conclusions

Tax and other incentives to influence business location have proliferated in the 1970s. The Sun Belt-Snow Belt competition to attract industry has intensified, so this subject has become increasingly important. But some major facts and questions are often neglected:

> Whether the level of employment in a community expands or contracts depends much more on its experience with firms which are already located in it than on attraction of new industry.[36] Focusing on tax incentives for new businesses represents a mistaken priority.

> The source of revenue to replace property taxes is crucial. For example, it is not sufficient to criticize the personal property tax as a bad tax. The distributional consequences of its elimination must also be analyzed, and they will depend on the source of replacement revenue. While the ramifications are rather complicated, the owners of businesses will often benefit when the personal property tax is eliminated.[37]

> What exactly is "business climate"? Many pay lip service to the concept, but it remains slippery. Until it is better understood, property tax incentives for business will remain controversial.

In many places the tax treatment of business suffers from a serious case of schizophrenia, providing relief on one hand and taking it away with the other. But usually not everything evens out in the end, so that taxes on some businesses are too high and on others too low. The resulting morass promotes neither efficiency nor equity. The taxation of business badly needs to be made more rational, and the benefits of tax incentives must be weighted against their costs. When this is done, most incentives will probably appear to be undesirable public policies.

Notes

1. This section draws heavily from Advisory Committee on Intergovernmental Relations, *Significant Features of Fiscal Federalism,* 1978-79 ed. (Washington, D.C.: 1979), table 31.

2. Property taxes represented $21.3 billion of the $62.0 billion of state-local taxes with an initial impact on business in 1977. Other business taxes were the sales and gross receipts tax, $15.1 billion; corporation income tax, $9.9 billion; unemployment tax, $8.6 billion; severance tax, $2.2 billion; and licenses and other taxes, $5.1 billion.

3. Commercial and industrial real property constituted 24.2 percent of the gross value of assessed realty in 1976, down from 27.7 percent in 1956. The entire drop was due to industrial rather than commercial property. U.S. Census Bureau, *1977 Census of Government* (Washington, D.C., 1978) vol. 2: *Taxable Property Values and Assessment/Sales Price Ratios,* p. 6.

4. This section is largely based on the discussion in Gary C. Cornia, William A. Testa, and Frederick D. Stocker, *State-Local Fiscal Incentives and Economic Development* (Columbus, Ohio: Academy for Contemporary Problems, 1978).

5. Paul E. Alyea, "Property-Tax Inducements to Attract Industry," in *Property Taxation USA*, ed. Richard W. Lindholm (Madison: University of Wisconsin Press, 1969), pp. 140-141. For a more extensive analysis, see Sandra Kanter, "A History of State Business Subsidies," *Proceedings of the Seventeenth Annual Conference on Taxation: 1977* (Columbus, Ohio: National Tax Association—Tax Institute of America, 1978), pp. 147-155.

6. Cornia, Testa, and Stocker, *State-Local Fiscal Incentives,* pp. 3-4; Conway Publications, Inc., *Industrial Development* 14, no. 1 (January-February 1979); International Association of Assessing Officers, *Assessment Practices in the United States* (Chicago, 1978), p. 293. Iowa's exemption program, enacted in 1979, is also counted in the text.

7. These costs may be partially offset by an increase in school aid from the state because the formula for distributing aid usually includes assessed property value. See chapter 5 for a further discussion of this point.

8. The 1977 Census of Governments reports figures on the composition of the personal property tax base for eighteen states in which commercial-industrial property constituted 69.5 percent of assessed personal property values. These figures may be misleading because utility property is not included with commercial-industrial property. In Michigan, one of the states not included in the eighteen shown, commercial-industrial property was 67.6 percent of the total and utility property was 31.9 percent. U.S. Census Bureau, *1977 Census of Governments,* vol. 2, p. 7.

9. U.S. Census Bureau, *1977 Census of Governments,* vol. 2, pp. 7-9; Steven J. Zellmer and Calvin A. Kent, "Trends in the Taxation of Personal Property," *State Government,* Winter 1979, p. 15. The fifteen states not exempting commercial-industrial property at all are Arkansas, Colorado, Georgia, Indiana, Louisiana, Massachusetts, Mississippi, Missouri, Montana, North Carolina, Ohio, Oklahoma, Texas, Virginia, and West Virginia. This list is based on a combination of the Zellmer-Kent and Census Bureau surveys.

10. Examples are Iowa, Washington, California, and Michigan. See chapter 12.

11. Harvey E. Brazer, "The Value of Industrial Property as a Subject of Taxation," *Canadian Public Administration* 14 (June 1961):137-141.

12. Robert Vaughan, *The Urban Impacts of Federal Policies,* vol. 2: *Economic Development* (Santa Monica, Calif.: The Rand Corporation, 1977), p. 72 and sources cited therein; Werner Z. Hirsch, "Local Impact of Industrialization on Local Schools," *Review of Economics and Statistics* 46 (May 1964):196; William H. Oakland, "Local Taxes and Intraurban Industrial Location: A Survey" in *Metropolitan Financing and Growth Management Policies,* ed. George E. Break (Madison: University of Wisconsin Press, 1978), pp. 24-28. Douglas E. Booth, "The Differential Impact of Manufacturing and Mercantile Activity on Local Government Expenditures and Revenues," *National Tax Journal* 31 (March 1978):33-43, found that manufacturing activity has a beneficial and mercantile activity a harmful fiscal impact. Despite the fact that a business itself may pay more in taxes than the costs which it imposes for services that it directly uses, communities do not necessarily enjoy a fiscal advantage when the secondary impacts of industrialization are taken into account, such as the costs of schooling for the children of employees.

13. Charles E. McLure, "The Interstate Exporting of State and Local Taxes: Estimates for 1962," *National Tax Journal* 20 (March 1967):65. Some of the exporting was due to federal deductibility.

14. Dick Netzer, "Property Tax Reform and Public Policy Reality," in *Property Taxation, Land Use, and Public Policy,* ed. Arthur D. Lynn (Madison: University of Wisconsin Press, 1976), p. 227.

15. See, for example, various issues of the Ralph Nader newspaper, *People and Taxes.*

16. The analysis of Jon Sonstelie of a proposed classified property tax for Washington, D.C., came to this conclusion. See "The Classified Property Tax," in *Technical Aspects of the District's Tax System* (Studies and Papers prepared for the District of Columbia Tax Revision Commission, 1978), pp. 233-260.

17. In a simplified general equilibrium model, the portion of the tax shifted to consumers is related directly to the differential between the national average property tax rate and the local tax rate. In a partial equilibrium framework, the greater the elasticity of supply and the smaller the elasticity of demand, the higher the proportion of the tax shifted to consumers. If labor is imperfectly

mobile, it may also bear some of the tax. The portion of the tax on land is borne by the landowner unless the supply of land is less than perfectly inelastic.

18. Brazer, "Industrial Property," pp. 146-7; Thomas F. Pogue and Larry G. Sgontz, "Value-Added vs. Property Taxation of Business: Effects on Industrial Location," *Land Economics* 47 (1971):150-157.

19. Statistics discussed here refer to sales-weighted assessment ratios, that is, ratios which weight sales according to how significant each type and value class of property is in the total tax base. The Census Bureau also reports unweighted median assessment ratios, which show less discrimination against business property than do the weighted ratios. For example, the median assessment ratio for commercial-industrial property nation wide was 34.6 compared to a ratio for all types of property of 31.3, an 11 percent disparity in contrast to the 15 percent disparity in the weighted ratios.

20. Since farm property usually has a considerably lower assessment ratio than other types, it might be proper to compare the treatment of commercial-industrial property only to nonfarm property. Where farm property is a large proportion of the tax base and is treated much more favorably than residential property, such a comparison would yield considerably different results from those discussed in the text. However, these conditions do not often exist, so the comparison between commercial-industrial and single-family residential assessment ratios produces results similar to those reported. Single-family homes are usually assessed at a higher rate than the average of all types of property but at a lower rate than businesses. Arkansas and Kentucky are the only states in which the assessment ratio for homes was higher than for commercial-industrial property while the all-types ratio was lower than for commercial-industrial property.

21. One state—West Virginia—had a large disparity between the treatment of business and other property, but its system of classification calls for discrimination in tax rates rather than assessment ratios. In addition, three states with classified property taxes are not included in the Census Bureau report because of the small number of sales of commercial-industrial property, and several states adopted classification after 1976. No state with classification for which data were available failed to have a large difference in assessment ratios between commercial-industrial property and other types.

22. Approximately 21 percent of the value of locally assessed taxable real property in 1976 had a market value of $750,000 or more, which was more than twice the amount of commercial-industrial property with a lower value. U.S. Census Bureau, *1977 Census of Governments*, vol. 2, pp. 59-60.

23. Daniel M. Holland and Oliver Oldman, "Estimating the Impact of Full Value Assessment on Taxes and Value of Real Estate in Boston," in *Metropolitan Financing*, ed. Break, p. 200.

24. Telephone communication with Dr. Gerald Auten, whose comments referred specifically to certain places in Missouri.

25. Unpublished study of Prince George's County, Maryland, by Tom Muller.

26. Cornia, Testa, and Stocker, *State-Local Fiscal Incentives,* discuss some of these issues, pp. 17-19; see also studies cited on p. 13.

27. Bernard L. Weinstein, "Tax Incentives for Growth, " *Society* 14, no. 3 (1977):73-75. Surveys of this literature include John F. Due, "Studies of State and Local Tax Influences on Location of Industry," *National Tax Journal* 14 (June 1961):163-173; Advisory Committee on Intergovernmental Relations, *State-Local Taxation and Industrial Location* (Washington, D.C.: Government Printing Office, 1967); and Cornia, Testa, and Stocker, *State-Local Fiscal Incentives.* Their conclusions are widely accepted, as in Vaughan, *Urban Impacts,* and George A. Reigeluth and Harold Wolman, "The Determinants and Implications of Communities' Changing Competitive Advantages: A Review of the Literature" (Urban Institute Working Paper, January 1979), pp. 50-51. However, Oakland, "A Survey," considers the conclusions of Due and Advisory Committee on Intergovernmental Relations to be "based upon introspection or casual empiricism" (p. 16). He concludes that his search of the literature "has failed to uncover any solid evidence for or against the proposition that intraurban location decisions of business firms are significantly affected by fiscal considerations" (p. 28). He criticizes existing econometric studies for lack of theoretical basis and implausible or weak results. However, his critique covers only the statistical research on this subject and ignores the sizable survey literature which also uncovers no significant effect of taxes on location decisions, so his criticism is probably overdone. One recent study has demonstrated that business taxes affected the rate of expansion of various industries in New York City, but it dealt with nonproperty taxes. See Ronald E. Griesen et al., "The Effect of Business Taxation on the Location of Industry," *Journal of Urban Economics* 4 (1977):170-185.

28. Tax differentials can be looked at in two ways. Cornia, Testa, and Stocker point out that variations in taxes are much smaller than variations in labor, construction, and energy costs (*State-Local Fiscal Incentives,* pp. 7-8). However, Oakland emphasizes that tax differentials are substantial in comparison with profits ("A Survey," p. 16).

29. Due, "State and Local Tax Influences," pp. 168-71; Roger W. Schmenner, *The Manufacturing Location Decision: Evidence from Cincinnati and New England* (Cambridge, Mass.: Harvard Business School, 1978), p. 5-32.

30. Joint Economic Committee, Congress of the United States, "Central City Businesses: Plans and Problems," (January 1979).

31. The majority view that within-region tax differences do affect location decisions to some degree is exemplified by Advisory Committee on Intergovernmental Relations. However, Schmenner found taxes to be of little, if any, importance within the two regions which he studies. Only one-quarter to one-third of firms which moved actually relocated in jurisdictions with lower tax rates from those which they abandoned (p. 5-27).

32. Daryl Hellman et al., *State Financial Incentives to Industry* (Lexington, Mass.: D.C. Heath, 1976).

33. Cornia, Testa, and Stocker, *State-Local Fiscal Incentives,* pp. 5-6. Outstanding recent examples are the packages developed by Pennsylvania and Ohio to attract Volkswagen and Honda plants.

34. See *Industrial Development,* January-February 1979, for a survey of more than fifty incentives available in various states.

35. Thomas Muller, "Central City Business Retention: Jobs, Taxes, and Investment Trends" (Paper presented at the Department of Commerce Round-table, February 22, 1978).

36. See, e.g., Schmenner, *The Manufacturing Location Decision,* and David Birch, *The Job Generation Process* (Cambridge, Mass.: M.I.T. Program on Neighborhood and Regional Change, 1979).

37. Netzer, *Economics of the Property Tax,* (Washington, D.C.: Brookings Institution, 1966), concludes that substituting the real for the personal property tax is likely to produce this result (pp. 155-163). If state general revenue is used as a replacement, the shift of the tax burden away from business is likely to be even greater.

7 Classification

A classified property tax is one in which different classes of property are taxed at different rates. Like nearly all types of property tax relief, its use increased in the 1970s, but it is still one of the less often employed methods of alleviating property tax burdens. Classification does not affect the total volume of property tax to be paid, but rather shifts the tax from some property to other property.

Description

The definition of classification is somewhat slippery. In a sense, most states have a classified property tax in that some kinds of personal property (including particularly household goods and intangibles like stocks and bonds) are taxed at lower rates than other property, if they are taxed at all. This is usually taken for granted now, so a property tax is regarded as classified only if real property is treated unevenly. Even this statement is misleading, since preferential assessment of farmland and exemptions or credits for homeowners and others are not considered to constitute classification. Moreover, as a result of nonuniform assessment practices, many states have had de facto classification of property in violation of laws requiring uniform treatment of all property.

Thus, Sonstelie, whose analysis of classification is the best recent treatment of it, was oversimplifying when he wrote that

> ... the distinguishing characteristic of the classified property tax is that the effective tax rate (the tax on a property as a percentage of its market value) is different for different classes of property. It therefore stands in stark contrast to the more common, uniform property tax in which the effective rate is the same for all taxable property.[1]

In fact, classification's distinguishing characteristic is not lack of uniformity per se, but rather that nonuniformity is enshrined in law either by assessing property in different classes at varying proportions of market value (that is, unequal assessment ratios) or by applying nonuniform tax rates to different classes of property.

West Virginia and the District of Columbia are the only places to specify different tax rates; all other states classify property through uneven assessment ratios. Iowa recently created a new wrinkle by limiting the annual statewide increase in assessments for farms and homes but not other classes of property, and Oregon also limits assessment increases in a manner which favors homes.

States differ greatly in how many separate classes of property they differentiate. At one extreme are those which distinguish only two classes; at the other is a state where there are over twenty classes. Homes and farms generally receive the most favored treatment under classification. If there is any differentiation among business, utilities tend to be treated more harshly.[2]

History, Current Extent of Use, and Costs

Classification of real property is currently in effect in fourteen states and the District of Columbia. This tally includes Iowa and Oregon, with their limits on assessment increases, and Illinois and Connecticut, where classification is used only in Cook County (which contains Chicago) and Hartford, respectively.

One of the first states to classify was Minnesota, which began with four categories of property in 1913. The number of classes in that state has increased gradually and at last count was over twenty. This experience led Rolland Hatfield, former commissioner of the Minnesota Department of Taxation, to write:

> . . . there is no logical stopping place once you start a classification of property. . . . The reason for this is that once you have classifications of property, experience has shown that it is extremely easy to add another class. This is because if the proposed new class is to be assessed at a lower fraction than the average of classes previously assessed, then all the people who will gain from that will appear in the legislature and will fill the halls to overflowing. If the legislation passes and you reduce the tax base, you increase everybody else's taxes, but they are not aware of it and they do not appear in opposition. . . Therefore, as you change the various classes in the classification system you bounce the little white ball of taxes around so that it shifts constantly every time you make a change.[3]

Sonstelie summarizes this argument as follows: ". . . the decision to classify may be the first step on a slippery slope."[4]

In 1934 three states (Minnesota, Montana, and West Virginia) classified, but there was little further interest in classification until the 1960s. Recent adoptions include Hawaii, 1961; Arizona, 1968; Alabama, 1972; Cook County, Illinois, 1973; Tennessee, 1973; South Carolina, 1976; Louisiana, Iowa, District of Columbia, Hartford, Connecticut, all 1978; and Massachusetts and Oregon, 1979.[5]

Classification does not entail a budget outlay for tax relief, but it does involve three kinds of costs. First, there are administrative costs because of the increased complexity of the property tax. In the District of Columbia, these costs were estimated at $150,000 to $253,000.[6]

Classification also involves costs through redistribution of tax burdens, since nonfavored classes of property must pay higher taxes as others pay less. These extra taxes usually represent substantial percentage increases in tax liability since the highest assessment ratio or tax rate is generally at least twice as high as that on the most favored types of property.

Finally, there may be resource misallocation costs because classification is not neutral.

Design Issues

The major design issues are how many classes to identify, the extent of difference in treatment of each class of property, how to handle mixed-use properties, whether to differentiate according to assessment ratio or tax rate, and whether to make the classification system static or dynamic.

Before these issues can be discussed, it is necessary to distinguish between two reasons for adopting classification. Some early proponents advocated classification as a means of bringing the property tax into greater accord with the principle of ability to pay. But, in fact, most states originally adopted classification as a means of legalizing the existing discriminatory pattern of assessment under the threat of a court order to follow the law requiring equal treatment of all classes of property.

Another consideration is the degree to which the tax system is neutral—how much it interferes with efficiency in the allocation of resources. Although it is relevant to the design of a classified property tax, discussion of neutrality is deferred to the next section.

Number of Classes and Extent of Differing Treatment

In the interest of keeping the tax system as uncomplicated as possible, it is desirable that the number of classes be held down. Simplicity not only reduces administrative costs but also tends to enhance public understanding.

If the purpose of classification is to legalize the existing unequal treatment of properties, the goal of simplicity must be balanced against the goal of reflecting the existing pattern of assessments. To achieve the latter goal may require a complex system.

Mixed-Use Property

A problem related to classification is how property should be treated whose use is near the borderline between two distinct classes, for example, a home located above a store. When the District of Columbia adopted classification, homes with rented apartments were treated like commercial property and subject to a higher tax rate than normal homes, which was widely criticized as unfair. Resolving these problems inevitably confronts sticky equity issues and complicates the assessment process.

Differing Assessment Ratios or
Tax Rates

One advantage of classifying by setting unequal assessment ratios is that it settles the classification issue so that it does not have to be addressed each year. On the other hand, the District of Columbia sets unequal nominal tax rates, which require reconsideration annually. This system heightens uncertainty about future policies, which tends to discourage investments of all kinds. A way of classifying by tax rates while avoiding uncertainty about relative tax rates is to specify a definite relationship between rates on each type of property (for example, commercial 20 percent higher than residential) and permit the whole structure of rates to rise or fall in parallel fashion each year. This system, which is used in West Virginia, enables assessments to be based on full market value. According to ACIR, full-value assessment "reduces the possibility of sloppy, politically oriented, or corrupt assessments"[7] because assessments can be directly compared with market values. Classification by setting unequal tax rates rather than unequal assessment ratios is also easier for citizens to understand.

Static or Dynamic Systems

Until 1978 all existing systems of classification were static in that they set unequal assessment ratios or nominal tax rates which did not change from one year to the next. A major reason for these laws in many cases was to perpetuate the existing division of relative tax burdens among each class of property—to avoid court-ordered reassessment which would have significantly redistributed those burdens. Traditional classification does not concern itself with shifts in taxes that occur because of differences in the rate of increase of assessments for different types of property when those differences reflect changes in underlying market values.

   Iowa, Oregon, and Hartford, Connecticut, have taken classification one step further by attempting to hold constant the relation of residential to certain other assessments. The Iowa law which took effect in 1978 ensures that total statewide home and farm assessments rise at the same percentage rate from year to year. Even this law does not ensure that relative taxes will remain unaffected because tax rates may vary; also, there is no provision for holding constant the share of taxes levied against nonresidential nonfarm property. Oregon's 1979 law limits all assessment increases for two broad categories of property—homes and all other property. Although the limit is the same for both, it benefits homes because their market value is rising faster. In Hartford, Connecticut, the proportion of taxes paid by residential property containing one to three dwelling units was held constant for two years beginning in 1978.

Assessment limits in California and Idaho are not considered to be classification systems because differences in the treatment of various classes of property resulting from the limits were unintended, at least by most of the citizens who voted for the tax rate and assessment limits in 1978. In fact, such assessment limits work to the disadvantage of homeowners, as explained in chapter 12.

Evaluation

Capitalization of the property tax must be considered in relation to all property tax relief policies, but it is particularly relevant to classification. If discriminatory assessment practices are long-standing, they will probably be reflected in property values. Owners who acquired their property after the practices were established are not affected by them, since preferential treatment has raised the property's value and unfavorable treatment has lowered it. To eliminate the discrimination in such cases will not necessarily improve the equity of the tax system.

To take the most recent case as an example, Massachusetts' assessment system for many years overassessed old business property and underassessed homes. If all property had been reassessed at a uniform rate, as ordered by a state court, it is estimated that there would have been a $265 million shift of taxes from business to residential property.[8] Changes in property values would have been much greater. To avoid these developments, classification was adopted in 1979.

The correct perspective from which to consider classification depends on the conditions under which it is introduced. If it is initiated in order to legalize an existing system of discriminatory assessment which would otherwise be changed to a uniform system, it avoids large shifts of tax burdens and property values. On the other hand, if it is begun when property has previously been treated uniformly, it will cause a shift of tax burdens, which will change property values.

States with a history of illegal discriminatory assessment practices face a devilish dilemma when a court orders that property must be treated uniformly. If they move toward uniformity, windfall capital gains and losses result. Nevertheless, this course was followed in such places as California and the District of Columbia in the late 1960s and early 1970s.[9] On the other hand, if they legalize the discrimination by adopting classification, they complicate their tax system and abandon the possibility of basing assessments on the full market value of property, which many observers believe is important if property tax fairness is to be achieved.

Three issues are related to this dilemma. First, which types of property are usually overassessed and underassessed when de facto discrimination exists? Although the answer differs from one state to another, it appears that often homes and farms are assessed lower than other types of property.[10] Since farms are now usually taken care of by assessing them on the basis of use value, homeowners may be the losers if uniformity of assessments is imposed.

Second, how long has the discriminatory system of assessments been in effect? If it is of recent origin, then a large proportion of current property owners have felt the effects of capitalizing the discrimination themselves. Therefore, it would not be unfair to reverse their recent capital gains or losses. However, if the discrimination is of longer standing, many of the current owners presumably acquired the property after the discrimination was already reflected in property values, so eliminating the discrimination could not be viewed with the same equanimity.[11]

Third, is it true that classification inevitably becomes increasingly complex, with ever more classes of property being differentiated? This view was noted above, but is classification always such a "slippery slope"? The argument definitely applies in Minnesota and Montana, but some other states have not added additional categories after first enacting classification.[12] This issue is important because the "slippery slope" argument is sometimes used against classification by those who might find it acceptable if it were kept simple.[13]

In evaluating classification, one must consider both the distributional consequences and the effects on economic activity. A recent study of these issues in Washington, D.C., is of interest, although the Washington economy is different from that in most states because an unusually high proportion of the property tax may be exported. The study concluded that adopting a two-part classification, with residential property being taxed at a lower rate than commercial property, would make the tax system for Washington residents more progressive and would result in exporting a substantial proportion of the tax burden to nonresident consumers and property owners.[14] Classification would tend to stimulate housing construction at the expense of commercial activity, perhaps resulting in a deadweight loss from resource misallocation.[15] However, the effect of classification on neutrality cannot be unambiguously determined a priori. The magnitude of these distributional and allocational effects depends on supply and demand conditions.[16]

Classification must be compared to other methods of providing relief such as credits or exemptions.

1. Classification is a crude means of providing relief. It hides the burden of taxation by placing more of it on business, which then shifts at least some of it to consumers. This is particularly ludicrous when utilities are singled out for especially high tax rates, even though they possess a virtually automatic means of passing these taxes on to consumers in the form of higher utility rates.

2. Credits or exemptions can be made more progressive than classification. Classification's direct benefits are proportional to the value of property, while credits can be fashioned to target benefits in many other ways, such as on the basis of income and residency.

3. The benefits and costs of credits are much more obvious and easy to calculate, while those of classification are indirect and uncertain.

4. Credits do not complicate the assessment system, as classification by means of unequal assessment ratios does. Credits create their own complications, but it is preferable to avoid tampering with full-value assessments.

5. The cost of credits is usually financed by state taxes while the cost of classification impacts on local property.

On the basis of these differences, it appears that classification is not a wise means of providing property tax relief when starting from a situation of assessment uniformity. It is more appropriate when a state wishes to avoid windfall capital gains and losses resulting from imposition of uniformity on a discriminatory assessment system. But even in that situation serious consideration should be given to other means of cushioning the shifts of tax burdens which the end of discrimination would bring. If assessments are not too far from uniformity, classification can be avoided and credits can be used to offset tax increases; but if assessments deviate massively from uniformity, the balance may tilt in favor of classification. The choice between classification and credits involves judgments about the desirable degree of progressivity of tax burdens and of state financing of tax relief.

This entire discussion has been concerned with the static variety of classification which sets assessment ratios and tax rates. Iowa's and Oregon's system of holding constant the proportion of residential (and, in Iowa, farm) property by limiting changes of assessments raises some of the same questions but also encounters new ones. Like traditional classification, it sets different assessment ratios for favored types of property, but unlike customary classification it varies those ratios each year. Credits or exemptions could accomplish similar results, but they would not be automatic as the assessment limits are; this makes the assessment limits politically attractive because they avoid divisive annual battles about how to provide relief.

The major new question raised by Iowa-style assessment limits is, Why should the relationship between different kinds of property be frozen at its base-year level? If one kind of property rises much faster in value than other kinds, should not the share of the total tax bill levied against it become greater? But Iowa-style dynamic classification locks in the ratio of farm to home valuation, and Oregon's fixes the ratio of home valuations to all others.[17]

Conclusions

Classification is easy to adopt but complex for the assessor to administer and for the average citizen to understand. Except as a means of legalizing extremely uneven assessments which face court-ordered equalization, it should not be adopted.

Notes

1. Jon Sonstelie, "The Classified Property Tax," *Technical Aspects of the District's Tax System: Studies and Papers Prepared for the District of Columbia's Tax Revision Commission* (Submitted to the Committee on the District of Columbia of the U.S. House of Representatives, December 1, 1978), p. 233.

2. Alabama, Arizona, and Tennessee assess utilities at a higher rate than most other business property. U.S. Census Bureau, *1977 Census of Governments,* (Washington, D.C., 1978) vol. 2: *Taxable Property Values and Assessment/Sales Price Ratios,* pp. 281-283.

3. Rolland F. Hatfield, "Minnesota's Experience with Classification," in *The Property Tax: Problems and Potentials* (Princeton, N.J.: Tax Institute of America, 1967), p. 242. Reprinted with permission.

4. Sonstelie, "The Classified Property Tax," p. 237.

5. Dates indicate when classification was implemented or passed according to the International Association of Assessing Officers, "Classified Property Tax Systems in the U.S.," February 1977; see also Census Bureau, *Taxable Property Values*, pp. 281-282; Advisory Commission on Intergovernmental Relations, *The Property Tax in a Changing Environment* (Washington, D.C., 1974); Advisory Commission on Intergovernmental Relations, *The Role of the States in Strengthening the Property Tax* (Washington, D.C., 1963), vol. 2.

7. Advisory Commission on Intergovernmental Relations, *Changing Environment,* p. 6; Sonstelie, "The Classified Property Tax," p. 253. Information on West Virginia was provided by Fred Sapp.

8. Raymond G. Torto, "Estimating the Impact of Taxation by 100 Percent Valuation and by Classification in Massachusetts" (Mimeographed, 1978).

9. Frank Levy and Paul Zamolo, "The Preconditions of Proposition 13," in *Fiscal Choices,* ed. George E. Peterson (Washington, D.C.: The Urban Institute, 1979); Sonstelie, "The Classified Property Tax," p. 237.

10. See chapter 6 for a discussion of evidence on this issue. John Shannon, "The Property Tax: Reform or Relief?" in *Property Tax Reform,* ed. George E. Peterson (Washington: The Urban Institute, 1973), pp. 28-32; Henry J. Aaron, *Who Pays the Property Tax?* (Washington, D.C.: The Brookings Institution, 1975), pp. 59-62; Thomas G. Lyons, "The Classification Issue in Illinois," and W.R. Snodgrass, "The Classification Issue in Tennessee," in *The Property Tax: Problems and Potentials,* pp. 216-220 and 221-238, respectively.

11. Aaron, *Who Pays?* pp. 64-67. Even when assessment ratio studies find evidence of discrimination among classes of property, capitalization will not take place if property is reassessed at the proper ratio when it is sold. The implications of such a "welcome, stranger" system of assessing property were pointed out to me by Jerry Auten.

12. West Virginia, one of the earliest classification states, has not added new classes, nor have Alabama and Tennessee, since they classified their property in 1972 and 1973. However, Arizona doubled its classes from four to eight between 1968 and 1979, and Washington, D.C., added a third class in the second year in which it classified.

13. Sonstelie, "The Classified Property Tax," p. 254.

14. In personal correspondence Jon Sonstelie indicated that he does not believe that the results of his Washington study apply generally in jurisdictions with different types of tax bases (letter dated January 29, 1979).

15. The District of Columbia's Tax Revision Commission concluded that it is not possible to state unequivocally whether a classified or uniform property tax minimizes the distortions of private economic decisions. If the demand for commercial real estate is less sensitive to tax-induced price changes than the demand for residential real estate, neutrality favors substituting classification for an equal-yield increase in the uniform property. tax. See District of Columbia Tax Revision Commission, *Financing an Urban Government* (Washington, D.C., 1978), p. 72.

16. Sonstelie, "The Classified Property Tax," pp. 256-260.

17. The ratio of home to other assessed values could still change because of new construction of homes or other buildings. If there is more construction of homes, residential assessments would tend to increase relative to other assessments.

8 Limitations on Local Spending and Taxes

During the 1970s many states adopted new types of limits on local government expenditures or revenues. The Proposition 13 explosion in 1978 was only the most extreme of these controls.

Controls tend to be either very crude or very complex; many manage to combine both undesirable attributes. Controls must be viewed in at least three ways: as a tax measure, as a spending device, and as a challenge to traditional concepts of representative democracy.

Description

"If it moves, control it" might be the philosophy which has inspired state policymakers. Nearly everything which could be limited has been, in one state or another.

The most common type of *limit* is *on tax rates* (often referred to as millage limits). Limits on tax rates severely restrict property tax revenue when they cannot be avoided, but often they are set so high that they are irrelevant for many governments. They can be very restrictive when assessments are growing slowly but exert no restraining effect when assessments rise rapidly, as they often have in the middle and late 1970s.

Limits may be either general, applying to all taxing units, or specific, covering only particular types of local governments. As a rule, taxes to finance certain kinds of spending, such as debt service and insurance premiums, are exempt even from general limits. In some states, limitations differ depending on population.

Although tax rate limits have generally taken the form of ceilings which apply uniformly to broad categories of governments, in some recent cases limitations have frozen tax rates at their level at the time when the freeze was enacted. In this case, the limit could be substantially lower for some local governments than for others with similar functions

A more certain restraint on taxes can be provided by a *limit on property tax revenue* (sometimes referred to as a levy limit). Such controls usually limit the increase in revenue from one year to the next, either by some specified percentage mentioned in a law or else according to the rate of increase of some measure such as inflation or income. These revenue limits also generally allow property taxes for some government functions to be free of limits.

A third control, used particularly for school districts, is a *limit on expenditures.* When applied to schools, this device usually takes the form of a limit on the increase in expenditure per pupil. It is potentially very restrictive because it may permit fewer "escape routes" than limits on rates or levies.

The final control is a *limit on assessment increases.* By itself, such a limit would not effectively restrict tax increases because the tax rate could be raised to yield any desired amount of revenue. However, in conjunction with tax rate limits, assessment controls can effectively put a lid on local property tax revenues. Limits on assessment increases may be for all types of property or just certain classes; if the assessments on particular kinds of property are limited, this policy is akin to classification.

Some observers consider *full-disclosure laws* to be an additional category of controls. These laws do not really limit taxing power, but they do require that any increases budgeted for property tax revenue be given special publicity and that a special public hearing on the budget be held. Such laws guard against officials claiming to have held down taxes when revenue increases because of higher assessments; although these laws may promote greater public understanding of the true tax situation, they represent a very mild form of control at most.

History, Extent of Use, and Costs

Property tax rate limits have existed for more than a century,[1] having first been used by Rhode Island in 1870. Like homestead exemptions, their use expanded considerably during the Great Depression, but their spread halted after the 1930s.[2] As table 8-1 indicates, thirty states have tax rate limits for all three types of local government—cities, counties, and school districts. Eight states have limits for some of but not all these levels, and thirteen states have no rate limits.

Limits on property tax revenue increases are the next most popular device, being used in twenty-one states for cities and/or counties and thirteen states for school districts. All but four of these limitations were established in the 1970s.[3] As would be expected, states with a heavy reliance on the property tax at the beginning of the decade and states in which local expenditures rose relatively rapidly in the period 1967-1971 were more likely to impose controls.[4]

In addition, full disclosure provisions are in force in six states and the District of Columbia. Once again, they all date from the 1970s.

Eight states apply controls to school district spending, but New Jersey and Arizona are the only states to directly limit expenditures of cities and counties. One reason for this pattern is that school spending can easily be tied to annual changes in enrollment, while similar data on population served are seldom available for cities and counties. In addition, most expenditure controls on schools were instituted in the 1970s as part of packages which included major increases in state aid to school districts. Other types of local government seldom receive such large infusions of state aid at one time.

At least six states limit assessment increases—Maryland, Oregon, Idaho, Colorado, Iowa, and California.

Altogether, forty-three states apply controls to at least some of their local governments. In view of New England's legendary tradition of local independence, it is not surprising that four of the seven exceptions are in that region[5] (Connecticut, Rhode Island, Vermont, and New Hampshire). The other states with no controls are Tennessee, Maryland, and Hawaii, but the latter two follow full disclosure procedures.

Many states impose more than one type of control on certain governments, so that if one limit is ineffective, another may not be. Nineteen states use such multiple limits.

One reason that controls are popular is that they do not necessarily involve a budgetary cost to state government. However, if the limits are very severe, the state is likely to pick up the cost of some of the services which the controls would otherwise eliminate.

Where does Proposition 13 fit in? It involves two kinds of controls: a tax rate limit which is set far below the prevailing average level of rates and a limit on assessment increases. Its uniqueness lies not in its structure but in the great disparity between the tax revenue which it permits local governments to have in the future and that which they had in the past.

Design Issues[6]

Designers of controls face a dilemma. On one hand, it is desirable to make controls flexible enough so that they do not choke off vital government services. On the other hand, if they are to be effective, it is important to make them as "airtight" as possible. Excessively leaky controls may be worse than no controls at all—they limit nothing and waste resources in their administration.

The two principal issues in designing controls are deciding whether to limit tax rates, tax levies, or spending, and how much to limit them. The two questions are related. Two loose limits of different types (for example, one on tax rates and the other on tax levies) have much more in common than a tight limit and a loose limit of the same kind.

Tax Rate Limits

Three types of tax rate limits can be distinguished—loose uniform limits, tight uniform limits, and a tax rate freeze. All will be completely ineffective if local officials are free to change assessment ratios at will. Tax rate limits are

Table 8-1
State Limitations on Local Government Power to Raise Property Tax Revenue

States	No Limitations	Full Disclosure of Effect of Assessment Increases on Property Tax Rate[a]	Property Tax Rate Limitation[b]	Property Tax Levy Limitation[c] (Levy= Rate × Tax Base)	Expenditure Limitation	Assessment Limitation
Alabama			CMS	C		
Alaska			MS	M		
Arizona			M	CM	CMS	
Arkansas			CMS	CM		
California			CMS	CM	S	X
Colorado				CM	S	X
Connecticut	M			C		
Delaware	MS		C			
District of Columbia		M		C		
Florida		CMS	CMS			
Georgia			CMS			
Hawaii	C					
Idaho		C	CMS			X
Illinois			CMS			
Indiana			CMS	CMS		
Iowa			CMS		S	X
Kansas			CMS	CMS	S	
Kentucky			CMS	CMS		
Louisiana			CMS	CMS		
Maine	CM		S			

State						
Maryland	CM	CM		CMS		X
Massachusetts			CMS	CMS		
Michigan			MS	CMS		
Minnesota			CMS			
Mississippi			CMS			
Missouri		CM	CMS			
Montana			CMS		S	
Nebraska			CMS		S	
Nevada			CMS	CM		
New Hampshire	M					
New Jersey			CMS	CMS		
New Mexico			CMS			
New York			CM			
North Carolina					CMS	
North Dakota			CMS			
Ohio			CMS			
Oklahoma			CMS	CMS		
Oregon				CMS		
Pennsylvania			CMS			
Rhode Island	M					X
South Carolina			S	CMS		
South Dakota			CMS			
Tennessee		CMS	CMS			
Texas	CM		CMS	CMS		
Utah						
Vermont	M	CM				
Virginia			S			

Washington	CMS	CMS
West Virginia	CMS	CMS
Wisconsin	CMS	CM
Wyoming		S

Source: Advisory Commission on Intergovernmental Relations, *State Limitations on Local Taxes and Expenditures* (Washington, D.C., 1977), pp. 16-17; Kent McGuire et al., "School Finance at a Fourth Glance," Poster (Denver: Education Commission of the States, 1979); William H. Wilken and John J. Callahan, "State Limitations on Local Taxes and Spending: A Paper Tiger?" Unpublished paper for the National Conference of State Legislatures (Washington, D.C., 1978); Education Commission of the States, *School District Expenditure and Tax Controls* (Denver, 1978); International Association of Assessing Officers, *Property Tax Limits* (Chicago, 1978).

aUnder a full disclosure procedure, a property tax rate is established that will provide a levy equal to the previous year's when applied to some percentage of the current year's tax base. In order to increase the levy above the amount derived by using the established rate, the local governing board must advertise its intent to set a higher rate, hold public hearings, and then approve the higher rate by vote of the board.

bProperty tax rate limitation sets a maximum rate that may be applied against the assessed value of property.

cLevy limitation places a maximum on the amount of revenue that can be raised by the property tax (for example, 106 percent of the prior year levy).

C = Counties
M = Municipalities

S = School districts (in some states school districts have no independent taxing authority or depend on county government for taxes, in which case school districts are affected by the limits on the independent general government) appropriate only in those states where assessments are equalized so that each dollar of assessed value represents roughly the same amount of market value throughout the state (or, alternatively, where changes in assessments are limited by the state).

To illustrate the differences among the three types of rate limits, suppose that there are four cities, with property tax rates of 3, 2 1/2, 1 1/2, and 1/2 percent. An extremely loose uniform limit might set a ceiling of 4 percent; it would have no practical effect, but some states have such useless limits. A somewhat less liberal limit, but still a loose one, might be set at 3 percent. It would restrict only the city with the highest tax rate, and even its tax revenue could increase rapidly if assessments rose sharply. One kind of tight uniform limit would set a maximum rate of 3/4 percent which could be exceeded with voter approval. Such limits, affecting the great majority of local governments, have been in effect in Ohio and Oregon for many years. Proposition 13 represents an even tighter limit in that it cannot be exceeded even with voter approval. It corresponds to imposition of a 1 percent limit requiring sudden reduction in tax rates in all jurisdictions with higher rates. Finally, a tax freeze would limit all jurisdictions so that rates could be lowered but not raised.

A relatively loose limit on tax rates serves two purposes, one relative and the other absolute—to reduce tax rate disparities by placing an upper bound on them and to hold down taxes in the places with the highest tax rates. Only the governments with the highest tax rates are affected. Until 1978, this was the usual form of rate limitation.[7]

A tight limit on tax rates such as the 1 percent limit contained in Proposition 13 is radically different in that it affects virtually all governments. Imposed on a system in which prevailing tax rates are much higher than the new ceiling, it slashes tax burdens. Its impact is highly uneven, being much more restrictive (and providing more relief) where tax rates are high initially.

Proposition 13 as voted on also differed from traditional rate limits in that it specified a global tax ceiling, whereas usually each type of local government has its own separate maximum tax rate. Proposition 13 therefore required additional legislation to determine how the revenue from the 1 percent tax was to be divided among cities, counties, school districts, and special districts.

The third form of limit, the tax rate freeze, differs from the two uniform rate limits in that it does not bear down especially hard on the places with the highest tax rates. To the extent that there are valid reasons for these high rates (such as a small tax base or a strong desire among the population for services) this is appropriate. But the freeze also may be capricious in that the tax rates in the base year could be abnormally high or low because of transitory factors.

Although a Proposition 13-type limit on tax rates ensures a one-shot drop in property tax burdens, no rate limit by itself can ensure that property taxes will not rise rapidly if property values are increasing substantially. If that is to be guaranteed, rate limits must be accompanied by some other type of controls.

Property Tax Revenue Limits

This type of control usually takes the form of a limit on the annual increase of property tax revenue. Thus, it is relatively mild in that it does not reduce property taxes absolutely or keep them from rising in the future. Nor does it necessarily reduce government spending. However, depending on how low the maximum increase in revenue is set and other restrictions placed on local government, it may reduce spending in real terms (that is, adjusted for inflation).

Escape Valves

Limits on property tax rates or revenues often do not limit government revenue as much as they supposedly limit the property tax. First, taxes for certain purposes are usually exempted from the limits; examples are debt service, employee pensions, and tort liability.[8] Thus, even without shuffling revenue among budget categories, taxes will rise more than the apparent ceiling if the uncontrolled items experience above-average growth. In addition, budgetmakers can often shift certain spending from the controlled to the uncontrolled categories (one result being a tendency to increase indebtedness).

Another common development is increased reliance on revenue sources other than the property tax. Some states have combined the imposition of controls on localities with new authority to levy local income or sales taxes. More common is increased employment of user charges for refuse collection, libraries, recreation, and other services.

Finally, controls can usually be overridden in some manner, by a referendum of local voters, appeal to a state board, or simply holding an extra public hearing on the budget.

Thus, those who expect controls to hold down the rise in their total payments to local government by the advertised percentage are often disappointed. But this long recitation of ways in which controls may be circumvented should not be taken to mean that they are always ineffective. On the contrary, many of the avoidance mechanisms can be used only to a limited extent, and thus controls can reduce local government activity. Of course, if government services are cut, citizens may wind up paying for private substitutes.

Expenditure Limits

The surest way to reduce the size of government (or to keep it from growing) is to directly limit its expenditures. This type of control overcomes some of (but not all) the avoidance mechanisms discussed in the previous section. In particular, government cannot resort to nonproperty tax revenue to make up for the loss of property tax dollars. However, expenditure limits still face the issue of whether spending for certain purposes will be exempted. If exemptions are not allowed, controls can be even tougher than intended. Relatively uncontrollable costs such as pensions and medical insurance may go up so much as to consume a large share of the permitted increase in spending, leaving little money for wage increases and other increases in costs.[9]

Assessment Limits

By themselves, limits on assessment increases (or, what is equivalent, assessment rollbacks) do not limit local government activity. When they are combined with tax rate limits, they are similar to limits on tax levies: They restrict the property tax revenue which can be raised. There are several important differences between limits on assessments and levies. First, assessment limits may alter the distribution of the tax burden among taxpayers, as explained in chapter 7. In addition, in many states they automatically tend to increase state aid to school districts, which depends on assessed valuation, and thereby reduce property taxes.[10] Finally, the California and Idaho limits provide that when property is sold, its assessment can again reflect market value. This has the unfortunate effect of locking in property owners, that is, discouraging them from buying and selling as often as they otherwise would.

All assessment limits do violence to horizontal equity in that properties of similar value will be taxed differently. They also violate one aspect of vertical equity, since owners of property which is appreciating rapidly are better off than those whose property rises more slowly, other things being equal. However, limits do tend to avoid large year-to-year tax changes.

Final Words about Design Issues

The major issue which has not been discussed thus far is how tight or loose the controls should be. The answer depends in part on whether the objective is to reduce the size of local government, to keep it constant, or simply to ensure that it does not grow too fast. It also depends on what loopholes are permitted and on the amount of new construction taking place. (Revenue from new construction is usually exempted from controls.) Some states set a specific figure, such as 5, 7, or 9 percent, for their limits on revenue or spending growth. Others tie the limit to the rate of inflation or income growth. The problem is that cost increases and shifts in the demand for services may differ considerably from one part of the state to another. While tying the lid to the rate of inflation may sound as though it allows for the maintenance of existing services, it probably does not do so because inflation tends to affect local government budgets more than other parts of the economy.[11]

The level at which a tax rate limit should be set depends on similar considerations. The 1 percent limit in California could be applied in Idaho, where existing rates are lower, with greater ease than in Massachusetts, where rates are much higher. The rate which is feasible also depends on how much state aid can be made available to replace lost property tax revenue. In that respect, Idaho was at a considerable disadvantage relative to California.

Recent Effects of Limitations
on Taxes

There are no reliable statistical studies which measure the property tax relief provided by limitations such as many states enacted during the 1970s. Nevertheless, the restrictive effects of these limitations can be seen in a number of states.

Studies of city and county governments by ACIR and schools by Wilken and Callahan reached similar conclusions: the limitations in effect in the mid-1970s had small effects, if any, on local spending and taxes. The ACIR estimated that limitations reduced per capita spending by 6 to 8 percent but had no effect on local revenue diversification. Wilken and Callahan found no effect on school spending at all, leading them to suggest that limitations are "paper tigers."[12]

These studies are useful in confirming that many limitations are ineffective, but they both failed to differentiate between tight and loose limitations. They separated rate limits from expenditure or levy limits, but they ignored differences between limits which permitted tax increases of 15 percent and others which allowed no increase at all. They also failed to consider for how many years limits had been in effect or to identify states where rate limits could be circumvented by raising assessments.[13]

State-by-state analysis reveals that in some cases limits have substantially reduced property tax burdens compared to what they would have been. These results occurred in states where major increases in state aid took place. Where aid did not increase, limits appear to have had much smaller effects.

Arizona has had a 10 percent limitation on increases in city and county spending since 1921. The state has responded to problems caused by the limit, particularly in rapidly growing areas, by exempting certain parts of the budget. For example, in Mohave County, the fastest growing in the state, more than 70 percent of the budget is in exempt categories. The limitation has apparently not been very effective, since the level of Arizona's property tax is relatively high.[14]

California illustrates the difference between effective and ineffective limits. The controls implemented in 1973 did little to restrain local revenues because they offered local governments a choice of limits, one of which was a freeze on the tax rate. With rapidly rising assessments, revenues could increase substantially despite their inability to raise the tax rate. However, in the first year

Proposition 13 was in effect, property taxes were cut 57 percent, or $7 billion. Most of this relief was offset by state aid to local governments. This was the first time since the Depression that limitations led to large absolute decreases in property taxes.[15]

Indiana applied strict tax rate and levy freezes to local governments in 1973. In the following four years, property tax revenue rose only 3.1 percent, far more slowly than in any other state. The limitations were accompanied by a large increase in state aid to localities and limited use of local income taxes.[16]

Iowa provides a good example of the effect which limits can have. In 1967 the state began to increase aid to school districts with no controls on local spending. Although aid rose $110.9 million over the next four years, school property taxes increased $94.2 million as spending rose sharply. School spending was limited when another round of big aid increases began in 1971, and the results were very different. Aid rose $146.9 million in the following four years, but school property taxes fell $4.3 million. From 1976 to 1979 Iowa also placed 9 percent limits on levy increases by cities and counties, but their impact was apparently much smaller.[17]

Kansas is another state where limitations may have had some effect, although smaller than in Iowa and Indiana. Its limits, adopted in 1970, were the first of the wave which occurred during the 1970s. City and county tax levies were not allowed to rise, unless there was new construction, unless the revenue was for an exempt purpose such as pensions or debt service, or unless an increase was approved by the voters. School spending was also limited, but to a smaller extent, with annual increases in spending of as much as 15 percent possible in some cases. In the first seven years limits were in effect, property taxes rose 53 percent, considerably more slowly than in earlier years and clearly below the national average.

A review of states in which school finance reforms took place during the 1970-1975 period found that in Indiana, Iowa, Kansas, Maine, Minnesota, and Wisconsin limits and aid increases had produced measurable property tax relief.[18]

Prior to Proposition 13, limitations had not had a large impact on the amount of property tax collected nationally because the states with effective controls were generally not large. New Jersey was the biggest state with a strict limit, but its 5 percent cap on local spending did not go into effect until 1976. In its first year, property tax levies fell 2.6 percent.[19]

It is difficult to establish the extent to which trends were due to changes in aid rather than to controls. Controls often have many exemptions which in some cases undergo frequent changes. Thus, it is possible that limitations on non-school levies in Minnesota (1972, 6 percent), Wisconsin (1973, percentage increase of equalized property valuation statewide), and Washington (1974, 6 percent) had some restrictive effect, since all these states had small increases in property tax levies; but it is difficult to quantify their effects without an in-depth study.

Although all the states discussed in this section had limits on levies and expenditures, in some states tax rate limits were also restrictive. For example, North Dakota had the largest decrease in property tax revenue as a fraction of personal income of any state from 1971 to 1977. In part, this was due to a major increase in state aid to school districts, but in addition most local governments were restricted by tax rate limits, and assessments increased very slowly.

A comprehensive study of the effects of limitations would have to consider what proportion of taxes and spending involves governments which are at the limits, how much state and federal aid has been increased, and how difficult it is for governments to exceed limits through referenda or other means.

Evaluation

There are many different objectives which controls may be designed to achieve. Some possibilities include:

1. Reduce property taxes because there is too much reliance on them.
2. Reduce local taxes because there is too much reliance on local government as a revenue raiser.
3. Reduce all taxes because the government takes too large a share of income.
4. Reduce all payments to government (including nontax charges) either because its services are overextended or because it is inefficient (and controls tend to increase efficiency).
5. Reduce the variation in taxes among different locations, to improve either equity or the efficiency of resource allocation.
6. Avoid sharp increases in property taxes.
7. Avoid sharp changes in the share of taxes borne by each class of property.

Controls must be evaluated in terms of how appropriate these objectives are deemed to be, how well they achieve these objectives, and what other (perhaps unintended) effects they may have.

Appropriateness of Objectives

In view of the diversity of state tax structures and value judgments about goals, it is impossible to generalize about what objectives ought to be pursued. Nevertheless, key issues can be placed in context.

It was shown in chapter 2 that property taxes have been rising more slowly than personal income or other state-local taxes in most states. On this basis, it is difficult to see the need for exotic new controls on property taxation per se.

Nevertheless, property tax controls might be desired as a means to speed up the relative rate of decrease or as a guarantee that property taxes will be lowered while some other revenue source is increased.[20]

The case for property tax relief as a means of shifting revenue raising away from local government is stronger, both in order to overcome fiscal disparities and to take account of benefit spillovers.[21] In this context, how property tax revenue will be replaced is crucial.

Limits on spending rather than on taxes raise a new set of issues. Several reasons have been suggested for imposing limits on local spending. Service levels may be excessive because voters overestimate benefits or underestimate costs of services, because certain interest groups have great political power at the local level, because of bureaucratic behavior, and for other reasons. On the other hand, costs may be excessive because services are provided by organizations not subject to the discipline of the market mechanism; hence, expenses tend to be bloated by waste, inefficiency, and/or corruption.[22]

The final two objectives listed at the beginning of this section—curbing sharp changes of absolute or relative property tax burdens—are relatively novel in that they have risen to prominence only in the past few years. When it is reflected in assessments, inflation causes sharp changes in tax burdens and tax shares. Political accommodations are often reached on the assumption that prevailing relative property values will continue, and assessment controls may be used to preserve those accommodations.

How Well Objectives Are Attained

Ladd recently argued that there are generally better means available for reaching whatever objectives are envisioned than controls. For example, if citizens lack adequate information about budgetary affairs, she advocates full disclosure legislation and perhaps referenda. If the problem is inefficiency, she suggests management and accounting reforms and changes in the civil service system.[23] However, most of these substitutes for controls either face great political obstacles or are unlikely to have much effect on government decisions. Full disclosure and more information tend to be ineffectual because relatively few citizens invest the time to inform themselves to a significant extent. Important problems with referenda are that they usually offer a very limited range of choices and that persons with extreme views are more likely to cast ballots than persons with moderate positions. Sometimes the countervailing forces to oppose local pressure groups (both public employees and service beneficiaries) are so weak that measures short of controls tend to produce few results.

Whether controls achieve their objectives depends on how they are designed and on external events. A limit on tax rates seems like an inappropriate policy if the objective is to slow the increase of property taxes, since it can be undermined by rising assessments; a better policy is a direct limit on property tax revenue increases. But a limit on revenue increases is not the best way of limiting the size of local government; controls on spending make more sense, unless it is desired to stimulate employment of user charges and nonproperty taxes. If the purpose of controls is to assist particular groups such as the elderly, homeowners, or owners of farmland, all the across-the-board measures discussed above are wrong. There should either be a limit on assessment increases for the particular types of property for which assistance is intended; or, better yet, some form of tax credit should be used. Across-the-board controls may give the greatest aid to unintended beneficiaries.

Other Effects of Controls

Limits on spending and taxing may vary considerably in terms of the incidence of tax savings among income groups. In most cases, controls result in a reduction of the nominal tax rate (millage rate); this is true of limits on spending and taxing as well as rate limits. As a result, *within each government unit* a proportional reduction in property taxation occurs. This means that all property taxpayers share in the reduction and that the more tax one would otherwise pay, the more benefit one receives.

How can this benefit distribution be characterized? In one sense, all benefit equally, since there is an equal percentage reduction for all. In another sense, the benefits are progressive because (assuming that the property tax is regressive) the benefits are a larger proportion of income for households with relatively low incomes.[24] Yet in a third sense, which is of the greatest practical importance, the benefits are strikingly pro-rich because the affluent receive by far the largest absolute benefits. This is especially true if one considers that much of the nonresidential property tax is not shifted to consumers or workers.

The preceding analysis pertains to a single government unit. One can imagine a situation in which the result is much different when an entire state is considered. For example, suppose that a fairly low tax rate limit is imposed, that high- and low-income groups are segregated into separate government units with a low tax rate in the high-income area and a high tax rate in the low-income area, and that the state government replaces much of the lost property tax revenue on a proportional basis. The residents of the low-income area would receive greater tax benefits than those in the high-income area because they have a greater proportionate reduction in their tax rate; their benefits would be greater in relation to prelimitation taxes and perhaps even in absolute terms.

The point of the preceding example is that from an intergovernmental perspective tax or expenditure limits appear more progressive if low-income persons tend to live in places with high tax rates. But not too much should be made of this example. High- and low-income families are not totally segregated. The distribution of business property can have a major impact on relative benefits from a tax limit. High-income areas have higher tax rates in some states. The distributional effects of rate limits must be examined on a case-by-case basis, since they are likely to differ substantially depending on local economic conditions and the prevailing tax situation. However, the basic fact that within government units tax savings are proportional to initial property tax bills is the starting point for all analyses and is likely to be a major element in the overall picture. Whether such across-the-board relief is desirable is dependent on the height of prevailing tax rates and other factors.

An important virtue of controls is that they can be used as a tool to stimulate reform of government structures. For example, in the aftermath of Proposition 13 California assumed the full financial responsibility for welfare and certain other poverty-related services. It also made special districts responsible to county governments by distributing their state aid through counties, a move long advocated by certain government reformers.[25] On the other hand, these changes tend to reduce local independence and are sometimes viewed as a disadvantage of controls. It has been speculated that controls tend to stimulate reliance on special districts, since such districts may provide a method of circumventing the controls; however, a recent study failed to find any relationship between controls and reliance on special districts.[26]

Similarly, controls on school district spending can be used to equalize differentials in school quality if they are tougher on higher-spending districts than on those with below-average spending, as, for example, in New Jersey and Iowa. The controls on school district spending in Iowa were also expected to squeeze small school districts particularly hard and thus induce school reorganization, but that expectation was not fulfilled.

Another important effect of Proposition 13-type controls is to discourage some forms of private development. Although it was not widely anticipated in advance, Proposition 13 results in a fiscal penalty to governments for traditional types of development, since the taxes collected at 1 percent tax rate are insufficient to cover the cost of infrastructure which has traditionally been provided by government. As a result, many governments are requiring developers to provide this infrastructure themselves, considerably increasing the "front end" costs for them. The result will apparently be less suburban sprawl.[27]

To summarize, tight controls tend to have far-reaching effects beyond limiting local taxes and spending. One must consider not only how well controls achieve the primary objectives which they seek to attain but also these other impacts.

Conclusions

Whereas other property tax relief policies simply reduce or redistribute taxes, controls have a threefold impact: they tend to reduce local government spending and autonomy as well as taxes. If one does not wish to reduce spending or if one places a very high value on retaining local government independence, controls are a poor choice.

As a device for reducing spending, controls raise several issues. First, how much money can be saved by increasing local government efficiency, so that an expenditure cut does not reduce services? The majority of persons who voted for Proposition 13 said that they did not expect that services would be decreased if it passed.[28] At the time this was interpreted as reflecting an impression of rampant waste and inefficiency. The public was correct about services not being affected much but for the wrong reason. A large infusion of state aid, not increased efficiency, prevented a major service reduction.

A second major question is, What services should be cut? Polls in California and other states showed that most people favored Proposition 13 even if it did mean cuts in services; but when asked about specific services, the majority favored reductions for few, if any, services.[29] The least popular services, such as welfare and social services, claim a relatively small share of property tax revenue. Few people endorsed decreases in money for schools, though they take nearly half of property tax dollars, or in police and fire protection, which also claim significant shares.

The only conclusion which one can draw is that most citizens are not well informed about the allocation of property tax revenue. A final key question is, Who will suffer most if services are cut? The greatest loss is very likely to be felt by those who rely on social services, public health and hospitals, and similar services. In general, the "have-nots" lose more from service cutbacks while the "haves" benefit most from the tax cuts.

As a tax reduction measure, controls are relatively crude. Many other ways of cutting taxes are available, differing greatly in how they distribute tax savings. But some types of controls do have a characteristic lacking in many other relief devices—they automatically provide relief which continues to grow over a period of time, while some other relief measures provide just one-shot relief or actually diminish over time. This is not necessarily a big advantage of controls, since changes may be necessary in allowable growth in order to take account of changing circumstances such as higher inflation than was originally foreseen. Controls may be compared to indexing the income tax in that they are automatic, but perhaps it is desirable to rely on discretionary relief measures covering one or two years at a time.

Finally, controls interfere with local autonomy more than other kinds of property tax relief. If one has faith in local democratic government to provide the quantity and quality of services which citizens desire, controls are unnecessary and undesirable. However, it appears that (except for controls on school districts in some cases) most citizens do not mind state restrictions which limit the power of local officials to determine taxes and spending.

The bottom line is that controls generally make more sense as a device to cut spending than taxes. If that is so, new forms of controls could be devised which separate the spending and taxing aspects. For example, property tax revenue in excess of some rate limit could go into a fund out of which tax relief is financed, with the relief taking the form of a circuit breaker, a homestead credit, aid to local governments, or some other device. Thus, spending would be controlled, and tax relief could take any form desired.

Several states stipulate that a referendum must be held before taxes can be increased. Although such a provision is not usually classified as a state-imposed control, it is likely to retard the rise of taxes (and reduce services and perhaps government waste). Since such laws maintain local control, they merit greater study as an alternative to rigid controls.[30]

The widespread use of limitations on spending and taxing other than loose rate limits is a very recent development. In part it is attributable to inflationary stresses and to the public disillusionment with government arising from Watergate, Vietnam, and the dashed hopes for the Great Society. The proportion of citizens believing that "government wastes a lot of money" rose from less than 50 percent in 1960 to 80 percent in 1978.[31] It is still too early to tell what the long-run effects of limitations on government operations and finance will be. But it seems clear, given the national mood, that they are likely to be around for many years to come, though probably in less extreme form than in California. The theme of this chapter is that the differences among limitations are highly significant and care must be taken to ensure that limitations which are adopted correspond to the problems they are supposed to solve.

Notes

1. This section draws heavily from Advisory Commission on Intergovernmental Relations, *State Limitations on Local Taxes and Expenditures* (Washington, D.C., 1977), and International Association of Assessing Officers, *Property Tax Limits* (Chicago, 1978). Information on schools is from Kent McGuire et al., *School Finance at a Fourth Glance* (Denver: Education Commission of the States, 1979); Education Commission of the States, *School District Expenditure and Tax Controls* (Denver, 1978); and William H. Wilken and John J. Callahan, "State Limitations on Local Taxes and Spending: A Paper Tiger?" (mimeographed, 1978). In a number of cases, the sources differed among themselves as to what limitations were in effect, and several compilers of these surveys acknowledged to the author that their reports were not fully comprehensive.

2. In 1962 the Advisory Commission on Intergovernmental Relations reported that no new overall property tax limitations had been enacted since the 1930s. See Advisory Commission on Intergovernmental Relations, *State Constitutional and Statutory Restrictions on Local Taxing Powers*, (Washington, D.C., 1962), p. 30.

3. The levy limits in Colorado, Arizona, Ohio, and Oregon are the only pre-1970 nonrate limits. The text does not count the levy limits in Iowa from 1976 to 1979; they have been replaced by limits on assessment increases. For a good discussion of Ohio's experience, see Richard A. Levin, "Property Tax Limits in Ohio" (Paper presented at meeting of National Association of Tax Administrators at Williamsburg, Virginia, June 2, 1977).

4. Helen F. Ladd, "An Economic Evaluation of State Limitations on Local Taxing and Spending Powers," *National Tax Journal* 31 (March 1978):2-3. This study deals only with limits in effect as of 1976. As the author acknowledges, the statistical procedure employed is subject to serious problems.

5. Although Rhode Island was the very first state to limit local tax rates, its limitation was repealed many years ago.

6. For more detailed discussion of design issues, see Advisory Commission on Intergovernmental Relations, *State Limitations,* and Wilken and Callahan, "A Paper Tiger?"

7. Although many limits were restrictive during the Depression, they became less so in the postwar period as assessments rose substantially. Advisory Commission on Intergovernmental Relations, *Restrictions on Local Taxing Powers,* pp. 53-62.

8. See Advisory Commission on Intergovernmental Relations, *State Limitations,* pp. 49-65, for a detailed list of exclusions from limits.

9. This has been the experience with New Jersey's 5 percent limit on city budget growth (*Wall Street Journal,* October 31, 1978, p. 22).

10. See the discussion of this point in chapter 1.

11. Most government activity is labor-intensive, and the rate of productivity improvement is relatively slow. The implicit GNP deflator state and local government expenditures (a price index for government costs) rose 277.2 percent between 1950 and 1977, far more than the overall GNP deflator, which increased just 163.5 percent during that period.

12. Advisory Commission on Intergovernmental Relations, *State Limitations,* pp. 19-23; John Shannon et al., "Recent Experience with Local Tax and Expenditure Controls," *National Tax Journal* 29 (September 1976):372-385; Wilken and Callahan, "A Paper Tiger?"

13. From 1971 to 1976 locally assessed realty increased in value more than 80 percent in eighteen states, a situation in which tax rate limits would not effectively restrain the increase of property tax revenue. John O. Behrens, "Again Some Facts for a Tax under Attacks" (Paper delivered at conference of National Association of Tax Administrators in Madison, Wisconsin, June 12, 1979), table 4.

14. *Wall Street Journal,* November 3, 1978.

15. In the 1930s in numerous states the limitations which were adopted forced reductions in property tax levies, but during most other periods limitations have generally moderated increases without causing large absolute decreases. Advisory Commission on Intergovernmental Relations, *Restrictions on Local Taxing Powers,* p. 37.

16. Advisory Commission on Intergovernmental Relations, *State Limitations*, pp. 27-32, contains brief descriptions of several of the states discussed here. Although its analysis emphasizes the role of local income taxes in Indiana, in fact they were much less important than increased state aid. In 1977 local income tax revenue totaled less than 3 percent of property tax revenue. All revenue figures are from U.S. Census Bureau, *Governmental Finances in 1976-77.*

17. Iowa Department of Public Instruction, "Statistical Analysis of State Financial Operation for Public School Districts from July 1, 1955 to June 30, 1973"; Iowa Comptroller, *Budget in Brief: 1979-81 Biennium* (Des Moines: State of Iowa, 1979).

18. The study assumed that property tax relief was provided in cases in which the state share of school costs rose while per pupil spending fell relative to the national average. Lawrence L. Brown et al., "School Finance in the Seventies: Achievements and Failures," in *Selected Papers in School Finance: 1978,* ed. Esther O. Tron (Washington, D.C.: Department of Health, Education, and Welfare, 1978), p. 74.

19. Nancy G. Beer, "1976 Municipal CAP Law: Review and Implications" (Princeton, N.J.: Woodrow Wilson School of Public and International Affairs, September 1977), p. 3.

20. Even opponents of limits such as Advisory Commission on Intergovernmental Relations and Ladd accept the value of controls temporarily when state aid is increased in some cases. See Advisory Commission on Intergovernmental Relations, *State Limitations,* pp. 7-8, and Ladd, "An Economic Evaluation," p. 14.

21. This point is, for example, forcefully made in Dick Netzer, "Is There Too Much Reliance on the Local Property Tax?" in *Property Tax Reform,* ed. George E. Peterson (Washington, D.C.: The Urban Institute, 1973), pp. 15-18.

22. Ladd, "An Economic Evaluation," pp. 3-5.

23. Ibid., pp. 6-7.

24. This is the position taken by Ladd, "An Economic Evaluation," p. 10: "Let us take . . . the view that the burden of the property tax is regressive. In this case a reduction in property taxes would benefit low income households more than high income households. . ."

25. David B. Walker, "Proposition 13 and California's System of Governance," *Intergovernmental Perspective,* Summer 1978, p. 14.

26. Advisory Commission on Intergovernmental Relations, *State Limitations,* pp. 23-24.

27. Neal R. Pierce, "Proposition 13: A Clamp on Land Use," *Washington Post.*

28. Cited in Seymour Martin Lipset and Earl Raab, "The Message of Proposition 13," *Commentary* 67 (September 1978):42-46.

29. *Newsweek,* June 19, 1978, p. 22. *Des Moines Register,* June 25, 1978, p. 1.

30. Referenda have several drawbacks. They tend to defeat one of the

frequent objectives of school district controls, which is to reduce inequalities between rich and poor districts [Dale Cattanach et al., "Tax and Expenditure Controls: The Price of School Finance Reform," in *School Finance Reform: A Legislator's Handbook,* eds. John J. Callahan and William K. Wilken (Washington, D.C.: National Conference of State Legislatures, 1976), p. 72; and Wilken and Callahan, "A Paper Tiger?" pp. 16-17]. Other problems with controls include voter apathy and the difficulty of framing options. Numerous school districts in Ohio, which has heavy reliance on referenda to set budgets, have had great difficulty maintaining quality programs (not to mention remaining open at all). See also Levin, "Limits in Ohio," pp. 15-19.

31. *Public Opinion,* July/August 1978.

9

State and Federal Grants to Local Governments and the Assumption of Certain Local Functions

Since states and the federal government rely heavily on taxes utilizing bases other than property and local governments draw most of their tax revenue from the property tax, an increase in state or federal responsibility for financing government services usually tends to relieve property taxes. In fact, increased state and federal aid has provided much more relief from property taxes than any other measure, although it is sometimes an unintended result.

Increasing state and federal financial responsibility as a means of providing property tax relief has several aspects which distinguish it from most alternative relief approaches. Unlike most other types of relief, it is provided by the federal government as well as state governments. Analysis is complicated because the effect of intergovernmental assistance in reducing taxes must be distinguished from its effect in increasing expenditures of recipient governments. The diversity of federalism also must be confronted, since the division of responsibilities between state and local governments varies tremendously among states.

Increased aid and the assumption of new responsibilities by higher levels of government are similar to local nonproperty taxes and user charges in that they provide relief to all types of property rather than selected categories. However, aid and the takeover of responsibilities can redistribute burdens among rich and poor areas, which local taxes cannot do. Local nonproperty taxes are discussed in chapter 10 and user charges in chapter 11.

Description

Shifting the burden of financing government to higher levels can take two forms. In one case, the higher level of government simply assumes responsibility for a function which previously was carried out by a local government. Welfare is the most prominent example in recent years, as states have increasingly taken over all the nonfederal costs of providing income maintenance for the poor.

It is more common for the higher level of government to provide financial assistance while the lower level of government continues to deliver the service. Intergovernmental grants can be classified in several ways, two of the major ones being according to whether they are intended to be used for designated purposes and whether recipient governments are required to match some proportion of the grant with their own funds.

The first distinction is between categorical grants, which are provided for specific purposes, and noncategorical grants, which are intended for general support. As explained below, categorical grants may have effects on government activity other than those intended by grantors, and those actual effects, rather than legal designations, must be analyzed.

The second distinction is between matching and nonmatching grants. Matching grants require that recipient governments expend some of their own funds in order to receive the grant. In some cases the match must represent an increase above previous expenditures, which is referred to as an effort maintenance requirement. Matching grants can be further divided into those which are open- and closed-ended, according to whether there is a limit on grant funding.

In practice, the most common federal grant is one which is categorical, matching, and closed-ended. The usual form of a state grant is categorical and nonmatching. However, during the 1970s an increasing proportion of grants from both levels of government were noncategorical and nonmatching. Welfare and medicaid are the major examples of open-ended, categorical, matching grants.[1]

History, Current Extent of Use, and Costs

Prior to the Great Depression, both federal and state aid to local governments were rather insignificant, amounting to less than one-eighth of local general revenue in 1927. Very little of the aid came from the federal government, as table 9-1 shows. Financial assistance increased sharply during the 1930s, with the states still accounting for more than 80 percent of total aid.

Table 9-1 also demonstrates the rapid increase in state and federal aid which occurred during the post-World War II period, particularly after 1962. In the fifteen years preceding 1976-1977, federal aid to local governments increased more than twentyfold and state aid rose to more than 5½ times its original level. As a result, federal aid jumped from 2 to 9.3 percent of total local general revenue and state aid rose from 28.4 to 33.7 percent. The intergovernmental revenue of localities had increased to such an extent by 1976-1977 that it was greater than the sum of all local taxes. In inflation-adjusted dollars, the increase was still impressive. From 1962 to 1977, after removing the effect of inflation, federal aid rose nearly ninefold and state aid 127 percent.

Table 9-1 gives a misleading impression of the extent to which the federal government aids local governments because it does not show the amount of state aid which is financed by the federal government. For example, in 1972 approximately one-fifth of aid from states to local governments was simply a "pass-through" of federal aid to states.[2]

Both the federal and state governments have one dominant type of local

Table 9-1
Federal and State Aid to Local Governments. Selected Years

Year	Amount (Millions)		Percentage of Total Local General Revenue	
	Federal Aid	State Aid	Federal Aid	State Aid
1902	$ 4	$ 52	0.4	6.1
1913	6	91	0.4	5.6
1922	9	312	0.2	8.1
1927	9	596	0.2	10.1
1932	10	801	0.2	14.1
1936	229	1,417	3.7	22.9
1940	278	1,654	4.0	23.8
1944	28	1,842	0.4	25.1
1948	218	3,283	1.9	28.9
1957	343	7,321	1.3	28.6
1962	763	10,879	2.0	28.4
1966-1967	1,753	18,434	3.0	31.7
1971-1972	4,551	35,143	4.3	33.4
1976-1977	16,637	60,311	9.3	33.7

Source: Prior to 1976-1977: U.S. Census Bureau, *1972 Census of Governments*, vol. 6, no. 4: *Topical Studies, Historical Statistics on Governmental Finances and Employment* (Washington, D.C., 1974). 1976-1977: U.S. Census Bureau, *Governmental Finances in 1976-77* (Washington, D.C., 1978).

government to which they provide aid, with more than half of federal aid going to municipalities and nearly half of state aid going to school districts, as indicated in table 9-2.

Overall, intergovernmental aid provided 43 percent of local government revenue in 1977. Except for townships, there is relatively little difference in the aggregate in terms of how dependent various types of governments are on aid from the federal and state governments. As table 9-3 shows, municipalities, counties, school districts, and special districts all derive approximately 40 to 50 percent of their general revenue from aid.

Major shifts have occurred in the composition of state aid over the years. Support for local education has always been the dominant objective of state aid, but its share of the state aid pie increased considerably during the 1940s and 1950s and has remained at about 60 percent since the early 1960s. Welfare aid, the second largest category, peaked in 1972; and its share of total aid has decreased considerably since then, primarily because the federal government assumed complete responsibility for aid to the aged, blind, and disabled. General government support, in third place, has fluctuated over the years, and is higher than it was in the 1960s but lower than in the 1940s. Highway aid, on the other hand, which once was the second most important type of aid, has been in a relative downtrend for fifty years.[3]

The makeup of federal aid has also changed considerably. Whereas 78 percent of federal grants to state and local governments in 1958 were for transportation and income security, these categories accounted for only 29

Table 9-2
Distribution of State and Federal Aid to Local Governments, 1977

	Percentage of Total		
Type of Government	Total	Federal	State
All	100.0	100.0	100.0
County	24.4	22.5	23.7
Municipality	31.4	53.4	23.6
School district	41.4	5.6	49.2
Special district	5.7	15.6	1.3
Township	2.5	3.0	2.2

Source: U.S. Census Bureau. *Governmental Finances in 1976-77* (Washington, D.C., 1978).

percent of total aid in 1978. Education, training, employment, and social services (26 percent in 1978 versus 7 percent in 1958), health (16 versus 4 percent), and general-purpose fiscal assistance (12 versus 2 percent) were the fastest-rising types of aid.[4]

There is a great deal of variation among states in terms of how dependent local governments are on outside aid. At one extreme are nine states in which aid exceeds the total general revenue that local governments raise themselves (New Mexico, Delaware, North Carolina, West Virginia, Wisconsin, Mississippi, Maine, Minnesota, and Arkansas), and at the other end of the spectrum are six states in which aid is less than half of locally raised general revenue (New Hampshire, South Dakota, Connecticut, Nebraska, Vermont, and Wyoming). In New Mexico, aid is nearly double self-raised revenue, while in New Hampshire it is less than one-third of locally raised revenue. Variations in state aid account for much more of these differences than do variations in federal aid.[5]

Statistics on intergovernmental aid such as those discussed above give a somewhat misleading impression of the extent to which local governments have been relieved of responsibility for financing services. For example, states which have assumed complete responsibility for financing the nonfederal share of

Table 9-3
Dependence on State and Federal Aid of Various Local Governments, 1977

Type of Government	Aid as Percentage of Total General Revenue
All	43.0
County	45.3
Municipality	39.6
School district	50.4
Special district	39.9
Township	29.7

Source: U.S. Census Bureau, *Governmental Finances in 1976-77* (Washington, D.C., 1978).

welfare costs are listed as providing no aid, while states like New York and California (prior to Proposition 13) which require localities to bear much of the burden of financing welfare appear to be providing considerable assistance. Likewise, Hawaii, where all schools are state-financed, is considered to offer no aid to local education.

Consequently, a preferable measure of the degree to which states have relieved localities of financial burdens should reflect both the degree to which a state has completely assumed functions and the extent of aid which it provides. In general, the more centralized a state-local fiscal system is, the lower property taxes will tend to be. There are numerous measures of centralization,[6] but the one which is most relevant to property tax relief is the proportion of state-local taxes collected by state government. Table 1-5 shows how centralized taxation is in each state. Except for Ohio, all the eleven most decentralized states have relatively high property taxes.[7] Then highly centralized states tend to have low property taxes, as table 9-4 illustrates.

During the period from 1959 to 1977 the proportion of state-local taxes

Table 9-4
State Dominance in Tax Collections and Relative Property Tax Levels, 1977

States with Lowest Proportion of State-Local Taxes Collected by State Government	Rank in Terms of Property Tax Revenue as a Proportion of Personal Income
1. New Hampshire	49
2. New Jersey	46
3. South Dakota	42
4. New York	45
5. Colorado	36
6. Massachusetts	50
7. Nebraska	41
8. Oregon	40
9. Ohio	23
10. California	48
11. Connecticut	39

States with Highest Proportion of State-Local Taxes Collected by State Government	Rank in Terms of Property Tax Revenue as a Proportion of Personal Income
51. Alaska	51
50. Delaware	7
49. New Mexico	6
48. Hawaii	9
47. West Virginia	4
46. Mississippi	12
45. Arkansas	7
44. South Carolina	10
43. Kentucky	5
42. Alabama	1
41. North Carolina	11

collected by the state government rose in every state except five. Four of the exceptions (Georgia, Hawaii, Louisiana, and Tennessee) had relatively centralized systems to start with and were still on the centralized end of the spectrum in 1977. New Hampshire stands alone as a state which resisted the centralizing trend even though it was decentralized to begin with. This pattern reflects the fact that New Hampshire is the only state without either a sales or an income tax.

Within states the centralizing tendency has been strongest for elementary and secondary schools and public welfare. Between 1961-1962 and 1977-1978, the state share of school costs rose from 40.5 to 48.3 percent, and state government now provides more than half of local school financing in the majority of states.

The states' share of nonfederal welfare costs jumped from 61.4 percent in 1942 to 71.8 percent in 1957 and 78.9 percent in 1976-1977. In thirty states, the state pays more than 90 percent of welfare costs, and New Hampshire, Montana, and Nevada are the only states in which the state finances less than half of welfare costs.

However, the centralizing tendency does not extend to all functions. The states' share of highway expenses dropped from 72.7 percent in 1942 to 70.9 percent in 1966 and 65.2 percent in 1977, while the share of health and hospital costs has fluctuated at close to 50 percent since 1942.[8]

Design Issues

Increased aid and the assumption of functions by higher levels of government differ from the relief mechanisms discussed in chapters 3 to 7 in several respects. First, they do not automatically provide any property tax relief, since lower taxes are conditional upon the actions of the local governments which receive the financial assistance. In some cases local governments may use the aid to raise their expenditures, for either the aided service or a different one. Second, to the extent that they do provide relief, aid and the assumption of functions lead to a reduction of the tax rate and thus relieve taxes for all types of property rather than for only selected categories. Third, even though aid is not targeted to particular types of property, the distribution of relief varies among jurisdictions depending on which functions are aided, which governments receive the aid, and the formula used in distributing funds among aided jurisdictions.

The first issue which must be discussed is the reasons for providing intergovernmental assistance. This leads to an analysis of the differing types of assistance, such as matching or nonmatching grants or a direct takeover of responsibilities. Next there is a discussion of restrictions that can be placed on the actions of local governments which either raise or lower the probability that property taxes will be reduced. This section concludes with an overview of the formulas which can be used in distributing aid among jurisdictions.

Reasons for Providing Intergovernment Assistance

Although the focus of this book is property tax relief, it is necessary to recognize that this is often not the purpose of intergovernmental assistance.[9] One of the major reasons for one government to provide aid to another is the existence of externalities, positive or negative effects which the provision of a service by one governmental jurisdiction may have on residents of another jurisdiction. Many government grants, such as those for education, highways, and welfare, are intended to stimulate the output of services which affect the well-being of large numbers of nonresidents. The presumption is that without outside financial support the level of such services would be less than desirable. Where externalities are primarily national, the national government is the appropriate source of financial support, but if their scope is more limited, the state may be the logical locus of responsibility.

A second major reason for providing intergovernmental aid is to reduce fiscal disparities which exist when there is a mismatch between the need for services and resources available to finance them. Affluent jurisdictions are able to provide superior services with lower tax rates compared to jurisdictions with small tax bases. Aid is an important means of evening out to some extent the variations in service levels and tax burdens which would otherwise occur.

There is a dispute as to whether intergovernmental aid is only a second-best solution to the problem of disparities.[10] On one hand, it can be argued that if undesirable differences exist in average community income, the best way to deal with this situation is with direct grants to individuals. When local governments are used as intermediaries, the distributional results are likely to differ from those achieved with grants directly to persons. But a complete solution to the problem of income inequality is so far off that it is reasonable to redistribute income among governments as a politically acceptable alternative. Even if the interpersonal distribution of income were considered acceptable, grants to the governments might be favored because of inequalities in the distribution of business property and as a means of stimulating the output of public services.[11]

Tax competition among local governments is a third reason why grants are thought to be useful. In some situations governments allegedly are forced to keep their tax rates lower than desirable because they are competing to attract industry. If this is a problem, grants can fill the shortfall of revenue which occurs.

The ultimate step in intergovernmental assistance is for a higher level of government to assume a function which was formerly carried out locally. There are three major reasons why services should be provided at high levels of government. First, the service may be a public good whose benefits flow over a broad area containing many governmental jurisdictions. Second, economies of scale may be so large that the service can be produced efficiently only by a large government. Third, redistributive services should be financed nationally in order to avoid migration problems. When a locality attempts to redistribute income, its high-income residents may move away and its low-income population may expand. To the extent that the national government does not fulfill its redistributive function, it should be assumed by the state rather than by local governments, once again because of potential migration problems. Since poverty is a national problem, fairness also requires that higher levels of government should be the ones which finance poverty-related services. Of the three reasons why responsibility for a particular service might be shifted from one level of government to another, the third one has been the most important in recent years because adjustments were made for the other two long ago.

The reasons why services should be more centralized must be balanced against the desirability of keeping service provision close to the people and avoiding diseconomies of scale. Thus, when a public good does not provide benefits over a wide area, economies of scale are not large, and redistribution is not an important consideration, provision of service should continue to be provided by a local government.

Various Types of Assistance

As noted previously, grants may be matching or nonmatching, categorical or noncategorical.[12] As an alternative to providing a grant, the higher level of government may provide the service itself.

As a general rule, matching grants should be used if the objective is to stimulate provision of a service because of externalities, and nonmatching grants should be used if the aim is to correct for fiscal disparities or to offset interjurisdictional tax competition. The logic behind this argument is that matching grants stimulate spending much more than nonmatching grants. Matching grants are analogous to a reduction in the price of a service, while nonmatching grants can be compared to an increase in community income. A reduction in price will normally result in more spending for a particular purpose than will an increase in income.

The foregoing analysis has to be qualified in a number of respects. For example, it is now clear that nonmatching grants do more to stimulate spending than would an equivalent increase in the income of a community. This is because of a tendency, labeled the "flypaper effect," for funds to stick where they are first received. Another complication arises from the fact that most matching grants are available in only a limited amount; that is, they are closed-ended rather than open-ended.

The most important implication of the theory of grants for the purpose of this book is that in order to provide maximum property tax relief, a grant should be nonmatching. If relief is the goal, the instrument used should stimulate spending as little as possible.

According to empirical estimates discussed below, grants vary widely in terms of how much spending they stimulate. Although some matching grants appear to result in more of an increase in spending than the amount of the grant, most grants result in a combination of spending increases and tax reduction.

Restrictions on Local
Government Activity

The objectives of various governments which have increased their aid to localities in recent years have been diametrically opposed. In many cases, the intention has been to encourage spending on a particular function, such as education, pollution control, public transportation, or community development. In these cases, restrictions were intended to avoid a lowering of taxes as a result of the grants. But in other situations when a government increased aid or assumed responsibility for an activity formerly financed locally, the major objective was to provide tax relief, so restrictions were imposed to avoid increases in local government spending.

The reason why grantors have difficulty ensuring that local governments act as they wish is a characteristic of funds known as *fungibility* which implies that revenue from one source can be substituted for revenue from another source. As someone once phrased it, "all money is green." For example, suppose that a state wishing to combat crime gives a nonmatching grant of $1 million to a city with the stipulation that it be used for police protection. If there are no restrictions on local activity, the city may use the $1 million in place of tax money which would have gone for this purpose, and thus lower taxes $1 million, increase nonpolice spending $1 million, or combine these alternatives in some way.

In the preceding example the government making the grant may impose an effort maintenance requirement stipulating that the local government cannot lower its previous level of spending. This requirement, however, will be ineffective to the extent that the grant is less than the amount by which the locality would normally increase its spending. If there were no inflation, effort maintenance requirements would be easier to enforce effectively, but if they are to inhibit local activity while costs are rapidly increasing, they must take inflation into account. It is rare for effort maintenance requirements to be designed in this manner, so that they normally do relatively little to prevent recipient governments from using grant funds for purposes other than the one designated in the grant, such as lowering taxes.

The probability that aid will actually lead to an increase in spending for the activity for which the grant is provided also depends on how much the locality was originally spending on the activity. If the grant is for a service which the local government would not otherwise provide, its result will be increased spending rather than reduced taxes.

Governments which want grants to be used for local tax reduction face a more manageable problem. Limitations on local expenditures or tax levies such as were discussed in chapter 8 can be used to guarantee that aid is passed along as relief to taxpayers. These limitations were used in numerous school finance reforms during the 1970s and occasionally for local general-purpose governments as well.[13]

When a state takes over a local function, the same situation arises as when aid is increased. Unless a restriction is placed on local governments they may increase their spending for other functions, tending to cancel out the tax relief which the state action was intended to produce.

Formulas: The Distribution of Tax
Relief among Jurisdictions

The distribution of tax relief among jurisdictions depends on which functions are aided, which governments receive aid, and the formula used in distributing funds among jurisdictions.

Many illustrations can be provided of how the functions and governments aided affect the distribution of relief. For example, as explained previously, there are compelling reasons why the burden of financing welfare and other poverty-related services should be assumed by the federal government or, if not by it, by state governments. However, the benefits from a takeover of welfare costs would be highly uneven. At the national level, California and New York would receive a large proportion of the benefits. Within states, because urban areas often have a disproportionate share of persons receiving welfare, urban areas would receive a large share of the financial gain. The pattern is similar for another prime candidate for state takeover, the costs of courts and court-appointed attorneys, which are higher in urban areas because of their crime rates and the large number of indigent defendants.

Many states have aid programs solely for municipal governments, which obviously discriminate against unincorporated rural areas. Aid for mass transit is also urban-oriented, because transit systems are located in cities. But programs for soil conservation or maintenance of rural rail lines are obviously rural-oriented.

The major fights are not, however, merely over which functions or governments will receive aid but also about how much goes to each type of aid program and how the aid is distributed.

Aid for education is by far the largest state program, and in forty-six states this aid is inversely related to assessed value per pupil. Since assessed value is a very imperfect measure of an area's ability to finance services, during the 1970s a number of states added income to their distribution formulas. There also has been a trend away from foundation programs and toward power equalizing.

Although both systems of education financing are based on a school district's property valuation, they differ in that power equalizing is more favorable to areas with higher tax rates. Since a foundation plan tends to stimulate local school spending less, it is preferable if the objective of reform is tax reduction. This is not surprising inasmuch as the impetus behind power equalizing was not to provide property tax relief but rather to enhance equality of educational opportunity while preserving local autonomy.[14]

Aside from aid for education, redistribution is not an important goal of state aid. In 1972 the ACIR estimated that approximately $15.5 billion (40 percent of all state aid, which amounted to $36.8 billion) was allocated on various bases designed to compensate for local fiscal capacity and/or effort. Fully $13.1 billion of the $15.5 billion of equalization grants was for public education. Of the rest, $1.7 billion was for general local government support, and $600 million was for other specific funding areas. Much of the aid which the ACIR considered to be equalizing was distributed according to population. Thus, aside from education, state governments apparently attempt little in the way of reducing fiscal disparities through their intergovernmental aid programs.[15] Rather, most of the aid is based on reimbursement by state government for certain costs incurred by local governments.

The most rural-oriented state program has been aid for highways because it is usually distributed according to land area and road mileage. For example, a study in Iowa found that in 1973 per capita highway aid was $21 in metropolitan counties and $77 in extremely rural counties.[16]

Because of the diminishing relative importance of highway aid, state aid has shifted away from its traditional pattern of rural favoritism. The ratio of per capita state aid to local governments in metropolitan areas to aid outside metropolitan areas rose from 0.85 in 1957 to 1.15 in 1972. However, as a proportion of all general revenue, state aid continued to be higher in non-metropolitan areas in 1972.

Federal aid is much more urban-oriented than state aid. Federal aid per capita to local governments inside metropolitan areas in 1972 was more than 2.5 times as high as it was to local governments outside metropolitan areas, while state aid per capita was less than 20 percent higher in metropolitan areas.[17]

Evaluation

The evaluation of aid and the assumption of functions by higher levels of government are divided into two parts. The first section addresses the question of the extent to which aid actually does lower property taxes as opposed to having some other effect. The second section compares aid to other property tax relief mechanisms.

How Much Relief?

In one sense, there is no question that a combination of aid and budget limitations can lower property taxes substantially, as evidenced most spectacularly by Proposition 13. Several other cases in which aid and limits have been combined were discussed in chapter 8.[18] A more complex and interesting issue the extent to which aid without accompanying limitations on local governments reduces property taxes.

Economists and political scientists have built up a voluminous literature during the 1960s and 1970s on the impact of intergovernmental assistance on state and local government activity. The largest group of studies has been statistical efforts employing multiple regression analysis. In addition, the Brookings Institution has issued several studies on general revenue sharing based on the informed opinion of monitors located in jurisdictions scattered across the country. Evidence has also been accumulated from opinion surveys of local officials and from trend analyses. Each of the four major approaches—statistical, monitoring, surveys, and trend analysis—has inherent shortcomings, and most of the studies have dealt with federal grants to state and local governments, so that they are not directly applicable to the current study, which is primarily concerned with local government finance. Therefore, it is impossible to draw precise conclusions about the extent to which property taxes have been lowered by aid. Nevertheless, the order of magnitude of tax reduction can be estimated, and it leaves no doubt that intergovernmental aid has been the single most important mechanism employed to relieve property taxes.

General revenue sharing (GRS) has been the subject of more studies than any other grant program, and these studies are suggestive of the impact of other nonmatching grants. Survey and monitoring studies generally indicate that 60 to 70 percent of GRS was added to spending, while trend analysis indicates a smaller expenditure effect, 50 to 60 percent. However, an econometric study by Gramlich estimated that only 36 percent went into higher expenditures.

Studies of nonmatching state grants to localities have produced somewhat inconsistent results. Separate studies of school aid in California, West Virginia, and Massachusetts agreed that 50 to 60 percent of the aid resulted in higher expenditures. These findings are particularly important because nearly half of all state aid goes to school districts. However, one study in Wisconsin concluded that each dollar of aid resulted in increased expenditures of $1.52. This result and others which indicate highly stimulative effects are suspect because of technical problems which bias their estimates upward.[19]

Studies of other federal nonmatching grant programs indicate that their stimulative effect varies widely. Whitman and Cline conclude that funds under the Comprehensive Employment and Training Act (CETA) and Anti-Recession

Fiscal Assistance (ARFA) had effects similar to those of general revenue sharing. However, Community Development Block Grants (CDBG) had a considerably stronger impact, with at least 85 percent of aid resulting in higher spending. The reason for this difference is apparently that the latter program funded activities which local governments would have been unlikely to fund on their own.[20]

The estimates of the impact of matching grants also vary from program to program. While certain grants appear to stimulate more local spending than the amount of the aid, most grants result in a combination of higher spending and lower local taxes and user charges. As expected, matching grants are more stimulative, on the average, than nonmatching grants.

Most of the estimates of the impact of aid cited here ignore the interplay between aid and state and federal mandates. For example, if a higher level of government requires localities to provide more service, their increased spending is a foregone conclusion. If aid is provided to defray part of or all the cost of meeting the mandate, its effect can be considered to be a reduction of revenue that must be raised locally.

Not all aid which does not result in higher spending flows into property tax relief. Approximately three-fourths of revenue sharing funds which did not result in higher spending went into tax reduction, with the other fourth leading to lower borrowing. Apparently most of the taxes reduced were on property, although user charges and nonproperty taxes were also relieved to some extent.

What does all this imply about the overall property tax situation? From 1971-1972 to 1976-1977, local governments received an increase of federal aid of $12.1 billion and state aid of $25.2 billion; during the previous five years, the comparable amounts were $2.8 billion and $16.7 billion, as shown in table 9-1. Two important conclusions are implied by these figures and the preceding analysis.

First, the increase of state aid has been much greater than that of federal aid in absolute terms, though not in percentages. This tends to increase the proportion of aid resulting in tax reduction for two reasons: State aid is less likely to be matching than federal aid,[21] and state aid is usually given for the support of more mundane local government activity than is federal aid, which sometimes has relatively esoteric objectives. Aid for unusual functions is more likely to result in spending than aid for more normal activity.

Second, intergovernmental aid has been far more important than any other mechanism for relieving property taxes. Even if one assumes conservatively that only one-fifth of the increase of aid resulted in lower property taxes, this amounts to $3.9 billion of relief from 1967 to 1972 and $7.4 billion of relief from 1972 to 1977, for a total of $11.4 billion in ten years. Compared to total property tax collections of $62.5 billion in 1977 or to the ten-year increase in local property taxes of $35.1 billion, this is an impressive figure. It makes the $950 million of circuit breaker relief in 1977 appear rather paltry.

*Comparisons with Other Forms
of Relief*

In many states the most important reason for increasing state aid is not directly
to relieve property taxes but rather to correct imbalances in the structure of
government. Horrendous fiscal disparities exist, resulting, for example, in great
variations in school quality between rich and poor areas. Poverty-related services
(such as police and fire protection, health services, and recreation) are often a
significant burden at the local level. Tax enclaves exist in which property owners
can shield themselves from costs which are therefore more onerous in neighboring governmental jurisdictions.

Correcting these problems which arise from overreliance on local governments to finance services does not necessarily imply relieving overall property
taxes. It does imply a shift of financial responsibility to state and federal
governments.[22] These higher governments could rely on property taxes to pay
for meeting their increased responsibilities, but that is hardly ever done. Instead,
there is usually a shift to sales and income taxes and away from the property tax.

The school finance reforms carried out in many states during the early
1970s illustrate the variety of objectives which state aid may serve. Eleven of
nineteen states which instituted major reforms provided significant property tax
relief, and ten of the nineteen states increased educational expenditures relative
to other states. In addition, ten of the states reduced disparities in local school
expenditures, and thirteen states reduced the correlation between expenditures
and school district wealth. Obviously, many states made progress in more than
one dimension, although no state was able to progress toward all four
objectives.[23]

Aside from its potentially useful role in overcoming intergovernmental fiscal
problems, how does aid compare to alternative means of relieving property
taxes? It has both pluses and minuses, with the balance depending on local
conditions and priorities.

On the positive side of the ledger, aid is an inexpensive method of relieving
property taxes in terms of administrative and compliance costs. Since it relieves
taxes by lowering the overall tax rate, there is no chance that a careless or
uninformed taxpayer will not get relief to which he is legally entitled.

Aid does not discriminate in terms of various types of property, which
could be considered an advantage if the tax burden is so high that all types of
property are judged to require relief. This lack of discrimination also accords
well with some concepts of fairness.

From other perspectives, aid is not such a desirable means of providing
property tax relief. For one thing, unless it is accompanied by an effective
limitation on local governments, much of the aid may not result in tax relief at
all, but rather in higher government spending.

The distribution of the benefits of aid is also controversial. Aid does nothing to reduce the regressivity of the property tax and provides much greater benefits to owners of valuable homes than of modest ones. Nonresidential property benefits along with homes, and therefore aid does not offset a shift in the share of taxes to residential property which may be occurring. In the short run, increased aid often does little on behalf of renters.

In some respects, aid is similar to increased use of nonproperty taxes. In fact, there is evidence that states to some extent treat them as alternatives.[24] Aid is superior because it tends to reduce fiscal disparities, while local nonproperty taxes may be favored by adherents of local government autonomy.

There are sound reasons for increasing state and federal aid to local governments, particularly state aid, and for higher levels of government to assume certain functions currently financed locally. Providing property tax relief is not necessarily one of those reasons. As a means of tax relief, aid must be contrasted with the other policies discussed in this book. Since it is the largest single source of relief from property taxes which has been used, the tax relief aspect of aid must not be overlooked.

At the time of this writing in mid-1979, the outlook for state and federal aid to localities is not very bright, as both state and federal governments must contend with "tax revolt fever." With the federal government pressured to reduce its budget deficit and the revenue of an increasing number of states subject to limitations or partial indexing,[25] intergovernmental aid is likely to grow at a much slower rate than in the past. As a result, a prime force for property tax relief will lose its power.

Notes

1. Categorical matching grants are seldom if ever used, for reasons explained later in the chapter.

2. In 1972 nominal federal aid to states was $26.8 billion, nominal federal-local aid was $4.6 billion, and nominal state-local aid was $35.1 billion. When $7.1 billion of pass-through funds is taken into account, net federal aid to states falls to $19.7 billion, net federal-local aid rises to $11.6 billion, and net state-local aid drops to $28.1 billion. Advisory Commission on Intergovernmental Relations, *The States and Intergovernmental Aids* (Washington, D.C.: Government Printing Office, 1977), p. 20. Unpublished research by Ross Stephens and Gerald Olsen suggests that the pass-through element may be even greater than indicated here.

3. Ibid., p. 10.

4. U.S. Office of Management and Budget, *Special Analyses of the 1980 Budget* (Washington, D.C. Government Printing Office, 1979), p. 223.

5. See table 2-3 for statistics on each state. All figures are for 1977, as

reported in Advisory Commission on Intergovernmental Relations, *Significant Features of Fiscal Federalism,* 1978-79 ed. (Washington, D.C.: Government Printing Office, 1979), table 57.

6. For a good discussion of centralization, see G. Ross Stephens, "State Centralization and the Erosion of Local Autonomy," *Journal of Politics* 41 (February 1974):44-76, and J. Fred Giertz, "Decentralization at the State and Local Level: An Empirical Analysis," *National Tax Journal* 29 (June 1976):201-209.

7. Ohio's property taxes are low because of its heavy reliance on nonproperty taxes and the limited scope of its public sector. Only two states had lower own-source state-local general revenue as a proportion of personal income in 1977.

8. Advisory Commission on Intergovernmental Relations, *Significant Features,* 1978-1979, tables 8, 13, 16, 18, 21; and Advisory Commission on Intergovernmental Relations, *The States and Intergovernmental Aids,* pp. 5-6. The state share of the nonfederal portion of welfare costs was 37.5 percent in New Hampshire, 44.4 percent in Montana, and 46.6 percent in Nevada in 1977. It was between 50 and 70 percent in California (prior to Proposition 13), Minnesota, Indiana, Ohio, and New York, and between 70 and 90 percent in Wisconsin, Iowa, North Dakota, South Dakota, Nebraska, Tennessee, Florida, Mississippi, New Mexico, Arizona, Wyoming, and Colorado.

9. For a good discussion of the rationale for intergovernmental assistance and the assignment of functions among levels of governments, see Wallace E. Oates, *Fiscal Federalism* (New York: Harcourt, Brace, Jovanovich, 1972).

10. James Heilbrun, "Poverty and Public Finance in the Older Central Cities," in *Readings in Urban Economics,* eds. Matthew Edel and Jerome Rothenberg (New York: MacMillan, 1972), pp. 541-544.

11. According to the "flypaper effect," discussed below, income distributed to governments does not result in the same pattern of spending as income distributed to individuals.

12. For a good brief review of this subject, see Edward M. Gramlich, "Intergovernmental Grants: A Review of the Empirical Literature," in *The Political Economy of Fiscal Federalism,* ed. Wallace E. Oates (Lexington, Mass.: D.C. Heath, 1976), pp. 219-239.

13. States which combined increased school aid with limitations include Iowa, Kansas, Minnesota, Florida, New Mexico, Maine, and Indiana. Indiana's limits and aid also affected city and county governments, as did California's Proposition 13. See chapter 8 of this book and Lawrence L. Brown et al., "School Finance Reform in the Seventies: Achievements and Failures," *Selected Papers in School Finance, 1978* ed., Esther Tron, (Washington, D.C.: Department of Health, Education, and Welfare, 1978).

14. Kent McGuire et al., *School Finance at a Fourth Glance* (Denver: Educational Commission of the States, 1979).

15. Advisory Commission on Intergovernmental Relations, *The States and Intergovernmental Aids,* pp. 23-27. More than 70 percent of nonequalizing state aid in 1972 was based on cost reimbursement.

16. Steven D. Gold, "A Scorecard for Rural-Urban Conflict: Geographic Income Redistribution by State Government" (Paper delivered at Midwest Economics Association meetings in St. Louis, Missouri, April 1976).

17. Alan K. Campbell and Seymour Sacks, *Metropolitan America* (New York: Free Press, 1967), pp. 77-81; and U.S. Census Bureau, *1972 Census of Governments,* vol. 5: *Local Government in Metropolitan Areas* (Washington, D.C.: Government Printing Office, 1975), table 9.

18. This section draws heavily on Ray D. Whitman and Robert J. Cline, "Fiscal Impact of Revenue Sharing in Comparison with Other Federal Aid: An Evaluation of Recent Empirical Findings" (Report prepared for the Office of Revenue Sharing, U.S. Department of the Treasury, under the auspices of The Urban Institute, Washington, D.C., November 1978); and Gramlich, "Intergovernmental Grants."

19. Many multiple regression studies of this subject have yielded biased results, tending to exaggerate the impact of aid on spending. For example, one problem is a simultaneous-equations bias arising from the failure to take into account the interaction between the level of local spending and grants received. Many of the studies have used models which were incompletely specified in other respects. See Whitman and Cline, "Fiscal Impact," pp. 45-79.

20. Ibid.

21. State and local governments provided roughly one dollar of matching funds for every three dollars of federal aid received in 1978, approximately the same ratio as in 1972. The constancy of this ratio occurred because the increase in general-purpose and broad-based aid was offset by a significant growth in programs such as Medicaid which require more than average matching aid. Hardly any state aid to localities is matching in the usual sense, although a large amount (nearly one-third in 1972) is provided on a cost-reimbursement basis, which is similar to a matching grant. See U.S. Office of Management and Budget, *Special Analyses,* p. 230, and Advisory Commission on Intergovernmental Relations, *The States and Intergovernmental Aids,* p. 32.

22. Redrawing the boundaries between local government jurisdictions would tend to ameliorate the problems arising from fragmented local governments, but there would still be a need for aid from overlying governments. In any case, redrawing the boundaries often faces prohibitive political problems.

23. Brown et al., "School Finance Reform," p. 74

24. States where localities derived a large proportion of their increased own-source revenues from nonproperty taxes tended to have a slow growth in the relative fiscal role of the state government during the 1962-1972 period. See Robert D. Reischauer, "In Defense of the Property Tax: The Case against an Increased Reliance on Local Nonproperty Taxes," *Proceedings of the Sixty-*

Seventh Annual Conference, 1974 (Columbus: National Tax Association, 975), pp. 290-292.

25. As of mid-1979, thirteen states had either limited the growth of its revenues or spending by law or constitutional amendment or had indexed their income tax.

10 Local Sales and Income Taxes

Local nonproperty taxes provide a means of dispensing property tax relief by shifting to other local government revenue sources. This distinguishes them from most other property tax relief mechanisms which are financed by state or federal governments. Thus, local sales and income taxes are frequently championed either by those who are dissatisfied with the amount of state financial aid or by those who fear the diminution of local autonomy which may accompany heavy reliance on it.

There are many possible ways to diversify local government revenue sources, but this chapter concentrates on two of the most commonly used methods—the local sales tax and the local income tax. A third method, user charges, is discussed in chapter 11.

Description[1]

A local sales tax is usually levied on substantially the same goods and services as a state's general sales tax. It is frequently collected with the state sales tax and then returned to the city or county which levied it. In more than two-thirds of the states in which a local sales tax is permitted, its revenue goes to the jurisdiction where the transaction took place; in other states, the revenue goes where deliveries are made.

The most common local sales tax rate is 1 percent, but it may be as little as 0.5 percent or as much as 4 percent.[2] In approximately half of the states which authorize local sales taxes, localities have an option as to what rate will be levied; elsewhere the state specifies the rate which must be used if the tax is employed.

Although local income taxes are permitted in far fewer states than local sales taxes, there is a much greater difference among them. The oldest local income taxes (in Pennsylvania, Ohio, and Kentucky) applied to the gross earnings of individuals, to net earnings of professionals, and to net profits of unincorporated businesses. They are administered locally and are levied at a uniform rate with no exemptions or deductions such as those which festoon the federal personal income tax. Administration is simple because employers withhold the tax from payrolls, eliminating the need for employees to file individual returns.

Most of the states adopting local income taxes in the 1960s and 1970s have changed this original model in one or more respects—several tax dividends, interest, and other nonlabor income, for example. Personal exemptions are often provided for, and sometimes deductions as well. One city taxes income at increasing marginal rates. An important improvement incorporated in some of the most recently enacted measures is that they are administered by the state government as supplements to the state income tax.

Workers usually must pay the tax even if they reside in a different community from where they work, although sometimes there is an arrangement for dividing the revenue between the two places. Occasionally the tax is payable solely to the place of residence.

A tax rate of 1 percent is most frequently used, but rates as low as 0.25 percent and as high as 4.3 percent can also be found.[3] Localities usually have some option as to how high the tax rate will be, although the state sets an upper bound.

In most states, local corporation income taxes accompany local personal income taxes, usually with an identical tax rate.

Other kinds of nonproperty taxes are not considered here because they individually provide relatively little revenue. However, in total these minor nonproperty taxes are quite important, accounting for 36.8 percent of local nonproperty tax revenue nationwide. Examples are taxes on public utilities, alcoholic beverages and tobacco products, and motor vehicle and operator's licenses.

History, Current Extent of Use, and Costs

History

The early local sales and income taxes were generally adopted in times of financial crisis. Although there were some earlier experiments with them, the oldest taxes still in effect date from the Depression of the 1930s. The first sales tax was passed by New York City in 1934, followed shortly thereafter by one in New Orleans. The oldest income tax was adopted in Philadelphia in 1939.[4]

The use of local sales and income taxes expanded steadily in the postwar period, with the most rapid increase taking place in the 1960s. Between 1963 and 1970 the number of states with local sales taxes doubled from thirteen to twenty-six. The progress of the local income tax can be seen by counting the number of large cities (those with a population over 50,000 in 1970) which use the tax. There were eleven such cities in 1950, twenty-four in 1960, and fifty-two in 1970.[5] These tabulations and others in this chapter do not include Washington, D.C., because of its unique situation.

The spread of local sales and income taxes slowed sharply in the 1970s. There was very limited use of local sales taxes in two additional states between 1970 and 1978. The only two states in which local income taxes expanded much were Maryland and Indiana, which broke precedent by granting the power to levy the tax to counties rather than cities. When Newark adopted an income tax in 1977, it was the first one of the nation's fifty largest cities to do so in a decade. These taxes became so unpopular, because of an increased perception that they discouraged business investment within a city, that Pittsburgh repealed its city income tax (though it subsequently reinstated it), and a reduction was seriously considered in Philadelphia, which has the highest local income tax rate in the country.

Local nonproperty taxes have recently been used in innovative ways. Indiana's local income taxes were part of a property tax relief package involving limitations on local taxes and increased aid to local governments. Local nonproperty taxes increasingly have been used to help finance local transit systems, as in the Atlanta, San Francisco, and Houston regions, where the local sales tax is used, and the Portland area, where the local income tax was adopted. Finally, Iowa authorized school districts to levy income taxes if they wished to exceed state-imposed restrictions on their spending, and numerous wealthy rural school districts have done so.

Current Extent of Use[6]

There are several different ways of describing the extent to which local nonproperty taxes are used. In 1977 they raised $14.519 billion, which was 19.4 percent of local tax revenue. Local general sales taxes provided 7.2 percent; local income taxes, 5.0 percent, and all other nonproperty taxes, 7.2 percent.[7] While these percentages are low, they represent increases from the past. In 1971 the corresponding figures were 15.4 percent overall, 5.4 percent sales, 4.0 percent income, and 6.0 percent other. These gains were due to the relatively high revenue elasticity of these taxes, increases in rates on existing taxes, adoption of the taxes by small governments in states where they had previously been authorized, and the adoption of local income taxes in Maryland and Indiana counties.

Local nonproperty taxes are considerably more important to cities than to other local governments. For cities they provided 39.9 percent of tax revenue in 1977; for counties, 18.8 percent; for townships, 8.3 percent; for special districts, 7.6 percent; and for school districts, 2.5 percent. See table 10-1.

Two qualifications add perspective to these figures. First, when user charges and state and federal aid are considered, local nonproperty taxes do not loom as large. While these taxes provide 19.4 percent of local tax revenue, they account for just 14.2 percent of total locally raised general revenue and 8.1 percent of total general revenue. Second, a few places account for a large share of the tax collected. To take the most outstanding examples, New York City alone accounts for 35.6 percent of local income tax revenue, various Pennsylvania

Table 10-1
Importance of Local Nonproperty Taxes, Various Years
(percent)

Type of Government	Local Nonproperty Tax Revenue Relative to:	Year					
		1976-1977	*1971-1972*	*1966-1967*	*1962*	*1957*	*1950*
All local governments	Local tax revenue	19.4	16.5	13.4	12.3	13.3	11.8
	Local general revenue from own sources	14.2	12.5	10.2	9.7	10.6	9.8
	Local general revenue from own sources	8.1	7.8	6.7	6.7	7.5	6.7
	All local general revenue						
Counties	Local tax revenue	18.8	14.4	7.9	6.5	6.3	—
	Local general revenue from own sources	13.1	10.6	6.0	5.2	5.1	—
	Local general revenue from own sources	7.2	6.1	3.6	3.2	3.2	—
	All local general revenue						
Municipalities	Local tax revenue	39.9	35.7	30.0	26.8	27.3	—
	Local general revenue from own sources	28.3	25.9	22.2	20.3	21.4	—
	Local general revenue from own sources	17.1	17.3	16.4	16.2	17.4	—
	All local general revenue						
Townships	Local tax revenue	8.3	6.6	7.2	6.7	6.4	—
	Local general revenue from own sources	7.3	5.8	6.4	6.1	5.8	—
	Local general revenue from own sources	5.2	4.5	4.8	4.7	4.4	—
	All local general revenue						
School districts	Local tax revenue	2.5	1.9	1.6	1.4	1.4	—
	Local general revenue from own sources	2.2	1.7	1.4	1.2	1.2	—
	Local general revenue from own sources	1.2	0.9	0.8	0.7	0.7	—
	All local general revenue						

Source: 1976-1977: U.S. Census Bureau, *Governmental Finances in 1976-77* (Washington, D.C., 1978); previous years: Robert D. Reischauer, "In Defense of the Property Tax: The Case against An Increased Reliance on Local Non-property Taxes," *Proceedings of the Conference on Taxation: 1974* (Columbus, Ohio: National Tax Association, 1975), p. 290.

governments take in another 20.2 percent of the income tax revenue, and California cities and counties raise 17.2 percent of the total general sales tax revenue. Seventeen of the twenty-two large cities which receive over half of their tax revenue from the local income tax are in Ohio.[8]

Local sales taxes are used in twenty-eight states, local income taxes in fourteen states, and neither is used in fourteen states. Included in this tabulation are six states (New York, Missouri, Ohio, Oregon, Alabama, and California) in which both are used. These figures include the recent limited use of income taxes in Iowa, Oregon, New Jersey, and California. There is also one state (Florida) where some local governments are authorized to use local sales taxes but have not chosen to do so.[9]

There are some pronounced regional differences. The sales tax is heavily used in the South and West. Nineteen of the twenty-four states west of the Mississippi River use a sales tax, but Missouri, Iowa, Oregon, and California are the only ones where income taxes are used (and in all they are used very sparingly). The income tax is mostly heavily used in the Middle Atlantic and North Central states. New England is unique in that not a single local sales or income tax is found in any state.

In many of the states mentioned above, only a minority of the governmental jurisdictions use a nonproperty tax and much of the population is not covered by one. In most states users tend to be large urban areas. But exceptions abound. In Alabama, California, Colorado, Illinois, Oklahoma, Texas, Utah, and Washington more than 100 jurisdictions use local sales taxes, while in Pennsylvania more than 3,700 and in Ohio more than 300 jurisdictions have local income taxes. Altogether, more than 4,300 local governments use local sales taxes and more than 4,200 use local income taxes.

Not surprisingly, there is a tradeoff between the use of a tax at the state and local levels. None of the eight states with the highest state sales taxes (Connecticut, Pennsylvania, Kentucky, Maine, Massachusetts, Mississippi, New Jersey, Rhode Island) permit local sales taxes. Since most of these states are in the Northeast, this may explain why local sales taxes are not used as heavily there as in the rest of the country.[10]

Table 10-2, which summarizes information on the use of local sales and income taxes, shows that local income taxes are usually levied by cities, although they are also used by some school districts, counties, and a transit district. Use of sales taxes is more varied. In half of the sales tax states, both cities and counties use them, and in seven states special districts or some other type of government levies them along with cities or counties. In only eight of the twenty-six states is use of local sales taxes limited to one type of government unit.

Among the forty-five largest cities in the country, twenty-four levied a general sales tax and twelve an income tax in 1977. New York City, St. Louis, and Kansas City were the only cities to levy both taxes. This tabulation is

Table 10-2
Use of Local Income and Sales Taxes

	Number of Jurisdictions					
	Sales			Income		
State	Cities	Counties	Other	Cities	Counties	Other or Indefinite
Alabama	240	25		6		
Alaska	80		6 boroughs			
Arizona	38					
Arkansas	3*					
California	394	58	1 transit district	2*		
Colorado	106	14	1 special district			
Delaware				1		
Georgia	2	14				
Illinois	1,240	102				
Indiana					38	
Iowa						21 school districts*
Kansas	12*	5*				
Kentucky				57	4	
Louisiana	112		19 parishes 52 school districts			
Maryland				1	23	
Michigan				16		
Minnesota	1					
Missouri	208*	1*	3 transit districts	2		
Nebraska	4*					
Nevada	13*					
New Jersey				1*		
New Mexico	92*	6*				
New York	24	44		1		
North Carolina		96				
Ohio		32	1 transit district	385		
Oklahoma	356					
Oregon			Number unknown[a]			1 transit district*
Pennsylvania						Over 3,500 cities, townships, and school systems
South Dakota	39*					
Tennessee	8*	90				
Texas	854		25 transit districts*			
Utah	175	29				
Virginia	38	96				
Washington	262	38				
Wisconsin			Number unknown[a]			
Wyoming		12*				

Source: Advisory Commission on Intergovernmental Relations, *Significant Features of*

Table 10-2 continued

Fiscal Federalism, 1976-77 ed., vol. 2: *Revenue and Debt* (Washington, D.C., 1977), pp. 186-187, 225-228; Commerce Clearing House, *State Tax Reporter* (Chicago, 1979).

Note: Unless noted by an asterisk, tabulation is as of July 1, 1976. The asterisk indicates that more recent information is included.

aRevenue in entire state is less than $50,000.

perhaps somewhat misleading because twelve of the largest cities are in California and Texas, where local sales taxes are universal. Cities which levy a local income tax tend to rely more heavily on it than do cities which levy a sales tax, as table 10-3 and appendix 10A show. Tulsa is the only city with more than 60 percent of its tax revenue from the sales tax, while five cities (Cincinnati, Columbus, Louisville, Philadelphia, and Toledo) derive more than 60 percent of their revenue from the income tax.

In summary, local sales taxes are used in more states and (excluding Pennsylvania's hordes of tiny governments levying income taxes) more jurisdictions than local income taxes, but income taxes tend to bulk larger in the fiscal situation of governments which do use them.

Costs

The cost of administering local nonproperty taxes depends on their complexity and whether it is done locally or by the state. For example, a flat-rate payroll tax is less expensive to administer than an income tax which covers the nonlabor income of individuals and the net profits of businesses. A supplement to a state tax is less expensive than a locally administered tax.

Three other important generalizations can be made about administrative cost. First, there are significant economies of scale, so that administrative cost as a percentage of revenue tends to fall as the size of the locality increases. For

Table 10-3
Proportion of Total Tax Revenue from Local Sales or Income Tax, Forty-five Largest Cities, 1976-1977

Proportion of Tax Revenue (Percent)	Number of Cities	
	Sales Tax	Income Tax
None	21	33
Under 20	9	1
20-39.9	10	5
40-59.9	4	1
Over 60	1	5
Total	45	45

Source: Appendix 10A.

example, in Pennsylvania the average collection costs ranged from 6 percent of revenues collected in jurisdictions where revenues were less than $50,000 to 3.9 percent in jurisdictions which collected more than $200,000.

Second, local sales taxes tend to be less expensive to administer locally than local income taxes. The average administrative cost of income taxes as a percentage of net revenues has been estimated at 4.5 percent in Pennsylvania, 2.2 percent in Detroit, and less than 1 percent in New York City. According to the ACIR, the administrative costs of sales taxes are lower.

Third, the costs are not so high as to rule out local income or sales taxes as local government tax sources.

The statements made about administrative costs also apply to the compliance costs which face individuals and firms. State administration and a common tax base lower costs substantially.[11]

Design Issues

In one of the most striking shifts in its history, in 1974 the Advisory Commission on Intergovernmental Relations advocated increased use of local nonproperty taxes, reversing a long-standing attitude which was "fairly negative" toward them. The fundamental arguments for and against this shift are evaluated in the next section of this chapter, but the ACIR's recommendations rested heavily on how it felt local sales and income taxes should be designed. Among its recommendations, the ACIR said that states should (1) provide a uniform local tax base which conforms to that of the state if the state imposes the tax; (2) collect and administer the local income or sales tax; (3) encourage widespread or universal coverage; (4) allow local flexibility in setting rates subject to state limits; and (5) take steps to reduce local fiscal disparities both by means of state aid and by redistributing local revenues.[12]

This discussion of design issues considers some of the major issues raised by the first two ACIR recommendations as well as related matters. The other three recommendations are considered in conjunction with the overall evaluation of local nonproperty taxes in the final section of this chapter.

The criteria for considering how local sales and income taxes should be designed are the same ones which must be used in evaluating the taxes themselves—horizontal and vertical equity, neutrality, administrative cost, and compliance cost.

Income Tax

The five major questions in designing a local income tax involve the definition of income which is subject to tax; whether personal exemptions, credits, or deductions should be allowed; whether rates should be graduated; how nonresidents should be treated; and whether the tax should be locally administered.

Income Subject to Tax. There is a continuum of possible tax bases ranging from those which are very narrow to others which are very comprehensive. At one extreme is a tax solely on payrolls. It is objectionable on grounds of horizontal and vertical equity. At each income level, households with considerable investment income would pay less tax than other households whose income was primarily from labor; those with investment income could also have a lower tax bill than others with lower total income whose income was solely wages and salaries. The Philadelphia-type income tax is somewhat broader in that it covers the profits of unincorporated business proprietors,[13] but the same criticisms can be made of it as of the pure payroll tax.

The best practical alternative is to define income in the same manner as the state. This can be done in the forty-one states which have broad-based income taxes. Elsewhere, local governments could follow the definitions of the federal government.[14] This broader measure brings interest, rent, dividends, and a portion of capital gains under the tax. It is not ideal, however, from an equity standpoint because of the many exclusions from the federal tax base, such as most of long-term capital gains, the imputed rent on owner-occupied housing, and most transfer payments.[15] Despite the superiority of a comprehensive definition of income, administrative and compliance costs would be so great as to render it unattractive until the federal income tax is itself reformed.

The difference between a payroll tax and one based on the federal definition of income is important from the viewpoint of vertical equity but not in terms of revenue in most cities. For example, Neenan found that inclusion of rent, interest, taxable capital gains, and dividends would have raised the revenue from the income tax only 5.3 percent in Kansas City and 6.6 percent in St. Louis.[16] Nationally, in 1975 gross wages and salaries constituted 83.9 percent of adjusted gross income reported on all returns but only 40 percent on returns with income over $100,000.[17] Thus, nonlabor income is much more important at high income levels than aggregate averages indicate.

Exemptions, Credits, Deductions. There are two advantages to providing a personal credit or exemption. They free from tax liability (or at least significantly reduce the burden of taxation on) households with very low incomes, and they make an allowance for family size. (With a uniform tax rate, exemptions and credits are equivalent in their effects, unlike the situation when tax rates are graduated.[18]) However, most local income taxes do not provide either a personal exemption or a credit. Michigan cities, New York City, Iowa school districts, and Maryland and Indiana counties are the only exceptions.

New York City, Maryland counties, and Iowa school districts have the only local income taxes which allow for nonbusiness deductions. Unless the tax is administered as a surtax on the state income tax, such deductions are best omitted in the interest of simplifying the taxing process.

Graduated Rates. Only the New York City income tax has graduated tax rates, although the surtaxes in Maryland and Iowa amount to the same thing. The employment of a uniform tax rate by all other income tax cities and counties is consistent with the strongly held view among academic economists that redistribution of income should not be a local government function.[19] Exemptions and credits also introduce a slight element of progression.

Treatment of Nonresidents. There are two issues in this area: How much tax, if any, should be paid by nonresidents who work in the jurisdiction levying the tax? And how should taxpayers work and live in different jurisdictions which each levy a local income tax be treated?

In most cases nonresidents must pay tax on their earnings where they work if their home government does not levy an income tax. In New York, Michigan cities, and Indiana counties nonresidents are taxed at a lower rate than resident workers. In Maryland and Iowa, however, the tax goes entirely to the place of residence.[20]

States differ in their treatment of persons who are subject to local income taxes both where they live and where they work. Pennsylvania law is peculiar in that Philadelphia receives all the tax on its commuters' earnings, while in the rest of the state all the tax goes to the city of residence, not that of employment. The fairest procedure is to divide the tax between the two places, but the division is usually made arbitrarily on a 50-50 basis rather than in some logical manner.[21]

State Administration. Maryland and Indiana counties and to a minor extent Iowa school districts derive revenue from local income taxes "piggybacked" onto state taxes. This procedure has much to recommend it. The local tax may be either a percentage of state tax liability, as in Maryland and Iowa, or a percentage of taxable income, as in Indiana. Some of the simplicity of state administration is lost if persons live and work in different jurisdictions and revenue does not go to the community of residence.[22]

Because the cost of administering an income tax locally tends to fall as a fraction of the total revenue generated as the size of a jurisdiction increases, the greatest gains from state administration are possible in states where many small governments use the tax. But even in larger cities and counties, state administration is clearly desirable on a cost basis.

Sales Tax[23]

The design issues for local sales taxes are simpler than for the local income tax. The three most important issues are whether the tax should be state-administered, whether the nexus for tax liability should be the location of the seller or the place of delivery, and how taxable sales should be defined.

All except four of the states in which local sales taxes are imposed provide for either mandatory or voluntary state administration and collection. The exceptions are Alaska (where there is no state sales tax), Arizona, Minnesota, and Louisiana. When offered the choice, some localities choose to administer the tax themselves.[24]

Most authorities recommend that the sales tax be paid according to where the purchase takes place in order to facilitate recordkeeping. Such a procedure tends to benefit jurisdictions with heavy concentrations of retail trade and hence exacerbates fiscal disparities.[25] As of 1977, fifteen states based the tax on the location of the seller and only five on that of delivery; the other ten had a mixed procedure.[26]

The question of how taxable sales are defined should really not be considered separately for local and state sales taxes. They should be (and usually are) defined the same way for both taxes. When a local sales tax is added to a state sales tax, however, the degree of regressivity of the sales tax becomes even more important than it otherwise is. States can reduce the regressivity by exempting food purchases or by providing an income tax credit. The exemption approach creates administrative and compliance problems, makes the tax less neutral, and does not target benefits. The credit approach is politically less appealing and often fails to reach some of the low-income households for whom the regressivity of the sales tax is most serious.

Do These Taxes Lower the Property Tax or Lead to More Local Spending?

Research on this issue has centered on local income taxes rather than local sales taxes. A study in the mid-1960s suggested that the local income tax was primarily a substitute for the property tax. In a comparison of cities with and without local income taxes, per capita property tax revenue was substantially lower in income tax cities in 1966 and had grown at a slower rate over the preceding decade. Moreover, total taxes per capita were also lower in income tax cities.[27] A more recent study came to the opposite conclusion—"taxes on earnings are not a substitute for, but an addition to, more traditional local revenue sources."[28]

Neither of these studies employed multivariate analysis to measure the effects of local nonproperty taxes on the property tax and the total tax bill. To carry out a complete analysis, it would be necessary to take into account such factors as differences in the assignment of functional responsibilities to cities, service levels, the extent to which taxes can be exported, and the availability of state or federal aid. Because such a study is beyond the scope of this book, what follows is an analysis of the relationship between per capita sales, income, and property taxes and the total per capita tax level.

The forty-five largest cities (excluding the District of Columbia) were divided into four groups according to size and into three groups according to whether they employed an income tax (twelve cities), sales tax (twenty-four cities) or neither (twelve cities). The three cities which levy both sales and income taxes (New York, St. Louis, and Kansas City) were then classified with the income tax cities because their income taxes yield considerably more revenue than their sales taxes. The median per capita levels of total taxes and property taxes alone are shown in tables 10-4 and 10-5.

The results are not surprising, although they differ from the conclusions of both previously mentioned studies. From table 10-4 it is clear that cities which levy local income or sales taxes do tend to have lower property tax levels. The only cell which is inconsistent with this generalization is the one for income tax cities with populations between 600,000 and 1 million. The reason for this exception is that one of the two cities included is Baltimore, whose property tax is particularly high because it is one of five cities in the sample responsible for running public schools and one of the few which has responsibility for functions normally carried out by counties.

The situation with regard to total tax collections as revealed in table 10-5 is more complex. In general, sales tax cities tend to have the lowest and income tax cities tend to have the highest overall per capita tax burdens. The principal explanation has to do with the fiscal situations of the respective cities. The great majority of cities using the sales tax are in the Sun Belt, are relatively young and healthy, and have relatively low spending. The income tax cities are all in the Northeast or North Central states (except for Missouri), have relatively old and poor populations, and are experiencing relatively great financial stress. One indication of the difference between the two groups is that twelve of the twenty-six sales tax cities gained population between 1970 and 1976, while all the income tax cities declined in population. Because of their problems, the income tax cities have relatively high spending and hence high taxes.

Table 10-4
Property Tax Collections in Cities with and without Local Sales and Income Taxes, 1976-1977

	Median per Capita Property Tax		
Population of City	Income Tax	Sales Tax	Neither Tax
Over 1,000,000	$125 (3)	$109 (3)	− (0)
600,000-999,999	148 (2)	61 (5)	$137 (5)
400,000-599,999	66 (5)	81 (5)	132 (3)
300,000-399,999	40 (2)	82 (8)	141 (4)

Source: U.S. Census Bureau, *City Government Finances, 1976-77* (Washington, D.C., 1978).
Note: Figures in cells are the median figures of per capita property tax for cities in each cell. Numbers in parentheses are number of cities in each cell. Three cities with both income and sales tax are classified with income tax cities.

Table 10-5
Total Local Tax Collections in Cities with and without Local Sales and Income Taxes, 1976-1977

Population of City	Median Total per Capita Tax		
	Income Tax	Sales Tax	Neither Tax
Over 1,000,000	$359 (3)	$211 (3)	− (0)
600,000-999,999	245 (2)	128 (5)	$141 (5)
400,000-599,999	239 (5)	196 (5)	205 (3)
300,000-399,999	142 (2)	143 (8)	175 (4)

Source: U.S. Census Bureau, *City Government Finances, 1976-77* (Washington, D.C., 1978).
Note: Figures in cells are the median figures of per capita total tax for cities in each cell. Numbers in parentheses are number of cities in each cell. Three cities with both income and sales tax are classified with income tax cities.

The cities with neither an income nor a sales tax are a mixed bag. They are scattered in all sections of the country. They include distressed cities like Boston and Buffalo which have relatively high tax burdens[29] and fiscally healthy cities like Portland, Jacksonville, and Miami.[30]

States can ensure that revenue from local sales or income taxes will go for property tax relief by placing strictures on local government action. For example, Indiana gave counties a choice: either levy a local income tax, in which case property tax levies are reduced and frozen, or do not levy a local income tax, in which case property tax rates are frozen (permitting revenue to rise only via new construction or reassessment). If a local income tax was levied, a portion of revenue from it was earmarked for property tax relief.[31]

Even if the nonproperty tax does not lead directly to lower property taxes in absolute terms, it may afford relief indirectly by averting an increase in property tax revenue to finance services. The only situation in which local nonproperty taxes do not either directly or indirectly finance property tax relief is that in which they are devoted entirely to increased government expenditures.

Sales, income, and other nonproperty taxes raised $14.519 billion for local governments in 1976-1977. Local property taxes would have had to be increased 24 percent to bring in that much revenue. This figure provides an upper bound on the amount of property tax relief provided by these taxes. To the extent that they lead to higher government spending or lower user charges, relief is less than $14.519 billion. It seems clear that these taxes do make a significant contribution to lowering property tax burdens.

Evaluation

The case for using local nonproperty taxes as a property tax relief device is complex because of the many factors which need to be considered. Local sales and income taxes must be compared to each other, to continued reliance on the property tax, and to increased state aid or a state takeover of local functions. We begin by analyzing how local sales and income taxes affect individual taxpayers considered narrowly—their horizontal and vertical equity, neutrality, and compliance costs. The second stage of the analysis considers the effect of these taxes on individual governmental units—their administrative cost, elasticity, and instability of revenue. The third stage considers broad intergovernmental issues—local autonomy, fiscal disparities, rate limits, arrangements for sharing revenue, and which governments should have the power to levy these taxes.

Vertical Equity

This criterion refers to whether households at different levels of economic well-being (usually as measured by income) are treated fairly, however that term is subjectively defined. It is difficult to analyze whether the average household at various income levels is better or worse off if a local income or local sales tax is substituted for a property tax, for three reasons.[32]

1. Sales and income taxes may be designed in many ways, and the differences have significant effects on each tax's incidence, as table 10-6 illustrates. A sales tax which does not exempt food but does exempt most services is quite regressive. A sales tax with the opposite characteristics is proportional over most income ranges although it is regressive for those with very low incomes. A payroll tax is progressive at low income levels because of the prevalence of transfer payments but regressive at high income levels because

Table 10-6
Incidence of Various Taxes by Income Class
(Expressed as percentage of income)

(a) *Property and Income Taxes, San Francisco, 1967*

Money Income Before Taxes	Property Tax[a]		Income Taxes of Various Types		
	Homeowners	Renters	Earned Income Only	Both Earned and Unearned Income	Supplement to State Tax
$ 2,064	14.7	5.0	0.24	0.34	0
3,354	9.8	3.9	0.57	0.65	0
4,902	6.0	3.0	0.71	0.82	0
6,450	5.6	3.6	0.82	0.88	0
7,804	5.0	2.1	0.87	0.94	0.2
9,675	4.7	1.8	0.92	0.97	0.5
12,642	3.8	1.5	0.92	0.98	0.7
17,415	3.5	1.2	0.89	0.96	1.1
35,217	2.7	0.6	0.87	1.00	3.2

Table 10-6 continued

(b)   Alternative Local Income Taxes, St. Louis, 1966

Money Income	Existing Ordinance	More Progressive Tax[b]
Under $2,000	0.927	0.486
$ 2,000-2,999	0.911	1.030
3,000-3,999	0.946	1.050
4,000-4,999	0.969	1.000
5,000-7,499	0.898	0.895
7,500-9,999	0.864	0.950
10,000 and over	0.661	0.859

(c)   Alternative Sales Taxes

Household Income	Food Taxable	Food Exempt
Under $1,000	1.51	0.93
$ 1,000- 1,999	0.75	0.46
2,000- 2,999	0.70	0.46
3,000- 3,999	0.73	0.51
4,000- 4,999	0.71	0.51
5,000- 5,999	0.69	0.49
6,000- 7,499	0.67	0.49
7,500- 9,999	0.64	0.48
10,000-14,999	0.60	0.46
15,000 and over	0.48	0.39

(d)   Property Tax Distributed in Proportion to Capital Income

Household Income	Property Tax
Under $3,000	7.2
3,000- 4,999	5.4
5,000- 9,999	3.6
10,000- 14,999	2.6
15,000- 19,999	2.9
20,000- 24,999	3.7
25,000- 49,999	5.7
50,000- 99,999	14.1
100,000-499,999	22.2
500,000-999,999	24.5
1,000,000 and over	18.2

Source: (*a*): R. Stafford Smith, *Local Income Taxes: Economic Effects and Equity* (Berkeley, Calif.: Institute of Governmental Studies, 1972), pp. 76-78. (*b*): William B. Neenan, *Political Economy of Urban Areas* (Chicago: Markham, 1972), p. 299. (*c*): James A. Papke and T.G. Shahen, "Optimal Consumption Tax Bases," *National Tax Journal*, September 1972, pp. 479-487. (*d*): Charles L. Schultze et al., *Setting National Priorities, The 1973 Budget* (Washington, D.C.: The Brookings Institution, 1972), p. 445.

[a]The estimates assume that all the tax on homes is paid by homeowners and 80 percent of the tax on rental housing is paid by tenants.

[b]The difference between the existing and the more progressive St. Louis income tax ordinance is that the latter taxes capital gains in full and provides for a $600 personal exemption.

of the exclusion of capital income. A flat-rate income tax on a base similar to federal adjusted gross income is also progressive at low income levels because of the exclusion of transfer payments, but it is close to proportional at higher income levels. Exemptions or credits make the tax more progressive, as do graduated rates.[33]

2. The incidence of the property tax varies considerably depending on local conditions. For example, according to the "new view," it tends to be more regressive, the higher the effective tax rate is above the national average; local assessing practices can also have a marked effect on regressivity. While low-value property is overassessed in most jurisdictions, the degree of overassessment varies considerably.[34]

Most of the comparisons in the literature between the incidence of a local sales or income tax and a local property tax are based on the "old view" of property tax incidence which exaggerated its regressivity. However, even according to the new view, the property tax tends to be regressive up to a family income of at least $15,000, as can be seen in table 10-6d.

3. The proportion of the tax which is paid by local households rather than businesses or nonresidents varies considerably depending on the design of the tax and local economic conditions. Two factors must be considered: how much of the tax is exported to commuters (shoppers and workers) and how much is paid by businesses rather than households. In most cities nonresidents directly pay a substantial proportion of the local income or sales tax, sometimes more than half. It is sometimes overlooked that they also pay some of the property tax in the form of business taxes shifted forward to consumers, but generally nonresidents will pay more of an income or sales tax than of property tax which produces equivalent revenue, lowering tax burdens on residents. But, on the other hand, usually considerably less of the sales or income tax is paid by business than is true under the property tax. Half or more of the property tax is often paid initially by businesses. But in the usual payroll tax none of the impact is on business; in a sales tax or broad-based income tax on both individual and business income, business usually pays a smaller share than it does under the property tax. Only if the tax rate on business income is much higher than on individual income will there not be a reduction in the share of taxes paid by business. Of course, shifting must be considered, but even when it is, business still tends to benefit from a substitution of the sales or income tax for the property tax.[35]

Thus, two offsetting factors affect the proportion of the tax burden on resident individuals. The increased ability to export taxes to nonresident individuals who commute into the jurisdiction levying the nonproperty tax is, to some degree, offset by the reduced share of taxes with an impact on business. Which effect is stronger depends on the structure of the tax (for example, the treatment of nonresident income) and the character of the local economy (such as the extent of commuting and the ratio of business income to business property).

If a higher percentage of the tax burden is borne by local residents, it implies that even low-income households could experience a higher tax burden when a progressive tax is substituted for a regressive tax.

The tendency of nonproperty tax to reduce business taxes can be counteracted. One method, proposed but not enacted in Iowa, would be to utilize the revenue from a local sales or income tax to increase the homestead credit. (A renter credit could also be raised, if the state has one.)

To summarize, the validity of all conclusions about tax incidence depends on local conditions. What is true in one city is not necessarily true elsewhere. However, in the average jurisdiction these statements can be made: If the proportion of taxes borne by local residents is held constant, the substitution of a local tax which is a supplement to a typical state income tax for a typical property tax will benefit the average person with below-average income. Substitution of a sales tax with food exempt and heavy taxation of services will be less beneficial for the person with below-average income, but it will either be of modest benefit or produce no significant change.

Horizontal Equity

According to the criterion which holds that "equals should be taxed equally," shifting from a property to an income tax is a move in the right direction. A study in New York City found that the dispersion of tax payments at each income level was considerably less for an income tax than for the existing property tax.[36] The income tax which the study considered was a supplement to the state income tax; a less comprehensive income tax would have poorer horizontal equity than the one studied, though perhaps better than the property tax. An income tax which did not permit deductions would have better horizontal equity than the one studied.

A movement from the property tax to the income tax would help homeowners at the expense of renters. This could be regarded as either an advantage or a disadvantage depending on one's perspective. Homeowners at each income level tend to pay much more property tax than renters, but they also tend to pay much less income tax.[37]

There are no empirical estimates as to how the horizontal equity of the sales tax compares to the property tax, but the sales tax is probably superior because consumption expenditures in general are less variable than consumption of housing.

Much of the horizontal inequity of the property tax referred to in this discussion is due to inaccurate assessments. For example, in 1976 in the average jurisdiction surveyed by the Census Bureau, each assessment ratio differed, on the average, by more than 20 percent from the median assessment ratio. This was a worse performance than in 1971, which in turn was worse than in 1966.[38]

Neutrality

There are all sorts of ways in which each of these taxes might interfere with neutrality, that is, change economic behavior. For example, to the extent that the property tax discourages investment in housing, changing to a sales or income tax might make the tax system more efficient. Most of these nonneutral effects are hypothetical and have not been shown to be of empirical significance.

However, one type of incentive created by these taxes has been frequently discussed and occasionally quantified—their effect on the location of households and business activity. One of the major shortcomings of local sales and income taxes in comparison with property taxes is said to be that their tax bases are considerably more mobile than that of the property tax.[39]

Numerous studies have concluded that local sales tax differentials do affect the location of retail sales. According to the best analysis, which analyzed 173 central cities of metropolitan areas, " . . .a one percent increase in the ratio of the city tax relative to the sales tax in the surrounding area will cause per capita retail sales to be between 1.69 and 10.97 percent lower" than they otherwise would be. The study also found that if the geographic area in which the tax is paid is broadened, the loss of sales is diminished.[40]

As for local income taxes, most research has suggested that they do not have much effect in causing people to flee places where they are levied. For example, a survey of recent movers in the Washington, D.C. metropolitan area found that relatively few persons considered tax differentials in deciding where to reside.[41] A survey of fifty-four municipal finance officers in cities employing local income taxes showed that nearly 90 percent thought that the tax had not resulted in any loss of individuals or businesses to other jurisdictions.[42]

On the other hand, a recent study of large cities found that those "which impose local income taxes lost eight percent of their resident work force between 1970 and 1976, compared to an overall employment growth of 10.2 percent in the average large city." The study concluded that these taxes contributed to business relocation from the urban core. However, it noted that the link between taxes and jobs is not unidirectional, since "cities facing revenue shortfalls added payroll taxes as a means to improve their fiscal position."[43] This is a classic example of the "chicken or egg" dilemma: Do income tax cities lose jobs because of the tax, or does the decline of their tax base induce them to turn to the income tax?

The extent of the loss of tax base depends in part on the magnitude of the tax differential: As long as tax rates are as low as at present, the outward movement is likely to be relatively minor. Resichauer probably expressed the consensus of professional opinion when he concluded that at relatively low rates these taxes do relatively little harm, but that their potential for heavier use is limited because of the wider tax rate differentials which would ensue.[44] Safeguards which could be adopted to keep differentials relatively small include constraints on maximum and minimum rates, limits on which governments are permitted to use these taxes, and state aid. These safeguards are discussed below. The fact that these taxes are deductible on state and local income taxes reduces the incentive of high-income individuals or businesses to migrate because of them.

Administrative and Compliance Costs

Obviously, the administrative and compliance costs of local sales and income taxes are much lower if they are state-administered. Even when they are locally administered, the cost of administration is only a small percentage of the revenue collected. Nevertheless, this administrative cost of a locally administered tax is considerable compared to the marginal administrative cost of raising additional property tax revenue, which is practically nil.[45]

Elasticity

The conventional wisdom of the 1960s was that income taxes have a considerably higher elasticity than sales taxes, which in turn have a higher elasticity than property taxes. In other words, revenue from nonproperty taxes tends to rise faster in response to economic growth than property tax revenue. To some extent, the sluggishness of the property tax base is due to the customary lag of assessments behind market values, but even with a well-administered property tax, its elasticity is lower.[46]

While the sluggish growth of the property tax base was a problem in earlier years, during the 1970s slow growth of property values was not a problem in most places. On the contrary, a rapid increase of property values was more of a problem than slow growth, since it tended to shift tax shares and led property taxes to rise more rapidly. Thus, although low elasticity was a negative factor in comparing the property tax with other taxes before 1970, it is no longer as serious a problem in most places.

Exceptions to these generalizations abound. In particular, many cities which experienced economic distress during the 1970s had very slow growth in their property tax base. Between 1971 and 1976 the per capita market value of property declined in St. Louis and rose just 1 percent in Detroit, 12 percent in Boston, and 31 percent in Buffalo. The growth of income and sales in these and other declining cities was considerably stronger than that of their property values because property values are more sensitive to population decline than are income and sales.[47] This factor weighs strongly in favor of nonproperty taxes in cities which are declining or stagnating but is not so important elsewhere.

Stability

In a noninflationary environment, one advantage of the property tax as opposed to income and sales taxes is that its revenue does not fluctuate with recessionary downswings in the economy. Cities dependent on local income or sales taxes, particularly income taxes, could experience drops in revenue during recessions, but those depending on property taxes are relatively immune to such ups and downs.

The prevalence of inflation changes the situation. Even in a recession revenue from the sales and income tax tends to rise, buoyed by price increases if not by real growth. However, when there is considerable inflation, unstable revenue may still be a problem in unusual cases. The 1974-1975 recession, the worst in the postwar period, provides some good examples. In the twelve large cities levying an income tax at that time, revenue rose more than 10 percent in six cities and from 5 to 10 percent in three cities between fiscal years 1974 and 1975. But in St. Louis it increased only 2 percent, in Philadelphia it dropped slightly, and in Detroit it fell more than 5 percent.

With their dependence on the sharply cyclical automobile industry, Michigan cities are especially vulnerable to a recession. In 1975, ten of the sixteen income tax cities in Michigan had decreases in income tax revenue. Pontiac's drop of 24 percent was the worst decline. In a period of inflation, stability is not as much of an advantage of the property tax as it formerly was, but it is still a virtue in cities with particularly volatile economies.[48]

There is a related factor which continues to hold true. Property tax revenue can be forecast with a high degree of accuracy, while sales and income tax revenue (particularly the latter) is subject to considerable uncertainty. The complexity which this introduces into the budgetary process increases the latitude for overly optimistic local officials to prepare unrealistic "balanced" budgets and thus slide their city into a fiscal crisis. The honesty which the property tax enforces on local officials is a "plus" for it.

Fiscal Disparities

One of the disadvantages of local income and sales taxes is the problem of fiscal disparities. Case studies in several states and metropolitan areas have consistently indicated that per capita income and per capita sales tend to vary among jurisdictions more than per capita property value.[49] Therefore, while these taxes bring in considerable revenue to places which are centers for employment or shopping, they bring in relatively little revenue to others. This problem can be alleviated to some extent if small jurisdictions are prevented from levying the tax and particularly if revenue is shared among local governments on some basis other than according to where it originated. These issues are discussed below.

Most studies of disparities do not address the issue in a comprehensive way, since they look at each tax separately. Even though income and sales are individually more variable than property values, a tax system which relied on more than just property alone might have smaller disparities. There are obviously many cities which are rich in all three respects and others which are poor in all three tax bases, but there are other cases in which variations are somewhat offsetting. Thus, disparities may not be as serious a problem as they sometimes appear. The situation differs from state to state depending on how structuraly fragmented local governments are. Studies that concentrate on California, where tax enclaves are common, have little relevance to places such as Iowa, where they are rare. A recent study in four metropolitan areas found, however, that local nonproperty taxes generally magnified, rather than offset, fiscal disparities arising from the property tax.[50]

Safeguards

The two major disadvantages of local sales and income taxes are fiscal disparities and the outmigration of the tax base in response to tax rate differentials. Both shortcomings can be mitigated in various ways. Four safeguards are recommended by the Advisory Commission on Intergovernmental Relations: (1) Set limits on the highest and lowest tax rates which may be used; (2) encourage the use of these taxes only by relatively large units of government; (3) share revenue among local governments; and (4) provide state aid to reduce fiscal disparities.

In specific terms, the ACIR suggests that states "encourage universal or widespread coverage" of these taxes in one of two ways: (1) mandate a minimum local levy and permit counties and those cities with at least 25,000 population to choose a higher rate subject to a specified maximum, or (2) give first option to adopt the tax to the local government of widest jurisdictional reach with sharing provisions for municipal governments. As part of this second option, if the larger unit of general government does not adopt the local sales or income tax, cities with populations of at least 25,000 should be allowed to do so.[51]

No states have adopted the safeguards proposed by the ACIR since they were proposed in 1974, but several states do have similar programs in effect from an earlier date. For example, in Utah, cities are allowed to impose the sales tax only if the overlying county has already done so. As a result, central cities of metropolitan areas benefit from the retail trade within their borders while the undesirable city-suburban tax differential is avoided. In New York State, the sales tax is imposed on a countywide basis, with its revenue being shared by cities within the county according to a formula.[52]

Consistent with the ACIR's views, the only two states initiating significant use of local income taxes in the 1970s, Indiana and Maryland, have authorized counties, rather than cities, to levy them.

While some sort of safeguards such as the ACIR suggests do seem desirable, it perhaps goes too far in proposing minimum rates. If all jurisdictions impose the local tax, it is equivalent to a state tax with revenue being returned to the jurisdiction where it originated. That is the situation with the local sales tax in California, Virginia, and Illinois. Such a system is certainly inferior to levying a state tax and distributing the revenue among localities according to need.[53] It eliminates the problem of tax differentials but does nothing about fiscal disparities.

Autonomy

An argument which was heard formerly but less often in recent years is that the property tax is a bulwark of local government independence. Reliance on local sales and income taxes would bring state controls. In the words of one authority, "We cannot abandon the property tax because local government could not survive without it."[54] Two reasons why such rhetoric is disappearing are that it exaggerates the threat to autonomy from limited restrictions such as the ACIR advocates and local governments are increasingly controlled by state governments regardless of local nonproperty tax policy. In fact, these taxes help to preserve local autonomy if the alternative is increased reliance on state aid.

Central City-Suburban Dimension

One of the most attractive aspects of local sales and income taxes from the viewpoint of central cities is the opportunity which they present to tax suburban commuters. Although suburbanites presumably pay some taxes indirectly to the central city through property taxes shifted forward by commercial enterprises, it is generally believed that suburbanites pay a higher proportion of nonproperty taxes. The extent to which suburbanites can be tapped by nonproperty taxes varies considerably among cities depending on the dominance of the central city as an employment and retailing center. At one extreme are cities such as Boston, Atlanta, and St. Louis, where an extremely high proportion of the workforce is commuters; at the other extreme are places like Jacksonville, Indianapolis, Phoenix, and Memphis with very few commuters.[55]

Aside from the opportunity for central cities to capture increased revenue from nonresidents, there is the larger question of whether central cities are "exploited" by their suburbs in the sense that suburbanites do not pay sufficiently for the central-city services which they use. It is difficult to answer this question because of the uncertainty as to how much of the property tax burden is exported to suburbanites and how valuable the services are which suburbanites use. Studies in Detroit and Washington, D.C., have concluded that there is exploitation, but one in San Francisco came to the opposite conclusion.[56]

Conclusions

The experience of Norway, Sweden, and Denmark with local income taxes provides a useful perspective. These three countries rely on local income taxes roughly to the same extent that U.S. local governments rely on property taxes. The problems of a mobile tax base, revenue instability, and loss of local autonomy are not generally considered serious, and the local tax system does operate satisfactorily. But the heavy reliance on income taxes at all levels of government contributes to another problem: the extremely high marginal tax rates to which most workers are subject. The high tax rates are resulting in increasing industrial absenteeism, a reluctance to work overtime, and a rising level of tax avoidance and evasion.[57]

The design of local nonproperty taxes requires care. An ideal local income or sales tax would differ considerably from those employed in most states. They should be state-administered, with tax bases conforming closely to the corresponding state taxes, and measures would be employed to alleviate fiscal disparities. Tax rate differentials should be limited, but they are not yet a serious problem with most existing local income and sales taxes.

Attention must also be paid to shifts in tax burdens if local nonproperty taxes are adopted. Unless offsetting steps are taken, burdens may shift from business to households and from homeowners to renters.

Local sales and income taxes tend not to excite enthusiastic reactions either pro or con. If the objective is to reduce the regressivity of the property tax, they are inferior to circuit breakers. If the goal is to diversify local revenue structures, they are inferior to state aid which is distributed according to local government need. But they are not clearly inferior to the property tax. As one advocate of local sales and income taxes says, "It is difficult to find any reason for its [the property tax's] fiscal preeminence."[58] Our review of criteria for evaluating these alternative taxes did not turn up any clinching arguments one way or the other, except in old, declining cities, where the property tax base is stagnating while the income and sales tax bases continue to grow.

Aside from the situation in these declining cities, one of the weightiest arguments in favor of sales and income taxes is the unpopularity of the property tax itself. If most citizens prefer to pay a relatively painless pay-as-you-go tax rather than the property tax, perhaps they should be allowed to. The alternative—to strip away illusions about "hidden" taxes—may not be achievable.

If it is not feasible to change public attitudes about the property tax, if the circuit breaker and redistributive state aid are not to be more widely used, and if the political demand for property tax relief continues to be heard, local nonproperty taxes are an attractive alternative.

In the United States, local nonproperty taxes are now an established part of the tax system in most states, but their use is still much less widespread than it could be. They have not been a particularly popular means of providing property tax relief in the 1970s. After expanding fairly rapidly in the 1950s and 1960s, local income and sales taxes spread much more slowly in the 1970s.

This is likely to change. One of the major factors tending to restrict the use of local sales and income taxes has been the reluctance of state legislatures to relinquish their priority access to sales and income taxes. In an era, such as the 1980s promise to be, of fiscal austerity, states are apt to be increasingly willing to permit localities to finance their own property tax relief.[59]

Notes

1. Advisory Commission on Intergovernmental Relations, *Local Revenue Diversification: Income, Sales Taxes, and User Charges* (Washington, D.C., 1974); Advisory Commission on Intergovernmental Relations, *Significant Features of Fiscal Federalism,* 1976-77 ed. Washington, D.C., 1977, vol. 2: *Revenue and Debt,* pp. 186-19, 225-230; Commerce Clearing House, *State Tax Reporter* (Chicago, 1979); Craig E. Reese, "Local Sales Taxation—Current Practices and Future Prospects," *Proceedings of the Seventieth Annual Conference, 1977* (Columbus: National Tax Association, 978) pp. 20-36.

2. The highest local sales taxes are in New York City and several Colorado resort areas.

3. The highest local income tax rate is 4.3125 percent in Philadelphia. New York City also has a tax rate of 4.3 percent for taxable income in excess of $25,000.

4. Charleston, South Carolina, had a local income tax in the nineteenth century. New York City adopted one in 1934 but repealed it the following year without ever collecting it. Advisory Commission on Intergovernmental Relations, *Local Revenue Diversification,* pp. 31, 51.

5. Advisory Commission on Intergovernmental Relations, *Local Revenue Diversification,* pp. 31, 53.

6. U.S. Census Bureau, *Governmental Finances in 1976-77* (Washington, D.C., 1978); U.S. Census Bureau, *City Government Finances in 1976-77* (Washington, D.C., 1978).

7. The Census Bureau's statistics are not fully revealing about the nonproperty tax revenue other than income and general sales taxes. The largest item is selective sales or gross receipts taxes on public utilities ($1.798 billion); other such taxes are on motor fuel ($75 million), alcoholic beverages ($144 million), tobacco products ($131 million), and other ($667 million). Revenue from motor vehicle and operators' licenses was $354 million, and all other taxes were $2.18 billion. U.S. Census Bureau, *Governmental Finances in 1976-77,* p. 19. One of the few discussions of minor local nonproperty taxes is in Marvin R. Brams, "Miscellaneous Revenues," in *Management Policies in Local Government Finance,* eds. J. Richard Aronson and Eli Schwartz (Chicago: International City Managers Association, 1975), pp. 146-165.

8. Data are for cities with populations of at least 50,000 in 1973-1974.

9. San Francisco's payroll tax is the only California local income tax. It differs from taxes in other states in that it is legally considered a tax on companies and not on workers. In Florida the sales tax may only be used for local transit systems. See John L. Mikesell, "Local Government Sales Taxes," in John F. Due, *State and Local Sales Taxation* (Chicago: Public Administration Service, 1970), p. 294, and Commerce Clearing House, *State Tax Reporter.*

10. Mississippi is a special case in that it formerly used local sales taxes extensively but prohibited them when it raised the state sales tax in 1968. Of revenue from the state tax 19 percent is returned to cities based on the place of collection. Mikesell, "Local Government Sales Taxes," p. 266.

11. Advisory Commission on Intergovernmental Relations, *Local Revenue Diversification,* p. 61; R. Strafford Smith, *Local Income Taxes: Economic Effects and Equity* (Berkeley, Calif.: Institute of Governmental Studies, 1972), pp. 24-28.

12. Advisory Commission on Intergovernmental Relations, *Local Revenue Diversification,* pp. 1-3.

13. The distinction between a payroll tax and a Philadelphia-style income tax is sometimes overlooked, but it is brought out by the Whites. See Melvin I. White and Anne White, "A Personal Income Tax for New York City: Equity and Economic Effects," in *Financing Government in New York City,* ed. Dick Netzer (New York: Temporary Commission on City Finances, City of New York, 1966), pp. 452-453.

14. Thirty-two states out of forty-one income tax states have tax bases which are very similar to that of the federal income tax, so there is relatively little difference between relying on the federal or the state definition of income. Advisory Commission on Intergovernmental Relations, *Significant Features,* pp. 206-207.

15. See, for example, Richard Goode, *The Individual Income Tax,* rev. ed. (Washington: The Brookings Institution, 1976). One difference between the federal and state income measures is the treatment of government bond interest. Many states tax state and local interest but exclude federal interest while the federal government does the opposite.

16. William B. Neenan, *Political Economy of Urban Areas* (Chicago: Markham, 1972), p. 312. In those two cities, the existing tax covers wages, salaries, commissions, and corporate and noncorporate business and professional profits. The tax on corporate profits was not part of the original Philadelphia income tax.

17. U.S. Treasury Department, *Statistics of Income: Individual Income Tax Returns, 1975* (Washington, D.C., 1978), p. 13. Part of the difference between wages and salaries and adjusted gross income is due to farm income, which would be relevant to some county income taxes but to few city income taxes.

18. With a graduated tax rate, an exemption provides a greater tax saving to taxpayers in higher marginal tax brackets, whereas a credit provides the same saving to all taxpayers.

19. See, for example, Richard Musgrave, *The Theory of Public Finance* (New York: McGraw-Hill, 1959), and Wallace E. Oates, *Fiscal Federalism* (New York: Harcourt Brace, 1972).

20. Albert L. Warren, "Integrating Local Nonproperty Taxes into the State Tax Structure," *Proceedings of the Sixty-seventh Annual Conference of the National Tax Association, 1974* (Columbus, Ohio, 1975), pp. 310-313. In Indiana, nonresidents pay the tax only if their home county has no income tax. Certain local governments in Pennsylvania and Kentucky may not tax nonresidents. Robbi Rice Dietrich, "Local Income Taxes: One Solution to Fiscal Dilemmas Facing Local Governments Today" (Regional Science Research Institute Discussion Paper, August 1978), p. 9.

21. Advisory Commission on Intergovernmental Relations, *Local Revenue Diversification*, pp. 56-58.

22. According to Stocker, administration of a "piggyback" income tax "becomes very complicated" if revenue does not go to the community of residence. On the other hand, administration of a locally administered income tax is complicated when revenue does not go to the community of employment. See Frederick D. Stocker, "Diversification of the Local Revenue System: Income and Sales Taxes, User Charges, Federal Grants," *National Tax Journal* 29 (September 1976):316.

23. See John L. Mikesell, "Local Government Sales Taxes," in John F. Due, *State and Local Sales Taxation* (Chicago: Public Administration Service, 1970).

24. Reese, "Local Sales Taxation," pp. 27-30.

25. Stocker, "Diversification," p. 317-318.

26. Reese, "Local Sales Taxation," pp. 27-30.

27. Elizabeth Deran, "Tax Structure in Cities Using the Income Tax," *National Tax Journal* 21 (June 1968).

28. Thomas Muller, "Central City Business Retention: Jobs, Taxes, and Investment Trends" (Report prepared for the Department of Commerce Urban Roundtable, February 22, 1978), p. 8.

29. Newark was one of the cities with neither tax at the time covered in the analysis, although it subsequently adopted an income tax.

30. Portland is covered by a regional income tax.

31. This system was instituted in 1973, and restrictions were eased somewhat in 1979. All the counties which elected to levy a local income tax are relatively rural ones. See John L. Mikesell, "Local Legislative Behavior in Tax Substitution," *Quarterly Review of Economics and Businesses* 6 (Winter 1974):83-91, for an analysis of which counties adopted the local income tax. One result of this local income tax system (together with other fiscal innovations) was that property taxes on farm real estate fell 7.4 percent between 1971 and 1977, the largest drop in any state. The effective property tax rate on farms fell from 1.34 to .57 percent, while the tax rate on homes fell from 1.96 to 1.66 percent. See chapter 13 for an analysis of relative home and farm tax rates.

32. Christopher H. Gadsden and Roger W. Schmenner also conclude that generalization is difficult because of the many variables which must be considered. See their article, "Municipal Income Taxation," in John R. Meyer and John M. Quigley, *Local Public Finance and the Fiscal Squeeze: A Case Study* (Cambridge, Mass.: Ballinger, 1977), pp. 74-78.

33. See White and White, "A Personal Income Tax," pp. 445-460; Neenan, *Political Economy*, pp. 298-301; R. Stafford Smith, *Local Income Taxes*, chapter 4.

34. U.S. Census Bureau, *1977 Census of Governments*, vol. 2: *Taxable Values and Assessment/Sales Price Ratios*, (Washington, D.C., 1978), tables 14 and 19.

35. Smith, *Local Income Taxes*, chapters 3, 4. According to one estimate, nonresidents pay 12 to 15 percent of city sales taxes. Approximately 25 percent of income taxes are paid by business firms, who shift half to nonresidents. In 1971 approximately 27 percent of the property tax base was commercial or industrial property in growing cities, while the proportion was 40 percent in cities with declining population. See Thomas Muller, *Growing and Declining Urban Areas: A Fiscal Comparison* (Washington: The Urban Institute, 1976), pp. 65-66, 115.

36. White and White, "A Personal Income Tax," pp. 460-465.

37. According to one recent estimate, the combined effect of property and income taxes is biased in favor of homeowners. See Helen F. Ladd, "The Role of the Property Tax: A Reassessment," in *Broad-Based Taxes: New Options and Sources*, ed. Richard A. Musgrave (Baltimore: Johns Hopkins, 1973), p. 68.

38. U.S. Census Bureau, *Census of Governments*, vol. 2, *Taxable Property Values and Assessment/Sales Price Ratios*, 1967, 1972, and 1977. (Washington, D.C., 1968, 1973, 1978). Inflation is probably a major cause of the increasing inaccuracy of assessments.

39. James A. Maxwell, *Financing State and Local Governments* (Washing-

ton: The Brookings Institution, 1969); Oates, *Fiscal Federalism;* Robert D. Reischauer, "In Defense of the Property Tax: The Case against an Increased Reliance on Local Non-property taxes," *Proceedings of the Sixty-seventh Annual Conference of the National Tax Association, 1974,* (Columbus, Ohio, 1975) p. 301.

40. John L. Mikesell, "Central Cities and Sales Tax Rate Differentials: The Border City Problem," *National Tax Journal* 33 (June 1970):213.

41. Stephen S. Fuller and Joan E. Towles, "Impact of Intraurban Tax Differentials on Business and Residential Location," in *Technical Aspects of the District's Tax System* (Studies and Papers prepared for the District of Columbia Tax Revision Commission, 1978), pp. 145-192.

42. Advisory Commission on Intergovernmental Relations, *Local Revenue Diversification,* p. 59. Some skepticism about this finding is warranted because an even higher percentage of respondents to the survey felt that the local sales tax had no adverse effect on the local tax base. This conflicts with the statistical findings of Mikesell and others that there is such an effect. See Advisory Council on Intergovernmental Relations, *Local Revenue Diversification,* p. 39.

43. Muller, "Central City Business Retention," p. 8.

44. Reischauer, "Defense," p. 306.

45. Comparisons of the total cost of administering the property tax with that of the sales or income tax are rather pointless, since completely eliminating the property tax is not a serious option in most places.

46. See, for example, Reischauer, "In Defense," p. 305.

47. George E. Peterson et al., *Urban Fiscal Monitoring* (Washington: The Urban Institute, 1979), chapters 2, 3.

48. Data on Michigan were provided by Roy Saper. For other cities data were obtained from U.S. Census Bureau, *City Government Finances in 1973-74, 1974-75.* Even before inflation escalated in the 1970s, city income tax revenue seldom dropped. In constant tax rate terms, Neenan points out that in the twenty years after it adopted the income tax in 1948, Columbus, Ohio, had increased revenue every year with only two exceptions—1950, when there was no change from 1949, and 1961, when revenue dipped 0.1 percent in the face of a 13.2 percent unemployment rate in the Columbus labor market. In the ten years following 1959, Dayton never experienced more than a tiny drop in revenue, including one year in which the local unemployment rate was 14.8 percent. Philadelphia's tax produced increased revenue every year up to 1970 with two exceptions when it moved sideways.

49. Reischauer, "In Defense," pp. 300-305; John H. Bowman and John L. Mikesell, "Fiscal Disparities and Major Local Non-property Taxes: Evidence from Revenue Diversification in Indiana, Maryland, Ohio and Virginia," *Proceedings of the Seventieth Conference of the National Tax Association,* 1977, pp. 412-422.

50. John H. Bowman and John L. Mikesell, "Revenue Diversification

within Metropolitan Areas: Effect in Disparities and Central City Suburban Fiscal Relationships" (Bloomington, Ind.: School of Public and Environmental Affairs, 1979).

51. Advisory Commission on Intergovernmental Relations, *Local Revenue Diversification,* pp. 2-3.

52. Stocker, "Diversification," p. 319; Advisory Commission on Intergovernmental Relations, *Local Revenue Diversification* p. 46.

53. Reischauer, "In Defense," p. 305; G. Ross Stephens, "The Suburban Impact of Earnings Tax Policies," *National Tax Journal* (September 1969):333.

54. L.L. Ecker-racz, *The Politics and Economics of State-Local Finances* (Englewood Cliffs, N.J.: Prentice-Hall, 1970), p. 78. Similar statements are made by Maxwell, Financing State and Local Governments, p. 128; James N. Buchanon, *The Public Finances,* 3d ed. (Homewood, Ill.: Irwin, 1970), p. 412; and John Due, *Government Finance* (Homewood, Ill.: Irwin, 1963), p. 368.

55. The daytime working population was 78 percent higher than the resident working population in Boston in 1970. Comparable figures were 73 percent in Atlanta and St. Louis, 3 percent in Jacksonville, 5 percent in Indianapolis, and 6 percent in Phoenix and Memphis. Since three of the four lowest cities recently underwent city-county consolidations, this illustrates the point that cities with little metropolitan government fragmentation tend to have small interjurisdictional externalities. See Peterson et al., *Urban Fiscal Monitoring,* chapter 3.

56. For Detroit, see Neenan, *Political Economy of Urban Areas,* chapters 3 to 5; for Washington, D.C., see Kenneth V. Greene et al., *Fiscal Interactions in a Metropolitan Area* (Washington: The Urban Institute, 1974); Smith, *Local Income Taxes,* chapter 7.

57. Steven D. Gold, "Scandinavian Local Income Taxation: Lessons for the United States?" *Public Finance Quarterly* (October 1977):471-488. Reliance on the local income tax may have contributed to a reduction of local autonomy in certain respects, as evidenced by consolidations of local governments, reliance on aid from the central government, and restrictions on allowable tax rates. See also Melvin Krauss, "The Swedish Tax Revolt," *Wall Street Journal,* February 1, 1979.

58. L.R. Gabler, "A Reconsideration of Local Sales and Income Taxes," *Proceedings of the Sixty-seventh Annual Conference of the National Tax Association,* 1974, p. 281.

59. This prediction was suggested to me by John Shannon.

Appendix 10A:
Sales and Income
Taxes in Large Cities

Table 10A-1

Relative Importance of Local Sales Tax in Individual City Tax Structures:
1972 and 1977

| City | Percentage of Tax Revenue | | Tax Rate (Percent) |
	1977	1972	1978
Austin	24.3	23.7	1
Buffalo	0	7.2	0
Chicago	14.1	14.1	1
Dallas	20.5	19.6	3a
Denver	25.8	22.3	1
El Paso	25.2	23.7	1
Fort Worth	25.8	25.0	1
Houston	17.5	5.6	1
Kansas City	19.8	22.5	1
Long Beach	19.5	19.5	1
Los Angeles	23.1	22.4	1.5
Nashville-Davidson	44.8	41.3	2b
New Orleans	14.4	13.6	4
New York	14.4	13.6	4
Oakland	19.7	22.1	1
Oklahoma City	53.7	37.8	2
Omaha	29.8	26.6	1.5
Phoenix	43.5	39.1	1
St. Louis	17.5	11.8	0.5
San Antonio	29.6	26.6	1
San Diego	31.1	29.2	1
San Francisco	9.8	13.3	1
San Jose	24.1	23.5	1
Seattle	16.2	14.4	0.5
Tulsa	65.7	55.5	2

Note: Cities included are those with population of at least 300,000 in 1976.

aIncludes county tax.

bAdditional 1 percent for schools.

Table 10A-2
Relative Importance of Local Income Tax in Individual City Tax Structures:
1972 and 1977

	Percentage of Tax Revenue		Tax Rate (Percent)
City	1977	1972	1978
Baltimore	25.3	14.2	50% of state tax
Cincinnati	65.8	57.7	2
Cleveland	55.8	47.8	1[a]
Columbus	82.7	78.2	1.5
Detroit	37.7	35.1	2[b]
Kansas City	31.6	37.0	1
Louisville	61.8	55.0	2.2[c]
New York	22.2	21.0	0.9 to 4.3[d]
Philadelphia	64.3	62.6	4 5/16
Pittsburgh	15.8	16.9	1
St. Louis	27.9	29.4	1
Toledo	80.0	74.9	1.5

[a]Raised to 1.5 percent in 1979.

[b]One-half percent on nonresidents.

[c]Includes school tax; lower for nonresidents of Jefferson County.

[d]Highest rate applies to taxable income over $25,000.

11 User Charges as Vehicles for Property Tax Relief

All cities and counties, and to a lesser extent school districts, rely on user charges as one of their sources of revenue. One of the avenues available for providing property tax relief is to increase reliance on user charges. Such a policy has been enthusiastically advocated by a number of economists, and in fact reliance on user charges has increased somewhat in the past decade. However, the extent to which they offer a viable mechanism for substantial property tax relief, in view of the political, administrative, and equity problems which confront them, is a controversial issue.

Description

A user charge is a payment in which there is a clear relationship to the service made available, as opposed to a tax, which is a payment for government services in general. User charges can be divided into several distinct categories. First, there are charges which are directly related to an individual's voluntary consumption of specific public services or products, such as an admission fee to a swimming pool or a charge for a map sold by a city or state. Included in this category are fees for government-operated utilities such as electricity and water companies and tuition for schools. Closely related to this first type of user charge are taxes on private goods which are essential complements to use of certain publicly provided goods, such as a tax on gasoline. A third type of user charge differs in that it is not voluntary but can be viewed as a payment for a specific government service. One example is special assessments, which are charges levied against particular property owners for such improvements as roads and sewers, on the theory that much of the benefit from these facilities benefits owners of property nearby rather than the general populace. Fees to pay for government inspections related to the protection of public health and safety provide other examples. In addition to these conventional user charges, some economists have proposed novel approaches which entail initiating charges for the pollution or congestion which individuals or firms create. Table 11-1 catalogs some of the major types of user fees employed by local governments.

State law often restricts user fees to the actual cost of providing the service in question. If the fee were higher than this actual cost, it would be considered to be a tax, and local governments generally are prohibited from levying any tax which has not been specifically authorized by the state government.

227

Table 11-1
Types of Fees, Charges, and Licenses

Police protection
Special patrol service fees
Parking fees and charges
Fees for fingerprints, copies
Payments for extra police service at stadiums, theaters, circuses
Transportation
Subway and bus fares
Bridge tolls
Landing and departure fees
Hangar rentals
Concession rentals
Parking meter receipts
Health and hospitals
Inoculation charges
X-ray charges
Hospital charges, including per diem rates and service charges
Ambulance charges
Concession rentals
Education
Charges for books
Charges for gymnasium uniforms or special equipment
Concession rentals
Recreation
Greens fees
Parking charges

Sanitation
Domestic and commercial trash collection fees
Industrial waste charges
Sewerage
sewerage system fees
Other public utility operations
Water meter permits
Water services charges
Electricity rates
Telephone booth rentals
Housing, neighborhood and commercial development
Street tree fees
Tract map filing fees
Street-lighting installations
Convention center revenues
Event charges
Scoreboard fees
Hall and meeting room leases
Concessions
Commodity sales
Salvage materials
Sales of maps
Sales of codes
Licenses and fees
Advertising vehicle
Amusements (ferris wheels, etc.)

Electrician—second class
Film storage
Foot peddler
Hucksters and itinerant peddlers
Heating equipment contractors
Junk dealer
Loading zone permit
Lumber dealer
Pawnbrokers
Plumbers—first class
Plumbers—second class
Pest eradicator
Poultry dealer
Produce dealer—itinerant
Pushcart
Rooming house and hotel
Second-hand dealer
Second-hand auto dealer
Sign inspection
Solicitation
Shooting gallery
Taxi
Taxi transfer license
Taxi driver
Theaters
Trees—Christmas
ending—coin
Vending—coin

Concession rentals
Admission fees or charges
Permit charges for tennis courts, etc.
Charges for specific recreation services
Picnic stove fees
Stadium gate tickets
Stadium club fees
Park development charges

Billiard and pool
Bowling alley
Circus and carnival
Coal dealers
Commercial combustion
Dances
Dog tags
Duplicate dog tags
Electrician—first class

Vault cleaners
Sound truck
Refuse hauler
Land fill
Sightseeing bus
Wrecking license

Source: Selma J. Mushkin and Richard M. Bird, "Public Prices: An Overview," in Selma J. Mushkin, *Public Prices for Public Products*, © The Urban Institute (Washington, D.C., 1972), pp. 7-8. Reprinted with permission.

**History, Current Extent of Use,
and Costs**

The data available on revenue from user charges are difficult to analyze because of the ambiguity of their definition. According to the Census Bureau, local governments collected $18.977 billion in current charges in 1976-1977, but this figure is not sufficiently inclusive. For example, it does not include special assessments or revenue from motor vehicle fuel taxes and licenses. Inclusion of these revenues brings the total to $20.268 billion, which represents 19.9 percent of all local general revenue excluding intergovernmental aid.

More controversial is the omission of $14.191 billion of revenue from government-operated utilities such as water, electricity, and natural gas. If these enterprises operated on a break-even basis, it would not be necessary to consider their impact on other local government operations. However, they often run at either a surplus, enabling taxes to be lower, or a deficit, imposing a burden on the rest of the budget. Liquor store sales, while listed separately from utility revenue, are similar in this respect to it.[1]

Table 11-2 shows the relative importance of the various types of charges levied by local governments. Aside from utilities, the major sources of revenue are charges for hospitals, sewerage, school lunch sales, air transportation, and institutions of higher education.

Revenue from user charges rose rapidly during the 1970s. Between 1970-1971 and 1976-1977 user charges increased about 91 percent, whether one counts utility revenue or not. This is just slightly below the increase in total general revenue of 94.6 percent during that period. In this context, reliance on user charges does not appear to have changed much. However, if federal and state aid is excluded, the picture changes. General revenue other than inter-governmental aid and user charges rose only 74.5 percent, considerably slower than user charges. Thus, user charges became increasingly important to local government budgets.[2]

The fastest growth occurred in charges for hospitals, institutions of higher education, sewerage, and air transportation. In all these cases a major explanation for the rapid increase in user fees was that local government expenditures for these functions were expanding rapidly. Reasons differ in each area. Spending for higher education increased because of the increased popularity of community colleges. Spending on sewage systems was stimulated by federal antipollution efforts, which required that local user charges carry a portion of the financial burden. Hospital spending was pushed upward by extraordinary inflation in medical costs. Increasing air travel stimulated spending on air transportation facilities.

None of the nonutility charges cover all the local government expenditures for particular purposes, as the last column of table 11-2 shows. Air and water transport and parking facilities come closest to breaking even. Charges for higher

Table 11-2
Local Government User Charges, 1970-1971, 1976-1977

Type of Charges	1976-1977	1970-1971	Percentage Increase	Proportion of Local Expenditure 1976-1977 (Percent)
	(Millions of Dollars)			
Current Charges	*18,977*	*9,819*	*93.3*	
Education	3,492	2,470	41.4	0.5
School lunch sales	1,622	1,442	12.5	
Institutions of higher education	1,043	396	163.4	20.7
Other	828	631	31.2	
Hospitals	5,722	2,569	122.7	69.2[a]
Sewerage	2,488	1,034	140.6	38.1
Sanitation other than sewerage	622	344	80.8	26.6
Parks and recreation	626	316	98.1	16.2
Natural resources	130	105	23.8	14.4
Housing and urban renewal	916	621	47.5	27.8
Air transportation	1,109	515	115.3	96.0
Water transport and terminals	415	216	92.1	80.6
Parking facilities	287	191	50.3	88.3
Other current charges	3,130	1,438	117.7	
Other General Revenue	*1,291*	*809*	*59.6*	
Special assessments	862	581	48.4	
Motor vehicle and operators' licenses	354	186	90.3	
Motor fuel taxes	75	42	78.6	
Total general revenue user charges	20,268	10,628	90.7	
Utility revenue	*14,191*	*7,296*	*94.5*	
Liquor stores revenue	*368*	*269*	*36.8*	
Grand total user charges	34,827	18,193	91.4	

Source: U.S. Census Bureau, *Governmental Finances, 1970-71* (Washington, D.C., 1972), *1976-77* (Washington, D.C., 1978).
[a]Does not include expenditures for hospitals not operated by local governments themselves. If they are included, the proportion of costs covered by charges is 64.9 percent.

education and parks and recreation provide about one-fifth or less of the revenue to finance those functions.

Reliance on user charges varies widely from state to state and city to city. Local governments in the South tend to rely on them much more heavily than do governments in the rest of the country, while New England uses them least. Local governments in Mississippi and Alabama obtain more funding from this source than from taxation. At the other extreme, Rhode Island's charges and miscellaneous general revenue account for only 8.5 percent of its local own-source general revenue.[3]

Small cities seem to rely on user charges to a greater extent than large cities. To some extent, this may be due to differences in the types of services which they are providing. Fees and charges tend to be used for some types of services but are difficult to apply to others either because the users are not clearly identifiable or because persons who do not pay cannot easily be excluded.[4]

It is also difficult to interpret figures showing differences in the reliance on user charges for particular cities; that is, cities with a high proportion of revenue from user charges may be providing unusual services. For example, Cincinnati derives more revenue from charges than any other large city because of tuition at a large municipally operated university.[5]

Design Issues

Once the government decides that it is not going to give services away at no direct cost to users, the problem arises of how much to charge. Space does not permit an exhaustive consideration of the best way to deal with this issue, but two topics are briefly discussed, one theoretical and the other practical.

There is a large literature on marginal cost pricing. In a perfectly competitive economy, products should be priced according to their marginal cost. If the price is set higher, some units of output for which benefit exceeds cost will not be produced, and thus too little will be available from society's point of view. If the price is set below marginal cost, too much will be produced, since for some output marginal cost will be higher than marginal benefit. However, if the price is set equal to marginal cost, the product is likely to require a public subsidy because marginal cost may be less than average cost. Theoretically, a non-distorting lump-sum tax could be used to finance this subsidy, but in actuality the financing mechanism would itself cause allocative distortions.

Marginal cost pricing implies that prices should not necessarily be constant at all times but rather should vary as marginal cost varies (peak-load pricing).

The desirability of marginal cost and peak-load pricing depends on the cost of administering a marginal cost pricing system. If administration costs are too high, the theoretical advantages of these pricing schemes cannot be realized.

Many governments employ so-called user charges which are in fact nothing of the sort. For example, a fee for refuse collection is often a flat annual charge which does not depend at all on how much refuse is actually collected from each household. Such a charge does nothing to realize the equity and efficiency benefits which user charges make possible. Rich and poor pay the charge equally, even though the average amount of refuse generated tends to be considerably higher in affluent neighborhoods than elsewhere and the cost of collection is higher in areas where homes are farther apart.[6]

A similar example relates to user charges for sewage. The most unfair, regressive, and inefficient method of charging for this service is to make all households pay a uniform fee. It is fairer, less regressive, and more efficient to charge for the service on the basis of the amount of water used; however, the metering required by this method entails an added administrative expense. Cities frequently attempt to exempt water used for sprinkling and other outdoor use by basing the charge on the use during winter months; such a procedure tends to help the affluent (who have larger lawns), but it aligns the charge more closely with actual sewage produced. Altogether there are at least seven other methods available for determining sewage charges.[7]

Evaluation

There are three reasons why increased employment of user charges may be desirable: efficiency, fairness, and revenue availability.

Efficiency

When goods or services are provided at prices which are less than the (marginal) cost of producing them, they tend to be overused. If the government provides sufficient output to meet the total demand at the subsidized price, there is a misallocation of resources. Moreover, if services are provided free, it is impossible to determine the efficient level of provision, since prices are not providing signals as to the value placed on the goods or services by the public.

Fairness

User charges are more consistent with the benefit principle of taxation than is financing out of general revenue. According to this concept, those who use a service should pay for it. The application of this principle might not only increase payments by nonresidents who use local services, but also improve horizontal equity by redistributing payments among local residents.

However, the benefit principle often conflicts with another concept of fairness, the ability-to-pay principle, which stipulates that a fair distribution of the cost of financing government should be based on the income and wealth of each household. In an ideal federal system, the national government would redistribute income by means of ability-to-pay taxation allowing local governments to rely heavily on benefit taxes.[8] But in practice the federal government has not yet eliminated poverty, so that local governments cannot be blind to ability to pay.

Revenue Availability

User charges may make it possible to lower taxes or to keep them from rising as fast as they otherwise would. Since this book is particularly concerned with property tax relief, this discussion will concentrate on the third reason for increased employment of user charges. Whatever their advantages from the viewpoints of equity and efficiency, if user charges do not provide property tax relief, they lie outside the bounds of this book.[9] Moreover, we consider the prospects for increased reliance on user charges only at the local level, since that is where most of the property tax is raised.

Some writers have been extremely optimistic about the potential for vastly increasing the revenue yield of user charges. For example, Stockfish estimated that Los Angeles city government in the later 1950s could have increased its revenues approximately 40 percent by rationalizing and increasing its user charges.[10] Other analysts have concluded that unless technology or the public attitudes which shape political realities change radically, the potential revenue from user charges is much more limited.[11] Nevertheless, all the writings on this subject indicate that untapped potential still exists for tax relief from increased user charges.

There is surprisingly little difference between the conclusions of Stockfish and the others. Most of the revenue which Stockfish envisioned came from raising rates on the municipal electric utility system and instituting a charge for refuse collection. Many cities do not have the first option because electricity is privately provided and have already adopted the second.[12]

User charges are not appropriate for many public services. According to Due, they are most suitable when (1) substantial waste results if the service is provided free of charge; (2) the service primarily benefits individuals rather than the community as a whole; (3) the cost of collecting charges is low; (4) the burden on individuals of paying for the services would not conflict with accepted principles of equity; in particular, an excessive burden is not placed upon the poor.[13]

To these four criteria, a fifth can be added—the user charge must be politically acceptable.[14] Cases can be cited in which mayors and city managers saw their popularity plummet when they had the temerity to propose charging the public for services which previously were provided free.[15]

Two factors weigh against user charges even if all the other criteria are satisfactorily met. First, they are not deductible in computing federal income tax liability, while income, sales, and property taxes are deductible. The value of this deductibility depends on whether a household itemizes deductions and on its marginal tax rate. For example, if a family filing a joint return has taxable income of $25,000, its marginal tax rate is 32 percent. Therefore, if it pays $100 of property tax to its city for refuse collection and if it itemizes, its federal income tax will be $32 lower, so that the net cost of paying for the service is $68. However, if it pays a $100 user charge for its refuse collection, its net cost is the full $100.[16]

The deductibility consideration is primarily relevant to high-income households, since they are most likely to itemize deductions. The whole issue is not nearly as significant as it was previously because of the recent increases in the standard deduction and personal exemptions which have led to a reduction in the proportion of income tax filers who itemize from 60 to about 25 percent.

Another disadvantage of user charges is that if a government relies on them rather than tax revenue, its federal revenue-sharing allocation is reduced. One of the factors which determines how much revenue sharing a government receives is its tax revenue. Since revenue from user charges is not considered, there is a penalty for governments which rely on them. The incentive to obtain revenue from taxes rather than user charges varies greatly among communities because of the complexities of the formulas by which revenue sharing is distributed. Normally each dollar of extra tax revenue yields an extra 3 to 20 cents of revenue sharing,[17] but some governments have no incentive at all to change their method of raising revenue, while others can garner more than a dollar in added revenue sharing for each dollar their tax revenue rises.

A major unresolved issue concerning user charges is how they are normally distributed among income groups. Some writers oppose greatly increasing reliance on them because of the burden it would place on the poor. This charge elicits several responses. First, there are undoubtedly cases in which services are provided on a subsidized basis or at no cost primarily to individuals or businesses which can afford to pay for them. Common examples include police who direct traffic at special events or for specific businesses, public golf courses, and commuter transit. In addition, while existing user fees are often regressive, it is maintained that if they were properly designed to reflect use and costs more accurately, they would not necessarily be regressive. An example is the provision of refuse collection discussed earlier. Finally, special arrangements can be made to subsidize needy families and individuals, as is often done for college tuition and hospital charges.[18]

When local governments face serious budget problems, they often have turned to increased employment of user changes. A spectacular example is the behavior of California governments following passage of Proposition 13. Many services which were formerly subsidized suddenly had to pay their own way. While these increased user charges in some cases represented significant costs to individuals and businesses, their aggregate impact was not overwhelming. A survey in late 1978 estimated that increased user charges offset less than 9 percent of property tax savings for cities, counties, and special districts.[19]

The California situation also suggests that increased user charges may have important effects on the actions of individuals and businesses. The sharply increased charges which some localities placed on new home sites to cover the costs to the community of added infrastructure necessitated by development may dampen the tendency for suburbs to sprawl.[20] Similarly, if the charge for refuse collection depends on how much trash and garbage are collected, there might be an increased problem of illegal dumping and litter.

As one writer noted a few years ago, the literature on this subject "is still somewhat underdeveloped."[21] Important questions about the distributional and behavioral effects of increased user charges are yet to be answered. While user charges can bring in considerably more revenue than they do at present in most places, their potential is limited by the nature of certain services, particularly education and police, as well as by political resistance to unconventional policies and lack of appreciation of the increased efficiencies which user charges could produce.

Notes

1. This analysis generally follows that in Charles J. Goetz, "The Revenue Potential of User-Related Charges in State and Local Governments," in *Broad-Based Taxes: New Options and Sources,* ed. Richard A. Musgrave (Baltimore, Md.: Johns Hopkins Press, 1973), pp. 114-116. Census Bureau statistics indicate that revenue from city water utilities and transit systems fall substantially short of expenditures, while electric utilities break even and gas utilities have higher revenues than expenditures. However, it is difficult to tell whether these patterns are due to borrowing to cover capital expenses, aid from higher levels of government, or subsidies from tax revenue. In the case of transit, subsidies as a proportion of operating cost increased from 15 percent in 1970 to 46 percent in 1975. Much of this expanded subsidy was due to increased federal and state aid and use of local nonproperty taxes. See U.S. Census Bureau, *City Government Finances in 1976-77,* (Washington, D.C., 1978) table 1, and Group of Experts on Traffic Policies for the Improvement of the Urban Environment, "Report on Study of Financing Urban Public Transport" (Working Document, Organization for Economic Cooperation and Development, January 26, 1979).

2. Over the entire period from 1955 to 1976, what the Census Bureau calls "current charges" has consistently tended to rise faster than locally imposed taxes. However, the ratio of public utility charges to taxes has fluctuated around a mildly declining trend. Combining these disparate trends, total local charges as a fraction of tax revenue rose from 1955 to 1963, fell from

1963 to 1971, and rose after 1971. In 1976 total charges were 68 percent of taxes versus 57 percent in 1955. Selma J. Muskin et al., "The Taxpayer Revolt: An Opportunity to Make Positive Changes in Local Government," in *Local Distress, State Surpluses: Proposition 13: Prelude to Fiscal Crisis or New Opportunities?* (Hearings before the Subcommittee of the City of the Committee on Banking, Finance, and Urban Affairs, House of Representatives, July 25-26, 1978), p. 677.

3. Table 2-6 shows the proportion of local general revenue excluding state and federal aid derived from user charges and miscellaneous general revenue in each state.

4. Current charges were 16.8 percent of taxes in cities with over 1 million population in 1974-1975 but 33.2 percent in cities with less than 50,000 population. If water and other utility revenue is included, the ratios rise to 39.9 and 95.3 percent, respectively. Selma J. Mushkin and Charles L. Vehorn, "User Fees and Charges," *Governmental Finance* 52 (November 1977):42-44.

5. For rankings of the intensity with which particular cities employ user charges, see Mushkin and Vehorn, ibid., pp. 45-46, and Frederick D. Stocker and Marc Posner, "User Charges: Their Role in Local Government Finance," *Proceedings of the Annual Conference on Taxation: 1974* (Columbus, Ohio: National Tax Association, 1975), pp. 406-413.

6. One study found that collection and disposal costs in high-income outlying areas of Baltimore were approximately four times greater than in low-income inner-city neighborhoods. Stephen L. Feldman, "Waste Collection Services: A Survey of Costs and Pricing," in *Public Prices for Public Products,* ed. Selma J. Mushkin (Washington, D.C., The Urban Institute, 1972), p. 227.

7. James A. Johnson, "The Distribution of the Burden of Sewer User Charges under Various Charge Formulas," *National Tax Journal* 22 (December 1969):472-485.

8. Wallace Oates, *Fiscal Federalism* (New York: Harcourt, Brace, Jovanovich, 1972).

9. For a discussion of efficiency and equity issues, see various articles in S.J. Mushkin, *Public Prices for Public Products,* and William W. Vickrey, "General and Specific Financing of Urban Services," in *Public Expenditure Decisions in the Urban Community* ed. Howard G. Schaller (Baltimore, Md.: Resources for the Future, 1963), pp. 62-89.

10. J.A. Stockfish, "Fees and Service Charges as a Source of City Revenues: A Case Study of Los Angeles," *National Tax Journal* 12 (June 1960):97-121.

11. Goetz, "Revenue Potential," p. 125. Thomas Muller and John Tilney, "Pricing and Delivery of Public Services: An Overview and Research Needs" (Washington: The Urban Institute, June 1977).

12. These two proposals accounted for about 64 percent of the increased revenue which Stockfish projected. Stockfish, "Fees and Service Charges," p. 121.

13. John F. Due and Ann F. Friedlander, *Government Finance: Economics of the Public Sector,* 5th ed. (Homewood, Ill.: Irwin, 1973), p. 101.

14. Muller and Tilney, "An Overview," p. 59.

15. Advisory Commission on Intergovernmental Relations, *Local Revenue Diversification: Income, Sales Taxes, and User Charges* (Washington, D.C., 1974), pp. 72-73.

16. The net cost of an expense which is deductible can be found by multiplying it by one minus the marginal tax rate. Since most state income taxes also allow this deduction, the relevant marginal tax rate is higher than the federal rate alone. For a further discussion of this point, see chapter 12.

17. The extreme cases occur when a local government is at one of the ceilings or floors which override the other factors in the revenue-sharing distribution formula. Robert D. Reischauer, "General Revenue Sharing—The Program's Incentives," in *Financing the New Federalism,* ed. Wallace E. Oates (Baltimore, Md.: Johns Hopkins Press, 1975), pp. 59-67, 71-74.

18. Selma J. Mushkin, "An Agenda for Research," in Mushkin, *Public Prices for Public Products,* pp. 440-443; Milton Z. Kafoglis, "Local Service Charges: Theory and Practice," in *State and Local Tax Problems,* ed. Harry L. Johnson (Knoxville: University of Tennessee Press, 1969), pp. 164-186.

19. *Wall Street Journal,* June 1, 1979, p. 1. User charges were probably even less significant in replacing school property taxes, but data were not available to substantiate that.

20. George E. Peterson and Thomas Muller, "Allocation of Development Costs between Homebuyers and Taxpayers" (Paper delivered at National Conference on Housing Costs sponsored by Department of Housing and Urban Development, February 1979).

21. Stocker and Posner, "User Charges," p. 419. This article also has a good brief bibliographical note.

12 Miscellaneous Forms of Relief

This chapter describes some of the major types of property tax relief which have not been covered adequately in previous chapters:

1. Complete exemption of religious, charitable, and governmental property
2. Phase-out of the personal property tax
3. Phase-out of the state property tax
4. Universal percentage credits
5. Itemized deductions on the federal and state income taxes
6. Limitations on assessment increases

These six types of relief have little in common with one another or, in some cases, with the other relief mechanisms described in previous chapters. To a major extent complete exemption differs from other types of relief in that it was established long ago, whereas most other relief programs have been undergoing substantial change in recent years. But the issue of payments to localities to replace part of the revenue foregone from exempt property has been an active one recently in several states. Phasing out the personal and state property taxes has been going on for decades but at different speeds. The personal property tax is still in its death throes while the state property tax is virtually dead in the great majority of states. The fourth type of relief, a credit which covers part of the tax liability of all property taxpayers, is a recent invention and is employed in only three states. Income tax deductions are an indirect form of relief but a very sizable one. Finally, assessment limits can affect both the amount and the distribution of taxes.

Complete Exemption of Governmental and Charitable Property

Governments and certain nonprofit organizations of a religious, charitable, and social nature have had complete tax exemptions for a long time.[1] In that sense, they have the ultimate in property tax relief. However, their privileged status is occasionally called into question. To the extent that these exempt organizations paid taxes or made some other financial contributions to local government, property tax relief could be provided to nonexempt property taxpayers. Although many organizations with exempt property do contribute financially to compensate for services which they receive, the amounts of money involved are generally rather small in relation to local budgets or foregone tax revenue.

How Much Property Is Exempt?

Balk, in his book *The Free List*, cites several estimates that one-third of potentially taxable real estate is tax exempt.[2] However, all estimates are necessarily imprecise because figures on exemptions are not compiled in most states[3] and because assessors generally devote little effort to keeping assessments of exempt property in line with current market conditions. Although usually it is assumed that the up-to-date value of exempt property would be much higher than that which is carried on the official rolls, such a conclusion is not universally assented to. One writer has argued that accurate assessed values for much exempt property in large cities "would be very low indeed, for often neither the sites nor the existing buildings have readily apparent alternative uses, and hence the market value must be low."[4] The real question is the degree to which exempt property is over- or underassessed relative to nonexempt property. The answer is likely to vary widely from city to city and for particular properties within each city.

This section is not concerned with some of the exempt property which is included in the one-third figure. Exemptions for homeowners, businesses, and owners of farmland have been covered elsewhere in this book, so they are beyond the scope of this discussion, which is concerned with property that is completely exempt because of the identity of its owner and its use. According to Netzer's estimate for 1966, the partial exemptions excluded here account for approximately 9 percent of the total value of exempt property. Quigley and Schmenner show that such partially exempt property is a much higher proportion in some states than in others.[5]

The great majority of completely exempt real property belongs to governments. Nationally, it is estimated that more than 85 percent of completely exempt property is governmental, with the rest belonging to eleemosynary organizations such as churches and charities.[6] To the extent that the exempt property within a locality belongs to the local government itself, clearly no property tax revenue is forgone by the exemption, and a city's own property is often substantial. For example, in Connecticut's three largest cities, Hartford, Bridgeport, and New Haven, tax exempt properties comprise about 25, 24, and 30 percent of total values, respectively. If the municipally owned properties are excluded, the percentages fall to 18, 15, and 25 percent.[7]

Thus, the commonly used one-third figure for the proportion of the property which is exempt can be quite misleading. The real property of eleemosynary organizations is valued at roughly 4 percent of taxable assessed valuations and governmentally owned property at 26 percent, with another 3 percent representing partial exemptions.[8]

Data from several states reveal three rather consistent patterns. First, the distribution of exempt property is highly uneven, with concentrations being found in older urban areas. Second, the proportion of property which is exempt tends to be considerably higher in central cities than in suburbs of metropolitan areas. Finally, the value of exempt property is growing faster than the value of taxable property. These patterns indicate that exemptions are becoming an increasing problem for some cities, particularly older ones.[9]

What Kinds of Property Are Exempt?

States differ greatly in how they define which property is exempt and the restrictions which they can place on its use. The major categories of exempt nongovernment property are churches, schools, hospitals, and cemeteries. Other organizations which often receive exemptions include YMCAs; chambers of commerce; lodges and fraternal organizations; camps; veterans' organizations and patriotic groups; professional associations and labor unions; artistic, historical, and literary societies; libraries, museums, and art galleries.[10]

The nature of property receiving eleemosynary exemptions varies considerably from state to state. In California, charitable organizations account for more than half of nongovernment exemptions, but in Iowa and Hawaii religious organizations are the most important beneficiaries of exemptions. Educational institutions account for the largest share of exemptions in Minnesota, New York, Oregon, Rhode Island, and the District of Columbia.[11]

A host of details specify exactly which kinds of property are exempt. Sometimes these are spelled out by law, but often assessment policy is based on judicial rulings. Consider, for example, religious property. Not only is the church or synagogue building exempt, but also the parsonage usually is. Further details concern the treatment of land adjacent to the church, parking lots, land held for future expansion, and property held for nonreligious purposes, such as income generation. In the area of education, questions concern the treatment of bookstores, fraternities, faculty housing, dormitories, sports facilities, and so forth.[12]

Critics of exemptions cite cases of outrageous abuses by some tax-exempt organizations. Religious sects have sold thousands of mail-order ordinations so that untrained ministers could declare their homes to be tax-exempt churches. One Hartford church purchased 121 acres of vacant land a number of years ago for $24,500. The land was exempted as a cemetary when one person was buried there. In 1966, when the land had risen in value to $607,000, the body was transferred to another resting place and the cemetary was sold.[13] Such chicanery probably involves only a very small proportion of exemptions. Less sensational but still disturbing are the frequent cases in which assessors grant exemptions, particularly for religious property, which are not prescribed by law.[14]

There are also cases in which the exemption of government property seems rather dubious. A glaring example is the World Trade Center in New York City, two of the world's tallest buildings, which is exempt because it was financed by the New York Port Authority. In this and similar situations, it is difficult to see what public purpose is served by subsidizing operations that are virtually indistinguishable from private enterprises.

Arguments for and against Exemptions

Exemptions amount to subsidies for exempt organizations. They can be criticized either because the organizations are unworthy of public support, because subsidies should not be financed by local governments, or because tax exemption is an inappropriate means of providing a subsidy.

Whether exempt organizations deserve public subsidies is a hotly debated issue for several reasons. To some extent the benefits which the organizations produce accrue to specific individuals, such as students, patients, or parishoners, who may be fully able to pay for the services which they are receiving. In other words, the benefits produced are private rather than public. On the other hand, it is argued that if the private organizations did not exist, their services would have to be provided by government, and the existing arrangement with only a small public subsidy through tax exemptions represents "a bargain" for the public. Moreover, the exemption minimizes the government's interference in the private sector and promotes a pluralist approach to satisfying society's needs. Advocates of exemptions also emphasize the value of the exempt organizations to the community. In the words of a prominent educator, it is exempt institutions which make a town a good place in which to live.[15]

Even if one believes that subsidies are justified because of the public goods produced by an organization, there are many situations in which it is inappropriate for such subsidies to be locally financed. Frequently the students at a university or patients in a hospital come primarily from outside the local government area,[16] so it would be more appropriate for a state or federal government to finance any subsidy which is warranted. A counterargument to this position points to the property which may locate in an area because of proximity to the tax-exempt institution. However, there is no guarantee that this other property will generate a large enough fiscal surplus to make up the costs of providing services to the tax-exempt buildings.

The final issue is whether property tax exemption is a rational way to support worthy organizations. It is widely believed that the exemption causes exempt bodies to overinvest in real estate compared to what they would own if there were no exemption available. Another damaging criticism is that wealthy organizations receive substantial benefit while poor, struggling entities which may be doing more good work may not benefit at all because they rent their facilities. Finally, cash subsidies are always more beneficial to recipients than benefits in kind. The major advantage of a tax exemption is that it minimizes interference by the government in the operations of exempt organizations. In the case of religious bodies, it avoids complications arising from the constitutional principle of the separation of church and state.[17]

The arguments in favor of and against exemptions certainly do not apply equally to all types of exempt property. In fact, some of the arguments for exemptions hardly seem to apply at all in many cases. If exemptions are to be reexamined, it should be on a case-by-case basis.

Policy Options

A wide variety of policies could be adopted to ameliorate the problems caused by exemptions. Many are already in use to a limited extent. Even vehement critics of exemptions generally regard it as futile to advocate their outright abolition,[18] but there are many less radical possibilities.

One of the less controversial policies is reimbursement by the state or federal government for exempt property. Thirty-six states either provide payments to localities in lieu of taxes or permit local taxation of some state land or buildings. However, the amounts of money involved are usually small, and only limited types of state property are involved. Most commonly payments are for land in rural areas such as state forests.[19]

The federal government also has a large number of programs for reimbursing localities for exempt property. Once again the payments involved are relatively small, in 1978 totaling only $1.04 billion.[20]

Connecticut broke new ground in 1978 with its PILOT (Payments In Lieu Of Taxes) program which distributed $10 million to cities to compensate for exempt hospitals and private educational institutions. Elsewhere, compensation programs are for exempt government property. In Connecticut there is an inverse correlation between a city's average income level and the proportion of exempt property in the tax base, so Connecticut's program distributes funds in a relatively unobjectionable way; but such a pattern does not necessarily exist in other states. Distribution of state aid according to a city's exempt property valuation should be compared with other formulas for distributing aid.[21]

Another way of dealing with tax exemptions is for exempt organizations to pay for services which they receive through user charges. In many cases, such payments are made voluntarily. Occasionally cities do not charge for services such as water and sewage even though property tax exemption does not imply exemption from such ordinary charges. Netzer questions whether payments other than for utility-type services would be significant in many cases, since the marginal cost of services is often much lower than average costs.[22]

Many other proposals could be adopted, some of a more controversial nature. One would require localities to grant permission before taxable property could be bought by a tax-exempt organization. Another would provide for a "phase-in" period in such situations. A third option would phase out exemptions after a specified number of years, perhaps to be replaced by cash subsidies. Other proposals would limit the number of acres or dollar value to property qualifying for an exemption.[23]

Even a simple proposal like making assessments of exempt property more accurate is controversial. Advocates claim it would facilitate evaluation of exemptions in terms of costs and benefits. Critics say it would be a waste of time and money.[24]

In the future there is likely to be a further increase in state and federal payments to compensate localities for exempt property, and user charges will be increasingly applied to make exempt organizations pay for some of the services which they receive. But revolutionary steps such as abolishing exemptions are likely to remain politically taboo for the foreseeable future.

Personal Property Tax Phase-out

The personal property tax has been in decline for more than a century. This tax which applies to all forms of property other than real estate can be considered as several separate taxes, on intangibles, household goods, and automobiles, farm machinery and livestock, and business inventories and machinery. The process of exempting each of these types of personal property is at different stages, with intangibles being least taxed and business machinery most taxed.

In 1976 personal property accounted for 12.2 percent of net taxable assessed value, a decline from 17.2 percent in 1956. This drop represented a continuation of a long-term trend traceable at least to the 1870s. Despite the clamor against the personal property tax, the fall in its share of total assessed valuation was considerably slower in 1966-1976 than it had been in 1956-1966.[25]

A recent survey found that eight states completely exempt personal property (Delaware, Hawaii, Illinois, Minnesota, New York, North Dakota, Pennsylvania, and South Dakota). Four of these states granted the blanket exemption in the 1968-1978 period. In addition, Iowa and New Jersey exempt some personal property and partially exempt the remainder. Other states tax only a few classes of personal property, such as farm equipment, inventories, and office equipment. Household goods, intangibles such as stocks and bonds, and goods in transit are the types of property which are exempt most often. Agricultural property such as livestock, farm implements, and seed are taxed more heavily than those kinds of property but less than business property.[26]

In this area more than in many others, there has been a sizable gap between legal coverage and actual practice. Much property which should be taxed is never assessed. For example, Netzer estimated that assessments of tangible personal property in 1961 amounted to only about one-fifth of the amount which was legally taxable.[27]

Unfortunately, little information is available at the national level which shows the effect of the exemptions which have been granted in recent years. The census of governments permits a comparison of the composition of the personal property tax base in 1966 and 1976 in fourteen states, and the proportion of taxable personal property which was commercial-industrial property underwent a large change in only one state.

The phase-out of the personal property tax is treated in two different ways in various states. In some cases, the property is simply exempted and real property consequently pays a greater tax (unless the tax rate is limited by law). However, elsewhere the state provides a credit for personal property tax payments, with financing from state revenue. For example, in 1977-1978 California's personal property tax credit (primarily for inventories) amounted to $420.1 million; for perspective, this cost was equal to more than half of that for the homeowners' exemption and more than five times the cost of the circuit breaker.[28] Michigan's personal property credit for inventories cost $130.7 million in 1977. Altogether, at least twelve states reimbursed local governments for personal property tax revenue lost because of exemptions in 1977, and the total cost of these exemptions was of the same order of magnitude as circuit breakers for homeowners and renters.[29] However, often the reimbursement is for less than the revenue which would have been received if the treatment of personal property had not been changed because its taxes would have continued to rise.

Iowa's experience illustrates what a muddle personal property taxation is. The proportion of property tax revenue from personal property fell from 16.3 to 2.1 percent between 1962 and 1977. Near the beginning of this period, household personal property (except boats) was exempted. Then in 1967 the state provided a partial credit for the remaining personal property tax. This credit increased in 1973 and was scheduled to rise further over the next ten years until it covered all personal property tax liability.[30]

But not all personal property was treated equally. Livestock was exempted fully in 1973, with the state replacing most of the lost revenue. Some other types of personal property, such as computers, were redefined as real property, so that they did not benefit from the personal property tax phase-out at all.

After several years, the credit covered virtually the entire personal property tax in some counties but less than half of the tax liability in other counties. An absurd situation arose in which every owner of personal property had to complete a credit application annually and assessors had substantial paperwork although most owners had no tax liability. In some counties the administrative cost of the tax was said to exceed the revenue collected. By 1977 there were calls for the immediate phase-out of the remaining tax, with the $29.1 million cost being replaced by general state revenue. Instead the phase-out was suspended for two years because of the limited revenue available in the state budget. At that point the cost of the credit was $38.6 million.[31]

Intangibles (stocks and bonds, bank accounts, mortgages, and so on) are the least taxed form of personal property. Eight states are reported to place some taxes on intangibles, but a recent study found that evasion is very widespread.[32]

There are compelling reasons for exempting much of personal property. For one thing, it is often easily concealed, making it expensive to administer the tax relatively comprehensively. Since personal property is generally more mobile than real property, the personal property tax is likely to cause greater allocational inefficiency. Finally, the tax seriously violates horizontal equity, with companies in industries requiring large inventories or a high ratio of machinery to real estate paying much higher taxes than others. Nevertheless, before advocating the phase-out of the personal property tax, one must consider how it will be replaced. According to one analysis, if the alternative revenue source is the real property tax, its incidence may be more regressive than the personal property tax; if the alternative is the personal or corporation income tax, the incidence of the alternative may be less regressive.[33]

Phase-out of the State Property Tax

One obvious way in which a state government might provide property tax relief would be to lower the property taxes that it levies for its own revenue. In fact, this is rarely a viable alternative because most state property taxes have already been eliminated.

In the nineteenth century, states as well as local governments relied on the property tax as an important source of revenue. At the turn of the century, for example, more than half of state tax revenue was derived from property taxation. However, at that time the scope of state activity was rather limited, so that the property tax was primarily a local tax, with 88.4 percent of property tax revenue going to local governments in 1902. As the states expanded their responsibilities in the twentieth century, they turned increasingly to other revenue sources, particularly the sales tax at first and later the income tax. Thus, in 1932, 92.6 percent of property tax revenue went to localities and in 1946, 95 percent.

The increasing concentration of property tax revenue at the local level continued in the postwar period. By 1972, 97.1 percent of property tax revenue was collected by local governments. In the following years a reversal took place as the percentage fell to 96.4 percent in 1977, but this was primarily due to levies on specific types of business property rather than general property taxation.[34]

In fact, more than half of the remaining state property tax revenue is related to specific property taxes rather than the general one. The most prominent example is in Alaska, where state taxes on oil and gas properties and reserves raised $409.8 million in 1977 and $173 million in 1978.[35]

There are seven states in which more than 10 percent of property tax revenue was levied by the state in 1977: Alaska, 76.4 percent; Washington, 32.4 percent; Arizona, 17.8 percent; Alabama, 15.5 percent; Nevada, 12.2 percent; New Mexico, 11.9 percent; and Kentucky, 11.1 percent. None of these states is noted for high property tax burdens on its general population,[36] perhaps indicating that to some extent state taxes substitute for rather than supplement local property taxes. Three of the seven states derive most of their state property tax revenue from specific property taxes (Alaska, Kentucky, and Nevada). Specific taxes account for between one-third and one-sixth of the tax in three others. Only in Alabama, which has the lowest overall property tax burdens in the nation, are specific taxes insignificant.

In the mid-1970s Maine experimented with a state property tax to carry much of the burden of school finance, but after a short period it resorted to more conventional taxes.

State property taxes accounted for less than 5 percent of total property taxation in thirty-eight states in 1977, and in some of the other states specific rather than general taxes bulked large. Thus, in most places state property taxes are so low that eliminating them cannot provide much additional property tax relief.

Universal Percentage Credits

Ohio, Indiana, and Wisconsin have adopted state-financed credits which pay a certain percentage of tax liability for all property owners. The Ohio credit is 10 percent, and the Indiana credit is 20 percent. Wisconsin's credit is a certain percentage of the tax liability which exists because the local tax rate exceeds half of the statewide average tax rate.[37]

The sums involved in these three programs are quite substantial. In 1977 total credits were $163.1 million in Ohio, $270.4 million in Indiana, and $210 million in Wisconsin.[38]

Such credits provide fast and direct relief. If they were unaccompanied by limitations, local governments might raise property taxes in their wake because part of any tax would automatically be paid by the state. However, each state providing these credits also imposes limits on local tax levies to prevent such action.

These credits have advantages and disadvantages. On the positive side, the distribution of their benefits is very clear and they are state-financed. However, they distribute blanket relief, ignoring (in Ohio and Indiana) differences among taxpayers in terms of the need for relief. Thus, their desirability is very controversial.

As a relief device, these credits are roughly equivalent to distributing aid to local governments which must then lower their tax rates by the amount of the aid. They differ primarily in the visibility of relief and avoiding local governments as a decision-making intermediary.[39]

The Wisconsin credits are targeted to a greater extent than those in the other two states since they favor property in high-tax-rate areas. In 1976 cities experienced a 17 percent savings from the credits while rural towns received credits equal to only 8.7 percent of gross property taxes. However, as in the other states, no distinction is made between residential and nonresidential property, and high-value property enjoys benefits proportionately greater than low-value property.[40]

Itemized Income Tax Deductions

The deductibility of property taxes on federal and state income taxes is one of the largest sources of property tax relief. It is also one of the most regressive (pro-rich) types of relief because benefits are limited to households which itemize deductions and are directly related to a taxpayer's marginal tax rate.

It is estimated that the deductibility of the property tax on owner-occupied homes saved taxpayers $5.5 billion on their federal income tax in fiscal year 1978 and $6.6 billion in fiscal year 1980. This is about one-fourth less than the deductibility of mortgage interest on owner-occupied homes is worth, but is more than five times the combined value of all residential circuit breakers.[41]

In addition, there is a further savings from the deductibility of the property tax on most state income taxes. Thirty-five of the forty-one states with income taxes permit this deduction, and the combined value of these state income tax deductions is approximately 15 percent of the value of the federal deductions.[42]

The tax savings from the deduction[43] are heavily skewed in favor of high-income groups, as table 12-1 shows. For example, in 1977 the reduction in federal income tax liability from the deduction averaged $17 for returns with income between $10,000 and $15,000, $309 for returns with income between $30,000 and $50,000, and $3,061 for returns with income over $200,000. The majority of benefits went to the politically potent households with incomes between $20,000 and $50,000.

The average value of the property tax deduction is much greater for high-income than for low-income households for three reasons: the probability of itemizing deductions rises as income increases because the standard deduction becomes less attractive, marginal tax rates increase from 14 to 70 percent, and the rate of home ownership rises. Consider, for example, three families: the first has an income of $10,000 and a $500 property tax bill; the second has an

Table 12-1

Distribution among Income Groups of Benefits from Deductibility of Real Estate Taxes on the Federal Income Tax, 1977

Expanded Income Class	Reduction of Income Tax per Return	Percentage of Total Reduction
$ 5,000 or less	$ 2	0.1
5,000- 10,000	4	1.8
10,000- 15,000	17	6.7
15,000- 20,000	45	12.7
20,000- 30,000	121	28.4
30,000- 50,000	309	26.0
50,000-100,000	689	16.1
100,000-200,000	1,278	6.0
200,000 and over	3,061	3.6
Total	48	100.0

Source: Tabulation by U.S. Treasury Department on request of Senator Edmund Muskie, reported in "Muskie News" press release, February 13, 1978.

income of $40,000 and $1,500 of property tax; and the third has an income of $300,000 and a $5,000 property tax. It is impossible to determine whether they itemize and what their marginal rates are without information on such matters as their other deductible expenses and the sources of their income. But if these families are typical, the first family would not itemize, the second might have a marginal tax rate of 36 percent, and the third might be in the 70 percent marginal bracket. If so, the first family would not receive any benefit from the deductibility of the property tax, and the value of the deduction would be $540 for the second family and $3,500 for the third family.

The distribution of the benefits of the deduction has become more concentrated among high-income households as a result of changes in the income tax during the 1970s, particularly the large increase in the standard deduction. Whereas in 1969 approximately 58 percent of tax returns were itemized, in 1978 the proportion of itemizers had fallen to about 25 percent. Because of this reduction and the decline in marginal tax rates, the revenue lost by the U.S. Treasury because of the deduction rose only slowly from $3.25 billion in 1972 to $3.7 billion in fiscal 1976; thereafter it rose rapidly to $6.6 billion in 1980.[44]

There is much to condemn about the deduction of property taxes on homes. This deduction contributes to the extreme favoritism in favor of homeowners and against renters under the federal and state income taxes. Together with the deduction for mortgage interest and the exclusion of the imputed rent on owner-occupied housing, it has provided a powerful incentive for families and individuals to own homes rather than rent. These subsidies to homeownership reduce the progressivity of the income tax. However, not all the effects of the deduction are bad. Because of it, differentials in property tax rates provide less of an incentive to move in order to lower one's tax burden. In addition, many people feel it is socially desirable to induce as much home-ownership as possible. But if the objective is to encourage households to own their own homes, there is no reason why the deduction should be unlimited.[45]

Limitations on Assessment Increases

Limitations on assessment increases are in effect in six states. They differ greatly in their design and effects. Some have characteristics of classification, while several restrict increases in property tax revenue through their interaction with tax rate limitations.

Beginning in 1978 California and in 1980 Idaho limit assessment increases on each piece of property to 2 percent per year unless the property is sold, at which time its assessment can raise it to market value. This limitation works to the disadvantage of homes because they are sold on the average every seven years or so, while business property is sold much less often. Over time, the proportion of taxes paid by homeowners will tend to rise considerably if these limits are not changed. Another undesirable result may be to "lock in" property owners, discouraging them from changing their residence for fear of higher property taxes.

Colorado's assessment limits are similar to those in California and Idaho in that they apply to individual pieces of property, but they affect relatively few properties because the increase permitted is rather high.[46] Colorado also avoids the "lock in effect" by not providing for revaluation at market value when property is sold.

The assessment limits in Iowa and Oregon deal with classes of property rather than individual parcels and work in favor of rather than against the interests of homeowners. However, they also introduce complexities and possible inequities.

Beginning in 1978, Iowa limited home and farm assessment increases statewide. In the first two years these assessments were allowed to rise 6 percent per year and in the following years 4 percent. Assessments throughout the state are rolled back by the same percentage (in 1978, 22 percent for homes and 4 percent for farms). These limits were intended to avoid a shift of the tax burden to residential property; in fact, they have resulted in an increase in the proportion of taxes paid by business property, whose assessment increases are not limited.[47]

Oregon's limits, begun in 1979, are similar to Iowa's except that all assessments are limited. However, the limit is calculated separately for homes and other property, resulting in a lower assessment ratio for homes because their uncontrolled assessments are rising faster than those of other property. However, the proportionate relationship between the *total* assessed valuation of existing homes and the assessed valuation of other property is preserved.

Maryland also placed a limitation on assessment increases in 1979. If total uncontrolled assessments increase more than 6 percent in a year, they are reduced by a uniform percentage so that the increase in total assessed valuation is 6 percent.

Assessment limitations may affect not only the distribution of taxes among classes of property but also the volume of taxes. Iowa's limits were considered a substitute for levy limits, which were abolished when the assessment limitations took effect, but they restrict revenue only when a government is at its tax rate limit, which many are not. The restrictive effect of assessment limits was unimportant in Oregon, because it retained its long-standing levy limits, and in Maryland, which has no tax rate limits. But the California and Idaho limits severely restrict the increase of property tax revenue for local governments because they are so low and all governments are affected by the 1 percent tax rate limit.

In addition to its limits, Maryland has another policy to cushion the impact of assessment increases. Beginning in 1976, the state has provided a credit for the increase in taxes resulting from an increase in a home's assessment of greater than 15 percent. However, the credit is for one year only, so that the following year the homeowner has to pay taxes on the full assessed value. Unlike the others, this type of limitation does not affect local government revenue at all, since the state fully finances the credit.

Assessment limitations appeal to some policymakers because they are a simple way of avoiding large changes in tax burdens, in terms of both their distribution and their size. However, they generally introduce inequities by causing unequal tax burdens for property owners whose situations are similar. They also complicate the assessment process and make it harder for citizens to understand government finance.

Because of the inequities of assessment limits, it is not surprising that two other states which experimented with them, Minnesota and New Mexico, abandoned them after state courts declared them unconstitutional. Both states limited the assessments of individual parcels of property rather than of whole classes. If limitations are to be used, the latter type is preferable because it does not result in unequal assessment ratios for different homes, although it does cause unequal assessment ratios for different classes of property.

Conclusions

The relief mechanisms discussed in this chapter are a mixed bag, but they include some very important programs. The revenue forgone as a result of complete exemptions for charitable and government property obviously exceeds the cost of all other forms of property tax relief, but these exemptions are so firmly established that it is quixotic to contemplate their elimination. Still, substantial revenue can be derived from exempt institutions in other ways, through either state and federal payments or user charges. The relief granted through income tax deductions is also very large, being exceeded only by the relief resulting from state and federal aid to local governments. Universal percentage credits are another sizable program in the three states where they are used, and personal property credits and exemptions also provide substantial benefits. Their not having their own chapter does not mean that they are insignificant.

Despite their magnitude, these relief measures do not provide property tax relief to low- and moderate-income households in an efficient manner. Income tax deductions provide benefits inversely with income, and the phase-out of the personal property tax usually provides a large share of benefits to businesses, with much of the relief not finding its way back to consumers. Similarly, universal percentage credits and any revenue derived from the existence of exempt government and eleemosynary property tends to lower the overall tax rate, providing untargeted relief. Thus, while these measures do have some advantages and might have a role as part of a politically expedient tax relief package, they are inappropriate policies if the impetus for relief comes from concern for the tax burdens on low- and moderate-income homeowners.

Notes

1. For historical sketches and sources of further information, see John M. Quigley and Roger W. Schmenner, "Property Tax Exemption and Public Policy," *Public Policy* 23 (Summer 1975):259-261; and Alfred Balk, *The Free List: Property without Taxes* (New York: Russell Sage Foundation, 1971), pp. 20-27.

2. Balk, *The Free List*, pp. 10-11. Sources using the one-third figure include *Fortune*, the International Association of Assessing Officers and Martin A. Larson and C. Stanley Lowell.

3. Balk reports that only eighteen states have compiled exemption valuations inventories and only twelve do so on a regular basis. The Census Bureau obtained data for seventeen states and the District of Columbia for 1976, which was the same number as in 1971, although the specific states reporting changed somewhat. Quigley and Schmenner obtained "complete" data for thirteen states and the District of Columbia in 1971 or other years and less complete data for eight other states. See Balk, *The Free List*, pp. 10-12; U.S. Census Bureau, *1977 Census of Governments*, vol. 2: *Taxable Property Values and Assessment/Sales Price Ratios* (Washington, D.C., 1978), p. 28; and Quigley and Schmenner, "Public Policy," pp. 262-263.

4. Dick Netzer, "Property Tax Exemptions and Their Effects: A Dissenting View," in National Tax Association, *1972 Proceedings of the Sixty-Fifth Annual Conference on Taxation*, 1973, p. 271.

5. Netzer, "A Dissenting View," p. 270; Quigley and Schmenner, "Public Policy," pp. 262-263. In personal correspondence Netzer pointed out that his estimates were based on national wealth data and are therefore not comparable to estimates derived from assessment rolls, such as most other writers on this subject.

6. Netzer, "A Dissenting View," pp. 270-271. Government property accounts for more than three-quarters of exempt property reported in Colorado, Hawaii, Nevada, Oregon, and the District of Columbia in 1976. But it constitutes only 34 percent of exemptions in Minnesota, 38 percent in New Jersey, 54 percent in Rhode Island, and 62 percent in New York. These are the only states for which a breakdown is provided in the 1977 census of governments. See U.S. Census Bureau, *Taxable Property Values,* p. 28.

7. Quigley and Schmenner, "Public Policy," pp. 264-265.

8. Netzer, "A Dissenting View," p. 270. Actually, Balk's one-third figure refers to exempt property as a percentage of all real property, while Netzer's is the ratio of exempt to all real property excluding exemptions. Balk's figure corresponds to one-half, not one-third, in terms of the ratio which Netzer uses.

9. Quigley and Schmenner, "Public Policy," pp. 261-272. The authors point out that the proportion of exemptions in Connecticut which are for local government property has declined, while the proportion for property belonging to other governments has increased during the past several decades.

10. Greater Hartford Chamber of Commerce, *Property Tax Exemptions for Non-profit Institutions: Problems and Proposals,* 1978. This study was prepared under the direction of Professor Richard D. Pomp of the University of Connecticut School of Law.

11. U.S. Census Bureau, *Taxable Property Values,* p. 28.

12. For an excellent survey of the legal status of the property of nonprofit institutions as of 1978, see Hartford, *Property Tax Exemptions.*

13. Balk, *The Free List,* p. 26. This particular case is repeated in the literature so often that it makes one skeptical as to how prevalent such outrages are.

14. Ibid., pp. 21-22.

15. For a critique of the arguments against exemptions, see Netzer, "A Dissenting View," The most widely cited attack on exemptions is Balk, *The Free List.* See also Henry Aaron, *Who Pays the Property Tax?* (Washington: D.C. Brookings Institution, 1975), pp. 81-85.

16. Quigley and Schmenner report illustrative data for four Connecticut cities. See their "Public Policy," pp. 276-277.

17. The Supreme Court upheld exemptions for churches in the *Waltz* case in 1970. For a discussion of the issues raised, see Boris I. Bittker, "Churches, Taxes, and the Constitution," *Yale Law Journal* 78 (July 1969):1285-1310; and Richard S. Kay, "Property Tax Exemptions and Alternatives: Constitutional Considerations," in Hartford, *Property Tax Exemptions,* pp. 20-27.

18. One writer who does advocate elimination of exemptions together with

explicit subsidies to organizations "that demonstrate genuine need, public concern, or both" is Diane Fuchs. See her article "Tax Exempt Property: The Key to Property Tax Reform," *Conference on Alternative State and Local Public Policies* (March 1978), p. 6. Balk dismisses such proposals as politically infeasible. See *The Free List,* p. 128.

19. Thirty-three states have payment programs and sixteen permit taxation of some state property. Thirteen states have both types of local reimbursement programs, and sixteen states have neither (Alabama, Alaska, Arizona, Delaware, Hawaii, Iowa, Kentucky, Maine, Nebraska, New Mexico, Oklahoma, Rhode Island, Tennessee, and West Virginia). Advisory Council on Intergovernmental Relations, *The Adequacy of Federal Compensation to Local Governments for Tax Exempt Federal Lands* (Washington, D.C., 1978), p. 23. The census of governments lists payments from states to local governments for government property in fifteen states; the total value of payments is $53.9 million in 1977, with $18.7 million in Massachusetts being the largest payment. In seven states the payments are less than $1 million. See U.S. Census Bureau, *1977 Census of Governments,* vol. 6, pt. 3: *State Payments to Local Governments,* (Washington, D.C., 1979) table 7.

20. Advisory Commission on Intergovernmental Relations, "Compensating Local Governments for Tax Exempt Federal and State Property," April 1977, p. 4.

21. The original draft of the PILOT bill is in Hartford, *Property Tax Exemptions,* pp. 29-30. See also Quigley and Schmenner, "Public Policy," p. 264.

22. Netzer, "A Dissenting View," pp. 272-273.

23. Richard Pomp, "Testimony," in Hartford, *Property Tax Exemptions,* pp. 6-7.

24. Balk, *The Free List,* pp. 128-131; Netzer, "A Dissenting View," p. 271; Aaron, *Who Pays?* pp. 83-85.

25. In 1966 personal property was 13.1 percent of net taxable assessed value. Dick Netzer, *Economics of the Property Tax* (Washington, D.C.: The Brook, 1966), p. 139; U.S. Census Bureau, *Taxable Property Values,* p. 6.

26. Stephen J. Zellmer and Calvin A. Kent, "Trends in the Taxation of Personal Property," *State Government* 52 (Winter 1979). See also U.S. Census Bureau, *Taxable Property Values,* p. 5. For a more detailed survey of exemptions of business personal property, see Advisory Commission on Intergovernmental Relations. *Significant Features of Fiscal Federalism,* 1973-74 ed. (Washington, D.C., 1974). Unfortunately, the latest Advisory Commission on Intergovernmental Relations, report is for July 1, 1973. For an analysis of farm personal property taxation, see Ann G. Sibold, *Taxes Levied on Farm Personal Property: 1960-72* (U.S. Department of Agriculture, Agricultural Economic Report no. 321, January 1976).

27. Netzer, *Economics of the Property Tax,* pp. 146-147.

28. California, Legislature Analyst, "An Analysis of Proposition 13: The Jarvis-Gann Property Tax Initiative" (May 1978), p. 20.

29. U.S. Census Bureau, *1977 Census of Governments,* vol. 6, no. 3: *State Payments to Local Governments* (Washington, D.C., 1979) table 7. Ten states distributed $822.8 million to local governments to cover the costs of credits or exemptions for inventories and other personal property in 1977 (California, Connecticut, Iowa, Maine, Michigan, Nebraska, New Hampshire, New Jersey, North Dakota, and Wisconsin). Minnesota and Oregon also made payments for this purpose to localities, but they were not shown separately in the census report. Information about Wisconsin was obtained by telephone.

30. Steven D. Gold, *A Citizen's Guide to Local Government Finance: Iowa at the Property Tax Crossroads* (Des Moines, Iowa: Drake University, 1977), pp. 34-37.

31. *Des Moines Register,* March 6, 1977; Gold, *A Citizen's Guide,* p. 39.

32. In only one state was the revenue from the intangibles tax equal to that which should have been paid, assuming full compliance, just on the corporate stock listed on the New York Stock Exchange in 1975. Bruce L. Jaffee, "State Taxation of Intangibles: The Problem of Evasion," *Public Finance Quarterly* 6 (October 1978):485-502. See also U.S. Census Bureau, *Taxable Property Values,* 1977, p. 8.

33. Netzer, *Economics of the Property Tax,* pp. 155-163.

34. U.S. Census Bureau, *1972 Census of Governments,* vol. 6 no. 4: *Historical Statistics on Governmental Finances and Employment* (Washington, D.C., 1974) tables 4 to 6; U.S. Census Bureau, *Governmental Finances in 1976-77* (Washington, D.C., 1978).

35. U.S. Census Bureau, *State Government Tax Collections in 1978* (Washington, D.C., 1979) table 10.

36. None was among the highest twenty states in terms of effective tax rates on homes in 1977.

37. Monroe H. Rosner and George R. Meadows, "The Wisconsin Property Tax" (Working paper prepared for April 28, 1978 meeting of the Wisconsin Tax Reform Commission), p. 51.

38. Ibid., p. 51; U.S. Census Bureau, *State Payments to Local Governments,* table 7.

39. For credits to be identical in their incidence to aid, it would be necessary for the aid to be distributed to all governments in proportion to their property tax collections. Aid is seldom distributed in that way.

40. Of the benefits of the Wisconsin credit 56 percent were for residential property in 1976. Rosner and Meadows, "The Wisconsin Property Tax," pp. 51, 53.

41. U.S. Office of Management and Budget, *Special Analyses of the 1980 Budget* (Washington, D.C.: Government Printing Office, 1979), p. 208.

42. George E. Peterson, *Federal Tax Policy and Urban Development*

(Washington, D.C.: The Urban Institute, forthcoming), lists Massachusetts, Illinois, and Michigan as states not permitting a deduction for real estate taxes in 1969. Pennsylvania, which first imposed an income tax subsequent to that date, also does not permit this deduction. State income taxes have much lower marginal rates than the federal income tax but a much higher percentage of filers who itemize because the standard deduction is usually considerably lower than for the federal income tax. In 1977, state income tax revenue was about 22 percent of federal income tax revenue.

43. The value of the deduction in terms of income tax reductions is equal to the amount of property tax paid multiplied by the marginal tax rate. To find the combined effect of the state and federal income taxes, the marginal rates should be added, but only if deductions are itemized.

44. George E. Peterson, "Federal Tax Policy and Urban Development," *Tax Notes,* January 1, 1979, p. 7; Joseph A. Pechman, *Federal Tax Policy,* 3d ed. (Washington, D.C.: The Brookings Institution, 1977), p. 355; Stanley S. Surrey, *Pathways to Tax Reform* (Cambridge, Mass.: Harvard University Press, 1973), p. 9. A surprising fact which illustrates the relatively narrow distribution of benefits from this deduction is that only 60 percent of homeowners itemized deductions in 1977. See William F. Hellmuth, "Preferences for Homeowners," in Joseph A. Pechman, *Comprehensive Income Taxation* (Washington, D.C.: The Brookings Institution, 1977), pp. 179-181.

45. For an analysis of the equity and incentive effects of the deduction, see Henry Aaron, *Shelter and Subsidies* (Washington, D.C.: The Brookings Institution, 1971).

46. In 1978 assessments could not be more than 140 percent of the 1974-1976 average or more than 125 percent of the 1977 assessment. This information was provided by Ronald B. Welch.

47. See chapter 14 for a further discussion of the Iowa limitations.

13 Rural-Urban Conflict

Economists have devoted considerable attention to studying the distributional impacts of government activity, but they have tended to concentrate on distribution across income groups or factors of production.[1] They have virtually ignored a dimension of distribution which is of tremendous political significance—the distribution between rural and urban areas.[2] That is the focus of this chapter. Although in our political system this issue is fought out within states, here the focus is on the national picture.

One difficulty which a book such as this one faces is defining urban and rural. As rough measures, one can use either of two census numbers—the percentage of the population living in urban places (population over 2,500) or the percentage of the population living in metropolitan areas (population over 50,000 in central city). Both measures produce some strange classifications; for example, Utah and Nevada are two of the most urban states. But in most cases they agree about how urban a state is, and in most cases their indications accord with common perceptions.

Within states it is more difficult to draw the line between rural and urban. At the urban pole are "the big cities," a term which should be understood in a relative sense. Vermont and Wyoming do not contain a single metropolitan area, but even they have cities which stand out from the rest in terms of size. At the rural pole are farm areas. However, the percentage of farm residents dips to 1 percent or less in some states, and most inhabitants of rural areas do not live on farms. Rather, they reside in what the Census Bureau calls "rural nonfarm" areas—towns with less than 2,500 people and scattered nonfarm residents. In some states this rural nonfarm segment of the population exceeds 50 percent of the total. The line between rural and urban is indistinct, falling somewhere in the gray area which runs from towns with 2,500 population to nonsuburban cities of 49,999. For the level of analysis in this chapter it is not necessary to be precise about this matter.[3]

The first section of this chapter discusses the various factors which affect the balance of property taxes between rural and urban areas. It discusses the causes, arising either from the natural working of the economy or from government policy, which make property tax burdens differ between rural and urban areas. The second section empirically examines the extent to which differences in rural and urban property tax rates can be accounted for by the factors discussed earlier.

Theoretical Framework

The property tax is primarily a local tax, so that its rate varies from place to place within a state. The effective tax rate, the property tax bill expressed as a percentage of the market value of property, will depend on the size of the tax base and the volume and cost of services to be financed. To the extent that cities tend to have less property in relation to their population, higher costs, and a higher demand for services, they will naturally tend to have higher property tax rates than rural areas.[4]

It is widely recognized that urban governments have higher costs and confront a greater demand for services than governments in rural areas,[5] but the value of property in relation to population requires some discussion. In 1971 the assessed value of property per capita outside metropolitan areas was only 82 percent of that inside metropolitan areas, a decline from 1961, when it was 89 percent of the metropolitan level. However, a great change occurred between 1971 and 1976, and by the latter year the assessed value of property per capita was 5 percent higher in nonmetropolitan areas.[6]

This shift in assessed values was related to the economic upswing which occurred in rural areas in the 1970s. Reversing a long-term trend, population rose somewhat faster outside metropolitan areas than inside them.[7] But the difference in the rate of increase of property values was much greater than the relatively small differences in population growth. Assessed value outside metropolitan areas as reported in the 1977 Census of Governments (for 1976) was 80 percent higher than that shown in the 1972 Census of Governments (for 1971), while the growth inside metropolitan areas was only 66 percent. However, many counties were reclassified as metropolitan during those five years. It is not known what percentage of the property tax base was reclassified, but in terms of population the shift changed the classification of 14 percent of the persons who were outside metropolitan areas in 1971.[8]

At any rate, by 1976 assessed value per capita was higher outside metropolitan areas than inside them in thirty-two of the forty-eight states which contain metropolitan areas.

The gap between rural and urban tax rates is also affected by state government policies, most of which have been discussed in other chapters. The most important policies are identified in the following analysis.

First, states define what property is taxable and how it is valued. Forty-four states have laws which ensure that farmland is assessed according to its use value rather than market value; this tends to reduce farm taxes but increase taxes for property located in small towns. Preferential farm assessment lowers the share of total assessed value which is agricultural and thus shifts the tax burden to other local property.

A less important way in which the definition of property affects relative rural-urban burdens is the extent to which personal property is taxable.

Residential personal property is exempt in most states, but farm personal property is still often taxed.

A third means by which the state affects relative property values is through its policing of assessment practices. While uniformity is the law in most states, it is often honored more in the breach than in the practice. Obviously if homes tend to have higher assessment ratios than other property, residential property will bear a higher share of the tax load; the reverse is also true.

Finally, the state can affect valuations by legalizing the de facto discrimination among classes of property which often occurs. Fourteen states now have classified property tax systems, usually providing the greatest tax breaks to homes and farms.

One comparison is particularly relevant to the subject of this chapter. In 1976 single-family homes were assessed at an average assessment ratio of 30.7 percent, nearly 38 percent higher than the average assessment ratio on acreage (unplatted vacant land), which was 22.3 percent.

Second, state laws set up the ground rules which define the borders between local government units. At one time it was common for rural areas to have their own school districts. As states pushed policies of school consolidation, farm areas, having large amounts of property and relatively few students, lost their status as tax enclaves and saw property tax rates increase considerably; the opposite happened in the towns which were part of the consolidations.[9]

More generally, states can affect taxes by how easy they make it for cities to annex surrounding areas. A city might seek to annex a wealthy rural area or industrial enclave for tax reasons.

Third, states define the functions which various levels of government must carry out. By assigning greater responsibilities to counties, the state can ease the fiscal problems of cities. By taking on responsibilities itself, the state can directly ease property taxes. In this context, it all depends on which services the state picks up. Assuming the cost of welfare or court-appointed attorneys would tend to help urban areas more, but having the state police substitute for the county sheriff is more beneficial in rural areas.

Fourth, states can limit property tax rates or levies as well as authorize nonproperty taxes. The restrictiveness of the limits can differ between rural and urban areas, since they may bear particularly hard on areas which initially had relatively high property tax rates. On the other hand, nonproperty taxes are employed much more often in big cities than in small ones. Rural-urban conflict enters here because farm areas prefer to allow cities to use local income taxes rather than local sales taxes, on the assumption that less of the burden will be exported to them.

Fifth, a very important factor is state policy for aiding local governments. Formulas for highway assistance usually favor rural areas heavily, but school aid formulas usually involve much more money. Rural areas are disadvantaged because most school aid formulas define school district wealth in terms of assessed valuation per pupil, which tends to be higher in farming areas. (It would be worse for them were it not for preferential assessment of farmland.) In the 1970s numerous states have added income as a factor, and thi₃ tends to reduce the favoritism toward city school districts.

The latest data for documenting the bias in the distribution of aid are for 1971. In that year state aid accounted for a higher percentage of local government revenue outside metropolitan areas than inside them.[10]

Sixth, another important policy is state aid to individual taxpayers, in the form of homestead exemptions or credits, circuit breakers, and other such devices. An important distinction should be made according to whether this aid is financed by the state or left to localities. If the aid is not financed by the state, then it forces other local property to pay higher taxes.

When aid is limited to homeowners, it provides greater per capita relief in rural areas, because renters tend to live in urban areas. But when the value of the relief depends on local tax rates, it tends to be higher in cities because rates are usually higher there.

Seventh, the property tax is not completely a local tax. Most states levy some sort of property tax, although its coverage is often very limited. To the extent that a statewide property tax is still employed, relative tax rates will be higher in property-rich areas.[11] As of 1976, in most states these areas are rural.

Nationally, only 3.6 percent of property tax revenue is levied by state governments, but in seven states the proportion exceeds 10 percent. More than three-fourths of the Alaskan property tax is paid to the state, as is nearly one-third of the property tax in Washington. Other states with large shares of property tax revenue going to the state are Alabama, Arizona, Kentucky, Nevada, and New Mexico.

Empirical Analysis

Unfortunately, it is very difficult to verify empirically many of the factors discussed in the first section. They could be examined in case studies for individual states, but here the objective is to analyze the national picture.

First, there is the question of how to measure relative rural and urban property tax burdens. Ideally, it would be desirable to compare tax rates on businesses in rural and urban areas, and to compare both to farm taxes. Data for such a study are not readily available.

A second mode of attack would be to compare levels of property taxation between metropolitan and nonmetropolitan areas in per capita terms and as a percentage of income. The most recent data for such a study are for 1971, so they miss the major changes which have occurred in the 1970s.[12]

The approach used here is to compare home and farm property taxes in each state. This methodology deals with only a portion of the subject, since it ignores differences between urban and rural areas in the tax treatment of homes and businesses. Other shortcomings are that it ignores the fact that homes are located in rural areas as well as urban places and that the interests of farmers and rural homeowners sometimes coincide and sometimes diverge. However, the farm versus home aspect is a major element in rural-urban conflict, so this approach does cover an important part of the subject.

Two measures are used to analyze the home-farm tax conflict: the ratio of effective tax rates and the ratio of assessment ratios. These measures are shown in table 13-1 along with the proportion of total property taxes levied on farm real estate and the percentage of population residing in urban areas.

There are great variations in the relative treatment of homes and farms. The effective tax rate on homes varies from 0.61 percent in Louisiana to 3.50 percent in Massachusetts. The effective tax rate on farms is lower in all states and varies from 0.14 in Alabama to 1.70 in Massachusetts. The ratio between the home and farm tax rates varies widely, from Wisconsin and California, where the home tax rate was 42 percent higher than the farm rate, to New Mexico, where the home rate was more than six times the farm rate.

There is a tendency for states in the South to have relatively high ratios, indicating rural favoritism, and for North Central states to have low ratios.

There is virtually no correlation between the ratio of tax rates and the proportion of a state's population living in urban areas or the proportion of income derived from farming. However, there is a weak negative correlation between the ratio and the proportion of the population living in large metropolitan areas.[13] This indicates a tendency for rural areas to be less favored in highly urban states.

Unfortunately, for the purpose of analyzing assessment ratios on farms the only data available are for acreage, a category which includes not only farms but also forests and other vacant unplatted land which is not used for agriculture. However, the great majority of acreage is agricultural.

Assessment ratios, like effective tax rates, differ greatly from state to state. At one extreme is Hawaii, where homes are assessed at a rate more than six times as great as acreage. At the other extreme are two states (New York and North Carolina) in which the home assessment ratio is lower than that on acreage. The relation of home to acreage assessment ratios is most favorable to acreage in the South and North Central regions and most favorable to homes in the Northeast.

The correlation between the two ratios is statistically significant but not very strong ($r = .33$). Because effective tax rates encompass not only differences in assessment ratios but also other influences affecting home and farm property taxes, this chapter concentrates on them.

Many of the policy variables discussed in the first section are difficult to quantify without a great deal of effort. For example, government fragmentation is expected to have an important effect on relative tax rates. If farms are completely separate from cities, they are likely to have lower tax rates than if

Table 13-1
Measures of Home and Farm Property Tax Burdens and Urbanization

State	Ratio of Home Effective Tax Rate to Farm Effective Tax Rate	Ratio of Average Home Assessment Ratio to Average Acreage Assessment Ratio	Percentage of Property Tax Revenue from Farm Real Estate	Percentage of Population in Urban Areas
Northeast	*2.14*	*1.41*	*1.2*	*77.3*
Connecticut	2.39	1.70	0.7	77.3
Maine	1.46	1.76	2.8	50.9
Massachusetts	2.06	1.41	0.4	84.6
New Hampshire	NA	1.44	1.2	56.5
New Jersey	3.45	1.39	0.5	88.9
New York	1.78	0.79	1.3	85.6
Pennsylvania	2.23	1.38	1.7	71.5
Rhode Island	NA	2.69	0.5	87.0
Vermont	NA	1.05	7.0	32.2
South	*3.20*	*1.66*	*4.3*	*59.6*
Alabama	5.29	2.00	3.6	58.4
Arkansas	4.03	2.46	13.0	50.0
Delaware	5.50	1.43	1.5	72.1
Florida	1.69	1.15	3.7	80.5
Georgia	2.35	1.61	4.6	60.3
Kentucky	3.20	1.22	8.1	52.4
Louisiana	2.54	1.91	3.9	66.1
Maryland	3.38	2.06	1.7	76.6
Mississippi	3.44	2.10	7.6	44.5
North Carolina	3.29	0.93	4.7	45.0
Oklahoma	2.50	2.64	12.1	68.0
South Carolina	2.34	1.68	3.6	47.6
Tennessee	3.04	1.53	5.9	58.8
Texas	4.18	1.63	5.7	79.8
Virginia	2.69	1.89	3.1	63.1
West Virginia	NA	1.59	1.6	39.0
North Central	*1.91*	*1.63*	*11.5*	*66.0*
Illinois	2.00	1.73	8.2	83.0
Indiana	2.91	2.12	6.8	64.9

Iowa	2.12	1.54	30.8	57.2
Kansas	1.83	1.67	17.6	66.1
Michigan	1.63	1.23	4.0	73.9
Minnesota	1.70	1.58	12.2	66.4
Missouri	2.79	1.76	9.0	70.1
Nebraska	2.73	1.86	27.5	61.6
North Dakota	1.91	1.30	42.0	44.3
Ohio	1.68	1.51	4.2	75.3
South Dakota	1.90	1.85	30.4	44.6
Wisconsin	1.42	1.20	10.8	65.9
West	*2.18*	*1.52*	*5.2*	*72.6*
Alaska	NA	1.24	0.1	48.8
Arizona	2.12	NA	3.0	79.5
California	1.42	1.35	3.6	90.9
Colorado	3.46	1.95	5.2	78.7
Hawaii	NA	6.20	3.7	83.0
Idaho	2.36	1.49	19.0	54.3
Montana	2.15	1.56	15.7	53.6
Nevada	2.38	1.95	1.9	80.9
New Mexico	6.60	1.88	5.9	70.0
Oregon	2.18	1.30	6.4	67.1
Utah	1.69	1.17	6.7	80.6
Washington	2.47	1.21	4.8	72.6
Wyoming	2.02	1.68	7.5	60.4

Sources: Home effective tax rates: Advisory Commission on Intergovernmental Relations, *Significant Features of Fiscal Federalism*, 1978-79 ed. (Washington, D.C., 1978). Farm effective tax rates and farm property tax paid: U.S. Department of Agriculture, *Farm Real Estate Taxes: 1976* (Washington, D.C., 1978). Total property tax revenue: U.S. Bureau of the Census, *Governmental Finances in 1976-77* (Washington, D.C., 1978). Percentage of population in urban areas: U.S. Bureau of the Census, *1970 Census of Population* (Washington, D.C., 1973). Assessment ratios: U.S. Bureau of the Census, *1977 Census of Governments*, vol. 2: *Taxable Property Values and Assessment/Sales Price Ratios* (Washington, D.C., 1978), table 9.

Notes: Effective tax rates are for taxes payable in 1977. Assessment ratios are for 1976. Percentage of property tax revenue from farm real estate is for 1977. Urban population is for 1970. Statistics for regions are medians.

they are included within city boundaries. A very crude way of measuring this effect is by population per government unit, but that hardly captures the complexity of the real world.

Another important factor is the type of preferential assessment program for agricultural property which is in effect. No national data are available on the different methods states employ to measure use value for property tax purposes or on the proportion of all farmland in a state which participates in the program. In some states, it is 100 percent; in others, less than 5 percent. A dummy variable was used if a state had a preferential assessment program, but such programs are so widespread that this variable cannot be expected to explain much.

The composition of the tax base also is difficult to handle. What matters is the breakdown of property value not statewide but rather within each community. Even when farms comprise a high proportion of property statewide, they may have low taxes if they are segregated from other types of property.

It is also difficult to measure how a state's controls on tax rates, tax levies, or expenditures impact on rural versus urban areas; how the assignment of responsibilities among local governments differs; and how aid programs are biased, if at all.

A multiple regression analysis was performed in an attempt to explain the ratio of home to farm effective property tax rates. The variables included are listed in table 13-2, together with the signs which were expected and rationales. Only forty-two states were included because data were lacking for some variables in eight states.[14]

The independent variables are able to account for only about one-third of the variation in the ratio of home to farm tax rates. Most of the variables had extremely low t statistics, indicating a lack of evidence that they were statistically related to the tax rate ratio. Table 13-3 reports the results of a regression containing all variables with a t statistic greater than 1.

One variable stands out as being of foremost importance—the proportion of own-source general revenue derived from property taxation. What this indicates is that when states deemphasize the property tax, rural areas are the greatest gainers. Two of the major explanations are that state aids to local governments tend to favor rural areas and that rural areas tend to be relatively property-rich, so that they usually benefit disproportionately when the property tax is deemphasized.

The proportion of the population which is urban has a statistically significant positive relation to the ratio of tax rates. This is contrary to the expectation that urban states would have tax relief policies more favorable to homeowners than rural states. A likely reason for the positive sign is that per capita spending and tax rates tend to rise as city size increases. Thus, this variable recognizes that cities tend to have relatively high tax rates on homes independent on tax relief policies. A related variable, the proportion of the

Table 13-2
Independent Variables Used in Regression Analysis

Variable	Expected Sign	Rationale
PTR as percent of total own-source GR	−	State aid favors rural areas; property-rich areas gain most from property tax relief.
State PTR as percent of total PTR	−	Rural areas tend to have greater property wealth.
Local nonproperty TR as percent of local own-source GR	−	Urban areas tend to make greater use of local nonproperty taxes and have larger sales and income tax bases.
Circuit breaker benefits as percent of PTR	+	Since state pays a portion of property tax liability of homeowners covered by circuit breakers, their effective tax rates should be higher; tax rate data used here do not reflect circuit breakers.
Percent of population urban (living in place with population over 2,500)	?	Two offsetting factors: urban states may adopt policies favoring homeowners, but larger cities tend to have higher tax rates.
Percent of population in SMSAs with population over 1 million	?	Same as for previous variable.
Ratio of SMSA per capita assessed value to non-SMSA per capita assessed value	−	The higher the property tax base, the lower the tax rate needed to obtain a given amount of revenue.
Ratio of SMSA median family income to non-SMSA median family income	+	Demand for government services is a function of income.
Average assessment ratio on single-family homes divided by average assessment ratio on acreage	+	Discrimination in assessment practices tends to result in corresponding differences in tax rates.

Other variables tested included proportion of the total market value of property which was residential, acreage, or commercial-industrial; proportion of personal income derived from farming; percent of population living on farms or in SMSAs; government units per person; the ratio of per capita residential property to per capita acreage property (in terms of market value); and dummy variables for preferential assessment of farmland, inclusion of assessed value as a determinant of state school aid, homestead exemption or credit, controls on local government spending or taxing other than rate limits, classification, and region of the country.

Source: Property tax and other revenue: U.S. Census Bureau, *Governmental Finances in 1976-77* (Washington, D.C., 1978). Assessment ratios and property tax base: U.S. Census Bureau, *1977 Census of Governments*, vol. 2: *Taxable Property Values and Assessment/Sales Price Ratios* (Washington, D.C., 1978). Population: U.S. Census Bureau. Median family Income: U.S. Census Bureau, *Current Population Reports, Consumer Income*

Table 13-2 continued

(Washington, D.C., 1978), p. 60, no. 110-113. Personal income derived from farming: *Survey of Current Business* vol. 58 (October 1978), pp. 32-41. Effective tax rate on homes and circuit breaker benefits: Advisory Commission on Intergovernmental Relations, *Significant Features of Fiscal Federalism*, 1978-79 ed. (Washington, D.C., 1979). Effective tax rate on farms: U.S. Department of Agriculture, *Farm Real Estate Taxes: 1976* (Washington, D.C., 1978). Dummy variables: see respective chapters of this book.

Note: PTR: Property Tax Revenue
      GR: General Revenue
      TR: Tax Revenue
      SMSA: Standard Metropolitan Statistical Area

population living in metropolitan areas with over 1 million people, appeared to have virtually no relationship to the ratio of tax rates. However, it was significant and positive in regressions to account for home and farm effective tax rates separately.

The circuit breaker variable has a significant negative relation to the tax ratio, contrary to expectations. The main explanation is that Michigan, which has one of the three largest circuit breakers and a very low tax ratio, has very generous provisions for farmers which are not reflected in the farm tax rate data. Thus, taxes actually paid by farmers are much lower than the data suggest. The same is true to a lesser extent in Wisconsin, another state with a low ratio.

The proportion of local government own-source revenue from nonproperty taxes has the expected negative relationship with the home-farm tax ratio. This implies that greater use is made of local income and sales taxes in urban than in rural areas.

The final variable, the ratio of the home to the farm assessment ratio, has the expected positive relation to the effective tax ratio. This was not, however, due to legal classification, since a dummy variable for states which classify property was not related to the tax ratio. Rather, the finding reflects either extralegal discrimination or farm preferential assessment laws.

The insignificance of many of the other variables can probably be traced to either data imperfections or insufficient variation in state data.

The conflict between owners of farms and homes can be looked at from another perspective—in terms of the proportion of statewide property tax revenue which is paid by farm real estate. In 1977, 5 percent of the property tax was paid by owners of farms nationwide. The proportion varied widely, exceeding 25 percent in four states and falling below 10 percent in thirty-eight states and below 3 percent in twelve. Thus, in most states farm property tax relief does not have a very great impact on the average city dweller's tax payments.

But the issue is very important to owners of farmland, having a large impact on their income and wealth. The laws passed since 1956 providing for preferential assessment of farmland initially seemed to do little more than

Table 13-3
Results of Regression to Explain Ratio of Home Effective Tax Rate to Farm Effective Tax Rate

Variable	Coefficient
Proportion of own-source state-local revenue derived from property taxation	−.091** (3.99)
Proportion of population living in urban places	.0243* (1.83)
Ratio of circuitbreaker benefits to total property tax revenue	−.0956* (1.70)
Proportion of local own-source general revenue derived from nonproperty taxes	−.3860 (1.50)
Ratio of assessment ratio for single-family housing to assessment ratio for acreage	.00612 (1.54)
Constant	2.710

$$R^2 = .34$$
$$F = 5.26$$

Note: Numbers in parentheses are t statistics. All proportions are multiplied by 100.
  *Significant at .10 level.
**Significant at .05 level.

legalize the de facto discrimination in assessments which already existed.[15] But in the 1970s those laws have been of tremendous value to farm owners, protecting them from higher assessments and taxes which they would have had to pay had their land been assessed according to its market value. Between 1971 and 1977, the share of property taxes paid by farm owners fell in thirty-seven of the fifty states, despite the fact that the value of farm property was rising much faster than the value of other types of property.

While the declining portion of the property tax load on farm owners is partially attributable to preferential assessment laws, the results suggest that many other types of tax relief policies also played a role. The ratio of home to farm assessment ratios accounted for relatively little of the variation of tax rates in 1977.

To perform a complete analysis of rural-urban conflict would require a case study in every state. This chapter presents a framework in which case studies can be pursued. Understanding of rural-urban conflict at the national level can also be advanced as better measures of the factors influencing relative tax rates are developed.

Notes

1. See, for example, W. Irwin Gillespie, "Effects of Public Expenditures on the Distribution of Income," in *Essays in Fiscal Federalism,* ed. R. Musgrave (Washington, D.C.: The Brookings Institution, 1965), and R. Musgrave et al., "The Distribution of Fiscal Burdens and Benefits," *Public Finance Quarterly* 2 (July 1974), pp. 259-311.

2. There are three case studies on this subject, of Texas, Missouri, and Iowa, respectively. See Daniel C. Morgan, "Fiscal Neglect of Urban Areas by a State Government," *Land Economics* 50 (May 1974):137-144; John H. Bowman, Harold A. Hovey, and Frederick D. Stocker, *Fiscal Equity: A Study of Comparative Revenue Payments, Fiscal Capacity, and Public Expenditure Benefits and Needs in Seven Areas of Missouri* (Columbus, Ohio: Battelle Memorial Institute, 1970); Steven D. Gold, "A Scorecard for Rural-Urban Conflict: Geographic Income Redistribution by State Government" (Paper presented at Midwest Economic Association meetings in St. Louis, April 1976).

3. Frederick D. Stocker, whose analysis of the fiscal problems of non-metropolitan areas is one of the best, uses "rural" and "nonmetropolitan" almost interchangeably, and that procedure is also followed here except when citing specific statistics, despite its lack of precision. See his "Fiscal Needs and Resources of Nonmetropolitan Communities," *International Assessor* 43 (March 1977):2-9.

4. For an analysis of factors affecting property tax rates in one state, see Steven D. Gold, "Geographic Variations of Property Tax Burdens: The Case of Iowa," *Nebraska Journal of Economics and Business,* Spring 1977, pp. 55-72.

5. The demand for services tends to be higher because of higher incomes and the externalities related to congestion. However, Stocker shows that much of the difference in per capita expenditures between metropolitan and non-metropolitan areas can be accounted for by higher wages paid in large cities. See "Fiscal Needs and Resources," pp. 4-5. Muller and Peterson show that wages also account for most of the differences in per capita expenditures among cities with varying density and population size. See their *Economic and Fiscal Costs* (Washington, D.C.: The Urban Institute, 1977), p. 47.

6. U.S. Census Bureau, *1972 Census of Governments, Taxable Property Values and Assessment-Sales Price Ratios,* vol. 2, pt. 1, (Washington, D.C., 1973) table 6; U.S. Census Bureau, *1977 Census of Governments, Taxable Property Values and Assessment-Sales Price Ratios Washington, D.C., 1978) vol. 2, table 3.*

7. See Calvin L. Beale's statement in *Special Study on Economic Change* (Hearings before the Joint Economic Committee of the U.S. Congress, May 31, 1978), pp. 83-93.

8. See sources cited in note 6 and U.S. Census Bureau, *Statistical Abstract of the United States: 1978* (Washington, D.C., 1978).

9. See, for example, Charles W. Meyer, "Geographic Inequalities in

Property Taxes in Iowa, 1962," *National Tax Journal* 18 (December 1965):388-397.

10. In 1971 state aid was 31.7 percent of general revenue inside metropolitan areas and 39.3 percent outside of them. However, this difference was less than in earlier years. In per capita terms, state aid was higher inside metropolitan areas in 1971, reversing the pattern in 1957 and 1962, as reported by Campbell and Sacks. See U.S. Census Bureau, *1972 Census of Governments,* vol. 5, *Local Government in Metropolitan Areas* (Washington, D.C., 1974) table 9. Alan K. Campbell and Seymour Sacks, *Metropolitan America* (New York: Free Press, 1967), pp. 77-81.

11. This analysis applies to taxes levied on all property statewide at a uniform rate. If a state property tax is limited to certain types of property (as it often is), the analysis is not applicable.

12. Per capita local property taxes were 56 percent higher inside metropolitan areas than outside them nationally in 1971-1972. The differential differed considerably among states.

13. The correlation coefficient is $-.22$, which is not quite statistically significant at the .05 level.

14. No home tax rates were available for Alaska, Hawaii, New Hampshire, Rhode Island, Vermont, and West Virginia. Wyoming was omitted because it had no metropolitan areas and Arizona because its assessment ratio data were incomplete.

15. See chapter 5 for evidence on this point.

14 Case Studies: California, Iowa, and Michigan

The preceding chapters have described and analyzed the various types of property tax relief provided across the country, but they have not been able to give much detail about any particular states. This chapter attempts to compensate for that omission by describing the experience of three states in greater depth. The three states covered—California, Iowa, and Michigan—have each been innovative in quite different ways.

In California, the major focus is on the precursors and results of Proposition 13. California adopted several property tax relief measures in the decade preceding 1978, but they were unable to prevent a great increase in property taxes. Other interesting features in California include its early and widespread use of local sales taxes and an elaborate program for preferential assessment of farmland.

Iowa is a farm state which has a long history of tinkering with the property tax, but it was not until the 1970s that it took a series of steps which dropped it off the list of states with the highest property tax burdens. The most unusual aspects of the Iowa experience are its use of tax credits not related to income and its program for limiting the annual increase of farm and home assessments. Both were explicitly intended to avoid large changes in property tax burdens among different classes of property.

Michigan's outstanding feature is its pioneering use of the circuit breaker as a property tax relief device without age or income limits. Only Minnesota's circuit breaker picks up a larger share of property tax liabilities. Elaborate city income taxes and a farm circuit breaker are other programs in which Michigan broke new ground.

As a group, these three states offer insights into the variety of ways in which activist states have responded to the persistent demand for property tax relief.

California

Until Proposition 13, California was a high-property-tax state and had been for many years.[1] Its postwar history is interesting because of the many property tax relief measures which were considered. Although some of these measures were adopted, they proved incapable of halting the tide of rising property taxes.

California was a leader in the use of local sales taxes. Their use was rather chaotic until 1956, when passage of the Bradley-Burns Act led to the statewide adoption of virtually uniform local sales taxes. Both cities and counties derive revenue from these taxes, but the bulk of the money goes to cities.[2]

Another area in which California pioneered is in tax relief for agriculture.[3] Its Williamson Act, passed in 1965, is one of the most elaborate in the country. As amended, the act provides for counties to set up agricultural zones in which participating property is assessed according to its use value rather than its market value. While most of the land in the program is used for agriculture, a small amount is recreational or has some other "open-space use."

In order to receive the lower assessment, the owner of the land must sign a contract committing the land to its designated use for at least ten years. Although most states now have a preferential assessment program for agriculture, California is one of the few which provides for such contracts and long-term commitments.

The law has apparently failed to achieve one of its major objectives, to slow down the conversion of land from agricultural to other uses. Although 30 percent of the privately owned nonurban land in California participates in the program, very little of this land is in areas threatened by urban expansion. Where development prospects are on the horizon, few landowners choose to participate. Thus, the main effect of the Williamson Act is to lower taxes for owners of farmland.[4]

Another type of relief in which California was in the forefront of state action was the circuit breaker. Its circuit breaker for senior citizens, adopted in 1967, is the third oldest in the nation. With eligibility extending up to $20,000 of gross income (or a lower amount of net income), its coverage is one of the broadest. Also, prior to the passage of Proposition 13 its benefits were among the highest in the nation. For example, the average benefit for elderly homeowners who participated in the circuit breaker was $266 in 1977, the second highest in the country. Of course, a major reason why benefits were so high is that property tax rates were also extremely high.[5]

The decade prior to 1978 is punctuated by a number of property-tax-limiting initiatives which appeared on the statewide ballot. Although most of these initiatives failed to pass, they often induced the legislature to pass bills which provided property tax relief of a milder sort than the initiative called for.

The first initiative in 1968 called for eliminating reliance on the property tax for "people-related services" (primarily education and welfare) and reducing such reliance for "property-related services." Among the reasons for the defeat of this initiative (which was sponsored by Philip Watson, the Los Angeles County Assessor) were uncertainty as to how services would be financed if it passed, the absence of persistent assessment increases, and general optimism about the economic outlook.

As an alternative to the Watson initiative, the legislature proposed California's first homestead exemption. It freed from taxation the first $750 of assessed value of owner occupied homes; this was equivalent to an exemption of $3,000 of market value. The exemption, financed by the state, was approved in the November election at which the Watson proposal was soundly defeated. A partial exemption for business inventories was also adopted.[6]

In 1970 there were two attempts to pass property-tax-related initiatives. One which was on the ballot called for increased state funding of schools and social welfare programs and an increase in the homestead exemption. It received less than 28 percent of the votes cast. The other proposal, sponsored by Howard Jarvis, failed to obtain enough signatures to appear on the ballot.

Another Watson initiative was voted on in 1972. Once more it was defeated, but again the legislature passed a relief bill. It increased the homestead exemption to $1,750 of assessed value ($7,000 of market value), raised the exemption of business inventories, provided a small tax credit for renters, placed a limit on local government tax rates, and revised the formula for aid to school districts, including a limit on expenditure increases.

The next important initiative was in 1973. It dealt not with property taxes but with state spending, which it sought to prevent from exceeding 7 ½ percent of state personal income. This proposal of Governor Reagan was defeated, 56 to 44 percent.

Sometime after 1973 housing prices began to inflate rapidly. Reliable statewide data are not available, but in the Los Angeles and San Francisco metropolitan areas prices increased at an annual rate of 14 to 15 percent between 1973 and 1977. This was considerably faster than in the rest of the country, although not very different from what was happening elsewhere in California. These price increases were reflected fairly rapidly in higher assessed values. As a result of assessment reforms enacted in the 1960s, California property assessments do not lag far behind sales prices as they do in many states.

Higher assessments led to higher property tax burdens. Although the average tax rate faced by California homeowners fell from $11.15 to $10.68 per $100 of assessed valuation between fiscal years 1974 and 1978, this 5 percent drop was not nearly enough to offset assessment increases. As a result, tax bills soared.

Despite the rapid increase in residential property tax bills, local government spending did not increase very rapidly. There are two explanations for this paradox. First, business property values rose much more slowly than home values. Thus, the composition of the property tax base changed considerably, with homes becoming an increasing proportion. Homes rose from 31.6 percent of net total assessed value in 1973-1974 to 43 percent in 1978-1979.[7] Consequently, home taxes rose much faster than business taxes.

A second reason why property taxes increased faster than local government spending has to do with the way that school aid is distributed. As assessed value increases, aid tends to decline because of the formula used for determining how much aid school districts receive. Therefore, escalating property values changed the mix of school revenues, increasing the share from property taxes.[8]

The limits placed on local taxing in 1972 did very little to restrict property taxes because they provided a choice as to whether tax rates or levies would be limited. Localities naturally chose the less restrictive alternative, tax-rate limits. This illustrates how restrictions which are not carefully designed may fail to achieve their intended objectives.

In 1977 the legislature expended considerable effort in attempting to pass another property tax relief program. A plan establishing a large circuit breaker passed in the assembly and fell two votes short of the required two-thirds majority needed in the senate, as all Republicans and two Democrats kept it from passing.[9] The legislature adjourned in September without taking action on property taxes, and an opportunity to preempt the budding tax revolt slipped away.

Aside from disagreement about how to distribute relief among taxpayers, the major problem in passing a tax relief bill was uncertainty about how much state revenue was available to finance it. As often happens in state deliberations, the available resources were underestimated. In January 1977, the state's budget surplus was estimated at $940 million. By June 1978, the estimates had swollen to more than $6 billion. It would certainly have been much easier to reach agreement on a tax relief program in 1977 if the scope of the available resources had been realized.[10]

Shortly after the legislature failed to act in 1977, Howard Jarvis and Paul Gann began circulating petitions for their initiative to limit property taxes. Their Proposition 13 contained four major elements:

> Each property's assessment for tax purposes would be based upon its market value in 1975, or at the time of the property's last sale, whichever came later.

> As long as a property was retained by the same owner, its assessment could increase by no more than 2 percent per year. At time of sale, the assessment could be increased to reflect the actual market price.

> The combined property taxes of a city, a county, a school district, etc., would be limited to 1 percent of a property's "full cash value" (which is its assessed value multiplied by 4). The only exception to this limit was made for property taxes needed to retire bond issues that were outstanding as of June, 1978.

> Any general state tax increase would require a two-thirds vote in the legislature (rather than the majority vote requirement previously in effect). Similarly, local governments could not increase property taxes above the 1 percent limit, but other local taxes could be increased subject to a two-thirds majority in a referendum.[11]

Since total property taxes on a typical California home in 1977 averaged 2.6 percent of market value, Proposition 13 implied a tremendous reduction in property tax levies.[12]

As an alternative, the 1978 legislature passed and the governor signed a bill providing $1.6 billion of property tax relief in 1979. This bill, developed by a legislator named Behr, targeted relief to homeowners and renters. It provided for (1) a 30 percent immediate property tax cut for homeowners, to be financed primarily from the state budget surplus; (2) a limit of property tax revenue growth to the rate of inflation; (3) increases in the circuit breaker for the elderly and tax credits for renters; and (4) a limitation tying the growth of state revenue to the increase of personal income.[13] Since this proposal included classification (taxing homes and businesses at different rates), it could not go into effect unless the voters approved a constitutional amendment in June 1978, the same election in which Proposition 13 was voted on. If both propositions passed, the Behr bill's provisions would not go into effect.

Victory for Proposition 13 was ensured in May 1978, when the Los Angeles assessor notified property owners of their new assessments. Many homes had increases of 50 to 100 percent. The total property tax roll increased 17.5 percent, although only one-third of all properties were reassessed.[14] Publicity concerning this order boosted substantially the popularity of Proposition 13, and it passed with nearly two-thirds of the vote.

In addition to all the other things which Proposition 13 had going for it, the opposition ran a poor campaign, emphasizing the cuts in services which would allegedly ensue and not analyzing its implications as a tax proposal.[15]

Within a few weeks of the passage of Proposition 13, the legislature passed a bill providing $4.2 billion of aid to local governments to replace much of the lost property tax revenue. Using a portion of the large state surplus, the state was able in the short run to confound the predictions of massive layoffs and drastically reduced services which had circulated before June 8.

The repercussions of Proposition 13 were widespread. We discuss first the direct tax effects, then the effect on the federal government's activity, the results on service and state and local employment, the impact on governmental reform, and the longer-term outlook.

Tax Effect

Only a minority of property tax savings went to homeowners. Determining how the benefits of Proposition 13 were distributed is somewhat complicated because one must consider not merely the direct tax savings but also the fact that property taxes are deductible on federal and state income taxes, so that income tax payments rose as property taxes fell. Also, a portion of business tax savings was passed on to consumers in lower prices.

Approximately 35 percent of the direct $7 billion property tax cut went to homeowners, with the remainder going to businesses and landlords; thus, the homeowners' share was $2.5 billion and that of business was $4.5 billion. Of the business property tax savings $416 million went to public utilities, which were forced to pass them on in lower rates to consumers. It is difficult to determine how much of the remaining business tax savings resulted in lower prices or avoidance of price increases, but according to newspaper accounts most of the benefits of lower taxes were retained by business and landlords.[16]

The tax savings which individual property owners received depended on how much property was owned, whether income taxes were itemized, how high their marginal income tax rate was, and the level of the local property tax rate. Savings were greatest for persons who owned a large amount of property in an area with a high tax rate but had a low income so that the marginal income tax rate was relatively low. Several generalizations can be stated. (1) The rich benefited more than the middle class in terms of total taxes saved per household, although their percentage tax reduction was less because they tend to have high income tax rates and live in areas with relatively low property tax rates. (2) Homeowners benefited much more than the 45 percent of households which are renters, since rents did not decrease dramatically, if at all. (3) Residents of rural areas benefited much less than residents of urban areas because their tax rates tend to be much lower.

These conclusions are open to debate. According to one view, if it were not for Proposition 13, there would have been a major reduction of state income tax rates. Thus, Proposition 13 shifted taxation from the regressive property tax to the progressive income tax and consequently was adverse to the interests of the rich. Likewise, it hurt suburbanites and aided residents of central cities and rural areas because suburbs have high income in proportion to their assessed value.[17] Whether this argument is correct depends on unverifiable speculation as to the magnitude and distribution of income tax reductions which might have occurred.

The Congressional Budget Office estimated that the result of Proposition 13 would be to increase federal revenues $628 million in fiscal year 1979 and $911 million in fiscal 1980. These estimates consist of two parts: income tax receipts would increase $1 billion in 1979 and $1.3 billion in 1980 because of lower property tax deductions, but they would be partially offset by reduced economic activity resulting from lower state and local government spending, and thus lower business and personal income tax payments.[18]

In addition to these federal revenue impacts, it was expected that California governments would lose federal aid in such areas as education, highways, transit, sewage treatment, child nutrition, and general revenue sharing, because to some extent the amount of aid received depends on the level of spending by the recipient governments. California's loss in some of these areas would be balanced by a gain in other parts of the country because a limited amount of revenue is distributed according to a formula. For example, one of the factors in distributing general revenue sharing is tax effort (tax revenue as a fraction of personal income). With lower taxes in California, its share of revenue sharing would drop and that of the rest of the country increase.

The revenue of California's local governments in the fiscal year beginning in July 1978 turned out to be much higher than was expected by most people when Proposition 13 passed. Aside from the infusion of state aid, additional revenue came from several sources. Assessments increased 9 percent rather than the 1.3 percent which had been forecast, as many assessors raised the values on properties which had been underassessed. In addition, local nonproperty tax revenues increased substantially. To some extent, this was a continuation of the existing pattern, since they had been rising at a rate of 10 percent per year since 1974. But cities, counties, and schools turned to new or increased user charges to an unprecedented extent. The fees most commonly increased were building and inspection fees, business licenses, recreation and park fees, utility charges (including sewer and water), planning department fees, charges for trash collection, and hotel-motel bed taxes. However, the significance of user fees should not be overemphasized. They probably offset less than 5 percent of the decreased property tax revenue.[19]

Effect on Services and Government Employment

The widespread impression is that government services were not seriously affected in 1978-1979. Predicted mass layoffs did not occur.

According to a *Los Angeles Times* survey, city and county budgets did not decrease but rose. As of October 1978, only 1 percent of full-time city and county workers had been laid off. School districts in the aggregate had somewhat lower spending, but they were able for the most part to limit employment cuts to their noninstructional staff. The services which cities cut most often were parks and recreation, libraries, street sweeping and maintenance, police, and street lighting. The prime candidates for county service reductions were libraries, social services, and parks. Health services were cut in many places.[20]

The fact that service cutbacks were relatively small does not imply that they were not serious for some groups of citizens. In many cities hospitals and neighborhood health centers serving poor persons were forced to curtail their services. Schools often sharply reduced or eliminated their after-school programs. According to reports published by the Coalition of American Public Employees, low-income families suffered the most from these measures.[21]

One reason why local governments were able to maintain a fairly high level of services despite only small increases in revenues was that wages were frozen. Since labor costs account for a majority of most budgets, the impact of inflation was blunted.

Effects on Government Organization
and Land Use

The aftershocks of Proposition 13 were significant and produced results which had not been widely foreseen. For example, fragmentation of local government responsibilities was alleviated because cities and special districts became dependent on overlying county governments for revenue. The state assumed all the cost of financing welfare, Medicaid, and food stamps and considerably increased its share of educational costs. In sum, there was a giant step away from local control of government and toward increased centralization of power at the state level; these are not results which conservatives usually strive to achieve.[22]

In addition, suburban sprawl may be curtailed because many local governments have imposed sizable new charges on developers, adding to the "up-front cost" of new housing subdivisions. Much of the local fiscal incentive for development evaporated because new construction could not "pay its own way" when the tax rate is limited to 1 percent.[23]

Residential mobility will also be curtailed to some extent because when a family moves from one home to another, its taxes take a big jump. While the tax on the original home was based on its value in 1975, the tax on the new home will be based on its current value, which is usually much higher.[24] However, economist William Oakland has expressed skepticism that the reduction in the rate at which houses are sold will be significant. One reason is that most property transfers involve employment transfers, retirement, or death, so that taxes are not an important consideration. Moreover, with the tax rate at 1 percent, "the maximum savings from maintaining ownership is 1 percent of the value of the home—a figure which may be small compared to the benefits of upgrading one's housing."[25]

Longer-run effects

At the time of this writing, it appears that the state surplus will be able to continue to replace lost property tax revenue for several more years, in part because of large reductions in state spending subsequent to the passage of Proposition 13. In addition, the state income tax is highly elastic, meaning that its revenue increases significantly faster than the growth of personal income, although a partial indexing of the income tax which was enacted in 1978 reduces the elasticity considerably. Income tax rates were reduced in 1979, but this was not a permanent cut and rates could rise to previous levels in subsequent years. However, unless new taxes are enacted, the government sector will probably have to shrink in the future, albeit gradually and perhaps in undramatic ways.[26]

It can be shown that under certain assumptions even in the long run the growth of local government spending will not be curtailed much by Proposition 13. One key assumption is that personal income will rise at least 10 percent per year, which is sufficient to finance a steady increase in state aid to localities. It is also important for homes to continue to escalate substantially in price and for the frequency with which homes are sold not to be significantly lowered. If these and certain other conditions exist, William Oakland shows that Proposition

13 may reduce the rate of growth of public services by less than 1 percent per year below what would have taken place in its absence.[27]

There are so many economic, political, and social factors to consider that no firm conclusions about the long-run effects of Proposition 13 can be stated yet.

Conclusions

The most important point to make about California is that it is a special case. Its extremely high property taxes provided the will, and its unique state surplus provided the way to make an enormous cut in property taxes. Most other states have neither such a high property tax burden nor such an easy means of financing relief.

California's high property taxes are indicated by evidence from several sources. According to the Federal Housing Authority, the effective tax rate on homes in California during the first three months of 1978 was exceeded in only four states, and these data probably understate California's relative tax rates. Moreover, California is one of a handful of places where the effective tax rate rose between 1975 and early 1978.[28] Another indication that California's tax burden was unusually high is that the ratio of property tax revenue to personal income was the fourth highest in the nation in 1977. Aggregate figures suggest that the property tax has been taking a smaller fraction of income than earlier in the 1970s in California, but when allowance is made for the increasing proportion of the tax which was paid by homeowners, the opposite pattern emerges. Property taxes on single-family dwellings in California rose from less than 2 percent of personal income in 1973-1974 to more than 2.5 percent of income in 1977-1978. This level and trend of taxes California rose from less than 2 percent of personal income in 1973-1974 to tax rates and proportion of income in 1977-1978. This level and trend of taxes are matched in few other states. There are other states with higher effective tax rates and proportion of income going to property taxes than California, but they did not experience the rapid increase in home values which occurred in California.[29]

The final factor which explains Proposition 13 is that its politicians failed to offset the trend toward higher property taxes. In this sense, it differs from act—is not really independent of the other two forces mentioned (the high tax burdens and large state surplus). Rather, the political failure was a large part of the reason why the other two existed.

Iowa

Iowa is a typical state in many respects, ranking twenty-fifth in population, area, and per capita income.[30] Yet, it is a state of contrasts. On one hand, it has one of the more farm-oriented state economies, with some of the best farmland anywhere and over 40 percent of its property tax base being agricultural. On the other hand, less than 15 percent of the labor force is engaged in farming. In 1970, 57 percent of the population lived in urban areas (population over 2,500) and 36 percent in metropolitan areas. These figures classify Iowa as less urban than the average state, but it is far from being the most rural.

The year 1967 marks the beginning of the period in which Iowa's property tax system underwent sweeping and turbulent change. At that time the property tax in Iowa was high by any measure—as a percentage of state-local revenue or personal income, in terms of the effective tax rate on homes and farms, or in relation to population.

In 1967 a momentous step was taken—a commitment to reform the property tax assessment system so that homes, farms, and businesses were assessed at the same percentage of their market value throughout the state. Previously all property was by law supposed to be assessed at 60 percent of its market value, but assessments had in fact been closer to 25 percent. The assessment standard varied widely among counties, so that homes or farms with equal market values often had very unequal assessed values. Henceforth all property was to be assessed at 27 percent of its market value, and the state was to issue periodic orders to equalize the treatment of property in all assessment jurisdictions.

If all property had been assessed at a uniform percentage of its market value, the agricultural sector would have suffered, because previously it had been assessed at a lower rate than other types of property. Therefore, the assessment of farmland was half on the basis of its market value and half on the basis of its "productivity" as calculated from the net income derived from it. As a result of this special provision, farm assessed values did not change much when the new law went into effect.

A second important step in 1967 was to massively increase state aid to school districts, with revenue coming from increases of the state sales and income taxes. As a result of the 1967 action, state aid tripled within two years, the state share of the cost of financing elementary and secondary education rose from 14.6 percent in 1966-1967 to 32.1 percent in 1968-1969, and the property tax's share fell from 82.4 to 61.7 percent.

Another 1967 property tax relief measure was creation of a personal property tax credit. Since it provided for the state to pay a portion of personal property tax liability, it relieved the tax of those with farm machinery or livestock and business equipment and inventories, which were the main types of personal property still subject to tax. Most of the household personal property tax had been exempted in previous years.

Despite all these 1967 actions, property taxes continued to march upward. Governor Robert Ray, who was elected five times over the 1968-1978 period, experienced his only close call in 1970, the result of dissatisfaction with rising property taxes. Property taxes increased more than 20 percent between 1969 and 1971.

In 1971 Ray proposed another large increase in state aid to school districts. In place of the previous complex distribution formula, Ray proposed a foundation aid program which required all school districts receiving state aid to levy a 30-mill property tax, with state aid filling the gap between the revenue derived from this uniform levy and a target level of revenue per pupil. The plan gave relatively little aid to school districts with high assessed value per pupil, most of which were in rural areas.

The legislation which finally passed called for only a 20-mill uniform levy, which increased the proportion of aid going to rural school districts. To obtain some rural support, a provision was included setting a minimum aid level of $200 per pupil for a number of years.

The final bill raised school aid substantially beginning in 1972 and provided for a further increase in aid over the next ten years, all of which was financed by an increase in income tax rates.

One other feature of the bill was very important. Because of the perception that much of the 1967 increase in aid had simply raised teacher salaries without providing much property tax relief, a strict limit was placed on how much expenditures per pupil could increase in any year. Barring large increases in assessments, the school aid plan eliminated schools as a future source of major property tax increases.

Several other small steps were taken to provide additional property tax relief in the early 1970s. A circuit breaker for elderly renters and homeowners was begun in 1973, supplanting a double homestead credit in effect since 1969. Whereas the former program provided benefits only for those with income under $4,000, eligibility for the circuit breaker extended to an income of $6,000. A small revenue-sharing program for cities was begun, with money being distributed on the basis of population. Finally, a plan was passed to phase out the personal property tax completely over a ten-year period.

All was quiet on the property tax front until August 1975, when the State Department of Revenue issued one of its periodic orders designed to equalize assessment ratios throughout the state. This order was the first one since the inflation of the 1970s had started to drive up the values of homes and farms across the state. The order called for average increases in the values of homes of 29 percent and farms of 52 percent.

Inflation affected the Iowa tax base to an unusual extent because its farm sector was large and booming. According to Iowa State University surveys, the average value per acre of Iowa farmland rose from $482 in 1972 to $1,368 in 1976. Inflation of home values was not as great as for Iowa farms or California homes, but it was still enormous by past standards.

The equalization order applied to assessed values as of January 1, 1975. These values were the basis for property taxes to be paid in the year beginning

July 1976. Thus, the 1976 legislature had an opportunity to avert the changes in taxes which would have occurred if the tax system had simply rolled on as it existed at the time.

Those changes would have been large. For one thing, homes and farms would have represented a considerably large share of the total property tax base and would have consequently paid more tax while business paid less tax. A second force worked through the school aid plan. Higher property values raised the revenue which the uniform 20-mill levy brought in and thus automatically reduced state aid to school districts by approximately $48 million. One result was higher property taxes throughout the state, but particularly in rural areas where property values had increased most. Another result was a $48 million windfall to the state treasury.

In January 1976, Governor Ray proposed to deal with this situation by increasing school aid $48 million and limiting increases in nonschool property tax revenue to a certain annual percentage rise. This proposal would have kept aggregate property taxes from rising because of higher valuations but did nothing about the tax shift to farms and homes from businesses.

For only the second time in thirty years, the legislature was controlled by Democrats, and the leaders in the Iowa House of Representatives developed an alternative plan. The Democrats called for increases in the homestead and agricultural land tax credits. The homestead credit, which had paid $62.50 of the property tax on the principal residence of each homeowner since the 1930s, would henceforth pay the tax on the first $4,500 of assessed value. (In 1975 Iowa had made assessed value equal to 100 percent of market value rather than 27 percent.) The agricultural land tax credit had originally passed as a means of cushioning the rise in farm taxes when rural and urban school districts consolidated in the 1940s. For many years the credit had been funded at $18 million, which was sufficient to pay less than one-third of the claims filed. The Iowa House Democratic plan called for raising the funding to $42 million. It also would have limited the credit to 200 acres of land per owner.

The Iowa House program, which also included an increase in the elderly circuit breaker and a credit for low-income renters, had a cost which was similar to that of the governor's program, but it had two differences. First, all the benefits were targeted to residential and farm property, so that there was no shift in favor of business property. Second, it was more progressive in that the total tax relief for any property owner was limited. If school aid were increased, tax relief would have been greater, the more property a person owned.

The plan passed by the legislature did not incorporate the 200-acre limitation on the agricultural land tax credit or the renter credit. It covered three years, and in the second and third years the method of assessing farmland would have been changed so that it was based solely on productivity rather than on a 50-50 basis with market value and productivity. However, Governor Ray vetoed most of the bill pertaining to the second and third years. Thus, the increased credits applied only to 1976-1977 taxes.

One of the governor's proposals which was retained was a limit on the annual increase in property tax levies for local governments other than schools.[31] The limits were 9 percent per year, with certain funds exempted. The intent of these limits, which remained in effect from July 1976 to June 1979, was partially subverted by local governments which transferred certain activities from controlled to uncontrolled funds. Many cities also adopted user charges for refuse collection to avoid the limits. However, it is generally believed that the limits did have some effect in holding down property tax levies, particularly for cities.

Since the 1976 law covered only one year, property taxes were again at the head of the legislative agenda in 1977. The legislature also was confronted with the certainty that another equalization order mandating large increases in farm and home assessments would be issued later in the year to take effect January 1, 1978.

Governor Ray's 1977 proposals were surprising on two accounts. First, he proposed that the increased home and farm tax credits be made permanent, although he had opposed them previously. More significantly, he proposed that the increase of farm and home valuations be limited to 5 percent per year. The stated rationale for these limitations was not to avoid large shifts in the proportion of taxes paid by different classes of property but rather to avoid large jumps in assessments from one year to the next.

The legislature changed the governor's proposal in two major respects. It limited annual assessment increases to 6 percent on an aggregate statewide basis rather than within each assessment jurisdiction. This modification ensured that the limits did not interfere with assessment equalization for homes. For example, if the jurisdictional limit proposed by the governor had passed, a home in Des Moines might have been assessed at 60 percent of its value while one in Sioux City was assessed at 70 percent, which many persons would consider unfair. Under the system which was passed, all homes in the state are assessed at the same percentage of their market value. For 1978, this percentage was 78 percent, a figure which made the aggregate statewide increase in assessments 6 percent.

The second major change made by the legislature was to assess farmland completely on the basis of its productivity, thus completing the transition begun in the 1960s from market- to use-value assessment. If this step had been taken by itself, it would have helped owners of farmland at the expense of all other property owners. However, in conjunction with the limits on assessment increases, the adverse effect on homeowners of the movement to productivity was greatly reduced.

The 1977 bill was limited to a two-year period. But in 1979 the assessment limits were made permanent. They were modified to ensure that home and farm assessments rise each year at the same rate (but not more than 4 percent per year after 1979).

There are two perspectives from which these assessment limits can be analyzed. If one compares the situation after the limits went into effect with that which existed previously, their effect is to maintain the status quo: big changes in tax burdens are avoided. But if one compares what would have happened with and without limits, their impact is much different. They avoided a major shift of taxes from business to owners of homes and farms. Thus, they are of great benefit to homes and farms but impose a large cost on business (some of which will subsequently be passed on to consumers).[32,33]

Some of the small programs discussed earlier expanded in the late 1970s. The income limit of the elderly circuit breaker, which originally was $6,000, was raised first to $8,000, then to $9,000, and later to $10,000. Revenue sharing for cities was increased and extended to counties.

One of the few types of property tax relief which is not significantly used in Iowa is local nonproperty taxation. Even in this area Iowa has been innovative. For several years the only way for a school district to exceed the school spending limit was to levy a local income tax following a voter referendum. Only one district voted on this option, and it was soundly defeated. However, when the law was changed so that half of the revenue to exceed the spending limit came from the property tax and half from the income tax, the option became more popular. In 1978-1979, twenty-one school districts had the extra tax in effect (as a surcharge to the taxpayer's state income tax). All are small, wealthy rural school districts. The explanation for the turnabout is that the income tax itself is paid completely by residents, with none on business or outside workers. Much of the property tax, however, is borne by nonresidents.

The Iowa experience illustrates how a state can deemphasize the property tax and avoid large increases in property tax burdens even when property values are soaring. Between 1971 and 1977 the property tax declined from 6.1 to 4.7 percent of personal income; the effective tax rate on homes dropped from 2.63 to 1.59 percent; and the effective tax rate on farms fell from 1.50 to 0.83 percent. Adjusted for inflation, per capita collections fell more than 12 percent. One development which facilitated these changes was the fourfold increase of state income tax revenue.

Iowa's method of limiting assessment increases for homes and farms reduces political conflicts about relative tax shares, but it raises some serious questions:

1. Is it fair that the ratio of farm to home assessments, which has changed substantially although gradually over the years, should be held constant at some particular level, even if relative market values change sharply?[34]
2. At what point does the increasing share of taxes levied against business property become too great?
3. How serious a drawback is it that the property tax system is made so complicated that few citizens can comprehend it?

Michigan

Prior to the adoption of its circuit breaker, the major novelty in Michigan's property tax relief program was its system of city income taxes.[35] The earlier local income taxes (in Pennsylvania, Ohio, Kentucky, Alabama, and Missouri) were primarily on wages and salaries, allowed no personal exemptions, and were designed by each city on its own. Detroit broke with precedent in 1962 by defining taxable income to include income from investments as well as income from labor; it also was the first city to allow a personal exemption. Both innovations tended to make the local income tax less regressive.

Two years later Michigan incorporated these provisions into its Uniform City Income Tax Ordinance, which set up a common structure to be used by all cities adopting a local income tax. All cities had a 1 percent tax on their residents' gross income minus personal exemptions of $600 per person. (In 1968 Detroit was granted special permission to levy a 2 percent tax.) The tax rate on nonresidents was just 0.5 percent, which was allowed as a tax credit for any city income tax that might be owed in the city of residence. Corporate profits were also taxed at a flat rate.[36]

As of 1978, sixteen cities levied the tax, but its adoption was far from universal. Two of the larger cities in the state, Detroit suburbs Dearborn and Livonia, are among those which do not levy the tax. The smallest income tax city in Michigan is Grayling (population: 2,100).

Circuit Breaker

Michigan's circuit breaker was far larger than any that had previously been adopted. Even at present only Minnesota and Oregon have programs which are larger in terms of per capita benefits or the proportion of the population covered. How can the adoption of such an extraordinary measure be explained?

The adoption of a circuit breaker in Michigan in May 1973 culminated several years of agitation to reform the tax system. The previous year voters turned down a proposal, 58 to 42 percent, that would have eliminated most school property taxes and substituted an increased state income tax. The public discussion of that referendum drew attention to the inequities of the property tax and thus increased receptivity to the concept of the circuit breaker.

Another key development was a sharp improvement in the state's fiscal situation, owing to economic recovery, the initiation of general revenue sharing by the federal government, and the beginning of a lottery by the state.

Thus, there was both a desire and a means to significantly increase property tax relief. The circuit breaker was a very popular idea at the time, riding the crest of its greatest popularity. Five states had adopted a circuit breaker in 1971, doubling the number which already had one on the books; and they were followed by three other states in 1972 and eight more in the first five months of 1973, not counting Michigan.[37]

Four other factors contributed to the decision to provide such a large circuit breaker. First, Michigan has traditionally been a fairly liberal state. Second, a large amount was already being spent on property tax relief for homeowners and renters, so that by eliminating those older programs the net cost of the circuit breaker could be held to less than it otherwise would have been. Third, the backers of the circuit breaker were politically adroit at stitching together a diverse coalition. Finally, the state had a sophisticated staff of economists able to make relatively accurate, detailed projections of program costs and benefits.

The circuit breaker proposal was part of a far-reaching package which overhauled many aspects of Michigan's tax system. Several groups which did not benefit from the circuit breaker did gain from other parts of the package. For example, the personal exemption on the income tax was increased from $1,200 to $1,500, for a cost to the state in 1974-1975 of $96 million; this increase reduced income tax payments $11.70 per person, because the income tax rate at that time was a flat 3.9 percent.[38] The intangibles tax was also lowered $6 million as part of the bill, and a credit was provided for business inventory tax payments at a cost of $49 million.

The cost of the circuit breaker in 1974-1975 was $205 million, but $159 million of existing property tax relief programs was repealed, so that the net property tax reduction was only $46 million. By contrast, the other tax cuts listed added up to $153 million. So the property tax relief portion of the tax reduction program accounted for less than one-fourth of the total $197 million cost.[39]

Design of the Circuit Breaker

The Michigan program provides a credit of up to $1,200 (originally $500 and raised to its present level in 1976) which is equal to 60 percent of the excess of local property taxes over 3.5 percent of total household income. The credit is 100 percent of the excess for persons who are 65 or older, and senior citizens with income below $3,000 receive a credit for their entire property tax bill (up to the maximum). The threshold above which benefits are received rises as the income of senior citizens rises from $3,000 to $6,000.

Seventeen percent of rent is assumed to be property taxes, so renters are covered by the program as well as homeowners. Special provisions are also made for blind persons, disabled veterans, and farmers. Particularly important is the special treatment of farmers. Farmers whose gross receipts from farm operations exceed their total household income may include property taxes on their farm in calculating their benefit. When the maximum benefit was raised from $500 to $1,200, many of the beneficiaries were farmers. Unfortunately, however, none of the data on the circuit breaker which are reported separate farmers from renters and homeowners. This tends to cloud the interpretation of figures on how benefits are distributed by income class.

The design of the circuit breaker represented a series of political and economic compromises. For example, it was estimated that nearly half of all households and the majority of moderate- and higher-income households would receive no benefit at all from the circuit breaker; lowering the proportion further would have increased the progressivity of the program but narrowed its political base and made it impossible to enact.[40] Another compromise involved the proportion of excess tax liability which was rebated. This percentage was finally set at 60 percent. If it was higher, it might seriously distort voters' decisions about whether to favor property tax increases. At a level of 100 percent, a person could vote for higher property taxes, secure in the knowledge that the state circuit breaker would pay them all.

The circuit breaker by itself would also tend to encourage use of the property tax and discourage adoption of local income taxes. However, since 1967 the state has provided an income tax credit for local income taxes paid, so that this bias is partially neutralized.

Table 14-1 summarizes experience during the first five years the circuit breaker was in effect. There are a number of interesting points.

Number of Recipients. Participation has tended to trend upward, with the number of persons in the program in 1977 being more than 22 percent higher than in the first year. Participation reflects both greater knowledge about the program and economic trends in the state. The 1974-1975 recession hit very hard in Michigan, and many workers who had not participated at first became eligible. The effects of recovery from the recession are also visible in the data since the number of nonelderly circuit breaker recipients dropped sharply in 1976. Senior citizen participation has increased each year as the population ages.

Benefits Paid. The cost to the state was only 75 percent of what had been expected in 1973, but by 1974 it was very close to the projection. By its fifth year the circuit breaker's cost was more than twice as high as when it started. The increase in benefits in 1976 was partially attributable to the increase in the maximum credit to $1,200.

Average Benefit. The average benefit increased each year in every category. The major reason is that property tax levies have increased faster than personal income.

There is some indication that property tax levies rose faster than they would have because the circuit breaker was available to relieve some of their burden.

Table 14-1

History of Michigan Circuit Breaker Benefits, 1973-1977

(Number of recipients and benefits paid in thousands.)

	General[a]	Senior Citizens[b]	Total[c]
1973			
Number of recipients	620.0	290.0	1,009.9
Benefits paid	$77,900.00	$60,000.00	$150,600.00
Average benefit	$125.65	$206.90	$149.12
1974			
Number of recipients	759.0	332.0	1,173.0
Benefits paid	$101,640.00	$87,510.00	$203,560.00
Average benefit	$133.91	$263.58	$173.54
1975			
Number of recipients	840.0	350.3	1,279.0
Benefits paid	$120,973.00	$94,650.00	$231,408.00
Average benefit	$144.02	$270.20	$180.93
1976			
Number of recipients	777.9	364.9	1,234.8
Benefits paid	$137,234.00	$120,891.60	$275,582.20
Average benefit	$176.42	$331.30	$223.18
1977			
Number of recipients	775.0	376.4	1,239.9
Benefits paid	$151,979.00	$136,134.00	$305,241.00
Average benefit	$196.10	$361.67	$246.18

Source: Michigan Department of Management and Budget.

[a]The general program is the regular circuit breaker for the nonelderly.

[b]The figures include the regular senior citizen circuit breaker and the special credit received by those who received higher benefits prior to 1973. The number in the latter category fell each year and was less than 2 percent of total elderly beneficiaries in 1976.

[c]The total includes categories not shown separately: the special credits for veterans, the blind, the disabled, and others.

Between 1972-1973 and 1976-1977, property tax revenue rose 43 percent in Michigan and only 37.9 percent in the rest of the country. School property tax levies rose particularly fast, increasing from 62.6 to 66.8 percent of total property taxes between 1972 and 1977. Although the state program for aiding school districts underwent a major overhaul in 1973, aid was not increased substantially, nor was school district spending limited as in California and Iowa. State property tax relief funding went into the cirucit breaker rather than school aid as in many other states.[41]

The next three tables summarize data on how the benefits of the program are distributed. Table 14-2 shows, as expected, that average benefits are considerably higher for elderly than for nonelderly households. It is perhaps somewhat surprising, however, that average benefits of those who receive the circuit breaker do not tend to decline as income rises but rather follow a U-shaped pattern, with highest benefits in the highest and lowest income groups.

Table 14-2
Average Benefits from Michigan Circuit Breaker by Income Level, 1976

Household Income	General	Elderly
$ 2,000 or less	$235	$348
2,001- 4,000	148	333
4,001- 6,000	154	337
6,001- 8,000	168	312
8,001-10,000	178	314
10,001-15,000	176	326
15,001-20,000	163	351
20,000-25,000	169	389
Over $25,000	237	492

Source: Estimated from data provided by Michigan Department of Management and Budget.

As explained in chapter 3, there are three explanations for this pattern. (1) Renters, who tend to have relatively low incomes, receive considerably lower benefits than homeowners.[42] (2) High-income persons tend to live in places where tax rates are relatively high. (3) A small number of households which own farms perhaps have considerable influence on the average benefit level above $25,000, since they tend to receive very high benefits.

Tables 14-3 and 14-4 put the progressivity of the circuit breaker in a different light. As table 14-3 shows, less than 10 percent of the benefits paid went to households with incomes over $25,000 and more than half went to households with income under $10,000. It is difficult to measure what proportion of all households receive benefits, but table 14-4 shows that the proportion seems to fall off sharply as income rises. It is surprising that only 57.9 percent of households with income under $5,000 claim the circuit breaker, but there is reason to believe that many low-income families which are eligible for the program do not participate. A study of welfare recipients shortly after

Table 14-3
Distribution of Total Circuit Breaker Benefits among Income and Age Groups, 1976
(percent of total benefits)

Household Income	General	Elderly
$ 5,000 or less	7.7	19.5
5,001-10,000	11.2	17.2
10,001-15,000	10.4	6.2
15,001-20,000	9.2	2.0
20,000-25,000	6.4	0.9
Over $25,000	8.2	1.1

Note: There was a small amount of funds in special programs for veterans, the blind, and the disabled.

Table 14-4
Participation in Circuit Breaker at Various Income Levels, 1976

Household Income	Percentage of Households Claiming Circuit Breaker
$ 5,000 or less	57.9
5,000- 9,999	56.4
10,000-14,999	34.2
15,000-19,999	34.5
20,000-24,999	31.8
$25,000 and over	28.1

Source: Correspondence with Roy C. Saper, Economic Analyst, Michigan Department of Management and Budget.

the program began in 1975 estimated that only 12.5 percent of eligible households were receiving benefits.[43]

The program tends to reduce the regressivity of the residential property tax considerably, as table 14-5 shows. As anticipated, the drop in the tax burden is particularly great for low-income households.

Table 14-5
Property Taxes as a Percentage of Household Income in 1976 for Michigan Taxpayers Claiming the Circuit Breaker
(percent)

Household Income	General Taxpayers		Senior Citizens	
	Rate before Tax Credits	Rate after Tax Credits	Rate before Tax Credits	Rate after Tax Credits
$ 2,000 or less	38.5	19.4	30.2	1.4
$ 2,001- 4,000	11.8	6.9	11.9	0.8
4,001- 6,000	8.6	5.5	9.3	2.6
6,001- 8,000	7.4	5.1	8.0	3.6
8,001-10,000	6.5	4.7	7.0	3.6
10,001-12,000	6.0	4.4	6.4	3.6
12,000-14,000	5.4	4.2	6.1	3.6
14,001-16,000	5.0	4.0	5.7	3.5
16,001-18,000	4.8	3.9	5.6	3.6
18,001-20,000	4.6	3.8	5.2	3.5
20,001-22,000	4.5	3.8	5.4	3.5
22,001-24,000	4.4	3.8	5.3	3.8
24,001-25,000	4.3	3.7	5.3	3.6
Over $25,000	4.5	3.9	5.8	4.4

Source: Michigan Department of Management and Budget.

Household income: The sum of federal adjusted gross income as defined in the Internal Revenue Code plus all income specifically excluded or exempt from the computations of the federal adjusted gross income. The term does not include the first $300 of gifts in cash or kind from nongovernmental sources. Income does not include surplus foods, relief in kind supplied by a government agency, payments, or credits under the Michigan Income Tax Act of 1967, or any government grant which has to be used by the claimant for rehabilitation of the homestead.

Farm Circuit Breaker

In 1974, one year after the general circuit breaker was begun, Michigan enacted an additional circuit breaker solely for farms. If an owner signs a contract to keep his land in farm use for at least ten years, all property tax in excess of 7 percent of household income will be paid by the state. Because of this program, Michigan is one of only six states which does not assess farmland on a preferential basis. Wisconsin is the only other state with a farm circuit breaker.

After a slow start, the farm circuit breaker program has become popular with many farmers. By the end of 1979, it was expected that 1 million out of the 8 million acres of agricultural land in active production would be covered by the program. The cost of the program in 1977-1978 was estimated at approximately $5 million, a small amount compared to the regular circuit breaker; the cost has increased rapidly as more farmers enrolled. If one of the objectives of the program was to preserve farmland at the urban fringe, it is not very well targeted. On the average, land in the program was 22.7 miles from the nearest urban center of 25,000 or more people.[44]

Recent Controversy

Statistical reports which compare property tax levels among the states seriously distort the true situation in Michigan. For example, in 1977 the property tax was said to be equal to 2.63 percent of the market value of homes and 1.61 percent of the market value of farm real estate, ranking Michigan fourth and third among the states, respectively. However, these estimates do not take the circuit breaker into account. When it is considered, the property tax burden on low- and moderate-income residents of Michigan appears much less severe. Even ignoring the circuit breaker, the Michigan property tax is equal to only 4.9 percent of personal income, ranking the state eighteenth nationwide. Thus, Michigan is not really a high-property-tax state in many respects.

But the availability of the circuit breaker is of no value to many Michigan residents. Thus, it would not be surprising if a revolt against the property tax took root among those who are ineligible for the circuit breaker without finding great sympathy among those who do receive it. That is what happened in 1978. A strong proposal (the Tisch Amendment) was on the ballot which would have caused a 50 percent reduction in property tax levies and limited assessment increases to 2½ percent per year. The Tisch proposal appears mild only in comparison to Proposition 13, but since Michigan did not have a large state budget surplus available to bankroll property tax relief, the tax revolt leaders realized that the California measure could not be precisely copied. This proposal received less than 40 percent approval in the November election.

However, a milder tax limitation measure did pass, 52 to 48 percent. The most important provision of the Headlee Amendment is to limit the increase in state revenue to the growth of personal income. It also requires the state to finance any new mandates to local governments, and it limits property taxes. Whenever assessments within a jurisdiction rise faster than the rate of inflation, tax rates must be rolled back so that the increase in property tax revenue is no greater than the inflation rate. If assessments rise slower than inflation within a jurisdiction, there is no millage rollback.

Conclusions

The three states discussed in this chapter offer a study in contrasts. In each a property tax revolt could have occurred. But Iowa and Michigan acted in time to avert excessive property tax increases for most homeowners and farmers. California did not. With the state surplus available as a cushion, Proposition 13 was irresistable.

These states also illustrate the diversity of the ways in which property tax relief can be provided. Chapter 15 summarizes in capsule form the property tax relief measures in the other states.

These states are not typical. They all began the 1970s with relatively high property taxes and have been more innovative than the average state in designing property tax relief. But more can be learned from the activist states than from those in which little occurred.

Notes

1. Much of this section is based on a study by Frank Levy and Paul Zamolo, "The Preconditions of Proposition 13" (Urban Institute Working Paper, January 1979).

2. John L. Mikesell, "Local Government Sales Taxes," in John F. Due, *State and Local Sales Taxation* (Chicago: Public Administration Service, 1970), p. 284.

3. John C. Keene et al., *Untaxing Open Space* (Washington, D.C.: Council on Environmental Quality, 1976), pp. 271-302.

4. According to one estimate, approximately $45 million to $50 million of tax was shifted from participating to nonparticipating property in 1973, a year in which total farm real estate taxes in California were approximately $307.7 million. Ibid., p. 286.

5. See table 3-1.

6. Because it was state-financed, this homestead relief is more properly referred to as a credit than an exemption, according to the analysis in chapter 4 of this book.

7. William H. Oakland, "Proposition 13—Genesis and Consequences," *Economics Review* (Federal Revenue Bank of San Francisco, Winter 1979), p. 22.

8. Ironically, as originally passed, the 1972 school aid program would not have operated in this manner because an allowance was made for increased assessments. However, the following year this provision was dropped as a quid pro quo for more generous treatment of districts with declining enrollments. Levy and Zamolo, "Preconditions," p. 38.

9. A two-thirds majority was needed because the bill appropriated funds for the fiscal year which was already underway. Four senators who abstained on the final 21-15 vote had reportedly promised to vote for the bill if their votes would pass it. See Dean Tipps, "Legislative Report—Big Mistakes in 'No' Campaign," *Tax Back Talk* (California Tax Reform Association newsletter, July 1978), p. 2.

10. The three sources of the increased surplus during this period were planned surpluses ($2.19 billion), revenue underestimates ($1.56 billion), and expenditure cuts enacted after Proposition 13 passed ($1.35 billion). There is considerable reason to believe that Governor Brown wanted the massive surplus to develop so that it could be disposed of in a manner which maximized its political value to him. Levy and Zamolo, "Preconditions," p. 42, 45.

11. Ibid., pp. 1-2. Reprinted with permission.

12. Ibid., p. 2.

13. Walter Heller, " 'Meat-Axe Radicalism' in California," *Wall Street Journal,* June 5, 1978.

14. John Shannon argues that this experience shows why it is unwise to assess property on a cyclical basis rather than all at once. Because of the school aid provisions discussed above, it would have been impossible to lower tax rates enough to offset the assessment increases and prevent large increases in property tax bills.

15. Tipps, "Legislative Report."

16. "Spending a Saving: California Firms Try to Decide How to Use Property-Tax Windfall," *Wall Street Journal,* June 29, 1978; "Business Bonanza: Companies' Big Saving from Proposition 13 Is Slow to Reach Public," *Wall Street Journal,* February 13, 1979.

17. Oakland, "Genesis," p. 19, claims that rural areas gain from Proposition 13 because they are relatively property-rich. However, they do not benefit as much as central cities, where property tax rates were much higher before July 1978.

18. Congressional Budget Office, "Proposition 13: Its Impact on the Nation's Economy, Federal Revenues, and Federal Expenditures," July 1978.

19. Oakland, "Genesis," pp. 13-15; *Los Angeles Times,* October 1, 1978. Prior to Proposition 13, California had relatively low user fees compared to

other states. Charges and miscellaneous general revenue accounted for 13.2 percent of local revenue in California versus 15.5 percent in other states in 1977. An article in the *Wall Street Journal* (June 1, 1979) conveyed the impression that user charges had offset a large proportion of the property tax savings from Proposition 13, but actually increased charges and local taxes amounted to only $195 million, according to a November 1978 survey. See Commission on Government Reform, *Final Report* (Sacramento, 1979), p. 23.

20. *Los Angeles Times* October 1, 1978; Commission on Government Reform, *Final Report.*

21. Coalition of American Public Employees, *CAPE Update,* Washington, D.C., February, March, and May 1979.

22. David B. Walker, "Proposition 13 and California's System of Governance," *Intergovernmental Perspective,* Summer 1978, pp. 13-15; Levy and Zamolo, "Preconditions," pp. 62-65; Oaklans, "Genesis," p. 19.

23. George E. Peterson and Thomas Muller, "Allocation of Development Costs between Homebuyers and Taxpayers" (Discussion paper presented at a National Conference on Housing Costs sponsored by the U.S. Department of Housing and Urban Development, February 1979).

24. The *Wall Street Journal* reports that this has already occurred to some extent. See "California Home Boom Is Slowing Down a Bit; Sales Lag May Spread," January 19, 1979.

25. Oakland, "Genesis," p. 24. However, the higher taxes resulting from the increased assessment must be paid each year, not just once, as the author implies.

26. Levy and Zamolo, "Preconditions," pp. 60-62.

27. Oakland, "Genesis," pp. 15-17.

28. Tabulations by the Advisory Commission on Intergovernmental Relations. The four higher states are Massachusetts, New Jersey, New York, and Nebraska. Michigan is also listed as having a higher tax rate, but its circuit breaker is not taken into account.

29. Oakland, "Genesis," p. 22. Oakland shows that the gap between state and local taxes as a percentage of personal income in California and the rest of the country widened sharply in the mid-1970s. Nonproperty taxes accounted for most of the difference. See pp. 21-22.

30. More extensive analysis of Iowa's property tax relief programs can be found in Steven D. Gold, *A Citizen's Guide to Local Government Finance: Iowa at the Property Tax Crossroads* (Des Moines, Iowa: Drake University, 1977) and *Evaluating Local Taxes and Government Spending: A Do-It-Yourself Manual* (Des Moines, Iowa: Drake University Press, 1978).

31. A full-disclosure approach was seriously considered in 1976 but had insufficient support. The limits which were enacted required that an extra public

hearing be held if property tax revenue increased more than 7 percent. The 9 percent limit could be exceeded only with approval of a state board.

32. According to preliminary estimates by the Polk-Des Moines Taxpayers Association, for example, property tax on the average Des Moines home rose 0.4 percent in 1979-1980 from the previous year, but the tax on the average commercial property rose 14.9 percent. If there had been no limits on residential assessment increases, the pattern would have been reversed, with taxes on homes increasing sharply and taxes on businesses being stable or falling.

33. The future viability of this system depends on what happens to farm income, which is the basis for determining farm productivity, which in turn determines not only farm assessments but also home assessments. If farm income continues far below the level it reached in 1973, "productivity" is likely to fall in the 1980s. However, assessments could be maintained by lowering the rate at which farm income is capitalized.

34. New construction could still cause the ratio of farm to home assessments to change, and varying tax rates could alter the proportions of taxes paid by each class of property.

35. The discussion of the early development of Michigan's circuit breaker relies heavily on an unpublished article by James W. Haughey, Gerald H. Miller, and Robert J. Kleine, "The Michigan Property Tax Circuitbreaker: Design and Cyclical Sensitivity," May 1974. Analysis of later trends was facilitated by the extremely generous assistance provided by Roy C. Saper, an economic analyst with the Michigan Office of Management and Budget.

36. William B. Neenan, *The Political Economy of Urban Areas* (Chicago: Markham, 1972), pp. 286-289.

37. John Shannon, "The Property Tax: Reform or Relief?" in *Property Tax Reform,* ed. G.E. Peterson, (Washington, D.C., The Urban Institute, 1973) p. 36.

38. The $300 increase in the personal exemption times 3.9 percent equals $11.70. When the tax rate increased to 4.6 percent a few years later, the value of the exemption rose further.

39. Haughey, Miller, and Kleine, "Design and Cyclical Sensitivity," p. 6.

40. Ibid., p. 11. In fact, in 1977 only 40 percent of all households received any circuit breaker benefit.

41. State of Michigan, *Economic Report of the Governor* (Lansing, 1979). For an analysis of school finance, see Harvey E. Brazer and Ann P. Anderson, "Michigan's School District Equalization Act of 1973: Its Background, Structure, and Effects," in *Selected Papers in School Finance,* ed. Esther O. Tron (Washington, D.C.: Department of Health, Education, and Welfare, 1976), pp. 41-88.

42. In 1976 average benefits for renters were $68 from the general circuit

breaker and $171 from the senior circuit breaker. Average benefits for home-owners were more than twice as great.

43. Robert W. Swanson, "Utilization of the 1973 Michigan Property Tax Credit by Welfare Recipients" (Unpublished article, Michigan Department of Social Services, April 1975).

44. The program is of particular value to affluent farmers; the average income of farmers in the program is $17,000, which is much higher than the average income of Michigan farmers. The average benefit paid is $1,800. For 60 percent of farmers who receive the farm and general circuit breaker, property tax liability is completely eliminated by the programs. Correspondence with Dennis J. Hall, the person responsible for administering the program in the Michigan Department of Natural Resources, February 13, 1979.

15 Capsule Summaries of the Property Tax Situation in Each State

This chapter provides a condensed description of the property tax relief situation in all fifty states and the District of Columbia. Table 1-5 summarizes the major programs available in each state, and the text provides a capsule discussion of the level of property taxes and key relief programs state by state.

Comments about how high property taxes are in each state are based on the five measures shown in table 2-6. The first three, which are referred to in this chapter as the "aggregate measures," relate property tax revenue to total state-local general revenue, population, and personal income in fiscal 1977. The other two measures are home and farm effective tax rates for 1978 and 1977, respectively.[1] States were ranked on each of these five measures, and comments refer to these rankings. In general, if a state is said to have a "very high" or "very low" rank, that means it is in the top ten or bottom ten, respectively. If its rank is "about average," its rank is from twentieth to thirtieth.

This chapter has two purposes. The first is to show that in most cases the level of property taxes in each state can be explained rather easily in terms of its property tax relief policies and other characteristics of its fiscal system—in particular the degree to which taxing authority is centralized at the state level, local revenue diversification, and the level of local government spending. The second purpose is to provide somewhat more detail about individual state policies than in the chapters which deal with specific tax relief devices.

For a summary of the major state relief policies, see table 1-5. In order to simplify the discussion, some aspects of each state's policies are not mentioned. For example, most states which provide homestead exemptions or credits for all age groups provide additional benefits for senior citizens. Many programs for senior citizens also include widows or disabled persons. Although most of these conditions are noted in chapter 4, they are not included here. Likewise, farm tax relief is omitted because it is nearly universal.

The definitions of the various policies should be familiar from previous chapters. Homestead exemptions and credits are programs for homeowners in which income either is not considered or is a criterion for eligibility but not a factor in determining how much benefit is received.[2] Circuit breakers are state-funded credits in which benefits depend on property tax paid and income. Classification is a system in which various types of real property are assessed at nonuniform ratios or taxed at unequal rates. Local sales and income taxes are local taxes which can be used to relieve pressure for property tax revenue.

State-imposed limits are shown for levies, spending, assessments, and full disclosure. Levy limits refer to limitations on property tax *revenue,* not tax rates. Limitations on tax rates are not shown in the table, although they are in effect in the majority of states. Assessment limits refer to limitations on annual increases in assessments, not simply to state dictates as to the rate at which property should be assessed. Finally, fiscal centralization is measured by the proportion of state-local taxes collected by the state government in 1977.

New England

This region has traditionally had the highest average property taxes in the nation, and it widened its lead in the 1970s. Its rank is due to a strong commitment to local control, which is manifested in a high degree of fiscal decentralization, a low level of state-financed relief, and the paucity of state-imposed limitations on local taxes and spending. Four of the seven states in the entire country which do not impose such limits are in this region. Another reason for high property taxes is the complete absence of local sales and income taxes.

Connecticut is a high-property-tax state. The most important reason is that the state government plays a relatively minor role in raising taxes. This is the eleventh most fiscally decentralized state, and it has no general income tax. There is a circuit breaker for the elderly, with the program reflected directly in a lower tax bill rather than being refunded separately as in most states. There is also a tax freeze program for the elderly, and in 1979 classification was authorized in Hartford only.

Maine property taxes are close to the national average, except for those on farms which are the third highest in the nation. Property taxes are unusually low compared to the rest of New England. primarily because Maine's fiscal centralization is relatively high for this region (though only average for the nation). The state experimented briefly with a state property tax to finance schools. There is a circuit breaker for the elderly. Credits for homeowners and renters were provided in 1979 on a one-time basis.

Massachusetts has the highest property taxes in the nation. (Alaska's higher rank on some measures is due to special oil-related revenues.) The major reasons are its high degree of fiscal decentralization and a high level of government spending. An exemption for all homeowners has been passed but is not yet in effect, but the exemption for poor elderly homeowners has the highest average benefit in the nation. Classification was approved by the voters in 1978. There is a deferral program. This is one of the few high-tax states without a circuit breaker; one was vetoed by Governor Dukakis in 1978. In 1979 a 4 percent limit was placed on increases in property tax revenues and local expenditures.

New Hampshire, the only state with neither an income nor a sales tax, has very high property taxes, as would be expected in the most fiscally decentralized state. The only relief program is a homestead exemption for all senior citizens.

Rhode Island property taxes are high. Its decentralization is close to the national average, it provides an exemption for all homeowners, and it has a circuit breaker for the elderly which was begun in 1977 and increased in 1978 and 1979. Some local governments have homestead exemptions, deferral programs, and tax freezes for the elderly, but these programs are not mandated by the state.

Vermont property tax is above average, but not extremely high for the 23 percent of all households which are covered by the circuit breaker. This program, which is open to all age groups, is funded entirely by general revenue sharing. No other relief programs are available, and fiscal centralization is close to the national average.

Mideast

Four of the six jurisdictions in this region have above-average tax rates on homes. In fact, property taxes in this region of economic decline have been climbing relative to those in the rest of the country. In each of these states and the District of Columbia the local income tax is used by at least one unit of government.

Delaware resembles the South in its extremely low property taxes and high degree of fiscal centralization. Only Alaska is more centralized in terms of revenue raising. Delaware has a homestead exemption for the elderly, and Wilmington, its only large city, has a local income tax. In only seven states do local governments generate a larger proportion of their own-source revenue from user charges and miscellaneous sources.

The *District of Columbia* has average or below-average property taxes, as is not surprising in view of its unique fiscal structure, which relies to a major extent on high income and sales taxes. It also employs virtually every variety of property tax relief invented. In addition to an all-age circuit breaker which covers households with incomes under $20,000 (with liberalized benefits for the elderly), it has a $9,000 homeowner's exemption, deferral, full disclosure, and classification.

Maryland property taxes are close to those in the average state except for its above-average home tax rates. It has some unusual relief programs. Its circuit breaker with no age limit was restricted to homeowners until 1979, when renters who are senior citizens were also made eligible. Local income taxes provide a higher proportion of local own-source revenue than in any other state; these taxes are levied by all counties (and the city of Baltimore) as piggyback supplements to the state income tax. Homeowners whose assessments rise more than 15 percent in a year receive a credit from the state for the excess increase.

Maryland was the first state to adopt preferential assessment of farmland in 1956. Although the state is one of the few which does not limit local taxes or spending, in 1979 it placed a limit on assessment increases and strengthened its full-disclosure law.

New Jersey has very high property taxes, but its reliance on the tax has been diminishing since it adopted a state income tax to finance expanded school aid and a limitation on local government expenditures in 1976. Its 5 percent lid on spending increases is nearly unique for nonschool governments. Even with the income tax in effect, New Jersey is the second most fiscally decentralized state. There is a homestead credit, and several years ago Newark became the first New Jersey city to levy an income tax.

New York is a high-property-tax state. In fact, it is the only state which ranks high in terms of both property taxes and nonproperty taxes as a percentage of income. The high degree of fiscal decentralization and the far above-average level of spending (only one state is higher in per capita terms) are two of the main reasons for its high property taxes. Local sales taxes are widely used by cities and counties, and New York City also levies a relatively high, progressive income tax. A circuit breaker for all age groups with an income ceiling of $12,000 was initiated in 1978, and elderly homeowners benefit from an exemption.

Pennsylvania has an effective tax rate on homes that is high, although other measures of property tax burdens are below average. Philadelphia pioneered local income taxes in 1939, and these taxes are still widely used throughout the state. The elderly are eligible for both a circuit breaker and a homestead exemption.

Great Lakes

This region is a hotbed of property tax relief ideas. It produced the first circuit breaker and the first large all-age circuit breaker, refinements in local income taxation, universal percentage tax credits, and elaborate limitations on local taxation. As a result, the Great Lakes states have moved away from their former position near the top of the list of states in terms of tax burdens.

Illinois property taxes are above average although not extremely high. The state is relatively decentralized (ranking thirteenth) but relieves pressure on the property tax with widespread use of local sales taxes. A homestead exemption for all age groups was passed in 1978, augmenting a previous exemption for the elderly and a circuit breaker for the elderly which has unusually broad coverage. The exemption has a unique design, applying to the increase in assessed valuation due to revaluation. The property tax is classified in Cook County, which contains Chicago, but not in the rest of the state.

Indiana property taxes are close to the national average, in contrast to its historically above-average levies. The turning point came in 1973 when a major overhaul of the tax system took place. Counties which chose to levy a local income tax had to freeze their property tax levy; counties which did not levy an income tax had to freeze their property tax rate. Only rural counties decided to levy the income tax. In addition, the state increased aid to local governments and provided a credit for 20 percent of each taxpayer's property tax bill; state taxes were increased to pay for this aid. As a result of this program, farm property taxes actually decreased between 1971 and 1977, while residential property taxes rose slowly. The small circuit breaker for the elderly has a low participation rate, and there is credit for renters. In 1979 the property tax limitations were modified to encourage greater use of local income taxes, and a 10 percent credit for all homeowners was enacted; it was scheduled to gradually decline and disappear in 1985.

Michigan ranks high in terms of effective tax rates and per capita burdens and above average on other measures, but these statistics overstate the true burdens because they overlook the two large circuit breakers which are available, one for residential taxes and the other for farm taxes. The Headlee Amendment passed in 1978 rolls back the tax rate when assessments increase at a rate faster than inflation. Sixteen cities employ local income taxes, a device for which Michigan developed some important innovations. See chapter 14 for a detailed discussion of Michigan's recent property tax history.

Ohio has a low effective tax rate for homes and is average or above average on other measures of property taxation. It is the only state with a decentralized fiscal system (ranking ninth lowest in the proportion of state-local taxes collected by state government) which does not have high property taxes. There are numerous explanations. Voter approval is needed to exceed fairly low tax rate limits, and the limits are automatically rolled back whenever assessments go up, leading to a relatively impoverished public sector. Significant use is made of both local sales and income taxes. Ohio is the only state in which both are widely used. Since 1971 a state-financed credit has paid 10 percent of all real property tax bills. There is a circuit breaker for the elderly.

Wisconsin has high effective tax rates on homes and farms and is above average according to other property tax measures. Although it pioneered the circuit breaker in 1964 and later was one of the first to extend it to all age groups, Wisconsin's circuit breaker has had a relatively small cost because it was restricted to families with low incomes. The income ceiling was raised from $9,300 to $14,000 in 1979. All governments are subject to limitations on levy increases, and schools also have spending limitations. The state finances a credit for a portion of all property tax liability to the extent that the tax rate exceeds half of the statewide average. In addition, a credit was enacted in 1979 which pays 12 percent of the property tax for homeowners or a portion of rent. At the same time, the itemized income tax deduction for state and local taxes was dropped.

Plains

The Plains states used to rival New England for the distinction of having the highest property taxes in the nation, but no other section of the country has taken greater strides to reduce reliance on the property tax in the 1970s. Five of the seven states decreased their effective tax rates on homes considerably faster than the national average between 1971 and 1978. Nebraska started out with high property taxes and remained near the top, while Missouri began with relatively low property taxes and provided relatively little relief.

Iowa property taxes, while still above average, are no longer extremely high as they once were. To some extent, this change resulted from a fairly standard infusion of state aid for schools in conjunction with a limitation on the increase in school spending. But Iowa was also unorthodox in increasing farm and home tax credits in 1976 and limiting increases in farm and home assessments beginning in 1978. From 1976 to 1979 Iowa placed levy limits on cities and counties, and it provides a circuit breaker for the elderly. For a further discussion, see chapter 14.

Kansas property tax rankings center on the national average with considerable difference from one measure to another. In the early 1970s it was one of the first states to adopt limitations on local property tax levies and also on school spending. A fairly decentralized state, it has limited use of local sales taxes. Beginning in 1978, eligibility for its circuit breaker extends not only to senior citizens but also to any younger family with a child under 18.

Minnesota is a leading contender for the dubious distinction of having the most complicated state property tax system. Great strides have been taken to reduce property tax burdens, so that the state is now just average on most measures.[3] The most distinctive feature of its property tax is its classification system, which is the oldest one and also the most elaborate in terms of different classes of property (more than twenty). All homeowners receive a homestead credit which pays 50 percent of their tax bill up to $550, some 63 percent of households receive circuit breaker benefits, and renters are eligible for a credit.[4] In addition, there are limitations on the increases of city and county tax levies and school spending. A limitation on assessment increases was declared unconstitutional in 1979 when challenged by a property owner who had purchased a newly constructed home.[5] One city (Duluth) levies a local sales tax. The fiscal system is relatively centralized (thirty-eighth in rank). A property tax freeze for senior citizens was dropped in 1977 when the circuit breaker was liberalized.

Missouri has lower-than-average property taxes as well as below-average nonproperty taxes, so that overall taxes take a smaller percentage of personal income than in any other state. It is relatively decentralized (rank: 14) and is one of the few states in which both sales and income taxes are used by cities. But the income tax is confined to the two largest cities while the sales tax is levied in 208 cities and one county. There is a circuit breaker for the elderly. In

1978, after property had not been revalued for many years, voters approved a constitutional amendment to permit a rollback of assessments after property finally is revalued because of a court order.

Nebraska stands as the highest property tax state in the Midwest, resisting the trend away from the property tax in several nearby states. The seventh most fiscally decentralized state, Nebraska has levy limits on cities and counties and a spending limit on school districts. There is a state-financed homestead exemption for all homeowners, with extra benefits for the elderly. A few large cities use the local sales tax.

North Dakota property taxes are somewhat below average, as might be expected in a state in which centralization is somewhat above average. The elderly may receive both a circuit breaker and a homestead exemption. North Dakota had the largest decrease in property tax revenue as a proportion of personal income of any state from 1971 to 1977, primarily as a result of greatly increased state aid for schools. Most cities and counties levy the maximum tax rate permitted, and assessments have increased very slowly.

South Dakota has a tax situation that contrasts sharply with that of its neighbor to the north. The third most decentralized state, South Dakota has above-average property taxes. There is a circuit breaker for the elderly and also use of a local sales tax in thirty-nine cities. The decline in property tax rates has been matched in few other states; between 1971 and 1978, the effective tax rate on homes fell from 2.71 to 1.66 percent.

Southeast

This region has traditionally had the lowest property taxes in the country, both because its taxes generally are low and because it derives a smaller proportion of its revenue from property taxes than most other areas. Because its rates were already low, the South has not participated much in the move toward relief mechanisms such as circuit breakers and levy and spending limitations. Most of these states are very centralized fiscally, and localities receive considerable revenue from charges, local nonproperty taxes, and state aid. Classification is more common here than in any other sections of the country, and homestead exemptions are widespread.

Alabama property taxes are among the lowest in the nation; only in terms of the effective tax rate on homes is it edged out of first place, and in that case by only four states. Its revenue structure is highly unusual. In terms of the proportion of locally raised general revenue from various sources, it ranks second for user charges, third for the sales tax, and fourth for miscellaneous taxes (those not on sales, income, or property). It also permits local income taxes, so that the proportion of locally raised revenue from the property tax is less than 20 percent. (Only two other states are under 40 percent.) Its low property taxes are also attributable to its high degree of fiscal centralization (rank: 41). There is an exemption for all homeowners. The property tax is classified, and county levy increases are subject to a limitation.

Arkansas property tax indicators are very low, with the exception of the effective tax rate on homes. This rate, which is slightly above the national average, is the highest in the South. This may explain why Arkansas is the only Southern state (excluding West Virginia) which has a circuit breaker for the elderly. Arkansas is typical of the South in being highly centralized (rank: 44), employing user charges heavily (rank: 3), and permitting a local sales tax, though it is used in only a few cities.

Florida ranks in terms of the aggregate indicators of property taxation as the highest in the Southeast, though it is below average for the nation. Its effective tax rate on homes is low, in part because of a homestead exemption. Florida originated the full-disclosure approach to call attention to increases in property tax levies. Its fiscal centralization is average for the nation as a whole, although it is decentralized compared to other Southern states. Heavy use of user charges helps to keep taxes down, but a local sales tax which is permitted for financing of transit systems has not been adopted by any locality. A deferral program is available.

Georgia property taxes are below average, ranking 14 to 19 on all measures. Its centralization is average, but it employs user charges heavily. Local sales taxes are also levied, and there is an exemption for all homeowners.

Kentucky has low property taxes despite the fact that it has one of the highest property taxes levied by a state government. Its tax system has several unusual features. It is the only state which indexes the homestead exemption. As a result of inflation, this locally financed exemption which is limited to senior citizens rose from $6,500 to $10,200 between 1974 and 1979. Kentucky's cities and a few counties make very heavy use of local income taxes; in only two states do such taxes provide a higher proportion of locally raised revenue. Despite its low property tax levels, in 1979 Kentucky imposed a 4 percent limit on annual increases of property tax revenues for all levels of government. Kentucky is one of the most fiscally centralized states, ranking 42 in the proportion of taxes collected by local governments.

Louisiana has extremely low property taxes. One of its unique features is the most generous homestead exemption in the nation; the $5,000 exemption would be worth $50,000 if homes were assessed at the legal rate of 10 percent of market value, but it is worth even more because assessments are lower. Also contributing to low home taxes is a system of classification. The local sales tax brings in a higher proportion of locally raised revenue than in any other state. Louisiana is relatively centralized (rank: 37), and school spending is subject to a limitation.

Mississippi also has low property taxes on all measures (rank: 6 to 12). Charges and miscellaneous general revenue account for 52 percent of locally raised funds, which is higher than in any other state. All homeowners receive an exemption, and the fiscal centralization is high (rank: 45).

North Carolina is another low-property-tax state (rank: 11 to 20). It is centralized (rank: 40), a homestead exemption is allowed only for the elderly, and sales taxes are widespread among counties.

South Carolina has a situation similar to that of many other Southern states. Property taxes are low (ranking from 6 to 13 on various measures) because of a centralized fiscal system (rank: 43) and heavy local use of user charges (42 percent of locally raised revenue). The property tax is classified, and elderly homeowners are eligible for an exemption.

Tennessee has below-average property taxes (rank varies from 12 to 29). Centralization is only slightly above average (rank: 30), but heavy use is made of local sales taxes by counties and some cities. The property tax is classified, and the homestead exemption is limited to the elderly. This is one of the few states with no state-imposed limits on local taxes or spending.

Virginia property taxes are below average (rank varies from 15 to 20) although it is the least centralized state in the South (rank: 22). One of the most unusual aspects of Virginia's tax system is that localities obtain a higher proportion of their revenue from taxes which are not on income, sales, or property than in any other state (16 percent). In addition, local sales taxes cover the entire state. Virginia is one of six states which provides for full disclosure of tax increases. Many local governments have homestead exemption or deferral programs for the elderly.

West Virginia has very low property taxes, ranking seventh or lower on all measures. A major reason is the very high degree of fiscal centralization (rank: 46). For decades West Virginia has had a system of classification in which unequal tax rates are set forth rather than unequal assessment procedures. In order to exceed the low rates set by law, a referendum must be approved by voters. With tax rates so low, the homestead exemption and circuit breaker (both of which are limited to the elderly) provide little benefit to recipients.

Southwest

It is not easy to generalize about the four states in this region. Some have very low property taxes, but others are above average. About the only thing which they have in common is utilization of local sales taxes.

Arizona property taxes are above average, despite the fact that it was one of the first states to adopt limitations on the increase in city and county property tax levies. It adopted classification in the early 1960s, at one time planning to use twenty-seven different classes, but settling on four classes when classification was enacted, later increased to six classes. Arizona limits school spending and has widespread city sales taxes. It had a circuit breaker for the elderly for a number of years but dropped property tax payments from its calculation in 1977, so now it is simply an income-conditioned tax credit. For a number of years a homestead credit has been provided, with its level depending on availability of state revenue.

New Mexico property tax ranks among the lowest on all indicators except the effective tax rate for homes, which is close to the national average. The low taxes in general are due to New Mexico's being the third most centralized state and to very sizable local revenue from charges. There is a circuit breaker for the elderly and also a low-income credit for all state-local taxes. Nearly all cities and some counties use sales taxes. A limitation on assessment increases was replaced by levy limits in 1979 after it was declared unconstitutional. School spending is also limited.

Oklahoma is a low-property-tax state, ranking between 8 and 11 on various indicators. In only one other state do local governments derive a higher percentage of their self-raised revenue from the sales tax, and Tulsa is more reliant on this tax than any other large city. All homeowners have an exemption on their home, but only the elderly are eligible for the circuit breaker. Fiscal centralization is above average (rank: 36).

Texas ranks close to the average on aggregate property tax measures but above average on the home effective tax rate and below average on the farm effective tax rate. The local sales tax is used by cities across the entire state and by numerous transit districts, and all homeowners receive an exemption. A sweeping constitutional amendment passed in 1978 provided for a full-disclosure process for tax increases and paved the way for expanded tax breaks for agriculture. Previously farmland was eligible for preferential assessment only if its owner derived more than half of his income from farming, which was the tightest restriction in any state farm program. Texas is relatively decentralized (rank: 17). There is a deferral program.

Rocky Mountain

The states in this region have relatively little in common other than mountains. Every state has a circuit breaker or homestead exemption for the elderly, but none has both. Just about every type of relief is used in one state, but none are found in more than three out of the five states.

Colorado property taxes are somewhat above average but not by much (rank between 30 and 36, except for the farm tax rate, which is 18). That taxes are not higher is somewhat surprising in view of the very high degree of fiscal decentralization (rank: 5), but sales taxes are used heavily. In fact, some small resort areas have the highest local sales tax rate in the country. Property tax levies have been limited for all categories of local government since 1977. There is a circuit breaker for the elderly and a deferral program.

Idaho is not a high-property-tax state (ranking from 19 to 26 on each measure), but this did not stop voters in November 1978 from passing a Proposition 13–type proposal, limiting taxes to 1 percent of assessed value and holding the rise in assessments to 2 percent per year unless a property was sold. Since Idaho did not have a large state surplus as California did, the practical effects of this measure were uncertain at the time of this writing. Prior to this proposal, Idaho was already relatively centralized (rank: 34). There is a circuit breaker for the elderly.

Montana has a tax situation that is somewhat masked by its heavy taxation of mineral property, which places it among the top ten states on aggregate property tax measures; its effective tax rates are below average. Another reason why the indicators differ is Montana's classification system, one of the two oldest in the nation. Montana is a decentralized state (rank: 13). There is a limitation on school spending. Full disclosure is in effect. Montana began to provide a homestead credit in 1977, but two years later the value of the credit was reduced because of the limited funds available in the state budget.

Utah has below-average property taxes, especially for homes (for which the effective tax rate ranks ninth). Heavy use is made of local sales taxes, and centralization is somewhat above average (rank: 31). There is a circuit breaker for the elderly and an optional deferral program. In 1979 a sweeping new relief program was enacted which provided for state-financed credits for homeowners and renters. The homeowner credit is 27 percent of the property tax bill, with a minimum credit of $100 and a maximum of $400. The credit for renters is 2.7 percent of rent, with a minimum of $100. In addition, school aid was increased, and limits were placed on property tax increases. However, it was uncertain whether sufficient state funds would be available in future years to continue the relief program in this form.

Wyoming's mineral-related industries pay about 60 percent of the property tax, causing a sharp contrast between aggregate measures and effective tax rates; the latter are very low. Centralization is slightly below average (rank: 18). A few counties levy local sales taxes. Senior citizens are eligible for a circuit breaker. An exemption for homeowners was enacted in 1979.

Far West

There is great diversity among the states in this region. One of the few common threads is that limitations on local levies or spending are widespread.

Alaska property taxes are distorted by oil revenue, which accounted for about three-quarters of property tax collections in 1977 and placed Alaska at the top of the rankings on the aggregate measures. A truer perspective is provided by the effective tax rate on homes, which was very close to the national average in 1978. Alaska is the most fiscally centralized state. The city sales tax is widespread; Alaska is the only state without a state sales tax in which localities levy one. City property tax levies are limited, and a homestead exemption is provided to the elderly.

California had high property taxes prior to Proposition 13, and they were rising much faster than in other states. The June 1978 tax revolt cut them 57 percent in one year. For a discussion of it, see chapter 14. Other features of the California tax system include a pioneering universal system of local sales taxation, an exemption for homeowners of all ages, a circuit breaker for the elderly, a school spending limit, an ineffective rate freeze for cities and counties following 1972, a renter credit, a relatively large deferral program, and an elaborate system of preferential assessment for farmland requiring the signing of a contract committing land to agriculture use. Prior to Proposition 13 California was very centralized (rank: 10), and per capita spending was usually high (rank: 4).

Hawaii is a very centralized state with state-operated and -financed schools. It has a unique system of classifying property, which some surveys do not consider to be classification. There is a homestead exemption and a renter credit. No limitations are imposed by the state on local spending or taxes.

Nevada is another state which voted in 1978 for a Proposition 13-type reform, but it will not take effect unless it is approved again by the voters in 1980. Its property taxes are close to average (rank: 25 to 36), as is its fiscal centralization (rank: 19). There is a circuit breaker for the elderly. Thirteen cities use local sales taxes.

Oregon property taxes seem to be high, ranking between 38 and 45 on various measures, but the circuit breaker reduces their burden substantially for the 60 percent of households which receive it. Far-reaching tax changes were defeated by the voters in 1978, but a major reform was enacted the following year, providing large state-financed credits for homeowners and renters. Oregon, one of only five states without a sales tax, was a very decentralized state fiscally in 1977 (rank: 8). Levy limits are in effect for cities, counties, and schools. Referenda on budgets are held annually in all cities, counties, and school districts. Two transit districts levy local income taxes. Assessment limits were enacted in 1979 in order to prevent homes from becoming a larger proportion of the tax base.

Washington property taxes are close to the national average even though it has one of the highest state property taxes. The state is fiscally centralized (rank: 39). Heavy use is made of local sales taxes. Cities, counties, and schools are all subject to levy limitations. The elderly homestead exemption varies according to income. A major property tax relief program in 1979 cut local property taxes, increased state aid to schools, and placed a limit on the increase of state property taxes.

Notes

1. See chapter 2 for a discussion of these measures.

2. Some states call their circuit breaker a homestead program, but in this chapter that is ignored.

3. According to FHA data, the effective tax rate on homes is below average, but a state official reported an estimate which is close to the national average.

4. The figures in the text are for 1980. In 1981 the homestead credit will be 55 percent of taxes up to $600. The estimate of the proportion of households receiving the circuit breaker is from the Minnesota Department of Revenue as of 1979. Using the method applied in other states, the proportion was 66 percent in 1977.

5. The new home had a market value similar to surrounding properties but a higher assessment because the assessments of the older properties had been held down by the limitation.

16 Summary and Conclusions

This chapter begins with a summary of trends in the use of different kinds of property tax relief measures. Next there is a discussion of whether relief in general is desirable and what kinds of relief are most appropriate. This leads to a description of major topics on which further research is needed. The prospects for future property tax relief are discussed in the final section.

Use of Property Tax Relief Devices

In the 1970s property tax revenue rose relatively slowly in comparison with other taxes, personal income, and real property values. While it increased, its inflation-adjusted rise was much more moderate than in earlier years. The major reason was state and federal policies which either intentionally or inadvertently provided property tax relief.

The greatest source of relief has been increased state and federal aid to local governments. The purpose of increasing aid often was to stimulate production of services rather than to relieve property taxes. However, because of the fungibility of aid, property tax relief was one of the results.[1] It is difficult to determine with precision how much of this aid actually resulted in lower property taxes rather than increased government spending or reduction of other taxes and charges. Nevertheless, the increase in aid has been so substantial that it surely has led to billions of dollars of property tax reduction. Empirical studies suggest that at least one-fifth of the increase in aid from 1970 to 1977 resulted in lower property taxes. This represents $9.5 billion, an impressive amount when compared to the total increase in property tax collections during the period of $28.5 billion.

State-imposed limitations on local spending and taxes have been another important source of tax relief. Proposition 13 alone cut property tax collections $7 billion. The aggregate effects of limitations have not been added up, but in places such as New Jersey, Iowa, and Indiana they certainly had a marked impact. Most often their effect has been to reduce tax increases rather than bring outright tax cuts.

Federal and state income tax deductions for property taxes on homes have been another major vehicle of property tax relief, saving taxpayers close to $4.8 billion in 1977. They are also the most regressive form of relief. For example, taxpayers with income between $50,000 and $100,000 saved an average of $689

311

on their federal income tax from this deduction in 1977 while taxpayers with income between $15,000 and $20,000 saved an average of $45.

Although the federal government is not usually thought of as providing property tax relief, it is significant that two of the three most important sources of relief heavily involve the federal government. It is also noteworthy that each of these three relief mechanisms provides relief which on a per household basis is worth much more to the affluent than to others.

Besides these three major policies there are a number of secondary ones. The mechanisms which are tied to residential property, primarily circuit breakers and homestead exemptions and credits, have grown rapidly but account for a relatively small proportion of existing property tax relief. Total benefits from state-funded homestead exemptions and credits are nearly as high as those for circuit breakers ($880 million versus $950 million in 1977). Exemptions for homeowners which are not funded by the state government provide additional benefits, as do credits for renters.

The other types of relief which expanded considerably in the 1970s are preferential assessment of farmland, percentage credits for all property owners, and exemptions or credits for personal property, each of which provide benefits worth hundreds of millions of dollars. Classification is in effect in more than twice as many states as a decade ago, providing relief for some and increasing burdens for others. Following their rapid expansion in the 1960s, local sales and income taxes were not authorized in many additional states in the 1970s, but their revenue grew faster than that of the property tax and contributed to reducing pressure to increase taxes on property. Tax exemptions to attract new business investment mushroomed.

Although relief measures have been discussed individually, they are inter-related in many ways. For example, limitations on local government spending and taxing are often accompanied by increases in state aid or authorization of new local sales or income taxes. Exemptions and preferential assessments shift tax burdens to nonfavored classes of property and usually increase state aid to school districts by lowering taxable assessed valuations. Homestead credits are usually subtracted from circuit breaker costs. Any program which affects tax rates thereby influences the value of exemptions. Thus, each state has its own property tax system, with unique forms of relief which play off against one another in complex ways.

To summarize, there was enormous activity in terms of property tax relief during the 1970s. Most relief was of an across-the-board type, lowering taxes in proportion to the amount of property taxes initially paid. Policies aimed at particular kinds of property—residential, farm, or business—provided smaller benefits than the general relief mechanisms.

New programs in which benefits are tilted in favor of those with relatively small amounts of property or low income tended to make the tax less regressive, but in the aggregate they did not offset the long-standing income tax deductions which favor those with high income. Thus, on balance, relief programs probably make the property tax more regressive.

Evaluation of Relief Policies

There are three separate issues to be considered in evaluating policies:

1. Why should there be any property tax relief?
2. Which mechanisms should be used in dispensing relief to each type of property?
3. What are the fiscal alternatives to property tax relief? That is, how would funds for property tax relief be used if the relief is not granted?

The first question was discussed in the first chapter; our answers are reviewed briefly here. The second question has been touched on in many of the preceding chapters; here we summarize our views and compare the merit of the different relief alternatives. The third question requires much further research.

Reasons for Relief

As explained in the first chapter, the political pressure for some form of property tax relief has frequently become so great that it is futile to argue against it. Thus, if an economist wants to contribute to practical policy formulation, he or she must often accept the demand for relief as given.

Aside from politics, there is a good case for certain types of relief. One set of arguments follows traditional lines, pointing out that the tax is regressive in many places for a majority of households, that in certain cities (particularly old, severely declining ones) the property tax base has been rather stagnant relative to income and sales, and that the tax may cause serious resource allocation problems.

A less conventional argument for relief justifies it as a means of preventing taxflation, excessive increases in tax burdens arising from inflation. These increases occur because assessments of homes tend to rise much faster than assessments of other property and because of the way in which state aid to school districts is distributed.

Two of the arguments for relief—to reduce the regressivity of the property tax and to offset excessive tax increases on homeowners arising from inflation— deny the basic idea underlying the property tax, which is that tax payments should be directly related to the value of property owned. The regressivity rationale for relief recognizes that while property ownership may be a valid component of ability to pay at middle and high income levels, at low income levels the ownership of property does not imply proportionate tax-paying ability.

The taxflation argument highlights an aspect of the property tax which only appears when (1) assessments are raised fairly regularly to reflect the rising market values of property and (2) inflation is high. Since assessment reform has reached most states in the relatively recent past, factors 1 and 2 have never occurred together previously. Normally shifts in assessments occur only slowly, so the division of the tax load between homes, businesses, and farms is quite stable.[2] When high inflation occurs in a state with a modern assessment system, the division of the total tax burden is apt to change sharply. Whether this is fair is a question that has not had to be confronted previously.

A different but related question is the appropriate tax treatment of individual homeowners whose homes increase sharply in value under conditions such as have occurred in the mid- and late 1970s. In this case, we have not only the question of the appropriate treatment of residential property versus business property but also the question of homeowners with large capital gains versus less fortunate homeowners whose homes rise little, if at all, in value. Even though their gain is "only on paper," the homeowners with the big gains are clearly better off, and it is reasonable for their share of taxes to increase. But whether it is still equitable for taxes to be related directly to the market values of homes is less certain.

The point of this discussion is that there is a significant difference between the issue of residential versus business tax shares and the issue of tax shares among homeowners. Homes and businesses are often assessed by different procedures which work to the disadvantage of homeowners, but all homeowners within a single assessment jurisdiction are presumably assessed by the same procedures. The rationale for moderating changes in the homeowner-business tax split is stronger than that for moderating shifts for one homeowner as compared to another.[3]

Mechanisms for Providing Relief

The major themes of this book are that property tax relief measures differ greatly in their effects and that therefore they should be carefully designed to achieve specific objectives.

The rationales discussed in the previous section suggest different answers to the question of who should get relief and how it should be provided.

If one wants to reduce regressivity, a circuit breaker is the most appropriate policy. A homestead credit is a second best alternative but is preferable to policies which provide relief by lowering the tax rate.

If overreliance on the unevenly distributed property tax base is the problem, then redistributive state aid is the best solution. If there is special concern for residential property, a circuit breaker or homestead credit can also help to even out spatial tax burdens because they provide more relief in jurisdictions with high tax rates.

If there is concern about the disincentive effects of the property tax on investment in housing and other buildings, state aid or local nonproperty taxes may be warranted. Targeted exemptions for businesses and homeowners making improvements may also be made available. But there is little evidence that any type of property tax relief of the magnitude usually considered has much effect on investment activity, so any initiatives should be taken very cautiously.

If offsetting the effects of taxflation on homeowners is the objective, several options are available. A threshold circuit breaker automatically cushions increases in taxes when they increase faster than income. On the other hand, a state can increase homestead and other credits by an amount sufficient to offset increases in tax levies. But such credits provide only one-shot relief and require periodic revision as long as inflation persists; they are not automatic like a circuit breaker. A third approach, which also operates automatically, is to place limitations on assessment increases. By analogy with the income tax, the circuit breaker and assessment limits operate automatically, like indexing, while increases of the homestead credit correspond to discretionary reductions of income tax rates.

Finally, if the problem is that local spending or taxes are rising too fast, limitations on them are appropriate. The limitations can be designed to reduce the size of public sector, to keep it from growing, or to change revenue sources without affecting the amount of government spending.

Despite this multiplicity of objectives, four generalizations about how relief should be designed can be made. After they are listed, the reasoning which underlies them is explained:

1. Relief should primarily be financed by the state government rather than by local governments.
2. Aside from political considerations, credits and aid to local governments seem to be the most desirable relief policies.
3. Policies which operate through the assessment process, such as exemptions, classification, preferential assessment for certain types of property, and limitations on assessment increases, should generally be avoided. Their objectives can be achieved better through credits.
4. Limitations on local taxing or spending are sometimes warranted.

State Financing

State financing is desirable because all tax relief is redistributive and redistribution should not normally be financed at the local level. There are two considerations. First, with state financing, it is possible to provide extra help to places with small tax bases. Without outside help, poor jurisdictions will not be able to finance as much tax relief as richer areas, even though relief may be more urgent in them. Second, as a general principle, actions mandated by the state should be financed by the state. It fosters irresponsibility for state officials to order relief and then not bear the responsibility of ensuring that it is financed.

Credits and Intergovernmental Aid

Credits are ideally suited for solving problems related to specific groups of property taxpayers. First, they target relief to particular kinds of property, such as homes, farms, or others. Second, they facilitate even more precise targeting, such as limiting benefits to those with a certain amount of income, property, or ratio of property tax to income. Third, their benefits and costs are easily calculated, in sharp contrast to policies like exemptions which operate through assessments, for which the benefits and costs are implicit and hard to measure. There is a direct analogy to the concept of tax expenditures in the field of income taxation. Credits make tax expenditures obvious, which is desirable if relief policies are to be rationally evaluated. State-financed credits appear annually in the state budget, while exemptions or preferential assessment provisions are not part of the budget, making it easy to overlook or to underestimate their cost.

Aid to local governments, rather than credits, is an appropriate policy if it is felt that property tax rates generally are excessive or if local governments are thought to rely too heavily on local financial support. Ideally, the aid should be distributed in a manner favoring poorer jurisdictions.

Assessment Policies

Exemptions, classification, preferential assessment of certain types of property, and limitations on assessment increases have effects which are relatively difficult to analyze because the amount of relief which they provide varies from one place to another, depending on the composition of the tax base. For example, a $5,000 homestead exemption would provide virtually no relief in a homogeneous, purely residential community, while it would reduce taxes on homes considerably if substantial nonresidential property were present. A corollary of this point is that the burden of paying for relief varies considerably from place to place. It is possible for a class of property to have higher taxes in one part of a state and lower taxes in another area as a result of the same policy.

Another effect of assessment-related policies, when tax rate limits are in effect, is to limit the ability of local government to raise revenue. This effect also is not consistent but varies from place to place depending on the composition of the tax base and how close the government is to the rate limit set by the state.

One case in which an assessment-related policy may be warranted is when a long-existing pattern of unequal assessment for different classes of property is declared illegal by a court. If this discriminatory treatment has been capitalized into property values, it may be better to legalize it by means of a classification system than to make assessments uniform, with all the windfall capital gains and losses that would entail.

The generally negative conclusions about assessment-related policies rest on economic arguments which assume that it is good to have explicit policies with costs and benefits that are apparent and easily measurable. It must be noted that this approach may have negative aspects from a political perspective.

Politically it is desirable to enact policies for which the benefits are apparent to the recipients while the costs are not obvious to the nonrecipients.[4] Policies which avoid sharp conflicts among important groups of constituents are also usually prized. Assessment-oriented approaches are better than credits in both respects. A person receiving an exemption is normally likely to be as aware of it as one who receives a credit; in fact, he is likely to overestimate its value by ignoring an increase in the overall tax rate which may occur as a result of the exemption. But those who do not receive exemptions or preferential assessments are less likely to know what relief for other parties is costing them than if a credit were provided.

What has been said applies not only to exemptions but even more to limitations on assessment increases and preferential assessment. The change in tax burdens resulting from these policies (compared to the taxes which would have been paid if assessments rose with market values) are substantial but very difficult to estimate accurately. Once enacted, they have been effective in reducing conflict about rising taxes and changes in the distribution of taxes.

Limitations on Spending or Taxing

States should be cautious about placing limitations on local fiscal activity because there is a presumption that local citizens are better able to weigh the benefits and costs of local government spending than are state officials. However, an increasing number of states have concluded that local officials cannot be trusted to make decisions about the size of their budgets, particularly when available revenues are being increased by state aid. Experience thus far suggests that most citizens do not object to such limitations once they are in effect, and few states have repealed them once they have been enacted.

Limitations should be flexible enough that they can be overridden without great difficulty. A simple majority of voters should probably be sufficient to exceed the limitation. It is also reasonable to permit a state appeals board to grant temporary exemptions in extenuating circumstances.

A different sort of limitation can be mentioned here. Most states place restrictions on the ability of local governments to raise revenue from sources other than the property tax. In the context of this book, removing such strictures is considered to be one way of making property tax relief available. Local nonproperty taxes are inferior to state aid, which redistributes resources from rich to poor areas, but they do have advantages for cities with many commuters or a relatively stagnant property tax base. Their circumscribed use is certainly justified.

The Cost of Property Tax Relief

The benefits of property tax relief must be balanced against its costs. Income or sales taxes may have to be increased to finance the relief, or reductions in those taxes may have to be forgone. If relief is granted directly to individual households, important objectives such as reducing fiscal disparities among school districts may be slighted. The other major areas of state spending are higher education, highways, and health and welfare, any or all of which may have reduced funding if money is pumped into property tax relief.

Unfortunately, little has been written about what the practical fiscal alternatives to property tax relief have been. One economist has suggested that a principal effect of Proposition 13 was to prevent a major cut in the state income tax.[5] Another has lamented that Oregon's large circuit breaker has contributed to that state's continuing heavy reliance on localities to finance schools.[6] In fact, nearly all the states with large circuit breakers are below average in the proportion of school costs financed by state aid.[7]

Apparently circuit breakers and other credits are usually initiated when states have sizable surpluses. In the 1970s state taxes have rarely been raised to finance them, although there are many cases in which states have raised taxes to finance increased aid to school districts.[8] This suggests that the latter policy is usually better able to generate greater political support.

One's final judgment about the desirability of property tax relief must depend not only on what form it takes but also on the desirability of politically feasible alternatives.

The Federal Role

The national government is deeply involved in property tax relief through the itemized deduction for home real estate taxes and through aid to local governments, but the case for further action to provide property tax relief is not very strong. The strongest argument against such relief is that reliance on the property tax varies greatly from one state to another. It would hardly be equitable to states which rely primarily on other revenue sources to tie federal aid to property taxation. Why penalize Hawaii, West Virginia, and Alabama? Why reward New Hampshire, Massachusetts, and New Jersey? There are more rational ways of distributing federal aid.[9]

Within each state there is much greater uniformity of fiscal structure than among states; that is, most cities within a single state have relatively similar revenue systems, but the same is not true of cities in different states. Thus state property tax relief makes more sense than federal property tax relief.

A second criticism of federal rather than state property tax relief is that the distribution of benefits among income groups may be different. A national reduction of property taxes may be regressive while a state or local reduction is progressive. This hypothesis arises from the differing implications of partial and general equilibrium models.[10]

A number of other arguments against federal property tax relief have been advanced.[11] Most of them apply equally to state-financed property tax relief. However, the two arguments mentioned above apply to federal but not state tax relief, and they create a strong presumption that relief should come from the state.

In reply to the criticism that federal property tax aid would vary widely and unfairly among states, advocates respond that many existing federal programs are directed at the needs of specific sections of the country. If aid took the form of support for a circuit breaker, a much larger share of benefits would be directed to households that need relief than is true for many other federal programs.[12]

Need for Further Research
and Information

Analysis of property tax relief alternatives is severely hampered by the lack of basic information on state-local fiscal systems. Because the administration of the property tax is a local responsibility in most states, accurate, comprehensive information is seldom available at the state level.

Information needs to be collected both by jurisdiction and by household. For each taxing jurisdiction in a state, data should be available on the composition of the tax base, exemptions, and the amount of tax paid by each class of property. With this information, it would be possible to tell how much tax is paid by each class of property statewide. Lacking such data, researchers often assume that taxes are proportional to assessed valuation, ignoring differences in tax rates levied across each state.

States also should conduct assessment ratio studies, not only for research purposes but also because they are essential to ensure that treatment of property throughout the state is relatively uniform. While the majority of states do carry out such studies, there are still many which do not.[13]

In addition to these jurisdictional data, states should compile data on a sample of households including information on their income, the value of property owned, the tax rate on the property, and credits or exemptions received. Ideally, these households should be tracked over a period of years to determine how their situation changes.

While both types of data are desirable, the jurisdictional data are much more readily available and in fact are collected in at least one state.[14] The household data are apparently not compiled in any state. Of course, whether it is worthwhile to accumulate any of this information depends on the types of relief programs contemplated. If only simple or small-scale programs are envisioned, there is no need for some of the basic information suggested above. However, many states are so deeply involved in expensive property tax relief programs that the expenditures required to upgrade their data base seem easily justifiable.

Aside from the lack of basic data on the property tax situation, there are many important issues on which research is needed. Here are some examples.

1. The relationships among the assessed and market values of homes, tax rates, and household income need to be clarified if the incidence of the property tax and relief measures is to be better understood. To what extent are the high tax rates which boost circuit breaker and homestead credit benefits due to a jurisdiction's low tax base rather than high expenditure levels?

2. The effects of relief programs of various types on the actions of homeowners, owners of farmland, and businesses should continue to be studied. Although existing studies generally find that relief programs have little, if any, effect on the behavior of recipients, the belief that such effects occur is often cited by advocates of the relief.

3. The extent to which local sales and income taxes provide property tax relief or support higher government spending merits further analysis.

4. The effects of various types of tax and spending limitations on local government fiscal activity and the treatment of public employees is an increasingly significant issue about which little is known.

5. The reasons why states follow different courses in providing property tax relief and which other programs are sacrificed in order to provide relief are largely unexplored issues.

Many other important questions need further analysis, such as the fiscal impact of state aid to localities, the administrative costs of various types of tax relief, reasons for the low participation rate in many circuit breaker programs and methods of increasing it, and the costs to local government of providing services to tax-exempt property.

If property tax relief continues to be a popular state policy, it is important that the data and research gaps identified here be filled.

Future Relief Prospects

The sweeping changes in state and local tax systems which occurred in the twelve months following the passage of Proposition 13 were so unprecedented that it is obviously somewhat rash to make predictions as to what may happen in the 1980s. As one economist recently said, the shelf life of predictions in this field is less than ten years.[15]

A number of important cross currents will affect the property tax in the 1980s. If inflation remains at high levels, as is likely, home assessments will continue to rise relatively rapidly. Since more and more states are relating assessments to current market values, the pressures already confronted in states which have had assessment reforms are likely to spread to states where property is seldom revalued.

Local spending will rise considerably more slowly than in the past. One reason is that the number of school-age children, after rising sharply in the wake of the postwar Baby Boom, will decrease substantially.[16] Since nearly half of the property tax goes to local schools, this factor alone should contribute to a substantial deceleration of property tax increases. In fact, local spending in the second half of the 1970s already was rising much more slowly than in earlier years.

The growth of state revenue will also slow. As of mid-1979, thirteen states had adopted limitations on state spending or revenue or had indexed their income tax.[17] Many more states are likely to follow. All these measures reduce the funds which states have available to finance property tax relief.

Thus, a potentially explosive situation is shaping up in which home assessments rise rapidly and become a larger proportion of the tax base while states have relatively limited resources to fund relief, with a slow increase in school spending relieving some of the pressure on taxes. Making the situation more strained, federal aid is expected to increase much more slowly than in the past because of pressure to reduce the federal budget deficit and shifting priorities.

In such a situation one obvious course would be to rely on relief which does not require state funds, such as limitations on local government spending or taxing. However, such limitations would not keep the composition of the tax base from changing. To prevent tax shifts, tax exemptions or limitations on assessment increases would be needed.

Such policies are precisely the type which was argued against earlier in this chapter. They complicate the property tax system so that it is very difficult to comprehend. The distribution of their benefits and costs is obscure. Except for exemptions, they do not reduce the regressivity of the property tax.

If stringest limitations are not placed on the growth of state budgets, much better choices are available. When revenue growth is excessive, states can make discretionary cuts in income, sales, or property taxes. In the austere atmosphere which presently exists, states can reasonably be trusted to make such tax reductions. If the property tax option is selected, analysis such as that in this book should be helpful in deciding how cuts should be made.

There is a world of difference between the distribution of property tax relief from Proposition 13 and the approaches taken in states like Michigan, Oregon, Iowa, and Utah. They should not be ignored.

Notes

1. Fungibility refers to the possibility of replacing revenue from one source with revenue from another. For example, if aid is given for purpose A, it may actually stimulate spending on B rather than on A if the recipient government reduces the amount of its own funds which it would have spent for A in the absence of the grant. See chapter 9 for further discussion of this subject.

2. The text makes few references to farm property because it is usually assessed according to its use value. If its assessments are based on sales prices of similar property, many of the statements with regard to homes would also apply to farms.

3. Although taxes levied on business property are ultimately paid by individuals (as consumers, suppliers, or owners of the business), it is valid to differentiate between taxes with an impact on homes and businesses because their incidence will often differ considerably. For a discussion of this point see chapter 6.

4. Anthony Downs, *An Economic Theory of Democracy* (New York: Harper & Row, 1956).

5. William H. Oakland, "Proposition 13—Genesis and Consequences," *Economic Review* (Federal Reserve Bank of San Francisco: Winter 1979), p. 19.

6. Richard W. Lindholm, "Property Taxation and Land Use Control Policies in Oregon," in *Metropolitan Financing and Growth Management Policies,* ed. George F. Break (Madison: University of Wisconsin Press, 1978), p. 47.

7. Nationally, the average state share of school finance costs was 48.3 percent in 1977-1978; it was 35.1 percent in Michigan, 31.5 percent in Oregon, 28.7 percent in Vermont, and 36.3 percent in Wisconsin. Minnesota (61.4 percent) was the only state with a high state share of school costs and a large circuit breaker, but it is one of the lowest states in terms of state responsibility for welfare costs. Some states with relatively low state spending for schools, such as Oregon and Wisconsin, nevertheless have relatively small disparities in spending among school districts, and their disparities are not strongly related to school district wealth. Thus, a small state role does not necessarily imply relatively serious spending inequities. Advisory Commission on Intergovernmental Relations, *Significant Features of Fiscal Federalism* 1978-79 ed. (Washington, D.C., 1979) tables 13 and 18. Lawrence L. Brown et al., "School Finance Reform in the Seventies: Achievements and Failures," in *Selected Papers in School Finance: 1978* ed. Esther O. Tron (Washington, D.C.: Department of Health, Education, and Welfare, 1978), pp. 61, 65.

8. Examples are Iowa, Indiana, Wisconsin, and New Jersey. In the 1930s, Iowa raised state taxes to finance a homestead credit.

9. Henry J. Aaron, "What Do Circuit-Breaker Laws Accomplish?" in *Property Tax Relief*, ed. George E. Peterson (Washington, D.C.: The Urban Institute, 1973), pp. 53-64.

10. See appendix 1A for an explanation of this point.

11. Aaron, "Circuit-Breaker Laws."

12. Examples of questionable federal programs include farm subsidies, water resource projects, and veterans' programs.

13. Advisory Commission on Intergovernmental Relations, *The Property Tax in a Changing Environment* (Washington, D.C., 1974), pp. 4, 14.

14. Iowa.

15. Dick Netzer, "The Property Tax in a New Environment" (Paper presented at Conference on Municipal Fiscal Stress, Miami, Fla., March 8-9, 1979).

16. After rising 50 percent from 1954 to 1976, public school enrollment is expected to drop 9 percent between 1976 and 1986. Actually, enrollment peaked in 1971 and had already decreased 4 percent by 1976. All figures are for grades kindergarten through twelfth. U.S. National Center for Educational Statistics, *Projections of Education Statistics to 1986-87* (Washington, D.C., 1978), p. 16.

17. State spending or revenue is limited in Tennessee, New Jersey, Arizona, Hawaii, Michigan, Texas, and Colorado. Indexing of the income tax has been passed in Colorado, California, Arizona, Wisconsin, Iowa, and Minnesota.

Index

About the Author

Steven David Gold is professor of economics at Drake University. He received a B.A. from Bucknell University in 1966 and a Ph.D. from the University of Michigan in 1972. He has served as a consultant on taxes, budgeting, and collective bargaining to cities and unions of city employees, and as an adviser to the Iowa Legislature.

His scholarly research has focused on two areas: the distributional effects of government services and taxes, and state and local tax issues. His articles have appeared in the *National Tax Journal, Public Finance Quarterly,* and other journals. He has directed projects in 1977-78 and 1979-80 to improve the understanding of Iowa citizens about local government finance, and has authored a book, *A Citizen's Guide to Local Government Finance: Iowa at the Property Tax Crossroads.* During 1978-79 he was a visiting scholar at The Urban Institute, in Washington, D.C. as a recipient of a Science Faculty Professional Development Fellowship from the National Science Foundation.